PORTRAITS

of

Leadership

Notable Americans Who Shaped Democracy

HARRY L. MUNSINGER, J.D., PH.D.

ISBN 978-1-957582-89-4 (paperback)
ISBN 978-1-957582-88-7 (eBook)

Printed in the United States of America

Contents

Introduction

My book introduces readers to American history through biographies of eighteen men and women who made significant contributions to our nation as Presidents, Senators, Secretaries of State, Treasury Secretary, or Supreme Court Justices. These leaders span the political spectrum from conservative Alexander Hamilton to liberal Ruth Bader Ginsburg, but each helped America grow and prosper. I begin with George Washington, America's first and perhaps greatest President, who led the American colonies to victory in the Revolutionary War and guided thirteen disparate states through crisis to form the Constitutional government we enjoy today. Next comes Alexander Hamilton, who served as Washington's first Treasury Secretary and put the federal government on a sound financial footing by establishing the First United States National Bank, assuming state and federal war debts, and issuing federal bonds to pay off the national debt.

John Adams, second President of the U.S., appears next. His was a steady hand on the tiller of our new nation during its early years, and guided the United States through difficult times after Washington retired. Adams established a strong navy, paid off the federal debt, kept the country out of war, encouraged American manufacturing, and nominated John Marshall Chief Justice of the U.S. Supreme Court. John Marshall, the next great American leader, was perhaps the most important Chief Justice of the Supreme Court in history. He established the Court as an equal branch of government and gave it the authority to interpret the U.S. Constitution and evaluate the constitutionality of state and federal laws. Thomas Jefferson, third President of the United States, comes next. He supported agriculture over manufacturing, drafted the Declaration of Independence, championed democracy, and encouraged equality among all men, even though he owned slaves.

Next comes President Andrew Jackson, who expanded Jefferson's championing of the common man against those with money and power. He lowered federal tariffs to keep Southern states in the

Union, opposed the Doctrine of Nullification, which said that states could pick-and-choose which federal laws to follow, and closed the Second United States National Bank. Jackson was a war hero in the Battle of New Orleans, supported removal of Native American tribes west of the Mississippi River, and owned slaves all his life. Senator Daniel Webster, an American lawyer, and statesman follows Jackson. He opposed slavery, expanded the meaning of the U.S. Constitution, and worked tirelessly to preserve the Union. Webster was clearly qualified to be President but never won the job because he opposed slavery.

President Abraham Lincoln, the only rival of George Washington as the greatest American President, appears next. He led the North during the Civil War, saved the Union, abolished slavery, and was assassinated by a Southern sympathizer soon after the war ended. Following Lincoln, I introduce Theodore Roosevelt, who expanded American power worldwide by speaking "softly and carrying a big stick." He fought in the Spanish-American War leading the Rough Riders up Kittle Hill in Cuba, negotiated the rights to build the Panama Canal, and added Hawaii, Panama, and Puerto Rico to U.S. territories. Justice Oliver Wendell Holmes, Jr. follows Theodore Roosevelt. He fought in the Civil War and served on the U.S. Supreme Court for decades, established several legal precedents, clarified the meaning of the common law, and expanded civil rights for most Americans.

President Woodrow Wilson, our next leader, introduced the income tax, established the Federal Reserve, and guided the United States in World War I. He personally participated in the Versailles Peace Treaty that ended the war and introduced the League of Nations to keep world peace. Unfortunately, he was felled by a stroke while campaigning for the Versailles Treaty and was unable to guide his dream to reality. Franklin Delano Roosevelt follows Wilson. He was the longest serving President in U.S. history, being elected to four terms. Roosevelt led the country during the Great Depression, guided the Allies to victory in World War II, and greatly expanded the scope and power of the federal government in all areas of American life.

Chief Justice Earl Warren comes next. He presided over the Supreme Court during some of its most turbulent times. The Warren Court unanimously ordered desegregated U.S. schools in the face of strong Southern opposition and expanded defendants' civil rights in the courtroom. The Warren Commission reviewed the Kennedy assassination and concluded that Lee Harvey Oswald was the lone shooter. The FBI and many Americans were skeptical of that conclusion, although it is generally accepted today. John Kennedy, our youngest elected President, guided the country through perilous time during the Cold War, navigated a peaceful end to the Cuban Missile Crisis, dealt with the Berlin Wall, negotiated arms control treaties with the Soviet Union, and sent ground troops to Vietnam to stop that country from being overrun by the North Vietnamese. He was assassinated in Dallas near the end of his first term in office.

Ronald Reagan won the Cold War, began development of the Strategic Defense Initiative to protect America from nuclear missiles, lowered income taxes, and presided over the longest economic recovery in American history. He was one of our most popular Presidents. Reagan nominated Sandra Day O'Connor as the first female Justice of the U.S. Supreme Court, and she served as a role model of a generation of young female attorneys. Barack Obama, the first Black President of the U.S., made history by guiding the country through the Great Recession, revising financial regulations to protect consumers and homeowners from financial malpractice, expanding medical health insurance for millions of uninsured Americans, and negotiating a limit on Iran's atomic bomb program. Justice Ruth Bader Ginsburg fought all her life for gender equality and developed the doctrine that the Fourteenth Amendment's Equal Protection Clause applied to women as well as minority Americans.

The United States developed from a weak confederation of states into the wealthy and powerful nation we know today under the guidance and leadership of these notable Americans. The current success of America was not assured when the Founding Fathers met at Philadelphia in 1787 to plan a new government, but they used enlightened leadership and self-interested compromise to create a republican government that has worked for over two centuries.

The dynamic energy and creative intellect of the American people have been guided by the talented leaders presented in my book. They applied their considerable talents during critical periods in American history to shape our Constitutional form of government, preserve the Union, free the slaves, defend the country against all enemies, protect civil rights, and heal tribal divisions.

George Washington

George Washington was born at Popes Creek, Virginia, on February 22, 1732, the first of six children of Augustine and Mary Ball Washington. [1] The family moved to Little Hunting Creek on the Potomac in 1735 and built a two-story house that later became part of Mount Vernon. Lawrence Washington inherited most of his father's estate, while George received some land and ten slaves when their father died. Washington received little formal education after his father died but did master reading, mathematics, trigonometry, surveying, drafting, and mapmaking on his own initiative. He earned a surveying license from the College of William and Mary in 1749, and became the official surveyor of Culpeper County, Virginia, later that year. [2]

Washington began buying land west of the Blue Ridge Mountains and was able to find exceptional properties as a surveyor because he was often the first person to visit the property. In 1750, his brother Lawrence contracted what was probably tuberculosis, and they traveled to Barbados seeking a healthier climate so he might recuperate. George Washington contacted a mild case of smallpox in Barbados that gave him lifelong immunity and probably saved his life during the Revolutionary War, because many soldiers died of smallpox at that time. Lawrence died at Mount Vernon on July 26, 1752, leaving twenty-five hundred acres of land and all his slaves to George. In 1763, Lieutenant Governor Dinwiddie asked Washington to lead Virginia militia into the Ohio Country to discuss peace with the Iroquois Confederacy, gather intelligence about French forces in the area, and ask them to leave. His force was met by French troops and escorted to Fort Le Boeuf, where Washington told the French commander he must leave. The French refused but gave Washington food and warmer clothing for his return trip to Virginia. [3]

Dinwiddie ordered Washington to attack the French forces near the Forks of the Ohio River and drive them out of the area with his militia. Scouts told Washington the French had over one thousand troops in the area, but Washington found only a small force of fifty men, which he attacked, killing several French soldiers. Dinwiddie was delighted with Washington's action, but his attack on the French forces triggered the French and Indian War, which lasted seven years and cost England and the colonies money and men.

French and Indian War. Washington's journal of his travels in the Ohio Country became a sensation in England when it was published. The British decided to drive the French from the Ohio Country by force and asked Washington to lead his Virginia Militia and one hundred South Carolina soldiers into the territory because he knew the country. A French army of over nine hundred men attacked Washington and forced him to surrender. [4] After this defeat, Washington served as an aide to General Braddock, who commanded the British Army sent to expel the French from the Ohio Country. Braddock's force of fourteen hundred men was ambushed in the forest by a powerful French and Indian band that fought a hit-and-run battle, killing over two-thirds of the English soldiers from ambush. Washington rallied his Virginia Militia, fought an effective rear-guard action, and saved the surviving British soldiers. [5]

He learned it was more effective to fight from ambush and retreat rather than use European tactics, which required companies of men to stand and shoot at each other in the open. Washington knew an ambush worked better on the frontier than fighting in compact units that made excellent targets. He was not included in British planning and the insult added to Washington's resentment over how the English treated colonial officers. Braddock's defeat also changed Washington's attitude toward English invincibility on the battlefield because he had seen how to defeat them by using ambush and hit-and-run tactics.

Following Braddock's defeat, the western frontier of Virginia was open to Indian attack. Many colonial settlers abandoned their cabins and moved to more established areas in western Virginia. In August 1755, the assembly in Williamsburg voted funds to raise a new regiment of militia and gave Washington command. [6] He received authority to appoint his own officers, recruit soldiers, and an expense account of one hundred pounds annually. Washington faced a difficult task defending three hundred fifty miles of frontier against Indian raids and worked hard to bring his militia up to British standards of training and equipment. Because Washington believed men were motivated by fear rather than kindness, he instituted the death penalty for desertion and forbade gambling, prostitution, and drinking in his army.

Washington was popular with his officers because he was courageous and fair. He wanted to go on the offensive against the French and Indians, but the Virginia Assembly ordered him to use defensive tactics. The British moved most of their soldiers north into Canada and left the Ohio Country to Washington's regiment. He wanted a royal commission but was only given command of the colonial militia. Washington believed professional soldiers were needed to defend the frontier against the French and was encouraged when several hundred Cherokee Indians joined his militia because they were fierce wilderness fighters and knew the country. The British paid ten pounds for each French scalp the Indians collected, and they were delighted to join the war. Washington had to leave his militia and return to Mount Vernon when he contracted dysentery and was unable to ride.

Marriage to Martha Custis. Washington traveled to Virginia to recover his health, improve Mount Vernon, and manage his estate. A friend and neighbor, Richard Chamberlayne, introduced him to the widow Custis, whose husband had died the previous year. Washington courted Martha with military efficiency, behaving as a wealthy plantation owner and military commander. [7] He probably seemed reliable, manly, and courageous to Martha. Washington was serious about the relationship and didn't waste time before he asked her to marry him. She quickly accepted the proposal.

Washington rose to the top of Virginia society through his marriage to Martha because she and her children owned thousands of acres of land and over three hundred slaves. She inherited one-third of her husband's land and slaves, while the remaining property was placed in trust to support her children, with Washington as custodian. Martha was short, petite, sensible, prudent, sociable, and an enormous asset to Washington's career because of her land, slaves, and social graces. By the spring of 1758, Washington had recovered sufficiently to return to command of his militia. He learned that the British were going to send a fleet and seven thousand men to attack Fort Duquesne, and he wanted to be part of the attack.

The British commander, General John Forbes, was a veteran officer with a favorable view of Washington. The Virginia Assembly raised another regiment of militia, increasing Washington's command to over two thousand men. He adopted the hit-and-run tactics of the Native Americans and dressed his militia in buckskin jackets to allow them to blend into the woods. He believed the Indians were better fighters in the wilderness than his colonials or the British soldiers because they were used to fighting in forested terrain. General Forbes assigned Washington to lead one of the three regiments spearheading the assault. After a lengthy siege, the French burned the fort and fled down the Ohio River. [8] Once the threat to Virginia's frontier was gone, Washington resigned his commission and returned to Mount Vernon to manage his plantation. The British made a serious mistake neglecting such a natural colonial leader, and Washington was embittered by the way British aristocrats treated him and other colonial officers.

On January 6, 1759, Washington won a seat in the House of Burgesses and was given a rousing welcome by his fellow members for service during the French and Indian War. Although Washington was able to face death on the battlefield, he was anxious about public speaking and preferred to wield power behind the scenes. George and Martha Washington apparently enjoyed a happy marriage, although they never produced children. Historians have speculated that Martha's health may have been damaged by a difficult birth, so she could not conceive afterward. However, it's more likely Washington was infertile because of smallpox. [9] The fact that he was childless helped assuage fears Washington might favor a hereditary monarchy because he had no son to inherit his title when he died.

Washington's Political Activities. Beginning in 1760, Washington became a harsh critic of English tax policies toward the colonies because they adversely affected his plantation. He became a leading supporter of American independence because of British taxes, a ban on American settlements west of the Allegheny Mountains, and England's attempts to monopolize the fur trade in the West. On December 16, 1773, a band of colonists dressed as Indians dumped English tea into Boston Harbor to protest the Townshend Acts. [10] In retaliation for the Boston Tea Party, Parliament closed Boston Harbor and passed the Coercive Acts, designed to punish Northern colonies. The coercion failed, increased the resistance of Americans against British taxes, and drove the colonies closer together in their fight against English policies.

In July 1774, George Washington and George Mason sponsored a resolution calling for a Continental Congress to manage colonial affairs. He was selected as a delegate to the First Continental Congress from Virginia, asked to organize the colonial militia to resist British aggression and enforce a colonial boycott of English goods. Washington hoped to find a diplomatic solution to the problems with England but believed war was a last resort. The House of Burgesses passed a resolution stating that it alone had the power to tax Virginians. The next day the English governor dissolved the House of Burgesses for seditious activities, but the members defied him and failed to disband.

Instead, the House of Burgesses enacted the Fairfax Resolves, which stated that citizens of England and the colonies need only obey laws that were enacted by their own representatives. [11] The Resolves launched Washington's political career in America. He attended the First Continental Congress in Philadelphia, and his quiet style appealed to delegates who wanted someone to lead them who was not hungry for power. Most delegates to the Continental Congress were not ready for independence until English troops attempted to arrest colonial leaders meeting in Concord, Massachusetts, and were killed from ambush on their way back to Boston by colonial militia hiding in the forests and behind walls. The Battles of Concord and Lexington triggered the Revolutionary War.

General Washington. Delegates gathered for the Second Continental Congress shortly after the battles near Boston and began preparing for war. Washington signaled he was ready to lead the Continental Army by wearing his militia uniform at the Congress. Because he was the only member of Congress with extensive military experience, Washington was the natural choice to be Commander of the Continental Army. [12] He inspired confidence among the other delegates, who felt Washington had the judgment and common sense to lead the colonies in their war against England. However, Washington knew the Continental Army was not ready to fight the most powerful nation on earth. He needed time, trained men, money, equipment, and the help of France if he hoped to defeat England.

Washington collected talented aides to help manage the army and immediately set out to arrange Boston's defenses. He found the Massachusetts militia had few trained men available to defend the city; however, Washington had to appear confident in the face of these difficulties. He was concerned that British troops might overwhelm his small army before the war got started. Having experience with smallpox, Washington inoculated his army by soaking thread in pus from mild smallpox cases and sewing it into his soldiers' skin. He also quarantined soldiers who showed symptoms of the disease, avoiding an epidemic among his troops and keeping them healthy and available to fight.

London sent General Thomas Gage and a large contingent of British soldiers to occupy Boston in 1775. Colonial militia surrounded the English Army camped in Boston, creating a stand-off. Washington instilled discipline and order in the troops and began planning for a major battle. General

Knox transported heavy artillery captured at Fort Ticonderoga to Boston, and Washington secretly placed the guns on Dorchester Heights above the city during the night. [13] The English quickly realized they were at a severe disadvantage under those large guns and abandoned Boston for New York City.

Battle of Long Island. Washington marched his army ahead of the British Army to Long Island to fortify the area in preparation for an English attack on New York. A plot to assassinate Washington was uncovered and the loyalists involved were arrested, tried, convicted, and hanged for sedition. English troops began arriving in New York on July 2, 1776, and eventually, thirty-two thousand English regulars and auxiliaries opposed Washington's small army of twenty-three thousand militia. Based on faulty intelligence, Washington decided to attack General Howe's troops on Long Island and was soundly defeated, losing over fifteen hundred men while inflicting only around four hundred casualties on the British. [14] Washington retreated across the Hudson River with his army to escape capture. When he arrived in New Jersey for winter camp, Washington only had around five thousand able-bodied men remaining in his army. General Howe decided to spend the winter in New York enjoying the comforts of a large city, but Washington remained in the field hoping to gain a victory over Hessian and British soldiers in New Jersey.

Howe had stationed a Hessian mercenary garrison at Trenton, New Jersey, to hold the east shore of the Delaware River against Washington, but they became complacent, believing the colonials would not attack during the winter months. Washington surprised the Trenton garrison by crossing the Delaware River on the night of December 25-26, 1776. The American troops killed or wounded about one hundred Hessians and captured another eight hundred. Washington repeated his surprise attack on January 3, killing or capturing almost three hundred British regulars at Princeton, New Jersey. [15] Colonel Alexander Hamilton handled Washington's artillery and shelled Nassau ahead of the assault. Washington was able to capture the British position with minimal losses to his own men. The victories at Trenton and Princeton convinced the English that America was not going to give up easily, and they began preparing for a long war in the colonies.

Washington developed a new strategy of hit-and-run ambushes to avoid losing his small army and fought a defensive war because he didn't have the men and materials to attack the English directly. In the spring of 1777, General Burgoyne moved south from Quebec and recaptured Fort Ticonderoga, intending to control the Hudson River Valley and divide New England from the other colonies. In the same year, General Howe defeated Washington at Brandywine Creek and Germantown outside Philadelphia. [16] Colonial General Gates won a victory at Saratoga, and some in the Continental Congress suggested he should be leading the Continental Army rather than Washington. However, most Congressmen believed the victory at Saratoga was won by General Benedict Arnold rather than General Gates and continued to support Washington as supreme commander. General Burgoyne's loss at Saratoga impressed the French court and Benjamin Franklin used the victory to convince France to join the war against England. [17]

The English stayed comfortably in Philadelphia during the winter of 1777, while Washington moved his army into rustic winter quarters at Valley Forge, twenty miles north of Philadelphia, which he described as dreary and uncomfortable. [18] Washington rented a small two-story mill house for his headquarters. Congress was bankrupt, so Washington had little money to cloth, feed, or pay his soldiers. The colonials endured a miserable winter at Valley Forge, and many deserted because they were not paid; there was little food and much disease. Washington had his men build crude huts for shelter, but the lack of food, wood, and warm clothing created terrible conditions. Washington stayed with his soldiers, sharing their poor food and hardships. The Continental Army's survival during the winter at Valley Forge owed much to Baron von Steuben, a Prussian soldier who instilled discipline and fighting spirit in the colonial army. Von Steuben and Alexander Hamilton drafted a book of drills and marches that taught precision and discipline in the ranks and raised the soldiers' morale.

On February 6, 1778, France recognized American independence and signed an alliance with the Americans against England. [19] America's fortunes had taken a major turn for the better. The British replaced General Howe with Henry Clinton, who reinforced English colonies in the West Indies and Florida and moved his headquarters to New York City. Washington, with twelve thousand men, decided to attack the retreating English north of New York. His troops retreated in the face of British fire, but Washington rallied them and fought the English to a draw. During the night, the British withdrew from the battlefield, giving Washington a much-needed victory. The Battle of Monmouth, as it was called, was won by hard fighting by the militia and good leadership by Washington. Moreover, the French were coming to help defeat the English.

French Assistance. The French Navy arrived in America on July 8, 1778, with twelve ships of the line, four frigates, and four thousand seasoned fighting men. Washington recognized the tremendous advantage the French ships and soldiers gave him, but his relationship with the French officers was sometimes difficult. Both sides expected more than was realistic; the Continental Army was not so large as the French believed, and France never sent the number of soldiers and ships Washington felt he needed to end the war. The French entered the war to damage England, not to help the Americans, and the two countries had different agendas. The French helped America just enough, so they didn't surrender but never committed the money and materials needed to finish the war quickly. The result was a long and difficult war for the colonists.

Just when the French arrived in America, General Benedict Arnold began passing secret information to Major John Andre to help the British capture West Point, an important American fort on the Hudson River. [20] Historians have speculated that Arnold was angry at Congress for not promoting him quickly enough, in debt, under pressure because he had been accused of profiteering from the war, and believed Washington didn't support him. Colonial militia captured Major Andre and found incriminating papers on his person from Arnold. General Arnold learned of Andre's capture, escaped to a British ship, and sailed to New York, while Major Andre was tried, convicted of spying for the British, and sentenced to death. Washington offered to trade Andre for Arnold, but General Clinton refused.

The years 1778-80 were slow times in the American Revolution because the Americans were short of money, and Washington was forced to remain on the defensive. Congress was printing money to fund the war, inflation was rampant, and American credit poor. Washington was waiting for a loan from France and the Netherlands to help pay for the war before he could attack. There were minor skirmishes during these years but few major battles. General Clinton moved half his troops to Georgia to begin a southern campaign against Savannah. In 1780, Clinton began an assault on Charleston, South Carolina, to conquer the southern colonies.

Victory at Yorktown. French General Rochambeau, who arrived in America with five thousand seasoned troops, ships, and supplies, advised Washington to avoid New York and instead attack General Cornwallis and his southern army because they were more vulnerable. Washington listened to this sage advice and sent his troops south in French ships. The French and American soldiers surrounded Cornwallis at Yorktown and defeated his army decisively after a lengthy siege. [21] Washington had little experience with siege warfare and gladly took advice from French General Rochambeau. The combined American and French forces cut off supplies to the city, dug encircling trenches, and forced Cornwallis to surrender on October 19, 1781. Washington captured over seven thousand British troops in the battle. The French allowed Washington to take credit for the defeat of the English, ending the Revolutionary War.

As Britain and America began peace negotiations, England withdrew troops from New York, Savannah, and Charleston. The Congressional treasury was empty, and American soldiers were pressuring Congress to pay them. Congress promised Continental officers a five-year bonus, and Washington submitted a bill to Congress for over four hundred thousand dollars in expenses he had paid supporting the army. After lengthy negotiations, the Treaty of Paris was signed, formalizing peace between America and England on September 3, 1783. Washington resigned his commission and returned to Mount Vernon.

Mount Vernon. Washington had been at Mount Vernon for only ten days during the entire Revolutionary War and was eager to withdraw from public life and manage his plantation. He organized a trip to the Ohio Country to inspect his land, and when he returned, Washington began renovating Mount Vernon and growing new crops. His finances were in poor shape because his creditors paid in depreciated Continental currency and he owed back taxes. Washington believed the United States was vulnerable to foreign intervention and needed a strong executive to administer the country. He was a humble man who did not seek power; he merely did his duty as a gentleman. Washington never actively sought high office—power fell into his lap because he was the most experienced and competent leader in America and his countrymen trusted the man.

Washington issued a memorandum entitled "Circular to State Governments," advising Congress and the states how to govern themselves after the war. [22] Washington began the memorandum by stating he wanted no political office but intended to retire. Next, he painted a bright future for America but worried that a weak confederacy of states would induce European nations to meddle in American affairs. Washington called for the union of all thirteen states into a single national government and argued against repudiation of public debts. He also suggested that each state maintain a standing militia rather than having a national army. Washington ended his memorandum by calling on Almighty God to bless this new nation with His protection.

Washington spent time organizing his wartime papers, managing Mount Vernon, and traveling to New York City after the war. He recommended establishing a military academy, resigned his commission, and retired to Mount Vernon to live the life of a wealthy planter. Washington avoided appearing ambitious for power and became a legend as a result. He had been commander-in-chief for over eight years and was tired of war and the responsibility of command. However, it soon became clear the Continental Congress was incapable of running the country, and a new form of government was needed to manage the nation's affairs, so Washington was called on to lead the nation at a Constitutional Convention and then as president.

The Constitutional Convention. Many leaders of American society were considering what form of government might better serve the country because the Continental Congress was clearly a failure. In September of 1786, delegates from five states met to discuss how to resolve trade disputes among the various states. Hamilton proposed that all thirteen states send delegates to a Constitutional Convention, but nothing came of his idea at the time. A rebellion in Massachusetts led by Daniel Shays convinced Washington that the Articles of Confederation needed to be changed, and he agreed to attend the Constitutional Convention. On December 4, 1786, he was nominated to lead the Virginia delegation in Philadelphia. [23] Washington was reluctant to attend, but James Madison and Henry Knox convinced him his presence was essential to the convention's success. Benjamin Franklin nominated Washington to chair the convention and he was unanimously elected to serve as president general, a nonpartisan role that suited his nature.

Governor Randolph of Virginia proposed a constitutional form of national government that would include executive, legislative, and judicial branches. A major dispute developed between small and large states that was ultimately resolved by giving each state equal representation in the Senate and proportional representation in the House of Representatives. The delegates mentioned slavery in the Constitution by agreeing to count three-fifths of a person for every slave when apportioning representation. They finally agreed on our present Constitution, with a president, a bicameral legislature containing two branches, and a judiciary appointed for life. The delegates' fear of a monarchy was assuaged by electing Washington the first President of the United States because he was trusted to not become an autocratic king. Washington supported the Constitution, and it was ultimately adopted on September 17, 1787, after lengthy discussions within the various states.

The Federalist Papers. Alexander Hamilton, James Madison, and John Jay published a series of articles supporting the Constitution, which became known as the Federalist Papers, and are now considered classic political writing about the U.S. Constitution. [24] Early in 1788, the Constitution had been adopted by Pennsylvania, New Jersey, Delaware, Georgia, and Connecticut. Later that year, Massachusetts, Maryland, South Carolina, and New Hampshire also ratified the Constitution for a total of nine states. The most opposition developed in New York and Virginia, but these two large states eventually ratified the document. Once the new Constitution was accepted, Washington waited to be asked if he would accept the presidency because he did not want to seem power-hungry. Hamilton worked hard to persuade Washington to accept the office, and he finally agreed.

President Washington. The Constitutional delegates all assumed Washington would be elected President and wanted him to define the duties associated with the office. Washington received a majority of electoral votes in every state, and John Adams received the next most votes to become Vice President. Washington was inaugurated on April 30,1789, in front of Federal Hall in New York City, at that time the capitol of America. He offered to serve without salary, but Congress insisted he accept $25,000 to defray expenses of the office. Understanding that every decision he made would establish a precedent, Washington followed basic principles of good government. He asked to be addressed as Mr. President rather than a more flowery title. Washington also established the custom of giving an inaugural address, speaking before Congress concerning the State of the Union, and designed a cabinet form of government to administer the nation.

Washington wanted to serve only one term as President, but there was so much political strife during his first four years in office that he decided to accept a second term to maintain domestic peace. He was a good administrator, conferred with his cabinet on a regular basis, and welcomed opposing ideas. Washington met personally with the public every Tuesday afternoon at 3 p.m. in the White House. He disliked political parties and remained neutral between the different political factions throughout his presidency. During his first term, Washington faced a number of difficult problems, including worthless Continental money, British forts in America, and Barbary pirates attacking American shipping in the Mediterranean. Congress established executive departments of State, War, Treasury, and Attorney General during his first year. Washington appointed Edmund Randolph Attorney General, Thomas Jefferson Secretary of State, Henry Knox Secretary of War, and Alexander Hamilton Secretary of the Treasury. [25] He used the cabinet as an advisory board and worked hard to avoid the appearance of being a power-hungry monarch.

After a few months in office, Washington developed a fever and a tumor on his left thigh that was life-threatening. He called on Dr. Bard, a well-known New York physician, to treat the condition. Dr. Bard removed the tumor and scraped away pus from the surgical wound. Washington recovered, but it took months for him to regain his strength. Washington's mother, Mary Ball Washington, drifted into a coma and died on August 25, 1789. [26] Washington was bothered most of his adult life with dentures because his teeth were prone to cavities, and he had them extracted to relieve the pain. His last tooth was pulled in 1796, and without that last tooth as an anchor, he often complained that his dentures didn't fit properly, distorted his face, and sometimes slipped out of his mouth. Washington stopped smiling because his dentures turned black from drinking port wine.

In spite of Washington's dislike of political parties, Jefferson formed the Republican Party and Hamilton the Federalist Party to further their political goals against each other. Washington favored Hamilton's ideas of establishing a National Bank and paying off state and federal debts accumulated during the Revolutionary War and rejected Jefferson's idea of encouraging only agriculture in America. He proclaimed November 26 a day of thanksgiving to encourage unity among all Americans. Slavery was already causing friction between the states because Kentucky and Tennessee were admitted to the Union as slave states in 1792 and 1796. Slavery in federal territories south of the Ohio River was guaranteed, and Washington signed the Fugitive Slave Act on February 12, 1793, allowing slave agents to cross state lines hunting escaped slaves. The Slave Trade Act of 1794 limited American involvement in the Atlantic slave trade. However, there were millions of slaves already in America, and their natural increase produced a ready supply of slave labor for southern plantation owners to use and sell. Jefferson and Hamilton often disagreed about policy.

Hamilton-Jefferson Feud. Washington's first term as president was devoted mainly to domestic issues such as resolving the national debt, establishing a national bank, developing a policy for dealing with Native Americans, and deciding where to place the new federal capitol. He delegated little authority to John Adams, his vice president, and didn't include him in cabinet affairs. Hamilton was Washington's primary advisor, and he proposed that the federal government assume all state and national debts accumulated during the war, establish a national bank, and issue federal bonds to pay off the debt. [27] Jefferson, the balancing power in Washington's cabinet, opposed Hamilton's plan and a deadlock developed. Jefferson and Hamilton forged a compromise in which the federal government established a national bank, assumed all national and state debts, and issued federal bonds; in return, the Federal capitol was located on the Potomac River near Georgetown, Virginia, at its present location in Washington, D.C.

Even though Washington received adulation from the public, he never let the praise swell his ego. He didn't want power or attention and was honest and open in his dealings. Washington paid attention to public opinion, however, and followed the mood of the country when it was clear. Shortly after his inauguration, Washington announced he would visit every state in the Union to learn first-hand the condition of the country. He rode in an open carriage, paying attention to roads, canals, agriculture, manufacturing, and the public mood. Unlike Jefferson, Washington supported industrial development in America, even though he was a southern planter. He returned to New York to give his first State of the Union Address to both houses of Congress personally in Federal Hall on January 8, 1790, establishing a precedent. Washington invited his cabinet and the Supreme Court Justices to attend, so all three branches of government were represented at the State of the Union Address.

Hamilton proposed that the government establish tariffs on imported goods to pay the national debt and fund the government. Washington approved Hamilton's plan, and it was passed by Congress. Pennsylvania Quakers filed a bill in Congress to outlaw the slave trade in America and authorize the abolition of slavery. Washington reacted with caution, knowing slavery was an explosive issue in the South. He didn't support the petition and Congress quietly tabled the bills rather than divide the country. Later that year, Washington contracted pneumonia and his physicians feared for his life. However, he rallied and was soon feeling fine. While Washington was ill, Hamilton was de-facto head of the government because there was no formal procedure to transfer power when the President was unable to handle his job, and Washington preferred Hamilton manage the country rather than John Adams. Jefferson, as Secretary of State, began to view Hamilton as a future rival for the presidency, making their feud even worse.

Congress delegated the location and construction of the new capitol to Washington, and he selected a site just north of Mount Vernon on the Potomac River. He profited personally from the choice because Washington owned large tracts of land in the area. While the new capitol was being constructed, the government was moved to Philadelphia, America's largest city at the time with over forty-five thousand residents. Washington lived in a four-story brick mansion owned by his friend Robert Morris while in Philadelphia. Hamilton ignited a rebellion among western farmers when he suggested a tax on whiskey to raise more money for the government. Hamilton also suggested Congress authorize the formation of a revenue office with agents to collect the tax on moonshine in the western states, creating a problem that exists even today. The farmers wanted to avoid the taxes on their whiskey, and the government wanted to collect the money.

The most divisive issue of Washington's first term was whether to favor Britain or France in foreign policy. Even though he had fought an eight-year war against the English, Washington realized he needed good relations with London because the Royal Navy controlled the Atlantic Ocean. Jefferson wanted America to favor France, and that difference created a feud with Hamilton, who established a back channel with London and negotiated an agreement in which King George named an ambassador to America. Many in America felt that because of the French Revolution, that country was a natural ally of the United States because it was a republic as opposed to the British monarchy. In 1790, Washington tried to negotiate a peace treaty with the Indians in the Ohio Country, but they continued raiding American settlements. As a result, Washington sent militia to subdue the Indians, but they were defeated, confirming Washington's belief that state militia were not competent soldiers.

Washington's second term was filled with domestic strife and problems caused by the French Revolution. Jefferson believed the French would remain peaceful during their revolution. Even after it turned into a bloody Reign of Terror, Jefferson continued to support France over England, claiming the terror was nothing but propaganda issued by England and the Federalists. On January 21, 1793, King Louis XVI was beheaded before a mob in the streets of Paris. Two weeks later, France declared war on England and Holland. When Washington received the news, he instructed Jefferson to keep America neutral. Washington issued a formal declaration of neutrality, but the French government sent a new minister to America named Edmond Genet, who immediately began issuing letters of marque to American ships so they could become privateers and attack English shipping. [28]

Jefferson supported the French actions and resigned as Secretary of State when Washington failed to support him. The President had a difficult time finding a replacement of Jefferson's caliber, finally settling on Edmund Randolph as his new Secretary of State. England intensified pressure on America by blockading the coast of Europe and stopping American ships to impress sailors into the English Navy, claiming they were British citizens. Washington sent John Jay to England as a special envoy with authority to negotiate a treaty with England and try to persuade the British to remove their forts from the United States.

At the same time, Pennsylvania farmers were rebelling against the whisky tax and burning revenue collectors' houses or shooting at them. Washington called a cabinet meeting and authorized calling out state militia to suppress the rebellion. Washington went into the field with the militia, although Hamilton took actual command of the troops. The country was economically well off and Washington didn't understand why the farmers were rebelling. After all, the tax had been voted lawfully by their own Congress. Washington inspected the militia, placed Hamilton in change, and went back to Philadelphia to manage the country. As he expected, the whiskey rebellion collapsed in the face of military force. When Hamilton returned to Philadelphia, he told Washington that he intended to resign from the Treasury at the end of the year and return to law practice.

The Jay Treaty. Meanwhile, special envoy John Jay had negotiated a treaty with England, so Washington called for a special session of Congress to debate and vote on the agreement. The treaty was not favorable to America because it didn't stop the British Navy impressing American sailors on the high seas and granted England most-favored-nation status for its manufactured goods in America while not extending the same benefit to American manufactured goods. However, the British agreed to abandon their forts on the Great Lakes, open the British West Indies to American commerce, compensate American merchants for goods confiscated by the British, and remain at peace with America. Congress passed and Washington signed the treaty, but there was strong opposition to it in the country. [29]

Washington's Farewell Address. Washington asked Hamilton to help draft his farewell address to be published at the end of his second term. In his address, Washington announced he would not be seeking a third term as President, called for national unity, law and order, and preservation of the Union. Washington decried the growth of political parties, saying they foster dissent. He supported a foreign policy based on national interests rather than friendship. Washington made no mention of slavery in his farewell address, acting in conjunction with southern plantation owners who wanted the subject avoided if at all possible. [30] Soon after Washington's farewell address to Congress, the presidential election of 1796 began. John Adams, Washington's vice president, collected seventy-one votes to win the presidency, while Jefferson was a close second with sixty-eight votes and became vice president under the election rules at the time.

Washington's accomplishments during his eight years as President are many. He and Hamilton restored America's credit, paid off state and federal war debts, created a national bank, a mint, a coast guard, a custom's service, a diplomatic corps, introduced tax and budget procedures, established a navy, avoided war, strengthened the army, subdued Native American uprisings, suppressed a rebellion against the whiskey tax, and followed the letter and spirit of the Constitution by establishing precedents for the new nation to follow. During his two terms, the economy boomed, tax receipts grew, his administration opened the Mississippi River to American commerce, negotiated a treaty with the Barbary pirates, and removed English forts from the Great Lakes. Perhaps more important, Washington showed that a republican form of government could work without becoming disorderly or authoritarian. And the new states of Vermont, Kentucky, and Tennessee were added to the Union.

After leaving office, Washington planned to organize the documents he accumulated during his years as Commander of the Army and President of the United States and remodel the main house at Mount Vernon. He also worked to repair his finances, renting his four farms at Mount Vernon, hiring a new manager for his estate, and converting the corn and rye grown on the estate into whiskey. Washington sold his land in Pennsylvania and personally asked creditors for payment of debts owed. He tried to stay out of politics and had no dealings with Jefferson, whom he hated because of the vile criticisms he had directed against Washington.

In December 1799, Washington spent five hours on horseback touring his farms around Mount Vernon in rain and snow. Soon after, he developed a sore throat and cough and spent the next day in his bed. Washington spent his last day in a simple but lovely bedroom and faced death with his usual poise. His physicians drained blood from Washington, believing that would heal him. In fact, it probably made him weaker and may have contributed to his death because modern experts estimate they drained almost five pints of blood (approximately half the body's total supply). Washington expired with dignity and self-respect on December 14, 1799. [31]

Alexander Hamilton.

H amilton was born January 11, 1755, in the West Indies. [32] His maternal grandparents owned a large sugar plantation and many slaves. His father, James Hamilton, was a minor Scottish Lord who moved to the West Indies to make his fortune in the sugar trade. Hamilton's parents never married because his mother was barred from remarrying because she was divorced. James Hamilton abandoned his family in 1765, and Alexander's mother ran a grocery store to support them until she contracted yellow fever and died when he was twelve. Hamilton lived with his uncle and worked as a clerk for the New York trading house of Beekman and Cruger in the West Indies. Later, he became the ward of Thomas Stevens, a wealthy merchant who provided him with advice and financial support. Some historians have speculated that Stevens was Hamilton's father, but there is no evidence to support the claim.

When the owners of Beekman and Cruger moved to New York, Hamilton was given total control of their trading business in the West Indies. He was a successful trader and manager but became bored working at a desk. When a hurricane came through the islands, Hamilton observed the storm first hand and wrote a letter to the local newspaper describing his experience. The letter was read by Hugh Knox, a preacher living in the Caribbean, who recognized Hamilton's intellectual potential and raised money to send him to America for a proper education. Hamilton was so successful in America he never returned to the West Indies.

Hamilton's Education. Hamilton attended King's College in New York (now Columbia University). He was a bright student and quickly developed an interest in colonial politics. Initially, Hamilton was loyal to the British crown but later argued that freedom from Britain was essential for the colonies because heavy taxes levied by Parliament were ruining them economically. He supported the Boston Tea Party and gave a speech at Princeton College in which he argued that destroying British tea proved the colonies were serious about freedom. He recommended the colonies boycott British manufactured goods and published *A Full Vindication of the Measures of Congress* in which he asserted that Americans have a natural right to manage their own affairs. [33]

The pamphlet made Hamilton an instant celebrity among colonial revolutionaries because he wrote well, thought clearly, and constructed arguments that impressed important people. When British troops marched out of Boston toward Concord and Lexington to capture leaders of the American Revolution, the local militia fought back, and the Revolution began. Hamilton joined the New York militia, taught himself military tactics and the handling of cannon. After the battles of Concord and Lexington, the Continental Congress began to prepare for war and named George Washington Commander-in-Chief of the Continental Army. General Washington marched his army to Long Island to defend New York City against invading British troops.

Hamilton fought with Washington in the First Battalion, Fifth Artillery, and his unit covered Washington's retreat after the British drove the Continental Army out of New York. Hamilton handled his guns well during the rear-guard action and Washington marked him for higher command or a staff position. Washington quickly realized his inexperienced militia could not win against hardened British troops in open battle, so he developed a strategy of guerilla strikes and retreats to damage the English troops and preserve his army. Washington attacked the British near Trenton and Princeton, New Jersey, after his retreat from New York and won both those winter battles. The victories raised American morale and Hamilton's profile.

After his victories in New Jersey, Washington sent a letter asking Hamilton to become his aide-de-camp. [34] Hamilton was reluctant to accept a desk job on Washington's staff because he wanted military glory and excitement. However, he couldn't refuse Washington because the general needed someone who could organize and supply the army. Moreover, Hamilton had the necessary skills acquired during his years managing the New York trading house and was a master of logistics, accounts, and finance. Washington needed Hamilton to put the army on a professional footing so it could defend America.

Washington relied on Hamilton to handle army logistics and draft clear memos explaining his requirements and strategy to Congress and his officers. Washington established a meritocracy in his army and Hamilton rose quickly because he was bright, talented, trustworthy, and energetic. He became indispensable to Washington, who relied on Hamilton and often assigned him sensitive tasks. A good example was when Washington sent Hamilton to tell General Gates he must surrender a regiment to Washington because they were needed elsewhere, and Gates was not using the men. Hamilton carried out this task expertly, convincing Gates to give Washington one of his better regiments rather than the under-strength unit Gates originally offered.

Washington and Hamilton agreed on most issues, but they had different views about enlisting slaves in the Continental Army. Washington was a Virginia slave owner who feared arming slaves might lead to a revolt and destroy the Southern plantation economy. Hamilton felt slavery was cruel and believed arming slaves to fight in the Revolutionary War was the first step toward granting them freedom. Even as late as 1864, Southern leaders refused to enlist slaves in the Confederate Army during the Civil War when the South was clearly losing because they were terrified of a slave revolt.

Benedict Arnold. General Arnold was commander of West Point, an important colonial military fortress in the Hudson River Valley. Washington and Hamilton visited West Point to inspect defenses and meet with Arnold to discuss the military situation, but he was not in the fort. While waiting for Arnold, a rider arrived with a message for Washington reporting that British Major Andre had been captured carrying a map and plans of West Point, apparently given him by General Arnold. When Arnold learned Andre had been arrested, he fled to a British ship in New York harbor to escape capture. [35] Hamilton went after Arnold with a military escort, but was too late; Arnold escaped trial for treason, but Major Andre was found guilty and shot as a British spy. Most Americans believed Benedict Arnold was the real traitor who should have been shot for treason, but he was under the protection of the British Army.

Hamilton and Washington had a serious misunderstanding when Washington asked to speak with him, and Hamilton replied that he would return in a few minutes after he delivered an important letter. Hamilton delivered the letter, but rather than returning immediately to see Washington, he spent time chatting with the Marquise de Lafayette. Washington was furious that Hamilton made him wait and told Hamilton he had disrespected his commander. Hamilton was surprised and said he did not realize he had disrespected Washington, but if that was how he felt, it was time for Hamilton to resign from his staff and take command of a regiment.

Washington soon realized his mistake and sent an apology to Hamilton later that day, but he was not willing to forgive Washington. Hamilton was angry, tired of being ordered around, felt insulted, and wanted an independent command. He also had a violent temper that created serious difficulties for him later in life. Hamilton never forgot the bitter quarrel and didn't forgive Washington until the newly elected president invited Hamilton to join his cabinet as Secretary of the Treasury years later. General Washington gave Hamilton command of an infantry unit and sent him to Yorktown to attack General Cornwallis. After heavy fighting, Washington ordered Hamilton's unit to make an assault on the English positions which was successful. Cornwallis surrendered his army to Washington later that day and the Revolutionary War was over.

Washington captured over eight thousand British prisoners during the battle. After lengthy negotiations, the Treaty of Paris was signed two years later, giving the colonies their independence from England under favorable terms. The French king was angry because the Americans negotiated a separate peace with England without consulting the French government. However, the Americans rightly pointed out they had only negotiated for themselves and had not harmed French interests. Besides, they got a good deal. However, America's troubles were far from over. The Continental Congress was not up to running a country.

The Continental Congress. At the beginning of the Revolution, the thirteen states drafted Articles of Confederation, forming a loose association of the states to manage and pay for the war. However, the Continental Congress was weak and could not even tax the states to fund the war. Congress had to beg for money and some governors refused to send any funds to the central government, claiming they needed the money to support their own militias. The Continental Congress resorted to printing money to finance the war, causing runaway inflation and saddling the country with enormous debts and a worthless currency after the war. America was essentially bankrupt after the war because the states would not cooperate to pay off the debts they had incurred. Hamilton proposed a convention to revise the Articles of Confederation and form a strong central government, but his suggestion was ignored for years.

Hamilton resigned from the army after the war, studied law, and passed the New York bar exam. While studying law, Hamilton began thinking about what kind of government America needed to manage its affairs effectively. He favored a strong central government rather than a weak association of states, but many Americans were wary of a strong government that could oppress them. However, Hamilton had seen first-hand how each state had favored its own interests rather than the common good during the war, and he believed the only solution was a strong executive to administer national affairs. Hamilton thought the country needed a strong central government that could coordinate policy, collect taxes, and defend the nation from foreign aggression. He published a paper outlining his ideas about managing the country's finances and paying off the national debt. Hamilton advocated establishing a central bank, nationalizing war debts, and issuing federal bonds to pay off the national debts and as a means for citizens to store wealth.

In 1783, Hamilton moved to New York and started a lucrative law practice on Wall Street. He defended unpopular cases, including American Tories, who had left the colonies during the war and now wanted to reclaim their property or receive compensation. One of his early clients was Elizabeth Rutgers, a wealthy widow who fled New York for Canada when war broke out. Her property was confiscated and leased to Benjamin Waddington and Evelyn Pierrepont. Hamilton settled Mrs. Rutgers' claim after the war and she was reimbursed for her land. Meanwhile, the Continental Congress was facing a rebellion in the Northeast because of taxes on farmers and an economic recession.

Shay's Rebellion. [36] In the 1780s, many Massachusetts farmers faced heavy debts accumulated buying land after the war. The post-war recession caused many indebted landowners to lose their farms and go to prison because they could not pay their debts (America had debtors' prisons at that time). These difficult economic conditions triggered an armed uprising against the banks. Daniel Shay, an ex-revolutionary soldier, led a group of angry farmers intent on liberating their imprisoned neighbors. However, the governor of Massachusetts hired mercenaries to crush the rebellion. Shay's uprising frightened state authorities and led to calls for a convention to revise the Articles of Confederation and strengthen the central government so it could deal with armed unrest. It appeared the time was right for Hamilton's idea of a strong central government to manage the country.

A Trade Convention organized earlier by James Madison had also called for a central government with power to regulate trade between the states, but the recommendation was ignored until armed farmers demanded debt relief. The rebellion frightened American leaders, who quickly scheduled a convention in Philadelphia to discuss forming a central government to replace the Continental Congress.

The Constitutional Convention. Hamilton was elected as a delegate to the Constitutional Convention from New York. Soon after the convention convened, Edmund Randolph proposed that a central government be formed with three separate but equal branches--legislative, executive, and judicial. Another plan proposed by William Paterson was to strengthen the Articles of Confederation but not to establish a strong executive who might become oppressive. After lengthy discussion, the delegates reached an impasse, so Hamilton rose to present his own ideas for a central government. He proposed a Senate and a Monarch, both with life tenure. Hamilton argued that because Senators and the Monarch would have lifetime authority, they would not become corrupt or oppressive. Delegates were astonished because Hamilton's proposal seemed too much like the English system of King and Parliament that they had just defeated to gain their freedom. Because his proposal was rejected, Hamilton left the convention, believing it would be a failure and the Continental Congress would persist.

Instead, delegates continued to debate what sort of central government they needed and finally agreed on a modified version of Randolph's plan, which included a President elected for four years, a Congress with two houses (Representatives elected for two-year terms and Senators for six-year terms), and a Federal Judiciary with lifetime appointments. Hamilton believed Randolph's plan was flawed but wanted it ratified because the alternative was a weak government under the Articles of Confederation. He worked hard to get the Constitution ratified by New York and wrote pamphlets arguing for acceptance of the new form of government.

The Federalist Papers. Alexander Hamilton, James Madison, and John Jay jointly wrote the *Federalist Papers* to convince Americans they should ratify the Constitution. Hamilton wrote fifty-one of the *Federalist Papers*, Madison penned twenty-nine, and Jay drafted five. Hamilton used the pen name Publius and argued that the choice facing the nation was between a weak coalition of states that could not govern or defend themselves and a strong central government that would allow the United States to maintain its independence and prosper economically. Hamilton also stressed that a strong central government would be good for the economy and give voters equal representation in their government. He highlighted the many problems associated with a weak Congress and urged his friends in New York to ratify the new Constitution.

The Federalist Papers explained the rights and duties of the legislative, executive, and judicial branches of government to a skeptical public. Hamilton argued that judicial review of congressional legislation (the power of the Supreme Court to declare legislation passed by Congress unconstitutional) would safeguard American freedoms from Congress and the President. The Federalist Papers were published during a heated political campaign to ratify the Constitution and were read by many Americans. [37] They supported ratification of the Constitution, exerted a strong influence on early political thinking, and still guide modern political philosophy. The *Federalist Papers* are regarded as classic political literature by most historians. A majority of the states ratified the Constitution, and George Washington was elected America's first president. His first job was to appoint competent people to his cabinet. One of his first appointments went to Hamilton as Secretary of the Treasury.

Secretary of the Treasury. President George Washington nominated Hamilton as his Secretary of the Treasury on September 11, 1789. [38] Hamilton had extensive experience in banking and finance because he had managed a Wall Street trading house in the West Indies and handled the finances of Washington's army during the Revolutionary War. He had written an essay about the need for a National Bank, had experience as a tax receiver (collector) for the State of New York, and helped found the Bank of New York. Hamilton was an enlightened choice to be the first Secretary of the Treasury because he understood finance and had clear ideas about how to handle the national debt and public finances. One of his first goals was to place tariffs on imported goods and establish a revenue service to collect taxes to fund the federal government.

To protect American manufacturing, Hamilton proposed that the United States impose stiff tariffs on foreign imports to encourage local businesses. He also established a custom service to operate in American ports and collect duties on cargo entering the U.S. Based on his experience working for Beekman and Cruger in the West Indies, Hamilton knew that ship captains would avoid paying custom duties if they could. To stop smuggling, Hamilton upgraded lighthouses on the East Coast and staffed them with customs agents to monitor ship traffic. He also authorized the building of guard boats to enforce his tariff duties, effectively founding the U.S. Coast Guard.

Once Hamilton had developed a revenue stream to pay for the federal government, he set to work paying off the nation's huge war debt. He wrote an outline of how he proposed to deal with the national debt in a paper titled *The Report on Public Credit.* [39] Hamilton wanted the federal government to assume all state and federal debts accumulated during the American Revolution and issue federal bonds that could be purchased through the treasury or any bank. His goal was to establish a national bond market where citizens could store their savings in a safe investment that earned interest. Hamilton's idea was supported by Northern states burdened with huge debts and opposed by Southern states that had generally paid their war debts through taxes on the sale of cotton and tobacco. Hamilton lobbied hard for his bill, but Congress was divided between the Northern and Southern states and couldn't reach an agreement.

Madison and Jefferson proposed a compromise to Hamilton: they would support passage of the Assumption Bill (as the debt statute was called) if the capitol of the new Republic was located in the South. Hamilton agreed, and he, Jefferson, and Madison asked Washington to support a bill moving the capitol to a special district between Virginia and Maryland called the District of Columbia (Washington D.C. today), in return for their support of the National Bank and federal bond market. Washington agreed and the Assumption Bill was passed.

After issuing federal bonds and establishing Washington D.C. as the new national capitol, Hamilton set out to charter a federal bank and develop an American currency. He proposed that the U.S. Dollar be minted in gold and silver to replace the British Pound as lawful currency in America, and he devised a system of smaller coins based on the decimal system. The penny, nickel, and dime are current examples of Hamilton's decimal money system. To raise additional revenue, Hamilton asked for a tax on whiskey, which caused serious problems in Pennsylvania.

The Whiskey Rebellion. Congress imposed a tax on whiskey to raise money for the federal government after the war, but Pennsylvania farmers objected. They had traditionally sold their moonshine without paying any tax and wanted to continue that practice, so in 1792 they attacked the federal revenue men who came to collect the new tax on moonshine. Hamilton asked Washington to authorize state militia to put down the rebellion, which he did. The militia successfully suppressed the Whiskey Rebellion, but Hamilton wanted the guilty farmers deported to set an example for others. Instead, Washington offered the farmers amnesty if they paid the tax. Hamilton had accomplished his main goals and believed Washington no longer supported him, so he resigned as Secretary of the Treasury and returned to his private law practice in New York in 1794. This was another example of his volatile personality, quick temper, and deep sense of personal honor that would cause him so much trouble all his life.

Hamilton continued corresponding with Washington and offering advice when asked but was no longer so close to the president as he had been while Secretary of the Treasury. At the end of his second term as President, Washington refused to run again, setting a precedent that was not broken until Franklin Roosevelt won third and fourth presidential terms during the Great Depression and Second World War. Washington asked Hamilton to help write his farewell address and Hamilton agreed. They collaborated in telling citizens to consider themselves Americans rather than Virginians or New Yorkers and to guard against foreign interference in American affairs. Washington returned to his plantation at Mount Vernon, Virginia and Hamilton continued his law practice in New York City.

Hamilton became active in the anti-slavery movement, founding the New York Society for the Manumission of Slaves, whose goal was to help Black slaves gain their freedom. [40] Hamilton urged New Yorkers to free their slaves and outlaw slavery in the state, but nothing happened at that time. Later, the issue of slavery would trigger the Civil War in 1860.

Presidential Politics. Alexander Hamilton and John Adams were both staunch Federalists, but they hated each other for purely personal reasons. During the presidential campaign of 1800, Hamilton wrote an article attacking Adams, who was running for a second term against Jefferson and Aaron Burr. Adams never forgave Hamilton for attacking him during the election, believing the attacks were a major factor in his defeat. After the votes were counted, Jefferson and Burr tied for electoral college votes, while Adams was a distant third. A tie in the Electoral College meant the House of Representatives selected the president, with each state having one vote. Hamilton was a member of the Electoral College from New York and he hated Burr, so he actively campaigned and voted for Jefferson. after thirty-six ballots, Jefferson was elected President of the U.S.

He immediately asked his new Secretary of the Treasury, Albert Gallatin, to review Treasury files and find something fraudulent or scandalous to use against Hamilton. Gallatin diligently searched Hamilton's files but found nothing wrong, much to Jefferson's disappointment. Although Hamilton's public life was honorable, his private life was scandalous.

Hamilton's Affair. During the Revolutionary War, Hamilton married Eliza Schuyler, the daughter of Phillip Schuyler, one of the wealthiest men in New York. Schuyler was concerned about Hamilton courting his daughter because he was a bastard son and not a member of New York's "upper class." Schuyler recognized Hamilton was bright, energetic, and an important figure in the U.S. Government, but he was reluctant to have his daughter marry below her social station. Schuyler finally consented and they were married in December 1780.

While he was serving as Secretary of the Treasury, Hamilton began an affair with Mrs. Maria Reynolds while his wife was in Albany with their children because of an epidemic raging in Philadelphia. Maria's husband was a speculator who lost his fortune during the recession following the war, so he forced his wife into prostitution to earn a living. Maria ran her business in the bedroom of their home, and when she learned of Hamilton's wandering eye, she came calling at his home. She told Hamilton her husband had left her for another woman and he wanted to believe her story because she was attractive and he liked pretty available women. He told Marie he would come to her home later with money. When he arrived, Mrs. Reynolds physically thanked Hamilton for his generosity. With Eliza living in Albany, Hamilton and Maria carried on a torrid affair in Washington, D.C.

After several months, Mr. Reynolds showed up at Hamilton's door asking for a job in the Treasury Department. Hamilton refused and vowed to end the affair, but Marie said she would tell Eliza about their sexual relationship if he did, so Hamilton continued the affair, hoping to avoid a scandal. Mr. Reynolds threatened Hamilton with exposure, so he gave Reynolds $1,000 to keep him quiet. Reynolds kept demanding more money, which is typical of blackmailers, and Hamilton didn't know what to do. While he was blackmailing Hamilton, Reynolds also defrauded a war veteran, was discovered and sent to jail. A friend of Reynolds met with Congressman Muhlenberg and told him about Hamilton and Mrs. Reynold's affair in hopes of getting Reynolds out of jail.

Muhlenberg was friendly with Jefferson, who was delighted to damage Hamilton's reputation by promptly spreading the gossip of his affair around Washington. Jefferson's friend James Monroe talked with Mrs. Reynolds and she confirmed the affair. Monroe then confronted Hamilton, who confessed, believing the scandal would go away if he was truthful. Instead, the matter got worse after Jefferson published a pamphlet claiming Hamilton embezzled money from the U.S. Treasury, using Mrs. Reynold's letters as proof. Hamilton denied the embezzlement accusations, saying the money he paid Mr. Reynolds came from his private funds rather than the Treasury. Washington society was shocked that Hamilton would do such a thing to his wife and family.

Hamilton tried to resolve the issue by meeting with Monroe, but they ended up arguing rather than compromising. Monroe denied he had sent letters to anyone about the affair because he had been in Europe at the time and knew nothing about the scandal. Hamilton called Monroe a liar and Monroe called Hamilton a scoundrel. Angry at Monroe and his unfortunate social situation, Hamilton became angry, challenged Monroe to a duel, and he promptly accepted. Monroe had second thoughts about the duel and turned to Aaron Burr to resolve the dispute.

Monroe gave Burr a letter for Hamilton, which said he had no intention of engaging in a duel. Hamilton accepted the letter as an apology and dropped the duel but decided to publish a pamphlet about the issue, which incensed Monroe all over again. He wrote an angry letter to Hamilton challenging him to another duel but never sent the letter. During this entire time Eliza remained loyal to Hamilton, saying he was a good husband and patriot who had been slandered by his Republican enemies. Hamilton was devoted to his family in spite of his sexual escapades, and Eliza stood by him to avoid public scandal and preserve her family. However, Hamilton's temper was about to lead to disaster.

Philip Hamilton's Duel. Hamilton's son Phillip got into a dispute defending his father's honor and died in a duel as a result. The altercation began during a Fourth of July celebration in New York City after a young Republican named George Eaker published a speech blaming Hamilton for almost starting a war with France. When Phillip read the speech, he was outraged and challenged Eaker to a dual. Phillip's friends advised him to respond to the insult in some other way, and when Alexander Hamilton heard about the duel, he advised his son to waste his shot by firing in the air rather than directly at Eaker. However, there was no guarantee Eaker would not shoot Phillip even if Philip fired in the air—a dangerous tactic in a duel.

Eaker and Phillip met on a sandbar near what is now Jersey City, New Jersey. Phillip followed his father's advice and refused to shoot. At first, Eaker didn't shoot either, then he fired and hit Phillip just above his right hip. The bullet went completely through Phillip's body, damaging several internal organs and causing severe blood loss. He was carried to a doctor but died the next day. Alexander Hamilton wrote a series of articles in *The Post* accusing Eaker of being a villain because Phillip had made it clear he had no intention of firing his pistol. Eaker was never tried for Phillip Hamilton's death, but his reputation was ruined. Hamilton must have felt guilty about the advice he gave Philip that got his son killed, but even so, he repeated the episode when he fought a duel with Aaron Burr and Hamilton was killed as a result of that decision.

Hamilton v. Burr. After Phillip's death, Hamilton decided to spend more time with his family to make amends. However, he didn't withdraw from politics and his hot temper led to a fatal duel with Aaron Burr on July 12, 1804. To appreciate what triggered the famous duel, we need to review the similar early histories of these two important Americans and how they became mortal enemies. [41] Hamilton and Burr both graduated from Ivy League schools (Hamilton from the college that become Columbia University and Burr from the college that became Princeton University). Both were orphaned as children and turned out to be exceptional students. After graduation, both studied law with prominent attorneys, opened law offices in New York, fought in the Revolutionary War, and entered New York politics at nearly the same time. Burr and Hamilton were both elected to the New York legislature, Hamilton was instrumental in passing the Constitution, and Aaron Burr supported passage of the 12th Amendment changing how presidents and vice presidents are elected.

Both Burr and Hamilton fought courageously during the American Revolution, earning reputations as American patriots. However, Burr believed General Washington didn't appreciate his talents and felt slighted by not being promoted or given command of troops while Hamilton earned promotions, served on Washington's staff, and commanded a regiment at Yorktown in the battle that won the war. Burr was finally promoted and led a regiment funded by William Malcolm, but he still felt slighted by Washington. Burr distinguished himself in several campaigns but always felt Washington had ignored him. Burr resigned from the army before the war ended.

After the war, Burr and Hamilton came into frequent contact in New York while practicing law. Hamilton lived modestly, even though his wife inherited a large family fortune, while Burr spent lavishly and was always in debt. Hamilton was a handsome and flamboyant lawyer, while Burr was bland and jealous of Hamilton. Burr took any case that came through his door because he needed money, while

Hamilton only represented wealthy clients who had interesting cases. Burr believed Hamilton was more successful and hated him for that as well as other perceived slights.

Hamilton and Burr served together in the New York Assembly and were interested in national issues. They were on opposite sides of the debate about ratifying the new U.S. Constitution, which Hamilton won, increasing Burr's jealousy and resentment. Burr was appointed New York Attorney General by Governor Clinton, while Hamilton served in Washington's cabinet as Secretary of the Treasury. Being Attorney General of New York was not an important job compared with being Secretary of the Treasury in Washington's cabinet—a further source of Burr's bitterness against Hamilton. Burr was eventually elected to the U.S. Senate from the state of New York and felt successful for the first time, but he never stopped hating Hamilton.

Jefferson, Madison, and Burr formed an alliance and were often on the other side of national issues against Hamilton, who was thin-skinned and volatile. During the presidential election of 1796, Hamilton and Burr clashed over political issues. Hamilton supported Thomas Pinckney, Governor of South Carolina, for president, while Burr supported Jefferson. Burr informed John Adams that Hamilton was supporting Pinckney, and Adams was furious because he wanted the nomination for himself. Adams never forgave Hamilton, and when Hamilton found out that Burr had turned Adams against him, he became furious with Burr. Bad blood was continuing to accumulate between these two important men.

Burr speculated in real estate and partnered with James Greenleaf to purchase land in New York state. Greenleaf was supposed to supply half the money for the land but backed out at the last minute, leaving Burr responsible for the entire contract. He couldn't pay for the land and was unable to find another partner. The landowner sued Burr for breach of contract and hired Hamilton to represent him. Burr was found guilty and ordered to pay the contract price for the land or go to jail. He was forced to sell everything he owned and mortgage his house to avoid debtors' prison. Burr was now impoverished and even more bitter at Hamilton but not about to stay on the sidelines. He started the Manhattan Water Company to supply drinking water to New York City and chartered a New York bank to recoup his fortune. The water company was not run properly and many New York citizens contracted yellow fever as a result.

In the presidential election of 1800, Adams and Jefferson were nominated by the two major parties as presidential candidates. Burr helped swing New York to Jefferson, and in return became Jefferson's running mate as vice president. At that time, vice-presidential candidates could accumulate electoral college votes and be elected president if they gained the most votes among all the candidates. Jefferson and Burr tied for electoral college votes and the matter went to the House of Representatives, which eventually elected Jefferson. In 1804, Jefferson selected a new vice president to replace Burr, who ran for Governor of New York. Hamilton wrote a series of vicious attacks against Burr during the election that turned him even more against Hamilton.

At a private party, Hamilton said Burr was a dangerous man who could not be trusted. A guest at the party published Hamilton's remarks in a letter to a newspaper. Hamilton denied the remarks, but Burr was furious when he learned of the comments and sent a letter demanding Hamilton explain his remarks. By this point in his life, Hamilton had been involved in at least six incidents that had almost resulted in a duel, but each time the deadly game had been averted by friends who advised the parties to apologize and forget the insults. However, Burr and Hamilton had a long fractious relationship and bad tempers, so their dispute was difficult to mediate. Hamilton hated Burr and felt guilty about the advice he gave his son Philip not to shoot so he refused to back down. Instead of trying to defuse the situation, Hamilton demanded a detailed analysis of what Burr wanted before he would respond.

Burr wrote an angry reply claiming Hamilton had slandered his honor and demanded an immediate apology. Rather than cool off, and consider the issue realistically, Hamilton wrote a nasty letter back to Burr. At this point it was clear there was no turning back. Hamilton chose Pendleton as his second and Burr selected Van Ness. Hamilton intended to use the same strategy he had recommended to his son Phillip—to fire in the air. Hamilton told Pendleton, who was shocked and advised him not to proceed because he would be killed. Historians have speculated that Hamilton was feeling guilty and depressed about Philip's death and wanted Burr to kill him, but most experts don't believe that's true. [42] However, Hamilton took several steps before the duel that indicate he may have been depressed and knew he would probably die. He arranged his affairs and drafted several letters to Eliza. He knew his wife would be financially comfortable because of an inheritance from her father and his own modest estate. Finally, Hamilton drafted his will the day before the duel.

Burr knew if he killed Hamilton, it would ruin his career, but he was determined to go through with the duel anyway because he was so angry at Hamilton and felt his honor had been sullied. Burr was an expert shot and practiced his marksmanship before the duel, while Hamilton did nothing to prepare for the deadly meeting. They met on neutral ground in New Jersey because dueling was illegal in New York. It was customary for New Yorkers to sail across the river to settle their disputes since New Jersey didn't enforce its ban on dueling. The evening before the duel, Pendleton visited Hamilton in hopes of dissuading him from going through with the encounter but was unsuccessful. Hamilton was accompanied by Pendleton and his personal physician at the duel.

Burr arrived first and Hamilton joined him shortly after. They drew lots to decide who would fire first and where each would stand. Hamilton won and irrationally chose the spot where the sun would be in his eyes, making it more difficult to see Burr and giving Burr a clear view of him unimpeded by sunlight—another sign that Hamilton was probably depressed and intended to die. Burr and Hamilton stood ten feet apart and assumed sideways positions to make it more difficult to hit the other party. Burr fired and Hamilton was hit in the stomach just above his hip. True to his word, Hamilton fired over Burr's head. Hamilton died on July 11, 1804, at the age of forty-nine. [43]

John Adams

John Adams was born October 30, 1735, in Braintree, Massachusetts, a few miles outside Boston. [44] His father was descended from Plymouth Rock settlers and the family lived in a five-room saltbox built in 1681 on a modest farm. John enrolled in Harvard College to study for the ministry. At that time, Harvard had four red brick buildings, a chapel, seven professors, and approximately one hundred students. He excelled at mathematics and science, joined a debating society, and discovered he had a talent for public speaking that served him well throughout his political career. After college, Adams studied law with James Putnam. [45] He lost his first case due to a drafting error and vowed to pay more attention to technical drafting and procedures by learning from more experienced lawyers in Boston.

Adams met Abigail Smith in 1759 and was not impressed with her at the time. [46] Later he realized how unusual she was and became interested in her as a wife. John's father died in May of 1761 from influenza and he inherited a house, forty acres, and one-third of his father's personal property-a substantial legacy at the time. Adams opened a law office in the house and married Abigail Smith on October 25, 1764, just before her twentieth birthday. Abigail was taught to read by her mother and loved to discuss political issues and books with Adams. Abigail's mother opposed their marriage, believing she would be marrying beneath her social class because Adams was not wealthy, but Abigail knew he was going to be a successful man and married him anyway. Adams said his marriage to Abigail was the single most important event in his life. They had two children, Abigail and John Quincy, who would also become president of the United States.

Adams wrote an essay entitled *"A Dissertation on the Canon and the Feudal Law"* that was printed in the Boston Gazette. [47] The article called on readers to be independent thinkers, support liberty, and protect their rights against British tyranny. Adams believed no one should be subject to taxes without his consent and opposed taxes levied by Parliament to pay for the French and Indian War. Soon after his essay appeared, Parliament repealed the Stamp Act, and the colonies were quiet for a few years until British troops arrived to keep order after England imposed new taxes on the colonies. Adams moved his law practice to Boston, became financially successful, and began buying land with his earnings. Having British troops stationed in Boston began to cause trouble.

The Boston Massacre. On March 5, 1770, a mob began throwing ice, snow, and insults at a squad of British soldiers who panicked and shot five of the colonials. Sam Adams immediately called the incident "The Boston Massacre," inflamed the public with pamphlets calling the British troops murderers, and issued a print of the slaughter showing colonists being shot in cold blood. [48] John Adams defended the British captain and soldiers who had fired on the crowd when their case came to trial, saying no man should be denied representation in a free country. Two trials were held, one for the captain and another for the soldiers. It was never proved that Captain Preston gave an order to fire, so he was found not guilty by the court. During Adams' closing argument in the second trial of the soldiers, he said the mob had provoked the soldiers and they had fired in self-defense. Adams listed some of the provocations, including hitting a soldier with a club, throwing sticks and stones, and shouting "kill them" at the troops. Four of the six soldiers were found not guilty and two were found guilty of manslaughter. Adams was roundly criticized by the Boston Gazette for defending the soldiers and lost several clients as a result. After tempers cooled, respect for Adams increased because of his courage in representing the British soldiers, and he was elected to the Massachusetts Legislature later that year.

The Boston Tea Party. Adams' law practice prospered as the country entered a quiet period, but then Parliament passed new taxes on the colonies. In response to these new taxes, angry American colonists dressed as Indians dumped English tea into Boston Harbor in December 1773 to protest taxes imposed by Parliament without consultation with the colonies. Adams was delighted with the action against English tyranny and said so in print. In 1774, he was selected as one of five delegates from Massachusetts to attend the First Continental Congress in Philadelphia. Because Massachusetts colonists were already revolting against England and Adams expected violence, he moved his wife and children back to Braintree for safety.

Soon after the battle at Bunker Hill, Adams penned a series of letters to the Boston Gazette arguing that Americans had the right to determine their own destiny and should be independent of Britain. General Washington ordered soldiers to take charge of the guns captured at Fort Ticonderoga and place them on the hills above Boston to threaten the English Army. The British recognized they were vulnerable in Boston because of the guns on the hill overlooking the city so they boarded ships and sailed to New York and safety. Washington moved his soldiers to Long Island to confront the English troops.

Meanwhile, the Continental Congress was meeting to discuss what to do about the British occupation of the colonies. Of the fifty-four delegates to Congress in the spring of 1775, almost all were college educated and about half were attorneys, such as Adams, or wealthy plantation owners. Adams was impressed by the exceptional talent he saw among the Congressional delegates. All meetings were held behind closed doors because there were British spies in Philadelphia trying to discover what the colonists were planning. Adams complained about the endless debates and labeled the Continental Congress an unwieldy body that got little done. He penned a list of goals for America that included an alliance with France, self-government, the development of powder mills in major cities, and a declaration of independence from Britain.

The Continental Congress was divided among those who wanted to stay united with Britain, those who secretly supported independence but were reluctant to voice their views openly, and those who wanted to be free of English rule and said so publicly. Delegates from six of the thirteen colonies, New York, New Jersey, Pennsylvania, Delaware, Maryland, and South Carolina, were instructed to vote "no" on independence by their legislatures, leaving the issue in doubt. Lord Dunmore, the English royal governor of Virginia, called on American slaves to revolt, promising them freedom if they would join the British Army in suppressing the American uprising. Southern delegates were outraged at British interference in slavery and supported independence for the colonies as a result. Benjamin Franklin, who was the most respected member of Congress, refused to speak in support of independence, so Adams assumed the lead among those arguing for freedom from Britain, even though he had been advised to allow the Virginia delegation to lead the debate because it was the most important colony. Opposition to independence was strongest among the Quakers of Pennsylvania who were pacifists.

Support for independence gained ground after Thomas Paine published *Common Sense,* calling for independence from England. [49] In February, Congress passed an embargo on exports to England and Silas Deane was sent to France to encourage that country to join America in the war against England. Benjamin Franklin went to Canada to see if America's northern neighbor would declare independence, but the Canadians refused. Congress passed a law disarming American Tories sympathetic to England and another that authorized privateers to capture British ships in the Atlantic. Adams advocated the creation of a colonial navy to defend the country, and on October 13, 1775, Congress authorized funds to build two heavy frigates, founding the United States Navy. [50]

Adams on Government. Adams published *Thoughts on Government* as a letter addressed to William Hooper. [51] He wrote that the job of government is to produce happiness for people, and the best form of government is a republic. He proposed a new federal government composed of two assemblies, one to represent the people and another smaller body to represent the states and act as a balance against momentary emotions. Adams also suggested the government needed an executive selected by the two houses to administer the government, have veto power over legislation, and the authority to appoint judges for life. Adams also wanted the executive to be commander-in-chief of the armed forces. He believed the president, congress, and the courts should be independent and balance each other to avoid one branch of government becoming too powerful. Adams also wanted the government to support education for all Americans. This was an enlightened view of government and was generally achieved during the Constitutional Convention of 1787. But in 1776, Congress had too many other priorities to change its form of government.

Shortly after Adams published his letter, word reached Philadelphia that a large British fleet had arrived in Halifax, Canada, and was awaiting reinforcements before sailing south to land troops in New York City. On May 9, 1776, Adams and Richard Henry Lee proposed a resolution before the Continental Congress that the colonies take over their own government from England and declare independence. After heated debate, the resolution was approved and the American colonies took a huge step toward independence. On June 7, 1776, Richard Henry Lee introduced a motion to the floor of Congress stating: [52]

"Resolved, That these United Colonies are, and of right ought to be, free and independent states, that they are absolved from all allegiance to the British Crown, and that all political connections between them and the state of Great Britain is, and ought to be, totally dissolved."

Adams seconded the motion, and after lengthy debate, a vote was scheduled for July 1, 1776, giving delegates time to receive instructions from their respective governments about how to vote. Congress asked Thomas Jefferson, John Adams, Roger Sherman, Robert Livingston, and Benjamin Franklin to draft a formal Declaration of Independence for Congress to consider. Adams suggested Jefferson write the first draft of the declaration so a Virginian could lead the effort. Jefferson borrowed heavily from a draft of the Virginia Constitution he was composing, as well as material from the Declaration of Rights for Virginia written by George Mason. The famous phrase "that man is born free and everywhere he is in chains" was first written by Rousseau and borrowed by Jefferson for the Declaration of Independence.

Adams delayed bringing the Declaration of Independence to a formal vote until the Pennsylvania delegation had received instructions from its legislature to support the motion. Debate began on July 1, 1776, and lasted three days. John Dickinson, a Quaker from Pennsylvania, argued it was premature to separate from England, and America should find a compromise with the British Crown. Adams rose in response and gave a compelling speech supporting independence. When a preliminary vote was taken, four delegations refused to approve the declaration, including the members from Pennsylvania, even though that legislature had instructed them to vote in favor of independence. Several delegations abstained, and others were divided. A final vote was postponed until a missing delegate from Delaware could arrive.

The Delaware delegate arrived early the next morning, mud-spattered and tired after riding all night. The Pennsylvania delegates opposing independence were absent from the meeting, the New York delegates abstained, and all other colonial delegations voted for independence, making the Declaration of Independence unopposed but not unanimous. The Declaration was kept secret because the signers had just committed treason against England and were at risk of execution if discovered. A large English fleet arrived off New York in late June of 1776, and on July 3, nine thousand British troops under General William Howe landed at Staten Island, where hundreds of American Tories welcomed them. By the middle of August, thirty thousand English soldiers were ashore in New York preparing to attack George Washington's army.

Opposing the British were approximately twenty thousand poorly equipped American militia and Continental Army soldiers digging in to defend the city. Adams, as head of the War Office, felt overwhelmed because he was responsible for everything from collecting ordinance, fortifying cities, promoting officers, recruiting enlisted men, paying and provisioning the troops, and supplying them with materials to fight. Congress printed paper money to pay for military supplies and inflation raged throughout the war. Basic necessities were in short supply and expensive when available, making life difficult for ordinary Americans during the war.

Adams was sent to France in February 1778, aboard the frigate *Boston,* to join Franklin in trying to convince France to join the American war against England. It took Adams six weeks to reach France, where he learned the country had already signed an alliance with America after General Horatio Gates' victory over the British at Saratoga. Franklin showed Adams around Paris, introduced him to important government officials, and got Adams invited to the right dinner parties. Adams was shocked by the forwardness of French women but liked their food and manners. Franklin was a favorite of the French because of his scientific achievements and humble dress. France and England never formally declared war, but they fought for years before the American Revolution was won.

Adams drafted documents and presented them for his fellow commissioners to debate, revise, and sign. They worked under a severe handicap because it took months for their letters to be answered by Congress while European delegates could communicate more quickly. Franklin and Adams often acted on their own without instructions, hoping Congress would agree with the decisions they made. Even though Franklin was getting older and had less energy, he was extremely popular in France and an effective advocate for America. Adams and Franklin nurtured the alliance with France throughout the war and believed it was an important part of winning independence from England. In September 1778, Congress named Franklin minister to the Court of Louis XVI and Adams returned to America.

He arrived in Boston on August 2, 1779, after an easy journey from France aboard the *Sensible.* The war was not going well for the colonies, however. After a harsh winter, the American army was better trained but short of men and still poorly armed. Adams drafted the Massachusetts Constitution that year and said it was one of his more important achievements. He wrote a preamble, a declaration of rights, and then the body of the Constitution. The Massachusetts government was based on Adams' proposals in *Thoughts on Government.* [53] He established three separate and equal branches: legislative, executive, and judicial. The government contained a House of Representatives and a Senate, an executive with veto power over legislation, and an independent judiciary appointed for life. The Massachusetts Constitutional Commission approved Adams' draft with only minor changes. The Massachusetts Constitution he drafted is the oldest active written constitution in the world.

As the Revolutionary War continued, Adams returned to France because Congress was worried that the French king was getting tired of the war and might seek a separate peace with England. Adams also visited the Dutch Republic to discuss a loan because America was insolvent and Holland favored American independence. Moreover, Dutch merchants had made fortunes trading with America and France during the war and Adams wanted to borrow some of that money for the American government. The Dutch government was hesitant to get involved in the American war because of English threats, so Adams traveled to Amsterdam where the banks were located. Dutch bankers were also frightened by English threats, so they stalled approval of a loan. Adams decided to take matters into his own hands and publicly announced the purpose of his mission to Holland before the Dutch had formally acknowledged him as an American delegate.

He was taking a huge risk because if the Dutch government decided not to recognize him, he would be sent home in disgrace. But Adams felt he had to do something to get money for Congress because the war was going badly, and the country needed a loan. Everything changed when news arrived in Europe that Washington had defeated Cornwallis at Yorktown, and the English had agreed to end the war. On February 26, 1782, Holland formally received Adams as minister from America and began discussing a loan. On June 11, 1782, Dutch banks issued a loan to America of two million dollars at five percent interest, which helped America establish credit in Europe and pay outstanding debts. Adams also signed a commercial treaty with Holland opening trade between the two countries.

In England, Lord North resigned as Prime Minister after the British surrender at Yorktown, and Lord Rockingham, a friend of America, took over the office. Charles Fox, who favored recognition of American independence, was named Foreign Secretary and he sent an envoy to America to discuss peace. John Jay, John Adams, and Benjamin Franklin were appointed by Congress to negotiate a treaty with England. They discussed the terms America wanted from England but refused to negotiate until the British recognized American independence. Adams was distressed to learn that Congress wanted the American delegation to involve the French government in the negotiations, and he threatened to resign if that happened. The American delegates decided on their own to negotiate a treaty without consulting the French.

Formal peace negotiations between America and England began on October 30, 1782. The major issues included independence, borders for the United States, navigation rights for America on the Mississippi River, claims by American Tories against the United States, and American fishing rights on the Grand Banks off Newfoundland. Adams especially wanted rights for Massachusetts fishing boats on the Grand Banks. The Americans asked for all the land between the Appalachian Mountains and the Mississippi River and the British agreed. Navigation rights on the Mississippi River were also approved quickly. Britain wanted compensation paid to Tories, but Americans hated them as traitors and stalled. After lengthy discussions, the U.S. proposed to allow each state to decide if they would recognize Tory debts, and the British reluctantly agreed in order to move the negotiations along.

Settlement of American fishing rights on the Grand Banks almost blocked agreement of the treaty, but Adams insisted that the ancient rights of Massachusetts fishermen be recognized, and the British finally conceded the point. The French were unhappy when they learned that America had signed a peace treaty with England without consulting them, even after Adams explained they had done nothing to impair French rights. In fact, the French thought the Americans had negotiated a good deal from the English and were impressed. On September 3, 1783, Adams, Jay, and Franklin signed the Treaty of Paris, ending the Revolutionary War; America was finally independent of England. [54] The United States established formal diplomatic relations with England and opened a ministry in London.

Minister to England. Adams was appointed minister to England after the peace treaty was signed. He met King George and was polite to the "tyrant." His family was also invited to meet the Queen. Adams found a suitable house for his family on Grosvenor Square near the West End of London, but Londoners rejected and ignored Adams. He socialized with other Americans and paid no attention to attacks in the London papers. American Tories spread nasty rumors about Adams at every opportunity, and he ignored them as well.

The major issues Adams faced in London involved debts owed by the various states to American Tories, compensation for slaves and other property confiscated by the British during the war, and the continuing presence of British troops in America. Britain was in no hurry to carry out the terms of the peace agreement it had made with the United States and viewed the new country as a weak adversary that could safely be ignored. Adams tried to open English ports to American ships without success. To make matters worse, American trade with France was also blocked to protect French merchants and manufacturers. Adams frequently corresponded with Jefferson, who was minister to the French Court. He was no more successful in opening trade with France than Adams was with England because they were negotiating from weakness against powerful countries with strong central governments that protected their own interests.

Another serious concern for Adams and Jefferson was raids on American shipping in the Mediterranean by Barbary pirates. Secretary of State John Jay instructed Adams and Jefferson to negotiate with the pirates and stop the raids. The Sultan of Tripoli's envoy met with Adams in London and said America needed to pay thirty thousand pounds to his country and three thousand pounds to him personally to stop the raids. Adams and Jefferson said that was too much, but the envoy told them it was his lowest price and they would have to negotiate treaties with the other Barbary states for comparable sums or face continued attacks on American shipping. Jefferson recommended war rather than paying tribute, but Adams argued it would be cheaper to pay rather than build a larger navy and fight a war with the North African nations in the Mediterranean. Congress took Adams' advice and paid the tribute.

Adams returned to Boston on June 17, 1788, and moved into a country house near Braintree he had just purchased for his family. Adams was delighted with the farm, but Abigail felt the house was too small and the ceilings too low after her experiences with elegant homes in London and Paris. Speculation in the U.S. about his political future was widespread, but Adams decided he would accept the nomination for vice president with George Washington in the new constitutional form of government, believing other offices were beneath his station. Everyone agreed that Washington would be the first President, and Adams was the natural choice for vice president because of his extensive foreign and domestic experience.

The President and Vice President were selected by electors from each state, who could vote for two candidates. The person with the most votes would be president and the other candidate would be vice president. If there was a tie, the decision would be made by the House of Representatives. Washington was elected president unanimously, and Adams was elected vice president. [55] His main duty as vice president was to preside over the Senate. Both Adams and Washington established numerous precedents as they proceeded because they were the first men to hold the offices of President and Vice President. Adams felt that something needed to be done to bring respect to the federal government, so he proposed grand titles for the major offices. However, Washington and the Senate decided to use the plain title of President of the United States to describe Washington's office. Adams understood President Washington was above criticism, so all negative feelings about government policies would be directed against him.

The major issues before Congress during Adam's first year as Vice President were where to place the new capitol and what to do about debts the Continental Congress and the states had incurred during the Revolutionary War. Secretary of the Treasury Hamilton proposed that the federal government establish a national bank, assume all state debts, and issue government bonds to pay off the debts and develop a national credit market. Washington and Congress agreed. Hamilton made a deal with Jefferson to move the capitol to Washington, D.C. in return for approval of the national bank and the issuance of federal debt. The vote on moving the capitol to Washington, D.C. was tied in the Senate, so Adams cast the deciding vote in favor of moving the government to Washington, D.C. While the new capitol was being constructed, the federal government moved to Philadelphia until the new buildings were complete.

Washington wanted to leave the presidency after one term and return to private life, but he was persuaded to accept a second term by Congressional leaders. Washington was reelected unanimously and Adams won the vice presidency again. The French Revolution broke out shortly after Washington took office for a second term and King Louis XVI was executed by the Committee of Public Safety. Adams was appalled by the mob violence in Paris and warned that unchecked legislative majorities were as dangerous as kings. On February 1, 1791, England declared war on France, starting a conflict that lasted for twenty years and tore Europe apart. President Washington announced that America would stay neutral in the war between England and France, but both countries attacked American shipping in the Atlantic and England blockaded Europe, causing a serious recession in America. Washington announced he would not accept a third term as President, so other candidates began to announce their interest in the office.

President Adams. John Adams and Thomas Jefferson were the leading candidates to replace President Washington after he decided not to run. Adams was expected to carry the New England states, Jefferson was strong in the South, and the Middle Atlantic states were likely to decide the election. When the votes were counted, Adams was elected President and Jefferson Vice President. Adams was inaugurated on March 4, 1797, with Washington and Jefferson standing beside him. The second President of the U.S. assumed office over sixteen states because Vermont, Kentucky, and Tennessee had been added to the union during Washington's presidency. Vermont was a free state, but Kentucky and Tennessee both entered the Union as slave states.

President Adams worked hard to avoid war with England and France, even though both navies were attacking American shipping in the Atlantic. Adams called Congress into special session to discuss dealing with the issue. Some called for an alliance with Great Britain and war against France, but President Adams wanted to resolve the disputes peacefully if possible. He did ask Congress for money to strengthen America's army and navy, just in case the country could not avoid war. Adams sent Elbridge

Gerry and John Marshall to Paris to negotiate a treaty with the French Revolutionary Government about attacks on U.S. shipping, but they ran into immediate difficulties with the French Foreign Minister.

French Foreign Minister Talleyrand didn't want to push the U.S. toward Britain by being too aggressive and was prepared to stop harassing American shipping, release their crews, and pay reparations for the cargo France had seized, but only if America would pay him a large bribe and loan money to France. The American envoys decided not to respond to Talleyrand's demands for money until France stopped harassing American shipping, so they were at an impasse from the very beginning of negotiations. Gerry began a series of secret meetings with Talleyrand and proposed to pay him a bribe to break the deadlock, but Marshall and Pinckney said "no." After months of unsuccessful negotiation, Marshall and Pinckney returned to America, leaving Gerry in France to continue talks with Talleyrand.

President Adams was angry at the French for the way it had treated his envoys and asked Congress to authorize additional money for the American Navy and coastal defenses. Congress refused funds until the American delegate's dispatches were published so they could see who was to blame for the failure. Adams was delighted to release the delegate's journal as the "XYZ Papers" because the document showed France had caused the impasse. [56] America's mood turned against France after the journal was published, in spite of Jefferson's efforts to blame the failure on Marshall. Congress quickly authorized funding for ten thousand troops and the construction of several heavy U.S. Navy frigates to protect the country. Marshall told Adams he didn't believe France wanted war with America because it was already busy fighting most of Europe, so Adams did nothing to provoke the French government, hoping to avoid war, and his tactic worked.

Adams also had to deal with the French who were living in America, including aristocrats who had fled France during the revolution, and refugees from San Domingo who had come to the U.S. following an uprising by slaves in that country. Some of the French were spies, and Adams wanted to limit their actions against America. To give the President authority to suppress the activities of French spies, Congress passed the Sedition Act designed to stop newspapers from libeling the government. It also authorized a tax on land to pay for the army and navy and established the Marine Corps within the U.S. Navy. Adams nominated George Washington commander of the new provisional army, although it was understood he would not lead troops in battle. The French Navy continued to capture American ships on the high seas and confiscate their cargos, much to Adams' dismay and American anger, but he avoided provoking the French into declaring war on America.

A problem arose for Adams when Washington said he wanted to name Alexander Hamilton the second-highest-ranking officer in the new army. Adams opposed the appointment because it would mean Hamilton was in command of the army. But since Hamilton had the support of Washington and because the ex-President was extremely popular with Congress and the people, Adams had no choice but to agree. After the English victory over the French in the Battle of the Nile, the threat of an invasion of America by France essentially vanished. On February 18, 1799, Adams made an important diplomatic move by nominating William Vans Murray minister to France and ordering him not to visit France without written assurances he would be received cordially, and a minister of equal rank would be appointed by France to represent that country in America. After some opposition in Congress, a compromise was reached naming Patrick Henry and Oliver Ellsworth in addition to Murray as ministers to France. The Senate immediately confirmed the appointments, and Adams waited to hear from France.

Adams soon learned that the American heavy frigate *Constellation* had captured the French frigate *L'Insurgent* in the first naval battle of the undeclared war with France and he was relieved. After that naval victory by the U.S., Talleyrand wrote a letter to Adams promising that the American ministers would be received by his government, so they went to Paris. Adams directed that the American Navy continue aggressive actions against French ships at sea while negotiations proceeded. On December 14, 1799, George Washington died at age sixty-seven from a sore throat and other complications. [57]

As a new century dawned, Napoleon seized power as First Counsel, making him the ruler of France and much of Europe. In the election of 1800, Adams ran for a second term as President against Jefferson and the government moved from Philadelphia to Washington D.C., even though there were neither schools nor churches and only a few hotels available in the city. The 1800 presidential campaign was nastier than usual, with rumors circulating that Jefferson was cohabiting with Sally Hemings, one of his Black slaves, while Adams was accused of being a monarchist friendly to the British. These criticisms were ironic because Jefferson lived on a plantation with hundreds of slaves while Adams was a farmer's son and despised slavery.

Near the end of the 1800 campaign, Hamilton published an open letter critical of Adams. Federalists were angry, believing Hamilton had lost his senses by attacking the President, who was a fellow member of Hamilton's party. Adams moved into the newly constructed White House in November 1800 and learned his mission to negotiate a treaty with France had succeeded. However, the news of his success was too late--Adams lost the presidential election. Jefferson collected seventy-three votes to Adams sixty-five. Aaron Burr also collected seventy-three votes, so the election was decided by the House of Representatives, where Jefferson won. Had the news of peace with France arrived earlier, Adams might have won a second term as President, but that was not to be.

Before Adams left office, he appointed John Marshall Chief Justice of the U.S. Supreme Court and the Senate promptly confirmed him. [58] Adams said later that naming Marshall Chief Justice was one of his best decisions as President. Adams left Washington, D.C., eight hours before Jefferson took the oath of office because they hated each other and Adams didn't want to see Jefferson inaugurated as the next President. Jefferson inherited a government without debts and at peace with the world. The American Navy had fifty powerful frigates and over five thousand officers and enlisted men to protect the country. During Adams' four years as president, there had been no scandal attached to his administration—all remarkable achievements.

Adams had to decide what to do with himself after losing his bid for a second term. He settled in as "Farmer John," caring for his land and reading. His son, John Quincy Adams, returned from a tour of Europe and established a law practice in Boston. Four months later, John Quincy was elected to the Massachusetts Senate. He later ran for the U.S. House of Representatives from Massachusetts but was defeated. John Adams lost all his savings when the English bank that held his money went bankrupt. At that time, ex-Presidents were not given a pension, so John and Abigail were destitute. John Quincy immediately gave his parents $13,000, bought the family farm, and allowed his parents to live there during their lifetimes. John Quincy also moved closer to his aging parents in Braintree to take care of them in their old age.

John Quincy Adams was elected to the U.S. Senate in time to vote for purchasing the Louisiana Territory, recently bought from France for $15 million, one of the great bargains of history. That summer, Vice President Aaron Burr killed Hamilton in a duel that shocked Washington, D.C. In 1804, President Jefferson won a second term as President by a landslide. John Quincy accepted a chair in rhetoric and oratory at Harvard College while serving in the U.S. Senate and John Adams began working on his autobiography. He reread Shakespeare, Cicero, and the Bible, settled into a comfortable domestic routine on his farm and carried on an active correspondence with American leaders. James Madison was elected the fourth president of the U.S., and he appointed John Quincy Adams ambassador to Russia.

Benjamin Rush engineered a reconciliation between John Adams and Thomas Jefferson in January 1812 now that both were retired. The reconciliation began with a letter from Adams to Jefferson, initiating an extraordinary correspondence discussing American history and institutions. [59] Each wrote the letters to express their own ideas for posterity. For example, on January 21, 1812, Jefferson wrote:

> "It carries me back to the times when beset with difficulties and dangers, we were fellow laborers in the same cause, struggling for what is most valuable to man, his right of self-government."

Adams responded on February 3, 1812:

> "[T]he Prospect of the Future, will depend on the Union, and how is that Union to be preserved? The Union is still to me an Object of as much Anxiety as ever Independence was."

Jefferson wrote on October 12, 1813:

> "In extracting the pure principles which he [Jesus} taught, we should have to strip off the artificial vestments in which they have been muffled by priests, who have travestied them into various forms, as instruments of riches and power for them … We must reduce their volume to the simple evangelists, select, even from them, the very words only of Jesus."

Adams wrote to Jefferson on June 20, 1815:

> "The question before the human race is, Whether the God of nature shall govern the World by his own laws, or Whether Priests and Kings shall rule it by fictitious miracles? Or, in other words, whether Authority is originally in the People? or whether it has descended for 1800 years in a succession of Popes and Bishops."

A remarkable set of letters discussing important questions of government, religion, and the nature of man.

By 1812, America was again at war with England. Jefferson gave credit to Adams when the American heavy frigates engaged several British ships in battles off the American coast. In November 1812, Rush sent Adams a copy of an important book he had written on *Diseases of the Mind*, one of the early seminal books in American psychiatry. Rush died the next year, apparently from typhus. Meanwhile, John Quincy received word he had been appointed to negotiate a treaty with Britain ending the War of 1812. John Adams sent letters to his son advising him during the negotiation.

Abigail Adams contracted typhoid fever and died on October 28, 1818. [60] John Adams said he had been blessed with the most exceptional woman in existence and was devastated by her death. He continued to enjoy good health, and John Quincy was appointed Secretary of State by President Monroe. John Quincy added Spanish Florida to American territory during his tenure as Secretary of State. Jefferson and Adams were getting along so well that Adams felt comfortable raising the issue of slavery with him. Jefferson said he was opposed to slavery but never supported the emancipation of slaves, didn't free his own slaves when he died, and didn't respond to Adams about the issue. Jefferson was occupied at the time with founding the University of Virginia, one of his proudest achievements. On August 14, 1821, two hundred West Point Cadets marched in front of Adams' house to show their respect for the ex-President.

In 1824, with President Monroe due to retire, John Quincy Adams became a candidate to replace him. Because neither John Quincy Adams nor Andrew Jackson received a majority of the electoral college votes, the contest was decided in the House of Representatives. Henry Clay, Speaker of the House, used his influence to elect John Quincy Adams sixth president of the United States. In 1826, fifty years after the founding of America, both Jefferson and Adams were invited to attend various events to celebrate the anniversary of independence from England, but neither man was able to travel because of age and poor health. Adams was ninety and Jefferson eighty-three at the time. Both were determined to see one more Fourth of July if possible. John Adams and Thomas Jefferson both died on July 4, 1816, fifty years after they signed the Declaration of Independence. [61]

John Marshall

John Marshall was born in a log cabin on September 24, 1755, in Germantown, Virginia. His formal education included one year of grammar school and six weeks of law school. [62] From these humble beginnings, he rose to become a military officer, prominent attorney, diplomat, Congressman, Secretary of State, and Chief Justice of the U.S. Supreme Court. [63] Chief Justice Marshall developed major legal doctrines that guide America today. He transformed a weak federal court into a co-equal branch of government that has the final say on the constitutionality of Congressional legislation and the meaning of the Constitution—extraordinary accomplishments for one man.

Marshall saw General George Washington transform the Continental Army from a group of poorly equipped men into a disciplined fighting force that eventually fought the British Army to a standstill. Later, as a diplomat, he negotiated with France, England, Spain, and the Barbary pirates from a position of military and political weakness. Marshall concluded that the perception of American strength and resolve was crucial in diplomacy and the key to avoiding war with other countries. When President Adams nominated Marshall Chief Justice of the U.S. Supreme Court, the federal judiciary was a minor branch of government that had little power. His opinion in *Marbury v Madison* made the Supreme Court a powerful equal branch of the U.S. government. [64] Before Marshall became Chief Justice, the Supreme Court decided few important cases, had little power and received no respect. Justices often resigned to run for an important state office. Marshall changed all that with his insightful analyses of legal issues in his Supreme Court opinions and made the Supreme Court the final arbiter of state statutes and the meaning of the U.S. Constitution.

No separate building had been constructed for the Supreme Court when Washington, D.C. was planned, so Marshall's Court met in the basement of the Congressional building. In spite of these humble beginnings, Marshall made the Supreme Court a powerful American institution. During his tenure the Court issued over one thousand opinions, many of them unanimous—an achievement never duplicated. Marshall authored over half the Court's opinions himself. He didn't favor a strict construction of the Constitution, believing it should evolve to meet the needs of later generations. Marshall defended the independence of the federal judiciary, the separation of powers within the federal government, the sanctity of contracts, and the supremacy of federal laws over state statutes. His rise to prominence began during the Revolutionary War.

Revolutionary Soldier. Marshall served in the Continental Army at Valley Forge during that first hard winter. [65] Morale was low, the troops had little equipment, and many were sick or dying from disease. Medical care was poor and soldiers were threatening to desert if they were not paid. The Continental dollar was losing value as Congress printed money to pay for the war and prospects looked dim. In spite of these hardships, John Marshall was upbeat and optimistic. He was an exceptional athlete who impressed his officers and men with fairness and intelligence. General Washington appointed Marshall deputy judge advocate, even though he had little legal experience. Marshall resolved disputes between soldiers and formed personal friendships with Washington, Hamilton, and other important Americans during his time in the army.

Marshall's Early Life. John Marshall was born sixty miles southwest of Washington, D.C., [66] the oldest of fifteen children. When he was around ten his family moved west near the Blue Ridge Mountains. His father taught Marshall self-reliance and the value of private property--principles that became the foundations of his judicial philosophy. Marshall's father and George Washington were hired by Lord Fairfax to survey more than five million acres in Northern Virginia and Lord Fairfax became a patron of the Marshall family. He helped John Marshall acquire land and develop a thriving law practice.

John Marshall's grandmother was descended from two of Virginia's leading families and was related to Thomas Jefferson. Marshall was unconcerned when Jefferson inherited the Randolph fortune while his own father received nothing from his grandmother's family because of primogeniture, where the first son inherits everything. Instead, Marshall made the most of his own talents, identified with the common man, and because of his distinguished maternal heritage, was able to interact comfortably with his social superiors. Marshall's parents taught him to read and write at an early age and he essentially educated himself. Lord Fairfax gave Marshall books, one of which was Blackstone's *Commentaries on the Laws of England*, which probably triggered his interest in the law.

Marshall saw first-hand that a confederation of state governments could not run a war and administer a nation effectively because the state legislatures could not agree about goals and means. He believed the United States needed a strong central government to manage its affairs. Marshall supported liberty, private property, national defense, and reconciliation with the British to protect the United States because America was a trading nation and needed freedom of the seas to prosper. Marshall met his future wife and decided to study law to be near her.

Attorney Marshall. Marshall visited Yorktown, where his father was stationed. He was introduced to Mary Ambler, fell in love, decided to enroll in law school to be near her, and attended lectures given by George Wythe. [67] Marshall read Blackstone's *Commentaries* and books by David Hume and other enlightenment thinkers in law school. After six weeks, Marshall learned Mary was moving to Richmond, so he withdrew from law school and followed her. Marshall took an examination and was admitted to practice law in Virginia. His law license was signed by Governor Thomas Jefferson. In 1781, Marshall was elected to a seat in the Virginia House of Burgesses, the state's governing body. This gave him a good reason to remain in Richmond and be close to Mary. When Mary turned sixteen, Marshall asked her to marry him, and to his surprise she refused. However, she quickly changed her mind and agreed to marry him. As a wedding gift, his father gave Marshall three horses and a slave.

Marshall worked with Richard Henry Lee and James Monroe in the Virginia House of Burgesses to pass bills. After a year, Marshall was elected to the powerful Council of State, the executive branch of Virginia's government, with the power to approve or veto actions taken by the governor. Marshall was the youngest member ever elected to the Council and was resented by some older men, although they acknowledged he was "clever." One of the earliest issues Marshall faced was whether the governor could dismiss a justice of the peace for misappropriating funds under a statute passed by the Virginia General Assembly. Marshall said he believed the statute was unconstitutional and, therefore, the justice could not be dismissed. The governor ultimately accepted the decision of the council, and Marshall's legal argument initiated the doctrine that legislative statutes are subordinate to the state's constitution, an idea he would strengthen later as Chief Justice of the Supreme Court in his famous opinion in *Marbury v. Madison.* [68] Marshall practiced law in Virginia.

Marshall's Law Practice. In 1786, Marshall bought Edmund Randolph's law practice, which was started by Thomas Jefferson. Marshall quickly earned a reputation as a skilled advocate. Most of his legal work involved defending colonial debtors against American Tory creditors trying to collect money for property confiscated during the Revolutionary War. His most important client was Lord Fairfax, the largest landholder in Virginia. During the war, Virginia confiscated five million acres of Lord Fairfax's land, believing he was a Tory sympathetic to England, a traitor, and therefore his land was forfeit. Marshall worked for years to regain title to these properties for Lord Fairfax's heirs and eventually purchased a sizable chunk of the land for himself. The Fairfax case came before the U.S. Supreme Court while Marshall was Chief Justice. He recused himself, although he helped write the opinion after the remaining Justices rendered a decision in favor of Fairfax. Marshall helped ratify the U.S. Constitution.

Ratifying the Constitution. Marshall was a delegate to the Virginia convention formed to ratify the U.S. Constitution. Other prominent Virginians, including James Monroe, James Madison, Richard Henry Lee, Edmund Randolph, and George Wythe, were also delegates. Marshall and Madison worked hard to get the Constitution ratified. Thomas Jefferson was an envoy to France at the time and missed the ratification, as did George Washington. Many delegates wanted to add a bill of rights to the Constitution, but Marshall and Madison feared that delaying passage might lead to rejection of the document. Madison was intellectual leader of the pro-constitution block of Virginia delegates, but Marshall was the group's public voice. He appealed to the delegates with well-reasoned arguments focused on the president's powers as commander in chief under Article II and the authority of the federal courts under Article III. Marshall argued in favor of a strong central government to defend the country and pointed out that because George Washington would be the first president and the federal courts would limit the power of Congress, state's rights would be protected from an authoritarian Congress.

The U.S. Constitution was adopted by a margin of 89 to 79 by the Virginia delegates and was adopted by a majority of the states. Marshall supported slavery, owned household slaves, and was concerned about what would happen to the country if slaves were freed. He wanted a gradual end to slavery and advocated sending freed slaves back to their native lands—a solution similar to Lincoln's own plan years later. President Adams sent Marshall to France in an effort to stop French seizure of American shipping.

Peace Delegate to France. In the spring of 1797, President John Adams sent Elbridge Gerry, Charles Pinckney, and John Marshall to France to negotiate an end to French seizures of American shipping. Thomas Jefferson believed France was a natural ally of the United States against Britain and wanted close ties with the French, but the commission failed to win an agreement with France because the French were stalling for time hoping they could defeat the British. Marshall visited John Adams on his way to Philadelphia to pay his respects. John and Abagail were impressed, believing Marshall to be an "honest man." Secretary of State Pickering sent Marshall a list of negotiating instructions concerning the issues he wanted resolved with the French. Included were the principle that goods traveling in a free ship are free and that the United States would not be bound by its treaty with France to intervene in the war with Britain because the French had attacked the English.

Marshall arrived in Amsterdam on August 29, 1797, and discovered that the Dutch were unhappy because Napoleon demanded almost 20 percent of the country's GDP to finance his wars in Europe. Marshall feared the same thing could happen to America if a foreign country gained influence in his country. He traveled to The Hague, where Charles Pinckney was living, and they became friends because both were Southern Federalists who supported President Adams. Marshall learned for the first time that Napoleon had seized power in France and was at war with most of Europe. After a few weeks, they grew tired of waiting for Gerry and went to Paris without him.

French Foreign Minister Talleyrand had trained for the clergy but turned against the church during the revolution. He became wealthy and powerful, rose quickly within the directorate, and was appointed minister to Britain by the revolutionary government. When France declared war on England, Talleyrand left for the U.S., where he stayed two years before being appointed French Foreign Minister and returning to Paris. Three months after his appointment, the American delegation arrived to discuss relations between the U.S. and revolutionary France.

Talleyrand was willing to stop harassing American shipping, release captured American crews, and pay reparations for the cargo seized if the Americans would give him a large bribe and loan money to France. After making the American delegation wait for days, Talleyrand sent a Dutch banker to visit the American commission informally and let them know what he wanted. The Dutch banker said France needed an apology from President Adams for a speech he had given earlier, the payment of French debts owed by the United States, a "loan" of thirty-two million Dutch guilders, and payment of a fifty-thousand-pound bribe to the Foreign Minister personally. The American delegation rejected these terms immediately.

Marshall also told the Dutch banker the U.S. would not respond formally to Talleyrand's demands until France stopped harassing American shipping. The Dutch banker said that until the Americans apologized for the speech by President Adams and agreed to a loan and bribe, France would continue to seize American ships—they were at an impasse before formal negotiations had even begun. Gerry went to see Talleyrand at his home and was told that the loan and bribe were essential if they wanted to stay in France. Talleyrand continued sending informal envoys to meet the American delegation, but they all failed because Talleyrand insisted on a loan to France and a bribe to him before he would begin formal negotiations and the Americans continued to say "no."

The Americans worried they would be arrested because they had not been formally recognized as diplomats in France and were therefore not immune from French law. Marshall drafted a memo to Talleyrand pointing out that the treaty between America and France allowed the U.S. to remain neutral because America was only obligated to join in defense of France if that country was attacked by England and France had started the war. He also argued that because of the unique geographical position of America, it was dependent on foreign trade and must avoid war with any foreign country. Talleyrand said French ships would continue to capture any neutral ships that carried British manufactured goods, including American boats until they paid him a bribe and gave France a loan. The delegation realized they were not likely to negotiate a treaty with France to stop U.S. ships being seized, so they discussed leaving France.

Gerry began a series of secret meetings with Talleyrand and proposed they pay the bribe to break the impasse. Marshall and Pinckney still said "no." They became concerned that Talleyrand intended to send them home and keep Gerry on in Paris for further negotiations because he was easier to deal with. However, they could not leave France because the government held their passports. After five more months of fruitless discussions, Marshall and Pinckney decided they should return to America. Marshall sent a final letter to Talleyrand arguing that a loan was impossible and requesting their passports. Before they left France, the American delegates decided to try one more time to make a deal.

The American delegates asked to meet personally with Talleyrand. To their surprise, he agreed. The day before the scheduled meeting, Gerry met with Talleyrand and was told there would be no formal negotiation until the loan and bribe were paid—the French position had not changed one bit. Talleyrand also said he preferred to negotiate with Gerry alone. The next day, the delegation met with Talleyrand and told him they would consider making a loan after the war was over, but Talleyrand rejected that proposal and terminated the meeting. A few days later Marshall and Pickney were ordered to leave France.

While negotiations with France were proceeding, the delegate's dispatches had arrived in America and President Adams became angry at the way Talleyrand was treating his envoys. Adams asked Congress for money to build ships and to fortify American defenses against attack by France. Congress refused until the delegate's dispatches were published. Adams was happy to comply and released the delegate's journal under the label "XYZ papers." The dispatches showed that France had caused the impasse in negotiations by making unreasonable demands on the American delegation. [69] America's mood turned against France.

When Marshall returned to America, he was hailed as a national hero for his firm stance against outrageous French demands. Marshall told Adams he did not believe France wanted war with America because Napoleon was busy fighting England and other European countries. On a visit to Mount Vernon to meet with Washington, Marshall was urged to run for Congress. He declined at first, but Washington persisted and finally persuaded Marshall to seek elected office. Jefferson didn't want Marshall in Congress and worked hard to defeat him. President Adams offered Marshall a seat on the Supreme Court that had recently become vacant, but Marshall declined because he felt being a Supreme Court Justice was not an important job at that time. The case of a British seaman arrested and sent to England caused Adams serious problems.

The Jonathan Robbins Affair. Jonathan Robbins, a British seaman, was arrested in South Carolina for murder aboard the British ship *Hermione,* extradited to England, tried, and hanged. To discredit President Adams, Jefferson and the Republican Congress alleged that Robbins was an American citizen and should not have been turned over to the British. They proposed a law to limit extradition under Jay's treaty. However, Representative Marshall argued in the House that it was the President's duty to extradite accused persons because as leader of the nation, he must follow all treaties that had been approved by the Senate since these treaties are the supreme law of the land according to the U.S. Constitution. Marshall won the day for Adams, and the Republican bill was defeated in the House of Representatives.

Shortly after the Robbins affair, President Adams fired his Secretary of State and nominated Marshall, who accepted the appointment. The Senate unanimously confirmed Marshall the next day. The job was important and paid enough for Marshall to support his family so he was delighted. [70] Marshall traveled by coach to the new capitol in Washington, D.C., and was not impressed. The swamp smelled bad, and construction was behind schedule and over budget. Marshall met with Adams in a tavern to discuss foreign issues, including difficulties with France, debts owed the English, attacks on American shipping by Barbary pirates in the Mediterranean, and Spain allowing France to use its ports for raiding American shipping. It was clear after this discussion that Marshall would face serious problems as U.S. Secretary of State.

Adams said he was leaving for home and Marshall would be responsible for running the government and overseeing construction of the capitol until Congress arrived in November. As Secretary of State, Marshall had extraordinary authority even when President Adams was in town. His office was the primary administrative agency of government; it issued passports, copyrights, land patents and oversaw the Justice Department because the Attorney General was simply a legal advisor to the President at that time. The State Department also ran the mint, handled the census, supervised U.S. territories, and published government documents. Marshall established his office in the Treasury building next to the White House and got to work immediately running the country.

Marshall's most pressing problem was how to deal with debts owed to Britain by Americans. The English ambassador wanted the U.S. government to pay England a lump sum to cover the debts, but

Marshall worried that France would be angry if America paid money to England while the two countries were at war. Marshall informed the British Ambassador that the U.S. was willing to pay no more than $2.5 million, much less than the claims were worth, and this tactic delayed the negotiations for months. The U.S. finally agreed to pay 600,000 pounds to England to settle Tory debts, a fraction of what was actually owed. By then, Thomas Jefferson was president, and he had to ask Congress for the money.

The next problem Marshall faced was the capture of American ships and taking of U.S. citizens by the British Navy as crewmen for their ships. Marshall instructed his ambassador to tell the English the U.S. wanted to remain neutral between France and England but stood ready to defend its shipping if necessary, although the American Navy was small compared with the massive British Navy. England refused to stop detaining U.S. ships and impressing American sailors. Disregard for the rights of U.S. ships on the high seas eventually led to the War of 1812 with England. However, that was in the future. Marshall also had to deal with French harassment of American shipping, but these negotiations were stalled while Napoleon won repeated victories over the European coalition. After many months of hard bargaining, the French and Americans finally reached an agreement that France would stop raiding American shipping, although compensation for past confiscations was postponed.

The other issue Marshall faced during his tenure as Secretary of State was how to handle the Barbary pirates who sailed from the North African coast and captured American ships. The pirates claimed to be customs agents of North African monarchs collecting fees for passage through the Mediterranean and they wanted to be paid to stop harassing American shipping. President Washington had paid ransom to these pirates because he had more pressing problems with the French and British. Marshall thought Washington's tactic sensible because it saved the U.S. millions of dollars in naval costs, and President Adams agreed. However, when Jefferson became president, he declared war against the Barbary pirates rather than pay bribes. The U.S. Navy and Marines soundly defeated the pirates, but at a huge financial cost. [71] Adams and Jefferson competed for the presidency in 1800, and Jefferson won. Before he left office, Adams placed Marshall on the Supreme Court as Chief Justice.

Chief Justice John Marshall. The presidential election of 1800 didn't produce a majority for any one candidate so the House of Representatives decided who would be the next president. It took thirty-six ballots before Jefferson won. After the election, Adams and Marshall began planning the transition to a new administration. Adams had approximately one month remaining in his term when Chief Justice Ellsworth resigned because of health problems, and during a meeting with Marshall, Adams said, "I believe I must nominate you." Marshall accepted the nomination and Adams submitted his name as the fourth Chief Justice of the U.S. Supreme Court. [72] At that time, the Supreme Court was a weak branch of the U.S. government and Justices often resigned to seek better opportunities, such as running for governor of a state or returning to a lucrative law practice. Marshall intended to change the status of the Supreme Court as Chief Justice, however.

The Court handled mainly Admiralty cases and disputes between the states during its early years because there were few federal statutes, and most legal disputes were governed by state law. Because there were no lower federal courts of appeal, the Supreme Court Justices rode circuit around the various states in addition to hearing cases in Washington, D.C. Before Jefferson was inaugurated, Congress approved a statute establishing six new circuit courts and reorganizing the federal judiciary, eliminating the need for Justices to ride circuit around the U.S. Additionally, the judicial statute organized federal courts into ten districts and expanded their powers to include individual property rights and creditors' rights.

When newly elected President Jefferson placed his hand on the Bible to take the oath of office, he faced his old enemy John Marshall as Chief Justice and recognized he might have a fight on his hands. Marshall convened his first session of the Supreme Court on February 2, 1801, in the Congressional basement where the Federal District Court and the D.C. Court of Appeals also met. In addition to Marshall, William Cushing, William Paterson, Samuel Chase, Bushrod Washington, and Alfred Moore made up the Supreme Court. Marshall wanted to forge a judicial consensus to withstand the pressures he saw coming from the executive and legislative branches controlled by Jefferson's Republican party, so he set out to befriend each of the Justices and learn about their personal lives so he could forge unanimous opinions on important cases.

Marshall moved all of the Justices into the same boarding house and met with them every evening over a glass of Madeira. He became friends with all the Justices and took a personal interest in their families. Marshall served on the Court for thirty-four years (longer than any other Chief Justice). He began the practice of issuing majority opinions rather than allowing each Justice to write individual opinions, as was the practice in England. Marshall believed the authority of the Court would be strengthened if it issued a single opinion, especially if the ruling was unanimous. He personally wrote over 500 decisions during his time on the Supreme Court. Marshall convinced his colleagues to issue unanimous decisions most of the time, giving the Court's opinions added authority on controversial cases.

The first important case for the Marshall Court occurred when the USS *Constitution* captured the armed French vessel *Amelia* and brought her into New York harbor as a prize. Navy Captain Talbot claimed half the value of the ship and cargo, even though the cargo was owned by a neutral Hamburg merchant. The parties were represented by two famous attorneys, Alexander Hamilton for Captain Talbot and Aaron Burr on behalf of the Hamburg merchant. The district court ruled for Talbot and the court of appeals for the Hamburg merchant Seeman, so the case came before the Supreme Court for final resolution.

The Justices heard four days of oral arguments and Marshall wrote a unanimous opinion for the Court. *Talbot v. Seeman* did much more than just decide whether Captain Talbot could collect a prize for capturing the French ship. The case also established the important principle that only Congress has the authority to declare war. [73] The Court ruled that *Amelia* was subject to seizure because Talbot had no way of knowing she carried a neutral cargo. Marshall decided that because *Amelia* was not an enemy vessel (America and France were not officially at war), the capture was illegal under international law. However, Marshall ruled that there was an implied contact between Talbot and Seeman, so the captain was entitled to compensation for the salvage of the cargo in the amount of one-sixth the value of the ship and its contents, less court costs. Marshall often used ordinary cases to announce sweeping legal rulings. The next case is a perfect example of this tactic.

Marbury v. Madison. [74] When President Jefferson took office, he found forty-two justice of the peace commissions neatly stacked on Marshall's desk waiting to be delivered. Jefferson refused to deliver the commissions, and among those not delivered was William Marbury's. At that time, Justices of the Peace notarized documents and arrested drunks, prostitutes, or runaway slaves. Marbury was independently wealthy and didn't need the income, so he likely filed the suit to embarrass Jefferson. The Republican Congress countered by abolishing the sixteen new federal circuit judges and canceling the Supreme Court's term for 1802 in an attempt to prevent the Court from ruling on Marbury's suit. The ploy didn't work because Chief Justice Marshall opposed President Jefferson.

The sixteen federal circuit judges sued in federal court, arguing their appointments were for life so they couldn't be fired except for cause. The Supreme Court Justices also considered refusing to ride circuit, but two Justices wouldn't strike, so that tactic failed. Before the Court had a chance to hear *Marbury*, the House of Representatives voted to impeach District Judge John Pickering as a warning to Marshall and the Court to avoid the case, but Marshall ignored the threat. When Marbury's case came before the Supreme Court, Secretary of State Madison refused to hire an attorney or appear to defend himself. Marbury's attorney had difficulty getting testimony about what had happened to the commissions because the Republican administration and Senate refused to answer questions. They all claimed a Fifth Amendment right to remain silent. Marshall knew the facts, but he was Chief Justice and could not testify in his own court. The case seemed at an impasse.

Marbury's attorney argued that the commissions vested when they were signed, and no one offered conflicting testimony supporting Secretary of State Madison's position, so Marbury won his case. Marshall wrote a unanimous opinion for the Court, holding that Marbury had a right to receive his commission once it was signed and the president had no right to deny delivery. He also argued that Marbury had a remedy because the Secretary of State had a duty to deliver the commissions and the president and his administration are not above the law. Marshall also held that according to the U.S. Constitution, the Supreme Court had original jurisdiction in cases involving ambassadors, public ministers, and states, therefore Congress could not change the Court's power and the statute dismissing the federal district courts was unconstitutional.

Near the end of his opinion, Marshall raised the most important issue before the Court: whether a Congressional statute or the U.S. Constitution is the supreme law of the land. Marshall asserted that the Constitution is supreme, and any Congressional statute inconsistent with the U.S. Constitution is null and void. *Marbury* established the important doctrines that the Supreme Court is the ultimate interpreter of the U.S. Constitution and that document is the supreme law of the land. Reaction to the decision was generally positive and neither Jefferson nor Madison dared challenge the doctrine that judicial review of Congressional acts is proper. In this simple case concerning a few justices of the peace, Marshall had established an important precedent and gained enormous power for his Court by asserting judicial authority where none had existed.

Territorial Sovereignty. *The Schooner Exchange v. McFaddon* [75] case raised the issue of whether American courts had jurisdiction over a claim against a foreign military vessel visiting an American port. The dispute began when the American schooner *Exchange* departed Baltimore for Spain and was captured on the high seas by a French privateer. Taken to a French port, the vessel was refitted as a warship and renamed the *Balaou*. En route to the West Indies, the ship was forced by a storm to enter Philadelphia harbor. John McFaddon, who owned the ship, filed suit in U.S. District Court, but the federal judge ruled that the vessel was immune because it was a foreign warship. The Court of Appeals ruled that the vessel had voluntarily entered an American port and had therefore subjected itself to American jurisdiction. The case went next to the U.S. Supreme Court.

The American government, trying to avoid a dispute with France while that country was engaged in a war with Britain, appealed the case to the U.S. Supreme Court, arguing that American courts didn't have jurisdiction over friendly foreign warships. Chief Justice Marshall delivered the unanimous decision of the court, arguing that jurisdiction within U.S. territory is exclusive and absolute and cannot be limited except by American actions or laws because only a sovereign can grant an exception to its territorial jurisdiction. Marshall next stated that American ports are open to all powers with whom America is at peace, so the seizure of the French ship in Philadelphia was illegal. Marshall ruled that the shipowner must seek redress from a political branch of government rather than the courts, nicely avoiding a serious dispute with France because Jefferson was not about to rule against Napoleon.

Martin v. Hunter's Lessee. This case began in 1791 as an action by Denny Martin against David Hunter for trespass to land Martin inherited from his uncle, Lord Fairfax. The State of Virginia expropriated Lord Fairfax's land during the Revolutionary War and sold it to Hunter. Martin wanted his inheritance so he sued Hunter. The case came before Virginia's highest court, which ruled that Martin didn't have good title to the land. He appealed the state court's decision to the U.S. Supreme Court. Marshall owned part of the disputed land so he recused himself from the case. However, Marshall helped Justice Story draft the unanimous decision for the Court once the other Justices decided the outcome. The decision, nominally written by Justice Story, held that the Treaty of Paris, which ended the Revolutionary War, restored good title to Martin based on the supremacy clause of Article VI of the Constitution because treaties are the supreme law of the land and the Treaty of Paris was superior to any Virginia state statute.

However, the Virginia Supreme Court refused to eject Hunter, arguing that the U.S. Supreme Court had no power to hear an appeal from a state Supreme Court and that the State of Virginia was co-equal with the U.S. Government. Martin appealed this state court decision to the U.S. Supreme Court, arguing that a state court is subordinate to the U.S. Supreme Court and state law is subordinate to federal law. Justice Story agreed, ruling that the U.S. Constitution was not ordained and established by the states in their sovereign capacities, but by 'the people. [76] Justice Story held that the U.S. Constitution limits the power of states and makes them subordinate to the U.S. Government. *Martin* established the doctrines that the U.S. Supreme Court is superior to state courts and that federal law is superior to state law. Maryland tested these doctrines a few years later when it levied a tax on the U.S. National Bank.

McCulloch v. Maryland. [77] In 1816, Congress established the Second Bank of the United States to restore the U.S. dollar and refinance national debts incurred during the War of 1812. Following the recession of 1819, Maryland imposed a tax on notes issued by the Second Bank of the United States to raise revenue for the state. McCulloch, manager of the Maryland branch of the Bank of the

United States, refused to pay the tax, claiming it was illegal. He was convicted of violating state law and appealed his conviction to the U.S. Supreme Court. Daniel Webster represented McCulloch and William Pinkney was lead attorney for the State of Maryland. The case raised a fundamental issue about the relationship of states to the federal government—if a state could tax a federal bank, what was the extent of federal supremacy?

In a unanimous decision, Marshall answered two questions: does the federal government have the authority to charter a national bank and does a state have the power to tax a federal bank? He ruled that although the Constitution does not explicitly give the federal government authority to charter a national bank, the document should be read broadly because it gives Congress "all necessary and proper" powers to carry out its express powers. Marshall believed that if the ends are legitimate, then any means used are legitimate. He ruled that it would be useful to have a national bank so Congress could tax and spend, therefore, it had the power to charter a national bank because it has explicit power to tax and spend.

Maryland argued that even if the national bank is legal, the state could still tax it. Marshall disagreed, ruling that the power to tax is the power to destroy so states have no authority to tax a national bank because of the Supremacy Clause. Marshall's decision in *McCulloch* reinforced slave states' worst fears that the federal government might someday use its supremacy power to outlaw slavery and lead to the Civil War. The next important case the Marshall Court heard involved the power of Congress to regulate interstate commerce.

Gibbons v. Ogden. Known as the great steamboat case, *Gibbons v. Ogden* established the doctrine that the power of Congress to regulate interstate commerce includes the right to regulate navigation on all U.S. waterways. Gibbons and Ogden were partners in a steamboat venture taking passengers from New York to New Jersey. They had a business dispute, and Gibbons withdrew from his partnership and opened a steamboat company under license from the federal government. Ogden sued in New York court and won an injunction against Gibbons, who appealed the state court judgment to the U.S. Supreme Court. The case raised two issues: does Congress have the power to regulate navigation and can the federal government regulate navigation within the waterways of New York state? [78]

Daniel Webster represented Gibbons and argued that Congress' power to regulate interstate commerce is comprehensive and exclusive. Ogden's attorney pointed out that nothing in the Constitution forbids the states from regulating commerce within their own waters and restricting navigation is not the same as prohibiting commerce. Marshall, writing for the Court, rejected a narrow reading of the Constitution, holding that limiting Congressional powers would cripple the federal government. He ruled that Article 1 gives Congress broad powers to regulate interstate commerce and defined commerce as all commercial transactions, including navigation. Marshall also held that the federal government can control interstate commerce wherever it exists. *Gibbons v. Ogden* gave the federal government primary jurisdiction over interstate commerce and made state laws subordinate to federal statutes. By this time, Marshall was getting old and his health was beginning to decline.

Marshall's Death. The winter of 1835 had been severe and the roads were icy when Marshall traveled through Virginia on his way home from Washington, D.C. His coach hit a patch of ice and rolled over, injuring Marshall's back. He was recovering slowly and decided to seek medical care in

Philadelphia. The physicians examined Marshall and determined that his back problem was minor, but he had an enlarged liver with abscesses that were preventing him from eating properly. Marshall only lived a few more weeks and died on July 6, 1835. [79]

Thomas Jefferson

Thomas Jefferson was born on April 13, 1743, near the Blue Ridge Mountains outside Charlottesville, Virginia. [80] Jefferson's father was a successful planter and surveyor, and his mother, Jane Randolph Jefferson, was a member of the prominent Randolph family of Virginia. Thomas Jefferson's earliest memory was of a horseback ride with one of his father's slaves into the Virginia wilderness when he was three. Jefferson's family moved to a larger plantation near Richmond, Virginia, when he was older, and Thomas received his early education from private tutors. The family moved back to western Virginia in 1752, and Jefferson attended a Presbyterian school, studying Latin, Greek, French, history, science, and the classics. Jefferson's father died when Thomas was fourteen, and he inherited approximately five thousand acres of Virginia land and around two hundred slaves.

Jefferson's Education. On the advice of his uncle, Peter Randolph, Jefferson enrolled in the College of William and Mary at Williamsburg in 1760, at the age of sixteen and earned a reputation as a serious student. [81] At William and Mary, the second oldest college in America (Harvard was established earlier), Jefferson studied natural philosophy and the Enlightenment, which favored reason and humanism as opposed to religion. Writers such as John Locke, Francis Bacon, and Montesquieu had a lasting effect on Jefferson's thinking about government and the nature of man.

After graduating from William and Mary, Jefferson studied law for five years with George Wythe, the most prominent attorney in Virginia, passed the Virginia bar exam, and began practicing in 1766. Jefferson mainly represented plantation owners in cases involving land sales and disputes about slaves. He was elected to the House of Burgesses, the legislature of colonial Virginia, in 1769. Jefferson studied agronomy and believed America should remain an agricultural economy because it was healthier for people. He began construction of Monticello, his hilltop mansion, in 1769 on land inherited from his father and remodeled it throughout his life.

Jefferson met and married Martha Wales Skelton, an attractive young widow whose dowry doubled his land and slave holdings, in 1772. [82] He practiced law for seven years before beginning work on American independence. Jefferson was an early advocate of colonial freedom from England and opposed taxation without direct representation in Parliament. Jefferson was elected as a delegate to the Continental Congress and arrived in Philadelphia on June 21, 1775, in a carriage pulled by four horses and attended by three slaves dressed in formal livery. He was the youngest member of the Virginia delegation to the Continental Congress and was relatively unknown at that time.

Jefferson was a replacement for Peyton Randolph, his political godfather, and was selected based on family ties rather than his own reputation, although he quickly showed himself to be an excellent writer. John Adams said Jefferson had "the reputation of a masterly pen" based on a pamphlet he published in 1775 entitled *A Summary View of the Rights of British America.* [83] In the pamphlet, Jefferson wrote that Parliament and King George have no authority to govern America and the colonies should be free to control their own destiny. Jefferson was angry because Britain sent troops to suppress lawful demonstrations and said that action infringed the natural rights of free men---ideas he had acquired from his studies of the Enlightenment.

Jefferson's arrival in Philadelphia highlighted the conflicts inherent in the author of the Declaration of Independence. The Declaration proclaimed that all men are created equal, but Jefferson came to Philadelphia with slaves. No one expected that a year later, Jefferson would be considered one of the most important delegates at the convention after he had drafted the Declaration of Independence. He was reluctant to speak in public, in sharp contrast with John Adams, who was an eloquent orator. The Virginia delegation was the most important group at the convention because Virginia was the largest and richest colony in America. The Virginia delegation was led by Edmond Pendleton and Patrick Henry, both master orators. In addition, George Washington, another Virginian, was leading the Continental Army against English troops in defense of the colonies.

Jefferson was a quiet scholar who preferred writing to public speaking. He published an estimate of the cost of war with England, based on his assumption the conflict would be over in six months and cost about three million dollars--a gross underestimate. When the convention opened, the colonies were already at war with England because of battles at Lexington, Concord, and Bunker Hill. However, the Declaration of Independence would not be signed for another year.

Moderates at the convention hoped for reconciliation with England, but the more radical elements, including John and Samuel Adams, wanted independence. The aggressive actions of the British Army in America drove more colonials toward independence every day. Jefferson already supported independence when he arrived in Philadelphia. His concern was how and when the colonies would break with England, not whether they should. The delegates to the Continental Congress were busy managing a war, raising an army, searching for alliances with France and Holland, and worrying about how to pay for the war. Jefferson published pamphlets aimed at the British Parliament and the American people arguing for independence. His goal was to convince fellow colonials that their future was with independence rather than King George.

Jefferson portrayed the colonies as innocent victims of English taxation and King George's unlawful interference in colonial affairs. He painted the English King and Parliament as evil conspirators threatening to take away colonial liberties through taxation and the stationing of British troops on American soil. John Dickinson, a Quaker delegate from Pennsylvania and leader of moderates in the Continental Congress, opposed independence. Dickinson was on a committee with Jefferson assigned to draft a statement outlining the reasons for independence from England. Dickinson believed that the extreme rhetoric Jefferson used would split Congress and make bipartisan support of independence impossible. Dickinson wanted to avoid a break with England and looked forward to eventual reconciliation with the mother country.

Jefferson drafted the Congressional resolution outlining the reasons for separating from England, and he resented changes to his work. However, Congress voted to add many of Dickinson's modifications before adopting Jefferson's resolution. He left the Continental Convention in disgust after it revised his resolution, returning to Monticello to attend his wife Martha, who was experiencing a difficult pregnancy. While at his hilltop home, Jefferson suffered serious migraines, which would trouble him throughout his life whenever he was under emotional pressure. His headache was likely triggered by the death of his mother and the turmoil associated with the Continental Congress. Jefferson had been estranged from his mother since the death of his father years before, and he may have felt both relief and guilt at her death. Jefferson recovered from his migraine after a few weeks and returned to the convention on May 14, 1776, knowing little of the historical events that were unfolding at Philadelphia. He considered going to Richmond to draft a state constitution for Virginia but ultimately decided his duty was in Philadelphia.

Jefferson was selected to draft the Declaration of Independence because he was the best writer at the convention, the Virginia Delegation was the leading group, and a Virginian had to be on the drafting committee. The committee included John Adams, Benjamin Franklin, Robert Livingston, Roger Sherman, and Thomas Jefferson. They delegated the drafting to Adams and Jefferson, with Adams assigning the initial drafting to Jefferson. Adams was leader of the Radical group of delegates who supported immediate independence and he felt the document would be subjected to greater scrutiny by the more moderate members of the convention if he drafted it, so he gave the job to Jefferson. That single decision made Jefferson a celebrity.

No one at the convention thought the Declaration of Independence would be an important document, so Adams didn't feel he was giving up much by assigning the work to Jefferson. Adams spent his time leading debates on the floor of Congress rather than drafting the Declaration of Independence because he felt debating independence was the more important job. After all, the decision to become independent of England had already been made through the actions of Congress in authorizing the raising of an army, appointing George Washington as its leader, and fighting the British at Lexington, Concord, and Bunker Hill. Most delegates viewed the Declaration of Independence as a formality and not really very important in the grand scheme of things. How wrong they were.

Jefferson spent May in Philadelphia drafting the Declaration. He wrote a scathing indictment of King George for his dictatorial handling of the colonies. The most controversial section of the Declaration was Jefferson's accusation that King George had perpetuated the slave trade in the colonies, which was not accurate, because King George was, in fact, inciting rebellion among American slaves by offering them freedom if they would join the English army. Jefferson was trying to have it both ways, by blaming King George for slavery in America and blaming him for emancipating slaves at the same time. He never reconciled his belief in the natural rights of men to be treated equally and his ownership of slaves.

Jefferson was assigned to draft the Declaration of Independence by default, and it would turn out to be his ticket to political fame. He wrote the Declaration in just a few days, using materials he had collected or written earlier. Jefferson showed his draft to Adams and Franklin, who made a few minor changes and then submitted it to the Continental Congress for debate and passage. Congress made several changes and deleted about one-quarter of Jefferson's draft, mainly dealing with King George. Jefferson regarded any change as a debasement of the document but had no authority to object. On July 4, 1776, Congress approved the revised Declaration of Independence, had copies made, and the members of the Continental Congress signed the document on August 2, 1776. They kept the Declaration of Independence secret because it was an act of treason against England and they would be hanged if discovered.

Congress deleted the entire section of Jefferson's draft dealing with slavery, believing it would divide the colonies. The delegates also deleted his argument that the original colonies were established by private initiative rather than royal charters because it was inaccurate. The most famous part of the Declaration of Independence states:

> "We hold these truths to be self-evident; that all men are created equal; that they are endowed by their Creator with certain inalienable Rights; that among these are life, liberty, and the pursuit of happiness; that to secure these rights, governments are instituted among men, deriving their just powers from the consent of the governed." [84]

The statement in the Declaration about equal rights for all men eventually triggered significant reforms in America, including the abolition of slavery, giving Blacks and women rights of citizenship, and producing a welfare state. Jefferson borrowed ideas from Aristotle, Cicero, Locke, and others, as well as his own earlier writings, in drafting the Declaration of Independence. He omitted Locke's natural right to property—substituting the pursuit of happiness instead. Jefferson borrowed from Locke's writings about the role of government in the affairs of man in drafting the Declaration. He returned to Monticello instead of joining the army to fight for independence and was criticized for appearing lukewarm about American freedom.

Jefferson strongly denied the charge because he was thin-skinned and took criticism personally. Later, he learned to ignore his critics and go on with his own affairs. Jefferson was asked to join Benjamin Franklin and Silas Deane as a member of the American delegation to France but declined, wanting to stay at Monticello to tend his crops and take care of his wife. Instead, Jefferson was elected Governor of Virginia in 1779 and dealt with economic and political problems caused by the war. Virginia suffered serious economic damage during the war because the English blockade limited the export of tobacco and cotton.

Virginia never met its assigned quota of enlistees into the Continental Army, primarily because it retained troops to protect the state against invasion. However, Jefferson approved sending Virginia's best militia to Detroit just before Benedict Arnold led an English army through Virginia, burning Richmond, attacking Charlottesville, and almost capturing Jefferson at Monticello. The legislature passed a resolution asking for an investigation into why Jefferson had allowed the English to invade Virginia, but the matter was dropped when emotions cooled.

His failures as governor were criticized during Jefferson's two campaigns for President in 1796 and 1800—although he won both elections. Jefferson's wife Martha died following her tenth pregnancy on September 6, 1782. [85] He promised Martha he would never remarry, and he stayed true to that promise. To recover from his grief over the death of his wife, Jefferson went to France as a minister to keep that country in the war against England.

Jefferson in Paris. Jefferson went to France in the summer of 1784 and promptly fell ill with a severe cold that lasted months. [86] He had difficulty learning to speak French, although he read the language easily. Jefferson began a lengthy correspondence with James Madison and James Monroe about American politics that would last a lifetime. He loved the food, culture, and architecture in Paris, and formed a close relationship with John Adams, although they would become bitter rivals for the presidency in later years. Adams and Jefferson dealt with the problem of Barbary pirates attacking American ships in the Mediterranean, worked with Franklin to keep France allied with America in its war against England, and searched for loans to pay for the war. Jefferson supported building and maintaining a naval force off the Barbary coast to stop raids on American shipping, but Adams said it would be cheaper to pay ransom.

Adams was posted to London, Franklin returned to America, and Jefferson assumed primary responsibility for American affairs in France after the Revolutionary War ended. [87] Jefferson hoped France would continue to support an independent United States, but it closed French ports to American shipping and imposed high tariffs on American tobacco and cotton to protect domestic producers and raise revenue. Jefferson was a passive partner while Adams negotiated a $400,000 loan from Dutch bankers, allowing America to consolidate its debts in Europe and pay ransom to the Barbary pirates. Jefferson was the ranking American diplomat in Europe and became famous as the champion of French culture. He also acquired considerable diplomatic experience during his time in France, which helped him later as secretary of state and president.

Barbary Pirates. Both Jefferson and Adams were seriously concerned about raids on American shipping in the Mediterranean by Barbary pirates. Secretary of State John Jay instructed Adams and Jefferson to resolve the issue by meeting with an envoy from the Sultan of Tripoli. The envoy told them if America wanted to avoid war, it must pay thirty thousand pounds to his country and three thousand pounds to him as a bribe. [88] Jefferson and Adams both felt that was too expensive, but the envoy said it was his lowest offer, and they would have to negotiate treaties with other Barbary states for comparable sums or face continued attacks. Jefferson recommended America wage naval war rather than pay tribute, but Adams argued that since America had no navy, it would be cheaper to pay rather than build ships and fight a war.

Jefferson was in Paris when the Constitutional Convention met in Philadelphia and drafted the American Constitution. His friend James Madison kept Jefferson informed of the proceedings and told him that America needed a stronger, more centralized federal government to survive. Shay's Rebellion against Massachusetts taxes was the proximate cause of the Convention because it showed the weakness of Congress to deal with domestic disturbances. Jefferson believed Shay's Rebellion was a sign of American political strength and issued his famous quote: "The tree of liberty must be refreshed from time to time with the blood of patriots and tyrants." [89] Many disagreed with that dictum.

Jefferson told Madison there were three major types of governments—the European model based on a powerful monarch; the English model, which looks to the people and Parliament for guidance; and the Native American model based on common values, small communities, and a local leader. Jefferson said he preferred the Native American model because he felt American society was homogenous and the people shared common values, so there was no need for a strong central government. However, the majority of Americans disagreed with Jefferson and drafted a Constitution that included a strong executive to administer the country.

Jefferson witnessed the dramatic changes in Paris before the French Revolution but failed to see how serious the situation had become for the French monarchy. He was optimistic that the king, nobles, and people of France would reach a compromise, give some freedom to the people, and maintain the monarchy. Jefferson was surprised when Paris erupted in riots and appalled by the violence of the mobs as they stormed government buildings. He continued to believe a peaceful political compromise would eventually be reached and was shocked by the French Reign of Terror. Jefferson eventually realized it was dangerous to stay in Paris and returned to America because he was interested in a cabinet appointment and wanted his daughters educated in the U.S. Washington offered Jefferson the post of Secretary of State in his new government in 1789, and he accepted.

Secretary of State Jefferson. [90] His service as Secretary of State coincided with turbulent times in American foreign policy and every decision Jefferson made set a precedent because he was the first man to hold the post under the new Constitutional form of government. During the early decades of the new government, Jefferson and Madison cooperated in establishing the Republican Party to oppose the Federalist policies of Hamilton and Washington. Madison led the fight against Hamilton's push for a national bank with support from Jefferson. Washington opposed the development of political parties, believing they would divide the country and make it more difficult to govern democratically.

Jefferson agreed with Hamilton, Adams, and Washington that the major task of the new government was domestic development and worked as Secretary of State to avoid foreign entanglements or war. However, even after the French Revolution and the rise of Napoleon, Jefferson favored France and opposed an alliance with England because there were still British troops stationed in America, and English ports were closed to American shipping. Jefferson believed England was in decline while France was on the rise under Napoleon. He was wrong. Napoleon was defeated by England, and during the reign of Queen Victoria, the United Kingdom became more powerful than any other nation in the world because of the Industrial Revolution and the Royal Navy. [91]

Secretary of State Jefferson was grateful for French help winning independence from England and favored France over England. Jefferson and Hamilton emerged as the dominant personalities in Washington's cabinet, with Hamilton favoring a strong central government and international ties, while Jefferson wanted a weak central government with strong states' rights and no foreign alliances. His feelings toward Hamilton were personal and political. Personally, Jefferson was jealous of Hamilton because he was a military hero and Jefferson had not served in the Revolutionary War. Politically, Hamilton and others attacked Jefferson for his Francophile leanings, while Madison and Monroe defended Jefferson and attacked Hamilton and Adams as monarchists who wanted to reinstate an English king in America. Jefferson believed he was spokesman for the common man as opposed to Federalist elites such as Adams and Hamilton. That was ironic because Jefferson lived as an aristocrat in his mansion at Monticello tended by hundreds of slaves.

Monticello. Jefferson was constantly in debt from overspending on good food, wine, travel, books, and rebuilding Monticello. When he left Washington's cabinet, Jefferson was sixty-five hundred pounds in debt. He returned to his plantation to pay off his debts by selling some slaves and managing his plantation more effectively. Jefferson owned nearly eleven thousand acres of land in Albemarle and Bedford counties and he sold some land to pay off part of his debt. However, Jefferson never really worried about money because he defined wealth in terms of land and slaves rather than dollars. He owned thousands of acres and hundreds of slaves for his entire life, but he never had enough money to pay all his debts.

Jefferson switched from growing tobacco to raising wheat and began systematic crop rotation to improve his depleted land. [92] The war between England and France provided a golden opportunity to ship wheat to both sides, but his economic plans failed because droughts, frosts, and heavy rains destroyed his crops year after year. Also, Jefferson only placed about one thousand acres under cultivation and that was not enough land to earn money to pay his debts. Jefferson's financial problems stemmed from spending too much on food, books, wine, travel, and rebuilding Monticello. No matter how much he earned selling wheat, land, and slaves, Jefferson always spent more. He never resolved his ideas of equality with the reality of owning slaves.

Jefferson on Slavery. All the work on Jefferson's plantation was done by slaves, but he was conflicted about the institution. He opposed slavery because it was incompatible with his republican values of equality, but at the same time, he needed slaves to work his plantation. Moreover, Jefferson never actively supported abolition of slavery in America. He was guilty of wishful thinking when he argued that slavery would naturally disappear in time. To be fair, no one had a realistic answer to the question of what would happen to slaves once they were free. Lincoln wanted to send them back to Africa or establish a colony in South America for freed slaves. Jefferson believed white and Black Americans could not live together in harmony because the history of slavery would forever separate the races. America is still dealing with this difficult issue.

Jefferson was also opposed to making the federal government supreme and believed Hamilton's scheme to establish a national debt was really a secret plan to make the central government more powerful. Jefferson wanted to eliminate public debt, stop issuing federal bonds, and close the National Bank. Adams and Jefferson were the leading candidates to replace Washington when he declined a third term as president. After a bitter political campaign, Adams won New England, Jefferson carried the South, and the Middle Atlantic states were split. When the votes were counted, Adams collected more votes, so he became president and Jefferson vice president. This created an uneasy truce between Federalist Adams and Republican Jefferson that would fracture in 1800 when they both ran for president again.

The major issues during Adam's first year in office were whether to move the capitol to the South and what to do about the debt states had incurred during the Revolutionary War. Hamilton proposed that the federal government establish a National Bank, assume all state debts, and issue government bonds to develop a national credit market. To get his legislation passed, Hamilton negotiated a deal with Jefferson to move the capitol to the District of Columbia in return for approval of the national bank. While the new capitol was being built, the government temporarily moved to Philadelphia.

President Jefferson. Jefferson and Aaron Burr ran for president in 1800 against Adams. Hamilton wrote a scathing attack against Adams that damaged his chance of being elected for a second term. As a result, Jefferson and Burr tied for electoral college votes at seventy-three each and Adams was a distant third. The Constitution requires that in case of a tie, the House of Representatives chooses electors from each state who select a president. After thirty-six ballots, Jefferson won over Burr. His election as president produced a less powerful federal government compared with the Washington and Adams administrations because Jefferson believed in a central government that allowed states more power to run their own affairs.

In his inaugural address, Jefferson suggested that the bitter party squabbles of earlier administrations should stop. He wanted to make the federal government small and simple rather than powerful and complicated. Jefferson inherited a nation at peace with England and France, few national debts, a powerful U.S. Navy of fifty ships, and a flourishing economy. Jefferson selected new men for his cabinet, including James Madison as Secretary of State and Albert Gallatin Secretary of the Treasury. Madison saw eye to eye with Jefferson on foreign policy, and Gallatin was a match for Hamilton on fiscal issues.

Jefferson continued Washington's staff model for the federal government where analysis of issues went through the cabinet head before being presented to the President for a decision. Jefferson only convened his cabinet when there was a crisis; otherwise, he worked individually with each cabinet member, making decisions once the issues had been analyzed and options developed. Most of the business in Jefferson's administration was done in writing rather than through face-to-face discussion. Jefferson tried to stay in the background and not exercise power openly. He wanted to pay off the remaining national debt, believing it was wrong for a nation to owe money, although he had no problem accumulating personal debts. Paying off the national debt was easy because American manufacturing, agriculture, and commerce grew rapidly, and custom taxes filled the federal accounts.

Jefferson appointed a smaller executive staff and felt Congress should be the leading branch of government as opposed to the President or the Judiciary. His attitude toward Native American people was paradoxical and similar to his attitude about slavery. Jefferson celebrated the cultures and government of Native American tribes and championed the idea that all men are equal, while relocating the Native Americans to reservations far away from their original hunting grounds and continuing to own and work slaves.

Two months after Jefferson assumed the presidency of the United States, Tripoli declared war on American shipping. Jefferson had always disliked paying tribute to the Barbary pirates, and now that he was president and had a powerful navy at his disposal, he went to war with the pirates. Because President Adams had built a strong American Navy, Jefferson had the means to carry out his preference for fighting. He dispatched a fleet of heavy frigates and several hundred U.S. Marines to the Mediterranean to fight the Barbary pirates, and eventually they stopped bothering American shipping. [93] Because Napoleon was fighting most of Europe, he needed money and decided to sell French possessions to America.

The Louisiana Purchase. When Spain sold its rights to the Mississippi River, New Orleans, and the Louisiana territory to Napoleon, Jefferson immediately contacted France and began negotiating to buy the properties from France. Jefferson believed America must control New Orleans, the Mississippi River, and territory west of the Mississippi to remain independent. He was so upset about French control of the Louisiana territory that he considered signing an alliance with England and declaring war on France to remove it from the continental U.S. if France would not sell the Louisiana Territory to America. Jefferson sent James Monroe to Paris to negotiate the purchase of the Louisiana Territory and authorized him to pay up to $10 million for the land. Jefferson even considered occupying New Orleans with the American Army if that was needed to convince France to sell.

None of that was necessary because Napoleon needed money. [94] Additionally, Napoleon's campaign to suppress a rebellion in Santa Domingo failed, contributing to the sale of the Louisiana Territory for $15 million. Jefferson immediately commissioned Meriwether Lewis to organize an expedition to explore and map the new territory. His purchase of the Louisiana Territory was a major change in attitude about executive power because Jefferson exceeded his authority by authorizing funds to buy the Louisiana Territory without Congressional approval. The acquisition was such a bargain that no one questioned his action. Jefferson continued his quarrels with Chief Justice John Marshall during his presidency.

Jefferson and Marshall. Jefferson opposed Marshall's doctrine of judicial review of Congressional statutes and the Supreme Court's right to interpret the U.S. Constitution. He thought Marshall had overstepped his authority and said so at every opportunity. However, as Madison pointed out, Marshall had convinced his colleagues on the Supreme Court of the doctrine of judicial review of Congressional statutes and the right of the Supreme Court to interpret the Constitution, so there was nothing Jefferson could do about it. Madison advised Jefferson to accept the situation and move on but to no avail. Jefferson continued to oppose Marshall, even proposing Congressional legislation that would allow Virginia to defy federal statutes, arguing that the right to determine their own internal affairs was reserved for the states in the Constitution. He sent the proposed legislation to Madison, who advised against submitting it to Congress. Madison told Jefferson to drop the entire scheme, and he wisely followed Madison's advice. During Jefferson's reelection campaign for a second term, rumors began circulating that he was cohabiting with one of his female slaves.

Jefferson's Personal Scandal. Following Hamilton's scandal with Mrs. Reynolds, newspaper editors considered the private life of any important political figure fair game, including President Jefferson. The editor of the Federalist *Port Folio* was the first to raise the sensational charge that Jefferson was having an affair with his Black slave Sally Hennings. The allegations were a reporter's dream because they could not be disproved. Given modern DNA evidence, it seems likely Jefferson did indeed sire children with Sally Heming, but at the time, the scandalous allegations were used mainly by Federalists to discredit Jefferson's character. Moreover, the accusations were plausible because many slaveowners indulged their sexual appetites with female slaves. Jefferson wanted a free press, but not that free.

He enjoyed many successes during his first term, but Jefferson's second four years as president were a disaster, primarily because of the war between France and England. The temporary peace had allowed American commerce to flourish, but after the war resumed, Jefferson closed American ports to English and French shipping, which caused a major recession in America and made Jefferson unpopular. In addition, Jefferson had to deal with a conspiracy by Aaron Burr, his former vice president, to establish an independent nation in the American Southwest. Jefferson was so eager to find Burr guilty he violated the man's constitutional rights. Chief Justice John Marshall saved Jefferson by finding Burr not guilty of treason against the U.S. in a trial before the Supreme Court. Burr's reputation was already ruined by his shooting of Alexander Hamilton in an earlier duel and Marshall believed there was no need to punish him further.

After Jefferson's second term, he returned to Monticello to retire and manage his plantation. He rode his favorite horse in the afternoon, entertained guests, and continued his correspondence with notable Americans, including John Adams, with whom he reconciled after they both retired. Their mutual friend Benjamin Rush engineered the reconciliation in January 1812. The reconciliation began through an exchange of letters from Adams to Jefferson, beginning an extraordinary correspondence about American history. [95]

On May 5, 1817, Jefferson wrote the following to Adams:

> "If by religion, we are to understand Sectarian dogmas, in which no two of them agree, then; your explanation on that hypothesis is just, 'that this would be the best of all possible worlds, if there were no religion in it."

On December 8, 1818, Adams wrote to Jefferson:

> "I believe in God and in his Wisdom and Benevolence: and I cannot conceive that such a Being would make such a Species as the human merely to live and die on this earth. If I did not believe a future State I should believe in no God."

A remarkable set of letters discussing important questions of religion, government, and the nature of man.

Jefferson's Last Years. His health declined as Jefferson aged and he feared senility and a loss of independence as he grew older. Jefferson worked to clarify his attitude toward slavery and consolidate his place in history. To this end, he claimed to be morally opposed to slavery based on the principles of equality for all men. Jefferson also wrote in his autobiography that he was opposed to slavery and that all Blacks should be free. Contrary to these grand words, however, Jefferson's behavior showed an ambivalence toward slavery. In spite of pressure from his Northern friends to support the abolition of slavery, Jefferson refused to take a stand for freeing slaves, continued to own slaves until the end of his life, and didn't free his slaves when he died.

When the issue of slavery in the new state of Missouri came before Congress, Jefferson avoided the issue by saying there is no plan for compensating slave owners and no clear idea of what to do with all those freed slaves afterward. The growing number of slaves in America made gradual emancipation unlikely and unworkable. Jefferson believed that allowing slavery to spread into the Western states would dilute Southern power and eventually result in the abolition of slavery in America, but many disagreed with this idea. He was also distressed that Northern politicians had taken the high moral ground on slavery because he wanted that honor for himself. However, Jefferson was in a moral bind: he was a Southern slaveholder who believed freeing slaves would not improve their situation, and at the same time, he believed all men were equal. He never found a satisfactory solution to this dilemma.

Jefferson faced serious financial difficulties in 1819 when the country went into recession and he had to sell his magnificent library to Congress for $23,950 to pay some of his debts. Even then, he was not able to pay all his creditors. During his last years, Jefferson founded the University of Virginia.

The University of Virginia. Jefferson designed and oversaw construction of the University of Virginia in 1819, and felt it was one of his proudest achievements. In 1976, the American Institute of Architecture recognized the University of Virginia as the "proudest achievement of American architecture in the past 200 years." Jefferson devoted his time and energy to designing and constructing the University the same way he devoted himself to rebuilding Monticello. He lobbied the Virginia legislature for money, oversaw the hiring of faculty, the building of a library, and designed a curriculum. Essentially, he created a model university for America.

In typical Jeffersonian fashion, he developed a plan that was far-reaching, brilliant, and unworkable. The Virginia legislature refused to supply all the funds needed to construct and operate his magnificent dream. Jefferson even insisted that only European scholars could supply the level of learning needed to make the university first-rate and refused to hire American professors. However, he found that leading scholars of Europe were not interested in moving to an unknown university in the wilderness. The legislature did authorize funds to begin building the University of Virginia on a smaller scale than Jefferson proposed, but he was disappointed not to achieve his dream.

In his final years, Jefferson had accumulated debts of over $100,000, the modern equivalent of several million dollars. Jefferson asked the Virginia legislature to authorize a public lottery, which would give him the chance to offer his farmland to the winner and keep Monticello. He drafted a petition to the legislature requesting a lottery, but it was rejected. A few weeks later, his friends lobbied the legislature and reversed the decision. Jefferson didn't live long enough to see his land go to the lottery winner, however. Knowing that the auctioneer would claim all his slaves, Jefferson freed five members of the Hemings family, although Sally Hemings was neither freed nor mentioned in his will. Jefferson died on July 4, 1816, fifty years after he signed the Declaration of Independence. [96]

Andrew Jackson

Andrew Jackson was born on March 15, 1767, near the North and South Carolina border to Scots-Irish parents who emigrated from Ulster, Ireland. Jackson's father died in a logging accident weeks before he was born. [97] Jackson is reported to have been a bully as a boy, although he protected smaller boys at times. During the Revolutionary War, Jackson served as a courier for the North Carolina militia and was captured by British troops in April of 1781. When young Jackson refused to polish an English officer's boots, the man slashed him on his left hand and head with a sword. [98] Jackson contracted smallpox and nearly starved to death while in captivity before his mother was able to get him released. His older brother died from smallpox, a wound to his head, and malnutrition, while Andrew recovered.

His mother died of cholera when Jackson was fourteen. After the Revolutionary War, he attended school in Waxhaw and received a rudimentary education, learning to read, write, and compute. Jackson worked as a saddle maker and school teacher until he inherited money from his mother or grandfather, and moved to Salisbury, North Carolina, to study law with attorney Spruce Macay. In September 1787, Jackson was admitted to the North Carolina bar and soon became an assistant prosecutor in the Western District of North Carolina, which later became the State of Tennessee. [99] Jackson fought his first duel in 1788, with both men firing in the air by prior agreement.

He moved to the small town of Nashville later in the year and lived as a boarder with widow Rachael Donelson. Jackson met her daughter, Rachel Donelson Robards, who was married to Captain Lewis Robards while boarding in the Donelson home. Robards and his wife separated in 1790, and Jackson married Rachel soon after, believing she was divorced. In fact, the divorce was not final when Andrew and Rachel married, so the union was illegal. [100] After Rachel's divorce became final, the couple remarried, although they had been living together before the divorce was even filed according to friends. Rachael was lively, spirited, beautiful, and appealed to Jackson—she was the love of his life and he never remarried after she died.

Jackson was elected as a delegate to the Tennessee Constitutional Convention in 1796, and after the territory was admitted as a state, he was elected to the U.S. House of Representatives from Tennessee. Jackson supported the rights of Tennessee residents against Native American tribes in the House and later as President. In 1797, Jackson was elected to the U.S. Senate but resigned after serving one year because he didn't like the policies of the Adams administration. When he returned to Tennessee, Jackson was elected to the state Supreme Court and served until he resigned in 1804. In addition to being an attorney and politician, Jackson ran The Hermitage, a large plantation in Tennessee. He owned slaves who worked the fields growing cotton. [101]

The scandal surrounding Jackson's marriage to Rachel triggered frequent salacious attacks on her, and he was quick to take offense when his wife was slandered. In May 1806, Charles Dickinson and Jackson had a dispute about a horse race, and Dickinson published an attack on Jackson's marriage in the local newspaper in retaliation. Incensed, Jackson challenged Dickinson to a duel. His opponent was an expert shot, so Jackson decided his best chance to survive the duel was to allow Dickinson to fire first, hoping that a hurried shot would spoil Dickinson's aim because Jackson planned to aim carefully and kill Dickinson if he survived the shot from his opponent. Facing each other at twenty-four feet, Dickinson fired quickly and hit Jackson in the chest near his heart. Jackson staggered, gathered himself, took careful aim, and killed Dickinson with his own shot. [102] His behavior during the duel outraged many in Tennessee, but Jackson ignored them because his tactic had succeeded—he killed his man and survived.

Shortly after recovering from his wound, Jackson met Aaron Burr, who was planning to conquer the Spanish territory of Florida and the city of New Orleans for his own ends. Jackson agreed to build five boats for Burr, provision them, and await orders from the Federal Government to attack Florida. While waiting for word from Washington, D.C., Jackson began to suspect something was not right about Burr's motives, so he sent a letter to Thomas Jefferson warning him of Burr's plans. Jefferson had Burr arrested and tried for treason. However, Burr was acquitted in 1807 by Chief Justice John Marshall after a trial in the Supreme Court. The incident showed two things about Jackson: he wanted to secure the United States against foreign threats, and he loved his country. He was forty-five when America went to war against Britain in 1812, and his actions during the war made Jackson a hero.

War of 1812. Tensions with England were high in 1812 because the British were stopping American merchant ships and forcing U.S. sailors to serve in the British Navy. Additionally, the U.S. had its eye on Florida, and Spain was an ally of England. When Congress declared war on June 18, 1812, Jackson was already a political and military leader. He had served as Tennessee Attorney General, Representative, Senator, and major general in the Tennessee militia. Jackson sent a letter to Washington offering to raise and lead twenty-five hundred volunteers to fight in the war. After several months of delay, his volunteers were finally called to duty by the federal government. In January 1813, Jackson set out for New Orleans with over two thousand men to defend the city against attack by British troops and Native Americans.

Before he arrived in New Orleans, Jackson was ordered to turn over his supplies to General Wilkinson, who commanded American soldiers in the area. He complied, and then marched his men back to Nashville, personally paying for provisions and ordering his officers to give up their horses so sick soldiers could ride. He then fought in the Creek War of 1813-14, also known as the Red Stick War and Creek Civil War (the Red Stick Indians were a Creek tribe who used red war clubs in battle). Jackson won several battles and was promoted to major general in the U.S. Army. With Madison's approval, Jackson imposed a treaty on the Creek Tribe, forcing them to surrender twenty-three million acres to the federal government.

After fighting a combined British and Spanish force in Florida, Jackson learned the British were planning to invade New Orleans, so he moved his men to the mouth of the Mississippi, arriving in the city on December 1, 1814. He imposed martial law on the city and formed an alliance with Jean Lafitte's smugglers to build defenses. The invading British forces, led by Admiral Cochrane and General Pakenham, numbered ten thousand experienced veterans of the Napoleonic Wars, while Jackson commanded under five thousand poorly equipped men. However, he was confident because his men would be fighting from strong defensive positions against British troops in the open.

The British launched a frontal assault on Jackson's well-prepared defenses on January 23, 1815, and their red coats made easy targets for American sharpshooters, who inflicted over two thousand casualties on the English, while the Americans sustained only seventy-one killed or wounded. [103] The British retreated and stopped fighting when they learned the war had already ended. His victory at New Orleans made Jackson a national hero. He was awarded a Congressional Gold Medal for his victory at New Orleans, and his heroic achievements in the war made Jackson a candidate for President a few years later.

After the War of 1812, Jackson commanded troops on the southern border of the U.S., negotiated treaties with the Cherokee and Chickasaw tribes, and gained large sections of land in Tennessee and Kentucky for the United States. He fought Native American tribes and escaped slaves to keep the area from becoming a refuge for Black slaves. Jackson invaded Florida on March 15, 1818, captured Pensacola, defeated the Seminole Nation, and captured two British agents who were working with the Native American tribes. Jackson executed both agents after a brief trial, causing a diplomatic incident with England. He was criticized by opposing politicians for invading Florida, even though John Quincy Adams, as Secretary of State, purchased Florida from Spain in 1819. A congressional investigation exonerated Jackson of wrongdoing.

Jackson returned to The Hermitage exhausted from years of hard campaigning, fearing he was dying. After a few months' rest, he recovered and began thinking about national politics. Jackson's main rivals at the time included John C. Calhoun, Henry Clay, and John Quincy Adams. He was disgusted by the corruption within the Monroe administration and angry at the Second Bank of the United States for causing the Panic of 1819. On July 22, 1819, the Tennessee legislature formally nominated Jackson for President, one of five candidates running that year. Jackson campaigned against federal corruption, vowed to restore honesty in the government, and was seen as a war hero for his victory at New Orleans. However, James Monroe won the Presidency that year, so Jackson had to wait for another election before he could achieve his dream.

In 1823, Jackson was elected to the Senate for a second time by the Tennessee legislature. [104] In the presidential election of 1824, Jackson won ninety-nine Electoral College votes, more than any other candidate, but still short of the one hundred thirty-one needed to win. The unsettled election was sent to the House of Representatives under authority of the Twelfth Amendment, which stated that only the top three vote-getters were eligible to be elected President. Henry Clay, who was Speaker of the House, hated Jackson, feeling he was a demagogue who would destroy the country, so he supported John Quincy Adams in the House of Representatives, and as a result, Adams won on the first ballot. Jackson supporters accused Clay of striking a corrupt bargain when Adams appointed him Secretary of State. In disgust, Jackson resigned from the Senate and returned to Tennessee.

At that time, America was moving from an economy based on small farms to one based on manufacturing. Railroads, canals, and roads were tying the country together, and immigration from England and Ireland filled the country with thousands of new workers. Regular steamship travel was established between Europe and America for the first time. Politically, the balance of power was changing, because Hamilton's Federalist Party had disappeared, and the Republican Party was divided into warring factions. Jackson saw an opportunity to further his own presidential ambitions by proposing that the people themselves should determine the policies of America rather than elite political leaders. He ran for the presidency again in 1828 against John Quincy Adams, and the campaign quickly turned personal and nasty. Jackson was called a slave trader, his opponents attacked his executing soldiers under his command in New Orleans, and accused him of eating the bodies of Native Americans he had killed in battle. In spite of these vicious attacks, Jackson won fifty-six percent of the popular vote and one hundred seventy-eight Electoral College votes to Adam's eighty-three in the election of 1828. John C. Calhoun was elected Vice President. [105] Soon after he won the presidency, Jackson suffered a terrible loss; Rachael Jackson died of a heart attack on December 22, 1828.

Jackson's opponents were mortified he was going to be the next President of the U.S. and immediately set about trying to block his agenda in Congress. On January 18, 1829, Jackson boarded the steamship *Pennsylvania* and sailed up the Cumberland River to Washington, D.C., arriving in the new capitol on February 11, 1829. Thus began the era of Jacksonian Democracy, which shifted political power from the ruling elites to ordinary Americans. Jackson supported agrarian interests, states' rights, and limited federal government. He opposed rich capitalists whom he feared would corrupt the government with their money through bribes. Jackson also rejected the idea that an independent and powerful Supreme Court had the authority to overturn Congressional bills.

President Jackson. Soon after Jackson arrived in Washington, D.C., he began selecting his cabinet. He appointed Martin Van Buren Secretary of State, John Eaton Secretary of War, Samuel Ingham Secretary of Treasury, John Branch Secretary of Navy, John Berrien Attorney General, and William Barry Postmaster General. [106] In his inaugural address, Jackson promised to strengthen state powers and respect the Constitution. After his speech, Jackson invited the public to the White House for an open house that became boisterous. He soon initiated investigations of corrupt officials within the government after he took office, indicting and convicting several in his first year as President. Jackson wanted an honest government so he asked Congress to tighten auditing of government accounts and limit the awarding of federal pensions to undeserving individuals. He called for abolition of the Electoral College, arguing that the popular vote should determine who is President of the U.S., a debate that is ongoing today.

Southern planters were growing fearful of a slave rebellion, and Jackson was sympathetic to their concerns since he owned slaves himself. Planters were also having economic troubles because the price of cotton was falling while the cost of manufactured goods kept climbing due to high federal tariffs. South Carolina and other slave states began discussing nullification: the idea that state governments have the right to ignore federal laws they didn't like and secede from the Union if they believe they were not getting fair treatment from the federal government. Most Southern politicians said they were not advocating leaving the Union but believed the threat of force was necessary to give them bargaining power with the federal government concerning tariffs and the Second Bank of the United States. President Jackson feared nullification would lead to dissolution of the Union and strongly opposed the idea. He also had to find a solution to Native American raids on white settlers.

Native American Removal. Jackson initiated a policy of removing Native American tribes to public lands west of the Mississippi by negotiating treaties with the Choctaw, Creek, Chickasaw, Seminole, Cherokee, Ottawa, Chippewa, and Potawatomi tribes. [107] Relations between white settlers and Native Americans had turned violent in recent years over territorial disputes and white voters wanted a permanent solution to the problem. Congress passed the Indian Removal Act in May of 1830, authorizing the President to buy tribal lands and move the Native Americans to public lands further west. The Seminole Tribes refused to move and fought back in 1835, triggering the Second Seminole War, which lasted six years. More than forty-five thousand Native Americans were relocated during Jackson's presidency. He believed the rights of white Americans were superior to Native Americans and acted accordingly.

In 1829, Georgia decided to move all Native Americans from the state, and Jackson didn't object because he thought they were violent savages who could not be trusted living close to white settlements. Relations between the races in America have always been tense, but this was a particularly difficult time. Native American tribes were seen as threats in their own right and also as potential allies of the French or British against American national interests. Also, Southern plantation owners worried about a slave rebellion and an alliance between Blacks and Native Americans. Jackson believed removing Native American tribes would ensure the security of white settlements, so he pursued the plan with vigor. To him, Indian tribes represented a violent element in American society that needed to be moved beyond the Mississippi River to make the country safe for white families.

Jackson also believed removing Native Americans from southern states would strengthen the U.S. border with Mexico by having white people living there rather than hostile Native American tribes who might join with Mexico to make war on America. Jackson believed tribes needed to be controlled by the federal government. He was neither a humanitarian nor a bigot but reflected the prevailing beliefs of his time. There were moral objections from clergy at the time about how the federal government was treating Native Americans, but most whites had a vested interest in acquiring land and they supported tribal removal.

Chief Justice John Marshall was sympathetic to Native Americans but announced that the Court would not hear their case against Georgia because the tribe had sued as a foreign nation when it was, in fact, a domestic dependent nation. In his opinion, Marshall described the relationship between the federal government and Native American tribes as similar to a guardian and ward. It was an important ruling, because prior to that, the federal government had generally treated tribes as sovereign peoples. Marshall was realistic enough to understand that the doctrine of Indian Removal couldn't be stopped by the Supreme Court because it was popular with voters. Jackson also wanted to build new roads and canals in the country, but needed money to do it, and began searching for new sources of funds other than high tariffs.

Internal Improvements. Jackson faced a dilemma in 1830: he wanted to build more infrastructure and also lower tariffs to placate Southern plantation owners, but he couldn't do both. High tariffs were a major source of federal funds and Jackson needed money to carry out his ambitious plans. He also worried that building a road or canal in one state would lead to criticism from other states that wanted similar improvements. Martin Van Buren advised Jackson to support only roads and canals that crossed state lines so he could not be accused of favoring one state. Jackson followed Van Buren's advice and approved the Cumberland Road, which was an interstate project, and supported a survey law that affected all the states. Southern states continued to press Congress to lower federal tariffs so they could import cheap foreign manufactured goods. Jackson was struggling with how to achieve these conflicting aims: he needed money to build roads and canals but didn't want to drive Southern states out of the Union with high tariffs. He didn't see how to resolve the issue until he had a chat with Martin Van Buren one afternoon.

Jackson and Van Buren were out riding together, ran into a thunderstorm, and retired to a tavern to wait for better weather. Van Buren was considering resigning as Secretary of State and told Jackson he wanted to leave his cabinet. Jackson immediately replied, "Never, sir." Van Buren pointed out that he wanted to run for President after Jackson left office, and believed he would have a better chance if he could run as an outsider. Jackson thought about that idea and decided he should force his entire cabinet to resign so he could reorganize his administration and strengthen his hand for the coming presidential campaign. He planned to oppose states' rights and lower federal tariffs after he was reelected. [108] He also needed to know what opposing politicians were thinking, so he organized a spy network in several Southern states.

During the Revolutionary War, Jackson needed to know what was happening with British soldiers to keep his family safe, so he began paying attention to information about the intentions and actions of opponents. He understood it was no different now that he was in the White House; he needed spies throughout the South feeding him information about what Senator Calhoun was doing and gauging the mood of Southern politicians. Jackson was hearing talk in South Carolina of rebellion against the federal government and he was worried. He discovered that Clay and Calhoun had devised a plan where they would both run multiple candidates against Jackson in the coming presidential election, hoping to deny him the votes needed to win in the Electoral College, and throw the election of 1832 into the House of Representatives, where Speaker Henry Clay could again deny Jackson the presidency.

Calhoun believed he could win enough votes and delegates in the South to keep Jackson from winning the Presidency outright in the Electoral College, and he was confident that Clay could swing the House of Representatives in his favor, and he would be the next President. However, Calhoun's strategy was risky because Jackson might garner enough support among North and Middle Atlantic states to win outright. During his campaign for the presidency, Jackson attacked the idea of nullification by saying that if states seceded from the Union, they would soon become colonies of powerful foreign nations and threaten the security of America. He promised to do everything in his power to prevent that happening if he were reelected. To preserve the Union, Jackson needed to block the Doctrine of Nullification among the Southern states.

The Nullification Doctrine. Jackson believed Americans need to live together, even if they didn't see eye-to-eye on every issue, and he wanted to expand the powers of the White House to keep the Union intact. The struggle over states' rights vs. the federal government was shaped by Andrew Jackson and John C. Calhoun, who both saw their positions as righteous. [109] Calhoun believed states had only ceded limited powers to the federal government when they signed the Constitution, while Jackson believed the states had ceded all their power to the people, and he represented them as President of the United States, since he was the only federal official elected by all the people. In October of 1830, supporters of states' rights took control of the South Carolina legislature and called a special convention to support the Doctrine of Nullification. In early 1831, Jackson announced he would seek a second term as President, strengthening his hand in dealing with Calhoun, who also wanted to be President.

Jackson argued that if Calhoun's Nullification Doctrine was accepted, the United States would revert to a confederacy and no longer be a united nation in which all the states followed national laws. The Nullification Doctrine would shift power to the states and produce chaos in America. Jackson also argued that nullification would weaken the federal government at the very time a strong central authority was needed to expand American civilization across the continent. Party politics became more divisive after 1830, and political machines much larger and more influential than in earlier times. Moreover, Jackson was expanding presidential powers to the point that his political opponents were suggesting Congress ought to impeach him as a tyrant. However, Jackson was too popular with ordinary voters to impeach and most Congressmen knew it. They began looking for an issue to use against Jackson and hit on rechartering the Second Bank of the United States during the presidential election.

Biddle's Bank. Jackson's political appeal was similar to Washington's; he instilled confidence that he was trustworthy and had the people's best interest at heart. Jackson believed the Second Bank of the United States had favored his rival, John Quincy Adams, during the earlier presidential election, and he wanted the practice stopped. Jackson accused Biddle of using the Second Bank of the United States to oppose his policies. [110] However, Biddle denied he favored any political party, saying he always acted in the interests of the country as a whole, although he admitted he was personally close to John Quincy Adams. Biddle also asserted that the Second Bank of the United States was an independent entity, under the control of neither Congress nor the President. Jackson disagreed and felt he had two options to deal with Biddle: remove federal deposits from the bank, or oppose renewal of its charter when it expired in 1836, killing the bank altogether.

Biddle believed Jackson would not dare do either of these things during an election year, but the President had other ideas, because he believed he spoke for the people and needed to redress their grievances against the bank. Biddle hoped to force Jackson to sign a bill recertifying the bank during the election of 1832, but he misjudged the President and the mood of most voters. The fight about recertifying the bank became a struggle for power in Washington, and Jackson intended to win by charging that Biddle had given loans to influential members of Congress to encourage them to vote for recertification. This charge of bank corruption strengthened Jackson's standing with the voters against Biddle and his bank. After Congress passed a bill recertifying the bank, Jackson vetoed it, saying that the purpose of government was to better the lives of all Americans, not enrich the few. Congress was unable to override his veto and Jackson won.

On top of all Jackson's other problems during the election of 1832, John Marshall issued a Supreme Court opinion supporting the Cherokee Nation against Georgia's incursions into its tribal lands. [111] Marshall ruled that the anti-Cherokee laws passed by Georgia were unconstitutional. However, Jackson refused to enforce the Supreme Court's decision, and the Georgia legislature continued to encroach on Cherokee lands. Marshall had no power to enforce his opinion on his own, so Jackson was able to increase White House power in relation to the judiciary and satisfy white voters that he was looking out for their interests. Jackson argued that the President should be free to formulate his own opinion on issues, and the people could decide who was right at the next election.

Jackson's opponents planned to run three candidates against him in the coming election, hoping that no one candidate would win a majority of the Electoral College votes and the choice of the next President would be shifted to the House of Representatives, where Henry Clay could control the outcome and elect Calhoun. During the campaign of 1832, both sides believed they were favored by the voters. Jackson thought that destroying the Second Bank of the United States, removing the Cherokee tribe from Georgia, lowering tariffs, and opposing nullification were popular issues with the voters. In contrast, Calhoun believed he was smarter than Jackson and suffered from overconfidence. In October of 1832, Jackson set out from The Hermitage on the first personal presidential campaign in American history to highlight his achievements and win the coming election.

Jackson and his running mate Van Buran traveled across the North East and Mid-Atlantic states, personally campaigning for the presidency, while Clay and Calhoun played by the old rules and didn't campaign personally. That tactic cost them dearly. Jackson held popular torchlight parades throughout the country while Clay and Calhoun stayed behind the scenes and allowed others to campaign for them. When the voting was over, Jackson won almost fifty-five percent of the popular vote, and collected two hundred nineteen Electoral College votes, more than enough to win the presidency for a second time. [112]

The Ordinance of Nullification. A week after Jackson won a second term as President, South Carolina's legislature nullified the Tariff of 1832, saying it would not collect the tax on imported goods within the state, directly challenging the authority of the federal government. [113] Would Jackson send troops to enforce the tariff or back down in the face of strong state opposition? He faced a difficult issue—how to preserve the Union without appearing to be a tyrant and forcing other Southern states to join South Carolina in leaving the Union. Jackson's men in South Carolina recommended he send loyal Southern men to take command of federal custom collection in South Carolina, but he decided to wait. In his annual State of the Union message Jackson sent to Congress in December, he argued for a peaceful resolution of the crisis. Jackson wanted to isolate South Carolina by appearing reasonable in the face of that state's threats, while at the same time, making secret military preparation to invade South Carolina if that became necessary. Jackson also issued a proclamation on December 10, 1832, stating that nullification contradicted the Constitution, and would destroy the United States.

Jackson didn't oppose states' rights. He believed in limited federal government, a debt-free nation, and the right of the people to act through their state government more often than through the federal government. But he firmly believed states didn't have the authority to dissolve the Union, and so he fought against South Carolina's plan to nullify federal tariffs. As 1832 came to a close, Calhoun resigned as Jackson's Vice President and the South Carolina legislature elected him to the U.S. Senate. Jackson feared other Southern states might follow South Carolina into secession because of the tariff issue and he walked a tight rope to avoid that happening. Virginia was the biggest threat because that state was evenly divided between those who wanted to secede and those who wanted to stay in the Union. James Madison believed nullification was unconstitutional, but John Marshall thought his home state might secede and he was worried that America might not survive if it did. Jackson appealed to Northern and Mid-Atlantic Senators for help.

Jackson needed support from Northern states on lowering tariffs to keep South Carolina in the Union, and he needed Southern states to acknowledge that these lower federal tariffs were legal. The President was also concerned that some Northern states might secede if he lowered tariffs too much. Jackson asked Congress to pass a bill lowering the tariff and giving him authority to order troops into South Carolina if lower tariffs didn't defuse the situation. Jackson wanted Congress to explicitly give him the power to use federal military force against South Carolina. His call for authority to use military force against South Carolina was not without prior precedent.

Twice before, in 1795 and again in 1807, Congress has passed laws giving the President authority to call out militia or use federal troops to enforce federal laws against a state. By asking for a specific authorization of military force in this case, Jackson was giving himself two options: if Congress failed to authorize the use of military force, he could blame the legislature and do nothing, or he could rely on these earlier laws and enforce federal law anyway. Jackson's strategy worked because other Southern states refused to support South Carolina, which stood alone against the federal government. To avoid war, Senator Clay was working on a compromise tariff bill to resolve the issue peacefully. On February 12, 1933, he rose in the Senate to make the case for reforming the tariff and stopping nullification rather than going to war.

Clay urged the Senate to rise above factionalism and reduce the tariff to give Southern states relief from economic hardship. Calhoun argued against Clay's compromise, while Daniel Webster spoke in support of Jackson and Clay. Webster argued that the American people fight as one, make peace as one, regulate commerce as one, and pass duties on imports as one. He pointed out that the purpose of the Constitution is to maintain unity among all the states. Clay's Compromise of 1833 included tariff reform for the South, though at a higher rate than they wanted, an authorization of force for Jackson if South Carolina didn't accept the compromise, and the distribution of free land revenues to Western states to buy their support. [114] Clay was hailed as the great compromiser, and even Jackson agreed Clay had saved the Union. Jackson supported the rights of states to govern their own people, but he supported the federal government's right to preserve the Union more strongly.

A week after Jackson's inauguration as President, the South Carolina legislature met to decide how to react to the Compromise of 1833. Some were defiant, but most legislators were realistic. Congress had given the President the power to use force to suppress succession, and they were not in a mood to test his resolve by going to war alone. South Carolina accepted the tariff but rejected Jackson's right to enforce federal law by force. Some Southern leaders argued that tariffs were not the real issue here, but that preservation of slavery was the true underlying cause of this dispute, and they feared that an all-powerful federal government would eventually abolish slavery in the South and the plantation owners will be forced to fight for their survival. They were right of course, and a generation later the American Civil War began. For now, however, the Union was preserved and Jackson was hailed as a hero by most and a villain by a few.

Assault on Jackson. On May 6, 1833, Robert Randolph, a disturbed former naval officer, assaulted Jackson on a steamship traveling to Fredericksburg, Virginia. [115] Randolph was subdued by fellow travelers, but not before he had struck Jackson in the face and drew blood. It turned out Jackson had dismissed Randolph from the Navy shortly before the attack for suspicion of stealing ship's funds and the man was angry. Americans were shocked that someone would assault a U.S. President, because that sort of behavior was more familiar in Ancient Rome or Europe where Kings and Dukes vied for power. In America, political conflicts were often initiated by wealthy groups of plantation or corporate owners who competed for favors from the government at the expense of the people, but they didn't resort to physical force to achieve their political ends. Jackson believed it was the job of the President to mediate among these groups and limit the power of interest groups so they would not take advantage of the country or the people.

Although Jackson had already defeated recertification of the Second Bank of the United States, he decided to withdraw all funds from the institution to weaken it and prevent rechartering at a later date. He believed that if federal funds were left on deposit in the bank, Biddle would use those monies secretly to influence Congress and get the bank rechartered. Jackson knew he risked impeachment by the House if he withdrew federal funds from the bank, but he did it anyway, believing he would be acquitted in the Senate. On December 23, 1833, Clay verbally attacked Jackson on the floor of the Senate, saying the President was trying to concentrate power in his own hands at the expense of Congress and the people. Clay accused Jackson of trying to establish an elected monarchy. To defend himself, Jackson took his case directly to the people by publishing articles in major papers explaining why he was withdrawing federal funds from the Second Bank of the United States. He argued that Biddle was an unelected official who was interfering in the workings of the American government and needed to be controlled. Clay criticized Jackson for appealing directly to the people, but Jackson ignored him and won the battle.

Jackson's plan was defeated in the Senate, where members were insulated from the will of the people, but the House of Representatives, whose members were elected directly by the people, overwhelmingly supported Jackson withdrawal of federal funds from Biddle's bank so he succeeded in his goal of destroying Biddle's bank. On April 4, 1834, the House voted that the bank should not be rechartered. Angry at Jackson for what they saw as unfair tactics, Senators submitted a resolution censoring Jackson for "exceeding his authority" by removing funds from the Second Bank of the United States. The censure would have no legal effect but was symbolically important to both sides. On March 28, 1834, the Senate voted twenty-eight to twenty to censure Jackson. [116]

Jackson attacked the Senate's censure by arguing that if it became a routine procedure, the tactic would unconstitutionally shift power from the Executive, which is an independent and equal branch of government, upsetting governmental checks and balances. Jackson argued that the President is the only official elected by all the people, and is their representative in government. He claimed the Senate's censure was an attack on his power to represent the people. Jackson wanted his protest entered into the Senate's record, but Clay was able to block that move by having a motion passed declining to enter his protest in the record.

In October of 1834, Jackson sent his annual message to Congress, saying that relations with France were tense because that country had refused to pay the United States monies agreed by treaty, and he intended to ask Congress to approve reprisals against French property if the monies were not paid in the coming year. The French minister to America wrote that if there was a war with the U.S., it would be important for France to win the first battle because the issue was not popular in America. The King of France recalled his ambassador and tensions grew between the two countries. France and America seemed to be at an impasse when England stepped in to mediate the dispute. The British resolved the matter quickly, pointing out that Jackson had included a conciliatory line in his message to Congress and urging the French to accept that as an apology and pay the funds due. France agreed to pay the debt, and the crisis was over. [117] The lesson Jackson took from this episode was that America must protect her honor and liberty by always being prepared for war.

Attempted Assassination. On January 9, 1835, as Jackson was walking out of the House chamber, Richard Lawrence, a well-dressed young man, raised a pistol and fired at him from ten feet away. [118] The cap exploded, but the powder didn't. Realizing the danger, Jackson rushed at Lawrence with his walking stick, while Lawrence withdrew another pistol and aimed at Jackson, but it also failed to fire. Two nearby Navy officers pushed Lawrence to the ground and subdued him. Jackson was probably saved from death by excess moisture in the Rotunda coming from an empty tomb waiting for the remains of George Washington. The pistols were examined later, and both fired when they were used in dry conditions. Jackson returned to the White House believing there were enemies all around him and that Lawrence was part of a plot by his political enemies to kill him. In the end, after being examined by two physicians, Lawrence was deemed to be mad.

By 1835, a majority of Americans opposed slavery and many Northern states were beginning to support abolition. Jackson opposed nullification and secession from the Union for any reason, but he supported Southern slavery and the removal of Native Americans west of the Mississippi River because he believed in democracy and freedom for white men, but not for Blacks or Native Americans. The American Anti-Slavery Society sent pamphlets to South Carolina through the U.S. Mail, and the

Postmaster had to decide what to do with them. After a story broke in the local paper, a Charleston mob broke into the post office and burned the pamphlets. Jackson supported suppressing the speech of anti-slavery voices to avoid an insurrection in the South. He also decided to not seek a third term as President.

The 1836 Presidential Election. For the first time in years, Jackson would not be a candidate for President of the U.S. because he was following George Washington's example of not running for a third term. Jackson supported Martin Van Buren for the office, but could not help him overtly, because as a champion of the people, he had to appear neutral rather than be seen as a kingmaker. Van Buren narrowly won the election of 1836, but he soon faced war with the Seminoles in Florida and Mexico over annexation of Texas. [119] Texas became a part of Mexico in 1821 after Spain ended three hundred years of rule of the area. Americans in Texas wanted to be free of Mexico and revolted in 1835 against their masters in Mexico.

When the Texas Revolution began, Jackson immediately began working quietly to bring the Texas Republic into the U.S. as a state. Santa Ana, powerful leader of Mexico, correctly believed the United States was encouraging the revolt, so he invaded Texas with around four thousand Mexican troops to stop the rebellion. American volunteers poured into Texas to fight the Mexican Army. Texas won its fight with Mexico, the United States suppressed the Seminole Tribe in Florida, and welcomed the Republic of Texas into the Union in 1845. In January 1837, a motion was filed in the Senate to expunge the censure of Jackson, undoing the Senate's criticism of him for withdrawing federal funds from the U.S. National Bank. The motion was approved, and the Senate's censure of Jackson was deleted from the Congressional Record.

March 4, 1837, dawned as a beautiful day in Washington D.C. as power was transferred from Andrew Jackson to Martin Van Buren. Van Buren said in his inaugural address that he didn't expect to match his giant predecessor in deeds but would work to be a President for all Americans. Jackson's age and failing health were taking their toll when he left the White House. He thanked God he had lived in a free country and turned from Washington, D.C., toward home. Back at The Hermitage, after leaving the White House, Jackson became religious. During his years in office, Jackson avoided joining a church because he wanted to maintain total separation of church and state. After leaving Washington, D.C., he joined the Baptist Church and attended regularly.

Van Buren's administration got off to a bad start because a financial panic and depression started soon after Jackson left the White House. Some blamed the depression on Jackson's order that only gold or silver could be used to buy public lands, a decree issued to slow fevered speculation in the land. In spite of this problem, Jackson's legend as a great President continued to grow over the years. In the spring of 1845, Jackson experienced a serious decline in his health, and by May of that year, he was too ill to attend church. Jackson had no fear of death, and continued to communicate with his many friends and admirers to the very end of his life. He died at six p.m. on June 8, 1845, at the age of seventy-eight years. [120]

Daniel Webster

Daniel Webster was born on January 18, 1782, in Salisbury, New Hampshire, in a frame house build by his father. [121] America had gained independence from Britain three months before when Lord Cornwallis surrendered to General Washington at Yorktown, Virginia. Webster's earliest memory was of a large barn floating down a flooded river on his father's farm. He worked in the fields while growing up but preferred reading to farming. Webster said he didn't know how he learned to read, although he believed his mother and sisters taught him at an early age. He had no memory of not being able to read, so he must have learned when he was very young.

When he was fourteen, Webster enrolled in Phillips Academy to begin his formal education. He entered near the end of the school year and studied grammar, arithmetic, and writing. Webster experienced difficulties at Phillips Academy because of his limited prior education. He developed the habit of reading for half an hour and then trying to recall important passages he had just read. He said this practice helped him recall a case or fact during a trial and was extremely helpful later in his life. Webster stayed at Phillips Academy for nine months but left for financial reasons. In 1797, he lived with Dr. Samuel Wood, the minister of an adjoining town where he received private tutoring in Latin to prepare for college.

After months of tutoring, Dr. Wood told Daniel he was ready to enter Dartmouth College, the major institution of higher learning in the state of New Hampshire. Entering Dartmouth required passing a test in English writing, translating English into Latin, and using basic arithmetic. Webster did well in English writing but barely passed the Latin and math exams. He was admitted primarily because of a strong recommendation from Dr. Wood. Webster studied Latin, Greek, English grammar, rhetoric, and critical thinking his first year at Dartmouth. He joined a debating society in his second year and worked hard on public speaking. [122] By the time he graduated, Webster was considered the best speaker on campus.

The leaders of Hanover, New Hampshire, asked him to deliver a Fourth of July oration, and the crowd cheered when he finished his speech. One critic said parts of his speech were excellent while other parts were empty. When Webster heard that comment, he vowed to work harder on the content of his speeches in the future. He earned good grades and was elected to Phi Beta Kappa upon graduation from Dartmouth College. Webster had to decide what to do with his life now that he had graduated. He loved books, but teaching, medicine, or the ministry didn't interest him, so his father suggested Webster study for law. There was a very fine lawyer named Thomas Thompson living near the Webster farm and he invited Webster to study law with him. Studying law in the 18th century involved reading a list of books, discussing cases, and helping around the law office, including cleaning and taking out the trash. Webster remained in Thompson's law office for several months before he had to leave for financial reasons.

Webster was offered a job teaching by the trustees of Fryeburg Academy in Maine and he accepted the position because he needed the money. The trustees were happy with his work and offered to double his salary and give him lodging if he would agree to stay for a second term. Webster wanted to return to studying law after he had saved a little money, so he refused the offer. He never learned to be prudent with money—regularly indulging his taste for luxury and falling into debt throughout his life. Webster began searching for an attorney who would take him as an assistant and approached Christopher Gore, one of the most prominent attorneys in Boston. Gore was kind enough to meet with Webster and listen to his appeal to become an assistant attorney in his office.

At the end of the interview, Webster asked Gore if he could become his clerk and study law and Gore replied that he only wanted to take on one or two clerks. Webster took that as a rejection and started to leave, but Gore said wait, hang up your hat, go into the next room, and begin studying—you can stay. Webster remained in Gore's law office for two years, studying cases, drafting contacts, and attending state Supreme Court sessions. Admission to the Boston Bar required proof of three years studying with an attorney, so Daniel asked for letters from attorneys certifying the time he had spent in their offices. Christopher Gore wrote a strong supporting letter for Webster and personally introduced him to judges of the Suffolk Court of Common Pleas. Gore stated that Webster was a diligent student of the law and would make a fine lawyer. Based on Gore's strong support, the judges admitted Webster to the bar without requiring him to take an examination. [123]

Webster established a law practice near his father's farm in Boscawen, a small New England town of fourteen hundred residents. His father was ill and Webster wanted to be close during his last years. He practiced law in Boscawen for two years and learned to adjust the level of his language to the audience he faced. When addressing a judge, Webster used legal language, but when he was before a jury, he used common English that was easy to understand. Webster's father died on April 22, 1806. Following his father's death, Webster asked his brother to take over his law practice so he could move to Portsmouth and open an office there. Portsmouth was the largest city in New Hampshire and Webster was ambitious to develop his law practice in a larger city, earn more money, and make his reputation.

In Portsmouth, Daniel met and fell in love with Grace Fletcher, a cousin of Reverend Dr. Buckminster. [124] To enhance his chances with Grace, Webster joined the Reverend's church so he could see the love of his life more often. After he had established his law practice and was economically successful, Webster asked Grace to marry him and she accepted. He became active in New Hampshire politics and his law practice flourished. Grace and Daniel married on May 29, 1808, returned to Portsmouth and bought a small frame house in the center of town. They lived in Portsmouth for nine years, while Daniel followed the superior court around the state, arguing cases in many different towns. [125] Farmers came from miles away to watch the drama in the court or listen to an interesting murder trial.

Webster learned how to explain a case in simple logical terms and connect personally with the jury by watching more experienced attorneys in Portsmouth. As his reputation grew, Webster's earnings increased and he was soon making over $2,000 annually. However, he was constantly in debt from overspending on food, drink, clothes, and other luxury items. Webster preferred England over France, even though the French had helped America win independence, because he felt the French were corrupt and would ruin America if they gained influence in the U.S. He became interested in politics and decided to run for a seat in the U.S. House of Representatives from New Hampshire.

Congressman Webster. Webster was nominated for a seat in the U.S. House of Representatives by the Federalist Party. He won, even though Republican James Madison was elected to a second presidential term by winning the South and many Middle Atlantic states. When Webster entered Congress, the War of 1812 had been going on for almost a year and it was becoming a disaster. The British had invaded America and were winning almost all the battles on land and at sea. [126] The American invasion of Canada failed and the U.S. lost control of Lake Champlain to the English. The English Navy blockaded the entire Eastern coast of America below New York City but spared New England shipping, hoping those manufacturing states would secede from the Union and make a separate peace with Britain. The plan failed and the New England states stayed in the Union.

Webster achieved little during his initial session in Congress and returned to his law practice at the end of the Congressional session. When he returned for another Congressional session in Washington, D.C., Webster learned his house in New Hampshire had burned, along with more than one hundred other dwellings in a major fire. Fortunately, his wife and children escaped unharmed, but his house and library were destroyed. The loss was financially devastating to Webster because he had no fire insurance on his home. He set about earning money to pay off his debts and buy another house. His political career helped him attract wealthier clients and his law practice prospered. As Webster became more prominent in legal circles, he often practiced before the U.S. Supreme Court and he won most of his cases before the Justices.

Webster's First Supreme Court Case. During his lifetime, Webster argued over two hundred cases before the U.S. Supreme Court. He took these cases to increase his income and influence the interpretation of the U.S. Constitution. His first appearance before the Supreme Court was to appeal an admiralty case, *The Grotius*, [127] and win a rehearing for his client. The case was later reversed in favor of

Webster's client, with the Supreme Court ruling that some act must be done that shows intent to sieze and retain a ship as a prize. After his initial success before the Supreme Court, Webster continued to enjoy victories for his clients, and his speeches and bills in the House of Representatives forced President Madison to repeal the embargo against Great Britain so Northern merchants could resume trading with England. Following repeal of the embargo act, Webster left Washington, D.C., and returned to New Hampshire to resettle his family and resume his law practice.

He rented a house and prepared for reelection to the House of Representatives on a platform of making peace with the English. Republicans attacked him as unpatriotic and a hinderance to the U.S. war effort against England. In spite of these attacks, Webster won another term representing New Hampshire in the U.S. House. Just before the election, a British Army invaded Washington, D.C., and burned many government buildings, including the White House. The New England states felt the federal government was not interested in protecting the North against attacks by the British, so they formed a committee to protect their homes. When Congress and the President moved back to Washington, D.C., after the British left, they discovered it would cost a fortune to rebuild the federal buildings burned by the British Army, and the war was not yet over.

The U.S. Government was facing a financial crisis and needed to raise taxes and find a way to borrow money to continue the war. The National Bank charter established by Alexander Hamilton had expired in 1811, and was not renewed because of opposition from Republicans such as Thomas Jefferson and James Madison. Because they needed money to support the war, Republicans now wanted to establish a new National Bank that could borrow money. However, the Republican bank bill failed in Congress, so Webster drafted a second bank bill that passed the House with a large majority. Southern states were concerned that Northern states intended to dissolve the Union, but Webster argued that Northern states were committed to staying in the Union and finishing the war with England. In later years, Webster was one of the strongest defenders of the Union when Southern states threatened to secede over the issues of high federal tariffs and slavery.

At the very end of the War of 1812, Andrew Jackson defeated a large British force attacking New Orleans. [128] More than two thousand British soldiers were killed, wounded, or captured, while Jackson claimed the loss of only a few dozen Americans. Days after the battle, Jackson learned that England had already signed a peace treaty ending the War of 1812. The United States exited from a difficult war with a decisive victory thanks to Andrew Jackson at New Orleans. Meanwhile, Webster's law practice was thriving and he was attracting important clients and political attention.

The Dartmouth College Case. Webster considered moving his law practice to Boston or New York but decided to stay in New Hampshire so he could continue representing the state in the House of Representatives. At the end of his second term in the House of Representatives, Webster moved his practice to Boston, where he accepted corporate and criminal cases and made a name for himself among the Boston social and legal elite. Shortly after moving to Boston, Webster received a letter from the President of Dartmouth asking him to represent the college in a dispute with the State of New Hampshire over ownership of the college. *Trustees of Dartmouth College v. William H. Woodward* [129] was an important case in American legal history because it clarified the contract clause of the U.S.

Constitution. The Supreme Court ruled that New Hampshire had violated the contract clause of the Constitution when it attempted to install a new Board of Trustees for Dartmouth College against the express terms of the founding charter.

The case began when the New Hampshire legislature passed a bill to take control of Dartmouth College, increase the number of trustees to twenty-five, and change its name to Dartmouth University. The New Hampshire legislature planned to establish schools of law, medicine, arts, and theology on the new campus, and convert the private college to a public university. The original college trustees refused to recognize the New Hampshire legislature's actions and filed suit in state court. Webster represented the original trustees and argued the case before the state's superior court. The three Republican judges of the New Hampshire Superior Court upheld the state legislature's actions, stating that Dartmouth College was a public institution subject to state regulation. The trustees immediately appealed to the U.S. Supreme Court and asked Webster to argue their case before that body.

Webster recommended transferring the case to a federal district court in order to claim the state's actions were unconstitutional under the New Hampshire Constitution as well as the U.S. Constitution. The trustees agreed with Webster's strategy, and he set about filing in federal district court to bring the state constitutional issues before the Supreme Court. When the Dartmouth Case came before the Supreme Court in March 1818, Webster spoke for four hours, laying out the issues that would make the case a classic in American jurisprudence. Webster argued that the Dartmouth College case involved Constitutional principles of private property and contract law because Reverend Wheelock had originally founded the school on his own land at his own expense, and therefore, the college was private and not a public institution.

Webster's argument that the original charter established Dartmouth College as a private, not a public corporation, meant that a private contract was involved and must be upheld. He argued that private corporations were protected by the contract clause of the U.S. and the New Hampshire Constitutions from interference by government entities and that the state legislature had violated Dartmouth College's rights by turning the private college into a public university. Chief Justice Marshall wrote the opinion for the Court and found for Dartmouth College Trustees, holding that the original royal charter established a private, not a public corporation, and therefore Dartmouth College was not subject to legislative regulation by the State of New Hampshire. Marshall also held that the state legislature's actions impaired the obligations of a contract and were a misuse of state power.

The Dartmouth College case limited the powers of a state to regulate private corporations, allowing entrepreneurs great latitude to grow their enterprises without state regulation. Webster learned how to structure a more effective legal argument by studying Marshall's well-reasoned opinion, which began with a major premise and then logically developed its arguments toward a conclusion. The Dartmouth College case was the turning point in Webster's legal career and made him famous throughout the country. His next case involved the Second U.S. National Bank.

McCulloch v. Maryland. Webster's next Supreme Court case, *McCulloch v. Maryland,*[130] concerned the legality of the Second U.S. National Bank established in 1816. The case made explicit Congress' implied powers under the Necessary and Proper Clause of Article 8 of the U.S. Constitution to pass legislation needed to carry out the enumerated powers of Congress. The Second Bank of the United States was established to finance debts incurred during the War of 1812. The case began in 1819 when Maryland imposed a tax on notes issued by the Second Bank of the United States. McCulloch, manager of the Maryland branch of the Second Bank of the United States, refused to pay the tax and was convicted of violating state law. He appealed his conviction to the U.S. Supreme Court.

Webster represented McCulloch before the Court and raised fundamental questions about the relationship of states to the federal government. He posed two basic issues to the Supreme Court: does the federal government have the power to charter a national bank, and does a state have the power to tax a federal bank? In his ruling, Chief Justice Marshal held that even though Article 8 of the Constitution does not explicitly give the federal government power to charter a national bank, it does give Congress "all necessary and proper" powers to carry out its express powers, so establishing a national bank is legal under the U.S. Constitution. Maryland argued that even if the national bank is legal, the state still had the power to tax any entity within its borders. Marshall disagreed, holding that the power to tax is the power to destroy, so states have no authority to tax a national bank because that would destroy the supremacy of the federal government over states. A complete win for Webster's client! His next case involved the regulation of interstate commerce by the federal government.

The Great Steamboat Case. *Gibbons v. Ogden*, decided in 1824, stood for the doctrine that Congress' power to regulate interstate commerce includes the right to regulate navigation on U.S. waterways. [131] Gibbons and Ogden were partners in a steamboat venture moving passengers between New York and New Jersey. They disagreed about business matters, and Gibbons left the partnership to establish a competing steamboat company under a license from the federal government to transport passengers between New York and New Jersey. Ogden sued Gibbons in state court and won an injunction against his new company. Webster appealed Gibbons' case to the U.S. Supreme Court and raised two issues: does Congress have the power to regulate navigation and can the federal government regulate navigation within the waterways of New York?

Webster argued that federal authority to regulate interstate commerce is comprehensive and exclusive, and that a state court cannot overrule the federal government's authority because of the Supremacy Clause of the U.S. Constitution. Ogden's attorney argued that nothing in the U.S. Constitution forbids a state from regulating commerce within its own waters and that restricting navigation is not the same as prohibiting commerce. Chief Justice Marshall rejected Ogden's arguments, ruling that a restricted reading of the U.S. Constitution would cripple the federal government's power to regulate interstate commerce. Marshall held that Article 1 of the U.S. Constitution gives Congress broad powers to regulate interstate commerce, including navigation on state waterways. He also ruled that the federal government's regulation of interstate commerce can be exercised wherever commerce exists. With each court win, Webster's political ambitions grew, and he began planning to run for the U.S. Senate to increase his power and reputation.

Senator Webster. When Webster returned to Washington for his third term in the House of Representatives, his friends suggested he run for the U.S. Senate. However, Webster was concerned that Jackson or Jefferson would defeat President Adams and deny him a second term, so running for the U.S.

Senate at this time might be premature. Webster kept his options open by working to elect Adams to another term as President rather than running for the Senate himself. Webster worked throughout New England to convince voters to support Adams, who was popular in the North. President Adams lost to Thomas Jefferson, but the Massachusetts Legislature still elected Webster by a two-thirds majority to be a Senator from Massachusetts because of his support for Adams.

Following his election to the Senate, Webster spent his summer at the Massachusetts shore with his wife Grace, resting and regaining their health. Grace had been ill for the past year and Webster wanted her to recover before he returned to Washington. She seemed to revive over the summer and decided to travel to Washington with Webster to attend his inauguration into the Senate. The family left for Washington in November, ran into bad weather, and were delayed. Webster's wife fell seriously ill, so they stopped in New York to give her a rest and consult a physician. The surgeon who examined his wife told Webster there was little hope Grace would survive because she had developed a cancerous tumor that killed her on January 21, 1828. [132]

When he arrived in Washington, Webster had difficulty concentrating and couldn't work because he was depressed by the loss of his wife, Grace. After a few weeks, his mood began to improve and he argued in favor of a tariff bill to protect infant American industries from foreign competition. Webster also became a strong supporter of infrastructure improvements to roads and canals so people and commodities could move around the country more easily and efficiently. When Jackson was inaugurated as President, Webster learned his older brother Ezekiel had died of a stroke or heart attack. That made two major personal losses in a single year for Webster and he was devastated emotionally.

A few months after his wife died, Webster began seeing Sarah Goodridge, a much younger miniaturist who had painted Webster's portrait years before. Rumors of Webster's sexual involvement with Sarah circulated throughout Washington, and he was accused of having a Black son and being a drunk by his political enemies. The charges were reported throughout the country and caused Webster significant personal distress. It's now generally believed Sarah Goodridge was Webster's mistress for a while before he married Caroline Le Roy, second daughter of Herman Le Roy, a wealthy New York merchant, on December 12, 1829, approximately two years after the death of his first wife. [133] Shortly after his marriage to Caroline, Webster began an important debate about slavery and the Union with Senator Hayne.

The Webster-Hayne Debate. [134] The original issue that triggered their debate was whether public land sales should be priced so they would be a significant source of revenue for the federal government or sold at a discount to attract more settlers to the Western territories. Webster supported selling public lands at affordable prices, but his hidden agenda in the debate with Senator Hayne was to argue against slavery and the right of any state to secede from the Union. He wanted to make a name for himself and run for President in the future. Because he feared an alliance of Western and Southern states in support of slavery, Webster reminded his listeners that the Northwest Ordinance of 1787 forbade introducing slavery into land northwest of the Ohio River. [135] By raising the issue of slavery in this indirect way, Webster shifted the debate from the sale of public lands to safeguarding the Union and dealing with slavery, both popular issues in New England and bound to make Webster an attractive candidate for President at a later date in that area of the country.

Hayne argued that slavery had a beneficial influence on Blacks because they were economically supported by their owners and that states retained all rights not specifically granted to the federal government in the U.S. Constitution. Hayne also said that the doctrine of states' rights was not a threat to the Union but a way to preserve it. Webster argued that slavery is inherently evil, but must be abolished by slave-holding states themselves since the federal government has no authority to emancipate slaves. He also argued for retaining Congressional representation of three-fifths a person for each slave living in the South. Webster pointed out that only the people have a right to overthrow a government that becomes oppressive, and if a state decided to secede, that would be illegal and mean civil war. Webster's speech was well received in the Senate and among Northern states, but was not popular among Southern states. While in the Senate, Webster attempted to recharter the Second Bank of the United States.

The National Bank Issue. Nicholas Biddle, president of the Second Bank of the United States, wanted its charter renewed during an election year because he believed Jackson would not dare oppose his bank during a presidential campaign. Jackson decided to wait and see what happened during the election and in Congress before he attacked Biddle and the bank. In spite of Jackson's caution, Webster took the lead in pushing the bank bill through the Senate. He argued that the Second Bank of the United States should be re-chartered because it had established American finances on a sound footing and supported American manufacturing. After six months of intense debate, the bank bill passed the Senate, but Jackson had been reelected by that time, so he vetoed the bill, accusing the rich and powerful of using the federal government for their own benefit.

Webster warned that if the bank was closed in four years, all its outstanding loans would be called, which would cause serious financial distress to farmers and the country. He also argued that the bank was constitutional by pointing out that the Supreme Court had already ruled on the issue in *McCulloch v. Maryland.* [136] Jackson responded that the Supreme Court is not the only branch of government that can interpret the Constitution—the president also has a voice in public issues, and he didn't agree with Marshall's ruling. Webster argued that Jackson was claiming the same powers as the king of England and said that Supreme Court precedent should be given great weight when deciding these issues. The Senate was unable to override Jackson's veto, so Webster's bank bill failed. Webster returned to his law practice and represented a group of investors in a toll bridge in Boston.

Charles River Bridge Case. [137] In 1785, Massachusetts issued a charter to a group of investors so they could build and operate a toll bridge across the Charles River. As Boston grew, citizens began asking for a toll-free bridge across the Charles River so they could travel to work and shopping without paying a fee. In 1828, Massachusetts chartered another company to build a new bridge parallel to the original Charles River Bridge and authorized the new company to charge tolls only until the cost of construction was recouped, and then the bridge would become free to all. The investors in the original bridge hired Webster to challenge the legality of building a competing bridge.

Webster argued before the Supreme Court that the original charter was a property right and could not be abridged without compensation. He pointed out that the dispute was between two private companies, and the government could not intervene and interfere with private property rights—arguments that had been winning ones in earlier cases before the Court. However, President Jackson had nominated and the Senate had confirmed several Republican Justices to the Supreme Court during his prior term, so Webster was likely to lose his case because of the shift in political opinion on the Court. Webster was aware of the shift in political attitude on the Court and urged his clients to compromise, but they refused, so he was forced to take the case before a hostile Supreme Court. To make matters worse, the cost of constructing the new bridge had been paid by the time the case went to the Supreme Court, so the dispute was between a bridge owned by the state and a bridge owned by a private company.

Webster pointed out that issuing a new charter was not an exercise of eminent domain by the state and should not be used to damage private property rights because that would be against the state constitution. The Court handed down a four to three decision declaring that Webster's clients didn't have an exclusive right to build bridges over the Charles River and a second charter to build a competing bridge was constitutional. The Supreme Court also ruled that the economy should be opened to competition because that would produce greater prosperity for all. The Charles River Bridge case recognized that community rights are superior to private property rights, a victory for Jacksonian Democracy, and a loss for Webster, his clients, and business owners in general. Webster was getting tired of practicing law and felt ready for a more important political career by this time in his life, so he positioned himself to become a member of President Harrison's cabinet and a possible campaign for President at the next election.

Secretary of State. In the election of 1840, Benjamin Harrison easily won the Presidency against Martin Van Buren. President Harrison asked Webster to be his Secretary of State or Secretary of the Treasury. Webster accepted the office of Secretary of State in the Harrison administration, the highest office below the President, and a possible step toward that office for Webster. He was politically ambitious and felt that being Secretary of State would help in his campaign for President after Harrison finished two terms. Before he could become Secretary of State, however, Webster had to deal with his personal debts.

Biddle, president of the Second Bank of the United States, negotiated a deal involving transferring Webster's western lands to investors in exchange for forgiving his debts. Webster didn't have clear title to the lands, so he traded diplomatic appointments for clear title to the land, a questionable practice today, but not unusual at the time. Webster also accepted a substantial personal loan from Isaac Jackson, a wealthy Philadelphia merchant, in exchange for an ambassadorship to Denmark. Today, diplomatic posts are given to large campaign donors rather than individuals who make personal loans to officeholders, so the appearance of bribery is not so clear.

Webster had a golden opportunity to be president of the U.S. during President Harrison's second term, because he was asked to run as vice president with Harrison in 1844 but turned down the opportunity because he didn't want to take second place on the ticket. As is well known, President Harrison died shortly after taking office, and Vice President Tyler became President. It must have been the height of irony and anguish for Webster to see Tyler become President when it could have been him if he had just accepted the office of Vice President. Such are the unexpected consequences of what appears to be an unimportant decision. As Secretary of State, Webster settled the boundary between Canada and the state of Maine.

The Webster-Ashburton Treaty. [138] After the American Revolution, Britain and America hadn't settled the boundary between the State of Maine and New Brunswick, Canada. When England selected a new Prime Minister, Secretary of State Webster saw a chance to resolve the issue under favorable terms for the U.S. His friend Lord Ashburton was appointed to negotiate the issue, so when he arrived in Washington and presented his credentials to President Tyler, Webster showed him around the new capitol. Ashburton and Webster then set to work negotiating the Maine/New Brunswick boundary. Webster didn't tell Ashburton that Jared Sparks, a professor of history at Harvard, had discovered a map in the French archives that strongly supported the British boundary claim. Webster ordered the State Department to buy the map, keep it secret, and hire Professor Sparks to discuss the map with Maine representatives to convince them they should compromise with New Brunswick.

To complicate negotiations, Congress was considering impeaching President Tyler and forcing Secretary Webster to resign. Ashburton knew of these political difficulties and pushed to settle the dispute before the political climate in America deteriorated further. Ashburton and Webster agreed on a new boundary between Maine and New Brunswick in four days of intense negotiations. Webster supported acceptance of the treaty by pointing out to Congress that the land conceded to Canada was of no commercial value, while the land received in return was fertile farmland that would be productive.

Additionally, Webster had acquired navigation rights on the St. John River for Maine lumbermen so they could move their logs to market more cheaply and efficiently, which pleased the people of Maine. The federal government also paid Maine and Massachusetts $125,000 to sweeten the deal and get them to accept the new boundary. Webster argued that neither country had a clear claim to the disputed territory and the only sensible path was a compromise. After Ashburton signed the treaty, he discovered the map proving the British claim, but by then it was too late.

Webster resigned as Secretary of State to run for another term in the Senate. Before he could campaign for the Senate, however, Webster needed to get out of debt again. A few of his rich friends raised $100,000 to pay off his most pressing obligations and Webster agreed to run for the Senate, saying if they wanted him in Congress, they could very well pay for it. The Massachusetts legislature unanimously elected him to the U.S. Senate for another term and Webster set out for Washington to argue a few cases before the Supreme Court after celebrating his sixty-third birthday. What to do about slavery in newly admitted states was a growing issue at this time and Webster wanted to resolve the issue in the next session of the Senate before it created a national crisis.

The 1850 Compromise. Before Webster took his seat in the Senate, President Tyler signed a bill admitting the Republic of Texas to the Union. Mexico immediately broke off diplomatic relations because it claimed Texas as Mexican territory, and the two countries were soon at war. The American Army invaded Mexico and occupied Mexico City. The Treaty of Guadalupe Hidalgo ended the Mexican War and gave the United States the territories of Arizona, California, New Mexico, Texas, Colorado, Nevada, and Utah. [139] Mexico also agreed to accept the Rio Grande as its border with Texas in return for a $15 million payment. President Polk submitted the treaty to the Senate and it was immediately ratified. However, Webster voting against ratification of the treaty because he was concerned about expanding slavery into several new Southern states and felt the issue could eventually destroy the Union if a procedure was not established for admitting slave and free states into the Union in a balanced fashion.

The addition of several new states and territories in the Southern part of the United States raised the issue of whether these new states would be free or slave when they joined the Union. Webster opposed slavery and wanted some of the new territories to be free, but Southern senators were pushing to allow each state to decide for itself whether to be free or slave by holding a vote. Webster wanted to admit California as a free state and decide the fate of the other territories later when attitudes might have changed. However, he didn't want to go to war over the issue, believing that good sense and Christian values would ultimately prevail and the South would eventually free its slaves. Henry Clay tried to build a compromise where California would be admitted as a free state and the other territories would be admitted later without any restrictions on their right to own slaves, but that effort failed in Congress.

Webster made an important speech in the Senate, saying he wanted to preserve the Union, but the two sides needed to compromise. He said the nation was facing dangerous times and then summarized how the nation had come to this perilous state. Webster finished by arguing that the North had a constitutional duty to capture and return escaped slaves to their Southern owners to avoid a war. He also listed grievances Northern States had against the South, saying the North had expected slavery to gradually become less important, but that was not happening. Webster argued that both the North and South were to blame for the problem of slavery and should compromise rather than destroy the Union. The speech was widely praised, except in Massachusetts, where Webster was criticized for abandoning that state's strong anti-slavery position. However, he was trying to forge a compromise to save the Union, not abolish slavery.

A special Senate commission proposed a compromise in which California was admitted as a free state, new territories were established in New Mexico and Utah without any statement about slavery, and adjustments were made to the boundary of Texas and New Mexico. In the middle of negotiations over the compromise, President Taylor died, and Vice President Millard Fillmore became President. Fillmore asked Webster and Clay to continue their work on a compromise settlement and offered Webster the position of Secretary of State in his new administration, which he accepted. However, Webster was again in debt and couldn't afford to abandon his law practice without help from his rich friends. They raised $20,000 for Webster so he could pay his most pressing debts and he accepted the position of Secretary of State again. He ignored the risk to his health by returning to Washington during the summer when diseases were rampant, because Webster believed the office of Secretary of State was his ticket to winning the presidency during the next election, and he was still interested in becoming President of the U.S.

However, Clay's compromise went down to defeat in the Senate as a single stand-alone bill. Senator Stephen Douglas of Illinois, chairman of the Committee on Territories, introduced a series of single bills containing all the provisions of Clay's compromise and Calhoun, Clay, and Webster joined forces to pass these bills one at a time. The first problem Webster faced as Secretary of State was a threat by Texas to take up arms to enforce its territorial rights against New Mexico. President Fillmore asked Webster to write a letter to Texas authorities saying the federal government would oppose any armed action against the New Mexico Territory. That threat from the federal government convinced Texas to wait while the Senate passed a Texas boundary bill to resolve the issue with New Mexico.

Next, the Senate agreed to admit California as a free state, abolish the slave trade in Washington, D.C., organize the New Mexico Territory, and pass a fugitive slave bill requiring all states to return slaves to their owners in the South. By September of 1850, Clay's entire compromise had become law and civil war was avoided for a decade. [140] Webster made one last try to become President, but he faced General Winfield Scott, who had won the Mexican War, and a sitting President in Fillmore, who had the advantage of experience and patronage, so his chances of winning seemed limited.

Exhausted from his labors at the State Department and his campaign for the Presidency, Webster left Washington for a vacation in Boston to regain his health. On the road, his carriage broke and Webster fell, striking his head on the ground. He was treated by a doctor and released to continue his trip, but Webster had suffered a subdural hematoma which caused him dizziness for months. His health declined and Webster was not able to campaign effectively for the presidency. He died on October 24, 1852, in Marshfield, Massachusetts. [141]

Abraham Lincoln

Lincoln was born February 12, 1809, in Hodgenville, Kentucky. [142] He attributed his energy, ambition, and intelligence to his mother, who was the illegitimate daughter of a wealthy Virginia plantation owner. His family had a history of trading, farming, and public service in America. Lincoln's grandfather moved from Virginia to Kentucky on the advice of Daniel Boone, who said the land was rich and fertile. The State of Kentucky followed the English doctrine of primogeniture, which meant Lincoln's father, who was a second son, inherited none of the five thousand acres his family owned, so Lincoln grew up in impoverished circumstances compared with his uncle's family.

Lincoln's father worked as a carpenter and cabinet maker, saved his money, and bought land in Hardin County, Kentucky. In 1806, he bought Sinking Spring Farm, a three-hundred-acre estate with a spring that bubbled from the bottom of a deep cave. Abraham Lincoln was born on that farm in a log cabin. His mother, Nancy, taught him to read and love books. His early memories were of working in the "big field" on his father's farm and attending a one-room school with his older sister for a few months when he was not working on his father's farm.

When Lincoln was seven years old, the family moved across the Ohio River to get away from slavery. Thomas Lincoln claimed a rich parcel of land in southern Indiana, built a fourteen by fourteen-foot log cabin, and blazed trees to mark his property. He returned to Kentucky and moved his family to Indiana just as the territory was admitted to the Union. Lincoln's father built a larger cabin on the land and hunted deer and bear during that first winter. Lincoln's father showed him how to handle an ax, and Lincoln helped clear trees and plant corn. Abraham's mother died of milk sickness (an illness caused by drinking milk from a cow that had eaten snakeroot) when he was nine years old. Within a year, Lincoln's father married Sarah Bush Johnston, a widow and mother of three children. Their marriage was a business arrangement rather than a romantic union—but it worked and Sarah was a good stepmother for Abraham Lincoln.

Sarah Johnston Lincoln brought her personal possessions, three children, and love into Lincoln's life. She organized the household, added a loft to the log cabin for sleeping, and blended the two families effectively. Sarah treated all the children fairly and was fond of Abraham. Although Sarah was illiterate, she believed education was important, so when a one-room school opened, she encouraged Lincoln to attend when he was not needed on the farm. Lincoln mastered the basics of reading, spelling, and arithmetic while at school, and taught himself for the remainder of his life by reading books. He became a good writer and neighbors asked him to draft letters for them. Lincoln read his mother's Bible and other books Sarah had brought from Kentucky. He was a natural storyteller and leader from an early age and had many friends.

By the time Lincoln was in his late teens, he decided he wanted to do something other than farming. In 1830, the Lincoln family moved to Sangamon County, Illinois, and a few months later Lincoln turned twenty-one and was free to determine his own future. Over the next ten years, he tried various jobs, including working as a clerk, soldier, carpenter, blacksmith, surveyor, postman, lawyer, and politician. [143] By the time he was thirty, Lincoln decided he wanted to be an attorney and politician. In the spring of 1832, friends in New Salem suggested Lincoln run for the Illinois state legislature, a post that required no experience at that time. Lincoln agreed to run, but lost his job when his employer went bankrupt and had to make other plans.

Lincoln joined the army because he believed military service would be good for his political career and he needed a job. He was elected to lead the company and said that was one of his proudest moments. Lincoln's military service was neither dangerous nor heroic, but it helped him later in his political career. He was honorably discharged and went back to Sangamon County to campaign for the state legislature. When the votes were counted, he was eighth in number of votes received, but only the first four candidates got seats in the legislature. Lincoln later said that was the only election he ever lost, and he vowed not to lose another one. At the moment, he needed a get a job and earn a living.

Postmaster. Lincoln partnered with his army friend, William Berry, to buy a general store in New Salem, Illinois. Lincoln helped customers and read books when business was slow, which was most of the time because the town was not growing. The only transaction of his store that made a profit was selling whiskey, so the store failed and Lincoln was again out of a job. He was considering leaving New Salem when his friends got him appointed postmaster for the town. Mail was delivered twice a week at that time, and it was Lincoln's job to distribute letters and collect the postage due since letters were paid for by the recipient in those days. The major attractions of the job, aside from an income, were meeting the people in the town, reading all the newspapers, and sending his own letters without cost to the recipient. Lincoln soon learned that the local surveyor was looking for an assistant, so he applied and got the job. He eventually took on complicated surveying work on his own after he learned the trade. His first love remained politics, however.

Attorney Lincoln. Lincoln ran for the state legislature in 1834 and was elected with the second-highest vote count. To prepare for his new job as a legislator, Lincoln began to study law by reading books. He joined the state legislature in December 1834 and learned that most of his colleagues had no experience in government. Lincoln quickly learned how to draft a statute and other members of the legislature were impressed with his mastery of English. After the first legislative session ended, Lincoln returned to New Salem to run the post office and read law. The ladies of New Salem decided Lincoln should be married, but only one woman interested him: Ann Rutledge, the daughter of a founder of the town. However, she was engaged to a man who had left for New York to straighten out his affairs. Lincoln made friends with Ann and bided his time because he noticed that correspondence from her fiancée had stopped after a few months. Lincoln finally asked Ann to marry him and she agreed. Unfortunately, she contracted typhoid fever and died on August 25, 1835, before they could be married. Lincoln was devastated, but still ran for reelection to the state legislature in 1836, and collected the most votes of any candidate in the county. He moved to Springfield to begin practicing law, having been admitted to the bar on September 9, 1836. [144] In 1837, Lincoln and Stuart opened a law office at No. 4 Hoffman's Row, Springfield, Illinois. [145]

Lincoln In Springfield. The capitol of Illinois was a frontier town in 1837, filled with log cabins and energetic people. Springfield had a high school, churches, doctors, and eleven attorneys. Lincoln easily made friends and had a thriving law practice because his partner was well known in the area. Most of their cases required common sense to resolve, so he had no difficulty practicing law. Lincoln traveled all over Illinois, trying cases in various counties and became a successful attorney, although he viewed law practice as a stepping stone to a political career. [146] Lincoln became the leader of the Whig contingent of the Illinois legislature and was active in the 1840 presidential campaign supporting Benjamin Harrison. He organized an effective get-out-the-vote campaign and met Mary Todd that year.

Mary Todd. Lincoln socialized with the elite of Springfield because he was a successful attorney. He met Mary Todd, daughter of a prosperous merchant and banker from Lexington, Ky., and was attracted to her. [147] Raised in luxury among slaves, Mary was cultured, graceful, and dignified. Lincoln liked Mary and had no difficulty interacting because she kept the conversation going. She had plenty of suitors but was interested in Lincoln, believing he was honest, courteous, and considerate. Lincoln and Mary became engaged before Christmas, and he immediately had second thoughts, wondering if he could afford to marry and if he was really in love with Mary. After some hesitation, Lincoln told Mary he didn't love her. She was heartbroken, but accepted the situation and broke off the engagement, saying she would leave the opportunity open if he changed his mind. Some of Lincoln's friends thought he was crazy, so they invited both of them to a social gathering and suggested they "Be friends again." Lincoln and Mary discovered they had much in common and renewed their relationship. Lincoln had a dispute with a state auditor and almost fought a duel with sabers.

A Saber Duel. While courting Mary, Lincoln wrote a series of anonymous letters making fun of an auditor, who demanded to know the author of the slanderous letters. Lincoln admitted he had written the letters and Shields asked for a retraction, or Lincoln would have to face a duel. Lincoln went to a friend for advice. His friend recommended Lincoln accept the duel because to back down would damage his reputation and honor. Lincoln accepted the challenge, and selected sabers, reasoning that his long arms would give him an advantage. [148] Dueling was outlawed in Illinois, so they arranged to meet in Missouri. Before the duel began, their friends convinced both parties to apologize and shake hands, avoiding possible injury or death. The incident taught Lincoln not to publish critical anonymous letters in the future.

Mary was impressed that Lincoln had taken responsibility for the anonymous letters and faced a duel, so they renewed their engagement and married in the Springfield home of Mary Todd's sister on November 4, 1842. [149] Lincoln and Mary moved into a room at Globe Tavern and he went to work practicing law. Lincoln took any case that came through the door, including bankruptcy, wills, land deeds, and legal disputes. Business was good and he moved to a new office the following year. Lincoln learned a lot from his new partner Logan, who was the leading lawyer in Sangamon County and a legal scholar. Lincoln argued their cases to juries because he was an excellent storyteller, while Logan drafted petitions and briefs for the court and did legal research for Lincoln's cases. In 1844, they dissolved the partnership because Logan wanted to go into business with his son. Lincoln asked his young associate Herndon to be his partner, because Lincoln wanted to run for the U.S. House of Representatives and needed someone to manage the office while he was away campaigning. However, Lincoln was not nominated by the party so he had to wait for another election cycle to run for a seat in the U.S. House of Representatives.

A year before the next election, Lincoln began campaigning for the nomination and collected endorsements from leading men all over the state as he rode circuit. Lincoln was nominated, won the election, and became a member of the U.S. House of Representatives from Illinois. [150] Because Henry Clay and Daniel Webster were getting older, Lincoln planned to become the next leader of the Whig Party. He made friends in Congress and found Washington D.C. interesting. With forty thousand inhabitants, it was the largest city Lincoln had ever seen. He was familiar with parliamentary procedures and enjoyed his time in the House of Representatives.

Lincoln was impressed with John Quincy Adams, whom he met in the House of Representatives, because he was an implacable foe of slavery and a former President. Lincoln wanted to know him better, but John Quincy died soon after Lincoln entered the House. In April 1846, fighting broke out between American and Mexican soldiers in territory between the Nueces and Rio Grande Rivers in Texas and the U.S. declared war on Mexico. In hard fighting, General Taylor defeated the Mexican Army repeatedly. By December 1847, the U.S. Army entered Mexico City, and the Mexican government surrendered. The Whig Party attacked President Polk for fighting an unnecessary war, but Lincoln supported the war and helped nominate General Taylor as the Whig candidate for President in the next election. Lincoln campaigned for him, and Taylor won the 1848 presidential election easily. Lincoln returned to Illinois to practice law at the end of his Congressional term.

Between 1849 and 1854, Lincoln practiced law in Springfield with Herndon and became the leading attorney in Illinois. In 1849, Lincoln's son Edward contracted tuberculosis and died—a devastating blow for Abraham and Mary. In 1854, Lincoln was retained by the powerful Illinois Central Railroad as their primary litigation attorney, and his income and political profile rose substantially. However, he was more interested in politics than practicing law and began looking around for a way to become even better known. Lincoln decided to debate Senator Stephen Douglas on the issue of slavery to raise his profile and advance his political career.

Douglas had just introduced the Kansas-Nebraska Act in the Senate, proposing that when these two territories were admitted into the union, the decision whether to allow slaves in each state should be based on a popular vote. Lincoln was against the idea, feeling the new territories should be admitted as free states to avoid the expansion of slavery. Lincoln ran for the Illinois state legislature again, knowing it would nominate a U.S. Senator for the next term, and he wanted that seat. Douglas made the case for letting voters decide whether a state was slave or free when admitted to the Union and Lincoln saw a chance to become better known by opposing Douglas on the issue. He had to wait for the right opportunity to initiate the debate with Douglas.

Lincoln and Douglas. Lincoln got his chance to debate Douglas when the Senator appeared in Springfield to support the Kansas-Nebraska Act. The open-air event was rained out, so Douglas spoke in the Illinois House building where Lincoln was a member. [151] The next day, Lincoln rose in the Illinois House and rebutted Douglas' arguments. He first attacked Douglas by arguing that Black slaves were men and needed to be treated with respect. He pointed out the injustice of slavery and contradicted Douglas' argument that state determination of the slavery issue was in the spirit of the Founding Fathers. Lincoln argued that the Founding Fathers believed all men are created equal, and since Blacks were men, they should not be slaves. Lincoln's speech was greeted with approval in the North when it was published in national newspapers, but was attacked in the South as radical and anti-slavery. In the fall election, a majority of new congressmen opposed the Kansas-Nebraska Act and it was defeated.

Lincoln campaigned hard to become the next Senator from Illinois but was not successful. When the legislature convened to vote for a Senator in 1855, Lincoln led with forty-five votes on the first ballot. However, after a few more votes, he began to lose ground, so Lincoln threw his support to another Whig candidate for the Senate named Trumbull. Lincoln was disappointed but took comfort in the fact that the election of Trumbull was a stinging defeat for Douglas. The anti-Kansas/Nebraska contingent agreed to support Lincoln in the next election to the Senate.

By the end of 1855, the Whig Party was no longer a viable political organization, so Lincoln organized a Republican Party in Illinois and wrote a platform that said Congress should have the power to exclude slavery from any territory. Lincoln gave a speech at the Republican Convention in which he stated that the issue of slavery was the primary cause of America's current problems and needed to be resolved. He recognized that the Republican Party faced formidable obstacles in the presidential election of 1856 because the Democrats had nominated James Buchanan, former Secretary of State, rather than Senator Douglas. Democrat Buchanan won the election because opposition votes were divided between Fremont and Fillmore. After the 1856 election, Lincoln maintained a low political profile and devoted himself to his law practice, all the time planning how to advance his own political ambitions.

Dred Scott Case. [152] Shortly after President Buchanan was inaugurated, the U.S. Supreme Court handed down a major pro-slavery decision. The case involved the fate of Dred Scott, a Missouri slave taken by his owner to the State of Illinois and the Minnesota Territory, both lands where slavery was prohibited. When he returned to Missouri, Scott's master died and the slave sued for his freedom, claiming he had been a resident of a free state and a free territory and therefore was no longer a slave. Chief Justice Roger Taney authored a seven to two opinion, ruling that Scott had no standing to sue because he was not a citizen of the United States but merely a slave. Taney also held that the Missouri Compromise was unconstitutional. Finally, Taney ruled that all slaves are property under the Fifth Amendment to the Constitution, and depriving an owner of his property is unconstitutional.

Anti-slavery groups were outraged at the Supreme Court ruling and predicted *Dred Scott* would allow slavery to expand into every state of the Union. Senator Douglas came to Illinois and defended the *Dred Scott* ruling as honest and conscientious. Lincoln attacked both Douglas and the *Dred Scott* ruling, arguing that the decision was wrong and Douglas was trying to extend slavery into every state. Lincoln said the Founding Fathers intended the Declaration of Independence to mean that all men should have equal rights to life, liberty, and the pursuit of happiness, including Black slaves because they are men. The issue of slavery became even more contentious when President Buchanan recommended that the Kansas Territory be admitted to the Union as a slave state. The admission of Kansas as a slave state would tip the balance of power in the Senate in favor of slavery, and Lincoln felt that would maintain slavery in America forever.

When the Republican state convention met in Springfield, they unanimously nominated Abraham Lincoln as their senatorial candidate to succeed Douglas. In his acceptance speech, Lincoln used the famous phrase "that a house divided against itself, half slave and half free, cannot stand." He accused Douglas of wanting to extend slavery into every state, claimed the Senator could not be trusted, and should be replaced. Lincoln's speech attracted national attention and was the most radical anti-slavery speech delivered by any major politician at the time. During the campaign for the Senate, Lincoln challenged Douglas to a series of debates, and Douglas agreed, producing the seven famous Lincoln-Douglas debates over slavery and the future of the Union. [153]

The Lincoln-Douglas Debates. Senator Douglas accused Lincoln of trying to establish an abolitionist party to outlaw slavery, but Lincoln said he didn't favor abolishing slavery or repealing the Fugitive Slave Act. Lincoln said he was willing to admit slave states into the Union in a balanced way and was not committed to abolishing slavery in the District of Columbia. He did argue that slavery is morally wrong and framed his disagreement with Douglas as a struggle between right and wrong. Northern parts of Illinois were Republican and supported Lincoln, while Southern sections of the state were Democratic and supported Douglas. Douglas was reelected U.S. Senator from Illinois and Lincoln began planning to run in the Presidential election of 1860.

In 1859, newspapers said Lincoln should be a candidate for president of the U.S., and he believed he had a chance to secure the Republican nomination because everyone knew him because of his debates with Douglas. Lincoln had the debates published as a book shortly before the Republican Party nominating convention of 1860, and it became an instant bestseller. Lincoln also prepared an autobiography in which he emphasized growing up in a log cabin, splitting rails, and practicing law. Lincoln embarked on a series of lectures along the East Coast to raise his political profile. He never openly campaigned for the nomination, because the custom at the time was that the office should seek the man, but his surrogates campaigned vigorously to have Lincoln nominated as the Republican candidate for President in 1860.

During the opening ceremony of the Republican Convention, Lincoln's supporters brought in two rails he had split years earlier and the crowd went wild. Lincoln's major competition was Seward, a popular candidate in the Northeast. However, the Republicans were looking for a presidential candidate who could win Pennsylvania, Indiana, and Illinois, and they believed Lincoln was that man. He had the right positions on major issues such as slavery and was a popular candidate in the Midwest. On the third ballot, members of the nominating convention began shifting to Lincoln, until finally the State of Ohio shifted four votes, pushing him over the top to be the Republican candidate for president of the U.S. [154]

Lincoln was almost assured of a victory in the presidential election of 1860 because the Democratic party nominated two candidates and split their votes. A crucial state in the election was Pennsylvania and Lincoln spent time in that state campaigning and uniting Republican voters. On election day, Lincoln won the Midwestern states, Pennsylvania, and New York, which assured his election as President of the United States. The Lincoln/Hamlin ticket won 180 Electoral College votes.

President Lincoln. Shortly after Lincoln was elected president, South Carolina voted to secede from the Union. Within a month every Southern state was debating secession. Some in the North felt the Southern states should be allowed to go their own way, but most Republicans were in favor of a compromise to keep the Union together. Because the old administration had no policy to deal with the political crisis, everyone looked to President Lincoln for a solution. However, he had no authority to act until the electors officially named him president. The country waited and watched the Union dissolve while Lincoln began selecting a cabinet to help him run the country.

Lincoln needed the support of William Seward, Salmon Chase, and Edward Bates if he wanted to lead a united Republican party through this crisis, so he asked Seward to be Secretary of State. Seward suggested Lincoln name two Southerners to his cabinet, but none would accept a cabinet position unless Lincoln said he would allow slavery in the new territories, which he was not willing to do. Lincoln made Chase Secretary of the Treasury and Bates accepted appointment as Attorney General. While Lincoln was putting his cabinet together, the Union was falling apart. By January 1861, South Carolina, Florida, Mississippi, Alabama, Georgia, and Louisiana had seceded, and Texas was expected to secede any day.

Seward tried to persuade Lincoln to compromise with the South, but he refused. On inauguration day, troops were stationed on capitol streets, and sharpshooters were positioned on buildings to prevent an assignation attempt against Lincoln. In his inaugural address, Lincoln stated that succession was illegal and he would enforce the law. [155] Lincoln urged Southern states to reconsider their votes for secession and stay in the Union. Instead, more Southern states seceded. Lincoln's immediate problem was what to do about Fort Sumpter in South Carolina. If he didn't resupply the fort, it would have to be abandoned, but he wanted the South to fire the first shot so he did nothing. Lincoln finally decided to send a fleet to resupply and reinforce Fort Sumpter, but by then Confederates had begun bombarding the fort, and it surrendered before supplies arrived. The American Civil War began and Lincoln avoided firing the first shot.

Lincoln asked Congress to authorize the enlistment of seventy-five thousand militiamen to suppress the rebellion, and many in Congress said his request was too small. Lincoln also needed troops immediately to protect Washington, D.C., but Maryland would not allow Union soldiers to cross her territory. To resolve the stand-off, the navy moved troops around Maryland by sea. They landed and traveled to the capitol by train. Several regiments were soon guarding Washington, D.C. Lincoln did not want to recognize the Confederacy because that would mean secession was legal, but he decreed that captured Confederate soldiers should be treated as war prisoners. He quickly imposed a blockade on all Southern ports to stop Confederates importing war materials and exporting cotton and tobacco. Lincoln believed the prosecution of the war was up to him and his cabinet, and Congress should keep hands-off.

Because Southern congressmen had withdrawn from Washington, the Republican Party dominated Congress and Lincoln could pass any bill he submitted. General Scott was appointed to command Union troops, and he proposed a blockade of all Southern coastal ports and sending an army down the Mississippi River to split the Confederacy in two. The blockade was begun, an army was formed to protect Washington, and a smaller army was sent West under General Grant to close the Mississippi River to Confederate shipping. The early battles of the Civil War went badly for the Union, mainly because Confederate generals were better tacticians and fought an aggressive campaign while Union generals were defensive and reluctant to fight. Lincoln appointed General McClellan to command the forces around Washington and rebuild the Union Army after its defeat at Bull Run, but the general refused to engage the enemy in battle until he had vastly superior numbers.

General McClellan procrastinated and trained rather than attacking. Even though Lincoln ordered him to take action, the general did nothing. The U.S. Navy triggered a serious diplomatic incident with Great Britain when two Confederate ministers were taken from an English ship on the high seas. The British demanded the Confederate diplomats be freed immediately. Both France and England were on the brink of going to war against the United States before Lincoln released the two diplomats. In 1861, things were looking bad for the Union because Confederate generals were winning battles and Lincoln's generals were too cautious. To remedy the situation, Lincoln began reading military strategy and tactics so he could select a general who would fight. Lincoln named Edwin Stanton as Secretary of War, and they immediately formed a good working relationship.

Lincoln issued War Order No. 1 which instructed all his commanders to begin a general advance against the enemy on February 22, 1861. Lincoln wanted his armies to threaten all Confederate positions simultaneously so the South could not move forces from one theatre to another on their interior lines. The plan worked at first and Union armies in the West began winning victories. General Grant cleared the Tennessee and Cumberland Rivers on his route to the Mississippi River.

In the South, the Confederate Navy sent the ironclad *Virginia* out of Norfolk harbor to sink Union ships blockading that port. If not stopped, the Confederate ironclad would break the Union blockade and allow the Confederacy to resupply its armies and raise money selling cotton and tobacco. The *Monitor*, a radically new Union ironclad ship, fought a lengthy battle with *Virginia,* and damaged the Confederate ironclad so badly it returned to port and never sailed again. The blockade was safe for the moment, but the land battle was not going well for Lincoln and the Union. The President was dissatisfied with McClellan, who would not attack, because he always claimed enemy forces were more numerous than his own troops. Lincoln learned that McClellan was badly mistaken when a Confederate Army withdrew from prepared fortifications and Union generals discovered that many of what appeared to be cannons were painted logs, and only about fifty thousand Confederate troops had been in the trenches, half the number McClellan had claimed opposed his army.

The question of what to do about slavery was constantly on Lincoln's mind. He considered sending freed slaves to a colony in Africa or South America, and a Quaker delegation met with him in 1862 to recommend that he emancipate all the slaves in the South. Lincoln thought freeing the slaves was premature because the war was going badly for the Union and the action would seem to be a desperate one.

General Grant was stalled at Vicksburg and having difficulty capturing the city while Stonewall Jackson was conducting a brilliant campaign in the Shenandoah Valley that diverted Union troops from other battles and relieved pressure on General Lee around Richmond. McClellan did nothing with his large army and repeatedly requested additional reinforcements, claiming General Lee had many more troops facing him. However, Lincoln knew from independent estimates that the Confederates were fewer in number than the Union Army. Lincoln had no confidence in McClellan and was considering replacing him, but he didn't know who to put in McClellan's place, so he waited for further developments before making a command change.

Emancipation. Lincoln reasoned that he had the authority to emancipate slaves because they were private property, and the Union had the right to confiscate private property found in conquered states. He discussed the issue with his cabinet, and they were divided on the wisdom of freeing the slaves because it might inflame the South even more. Lincoln decided to wait for a military victory before issuing his Emancipation Proclamation. However, no victory came. Instead, General Lee defeated the Union forces facing Richmond and then attacked into Maryland, threatening Washington, D.C. again. McClellan finally won a bloody victory over Lee at Antietam, and Lincoln decided it was time to emancipate the slaves. Reaction was predictable—most Northerners were delighted, Southerners were outraged, and leaders in the border states of Maryland, Kentucky, and Missouri believed emancipation was unconstitutional. Democrats in the North were opposed to emancipation, and the Republican Party lost seats in both houses of Congress in the midterm elections of 1862.

After the 1862 election, Lincoln replaced McClellan with Ambrose Burnside. A few months later Burnside ordered a frontal attack on Confederate troops dug in around Fredericksburg, and suffered the worst defeat in American military history. Lincoln immediately fired Burnside and considered naming Grant, as commander of the Union army. He finally appointed Joseph Hooker instead. In 1863, Lincoln was impressed by the French invention of a repeating rifle and recommended it be tested, and if found satisfactory, manufactured and issued to the Union army. The new repeating rifle helped the Union win the Civil War because it could be fired many times from a prone position without reloading compared with the single shot from a musket, which had to be reloaded standing up.

After Hooker was defeated at Chancellorsville, Lincoln selected General George Meade, one of his more experienced corps commanders, to replace him. Meade immediately followed Lee's army into

Pennsylvania and faced him on a field near the town of Gettysburg. On July 4, 1863, Lincoln learned that Lee had been defeated at Gettysburg and was retreating South. Shortly after, Grant captured Vicksburg and closed the Mississippi River to Confederate shipping. For a few days, it seems as if the Civil War might be over, but Meade didn't pursue Lee, who escaped with his army to fight another day. However, the tide of battle was turning in the Union's favor for the first time.

Lincoln's Gettysburg Address. Lincoln was invited to attend the dedication of a memorial cemetery at Gettysburg on November 19, 1863. In his address, Lincoln described the formation of the Union, dedicated the cemetery, and finished with an optimistic view of America's future. Lincoln made clear in his address that he was against a negotiated peace with the South, emphasizing that the United States was one nation and could not survive divided. He invoked the Declaration of Independence, which "brought forth …a new nation, conceived in Liberty, and dedicated to the proposition that all men are created equal." [156] Lincoln thought his address had not gone well, but when it was printed in the newspapers, everyone told him it was one of his best speeches.

By the fall of 1863, Lincoln's political position improved because the Union Army was winning battles, and the likelihood of England or France recognizing the Confederacy was declining. Lincoln began to discuss terms for how Southern states could be readmitted to the Union. He considered three options: withdraw the Emancipation Proclamation and offer a general amnesty in return for rejoining the Union; keep the Emancipation Proclamation in place and offer generous terms to Southern states that rejoined the Union; or treat the Confederacy as a conquered nation subject to the will of Congress and give former slaves equal rights under law.

In an address to Congress, Lincoln summarized what his administration had been doing over the past years to win the war, noted that over one hundred thousand former slaves were serving in the Union Army, and proposed amnesty and reconstruction for the South, including full pardons for all Confederates who had fought against the Union, and complete restoration of their property rights, except for ownership of slaves. High-ranking officials of the Confederacy would be required to take an oath of loyalty to the Union before they would be readmitted as citizens. His message contained something for everyone. Reconstruction would leave every Southern state intact and Northern Republicans were assured that slaves would be freed. The address was well received and became a major issue in the presidential campaign of 1864. Lincoln was so pleased with what Grant and Sherman had achieved that he gave General Grant control of the entire Union army.

General Grant. Lincoln wanted to name Grant commander of all the Union forces but was concerned he might be a presidential candidate in 1864, and Lincoln didn't want to run against a popular general who was winning battles. One of Lincoln's friends met with Grant and brought a letter to Lincoln stating that Grant was not interested in running for president. Lincoln was reassured and promptly promoted Grant to Lieutenant General, a rank not seen since George Washington's day, and named him General-in-Chief of the Union Armies. Lincoln wanted Grant to fight and win battles. The new commander reorganized the Union cavalry into a single corps under General Sheridan and developed a plan for simultaneous attacks on all the armies of the Confederacy. Grant was determined to destroy the Confederate Army and was willing to endure significant casualties in the process. Lincoln liked Grant because he fought.

Lincoln Reelected. The Republicans nominated Lincoln for a second term as President, and selected Andrew Johnson, a loyal Southern politician as Vice President. However, Lee was not finished; he fought a bloody battle in the Wilderness against Grant and then turned to threaten Washington, D.C. After hard fighting, General Early's fifteen thousand Confederate troops were driven from around the capitol, and Lincoln was able to proceed with his presidential campaign. The Democratic Party nominated General McClellan for president and he ran on a peace platform. In the middle of the Democratic Convention, word reached Lincoln by telegraph that Sherman had captured Atlanta and the Union Navy had taken Mobile, the last major Gulf port open to the Confederates. These victories and the nomination of McClellan as a peace candidate essentially assured Lincoln's second term. He won every state except New Jersey, Delaware, and Kentucky. McClellan collected under forty-five percent of the popular vote. Union Army soldiers voted overwhelmingly for Lincoln.

Southern leaders viewed Lincoln's reelection as a major disaster for the Confederacy and believed the South would lose unless something drastic was done. Various ideas were considered, including offering to emancipate slaves in return for recognition by England and France, enrolling slaves in the Confederate Army, and even murdering Lincoln. President Lincoln had more important things to worry about than his own safety, including the naming of a new Chief Justice of the Supreme Court to replace Roger Taney. Because Lincoln had already named four new Justices to the Court during his first term, adding a new Chief Justice would assure that a Republican Supreme Court would rule favorably on bills passed to implement reconstruction. The president selected Solomon P. Chase as his candidate for Chief Justice of the United States Supreme Court and the Senate promptly confirmed him.

Lincoln also sent Congress the Thirteenth Amendment to the Constitution authorizing emancipation of all slaves. The amendment was passed by Congress and sent to the states for ratification. Lincoln then called a meeting of his Cabinet to discuss terms for peace with the South. He proposed that as soon as the South surrendered, Confederate states would be readmitted into the Union, but he would not negotiate with the Confederate government while fighting continued. Lincoln felt the best way to bring the Southern states back into the Union was to establish friendly governments in each Southern state as it was conquered. Adoption of the Thirteenth Amendment helped Lincoln sell his reconstruction plan to Congress.

In his second inaugural address, Lincoln offered no prediction on when the war would be over, only saying he hoped it would end quickly. He ended his address with the famous words:

> "With malice toward none; with charity for all; with firmness in the right; as God gives us to see the right, let us strive on to finish the work we are in; to bind up the nation's wounds; … to do all which may achieve and cherish a just, and a lasting peace, among ourselves, and with all nations." [157]

After his inauguration, Lincoln took a vacation because he was exhausted. Then he went to see General Grant in the field to discuss the terms of surrender Grant should offer Lee. Lincoln told Grant he was not to negotiate with Lee unless the general was willing to surrender his army. Lincoln was concerned that unless the Confederate Army surrendered, there would be widespread violence in the South after the war. Lincoln was rejuvenated by his visit to Grant and sensed that the Civil War was almost over. He traveled to Richmond to see the Virginia statehouse where the Confederate Congress had met and sat in President Jefferson Davis' chair.

Lee Surrenders. On April 9, 1865, Lincoln learned that General Lee had surrendered his army at Appomattox. President Lincoln offered words of gratitude to Grant and the Union Army in a public speech at the White House and said he wanted no persecution of Confederate leaders. Additionally, Lincoln stated that he wanted to grant freed slaves the right to vote. John Wilkes Boothe, listening in the crowd, was angered by these words and vowed to kill Lincoln. He successfully shot Lincoln at Ford's Theatre on April 14, 1865. [158]

Theodore Roosevelt, Jr.

Theodore Roosevelt was born October 27, 1858, in New York City. [159] He suffered from childhood asthma and experienced recurring attacks but followed a program of exercise and weightlifting later in his life to strengthen his body and overcome the malady. Roosevelt saw Lincoln's funeral procession from the window of his grandfather's home in Union Square, New York, when he was six. He was home-schooled by tutors and studied geography, history, biology, German, French, mathematics, and classical languages. As was customary among their class, the Roosevelts sailed for Europe in 1869 on a Grand Tour. [160] They went to Scotland first, visiting Furness Abbey, a twelfth-century monastery. After Henry VIII broke with Rome, the abbey was abandoned and the stones used to construct other buildings, so little was left of the structure except the foundation.

The family traveled on to Edinburgh, visited the home of Sir Walter Scott, and journeyed south to York, Oxford, and London. The children were given riding lessons in Hyde Park and enjoyed the experience. They traveled across the English Channel to Amsterdam and up the Rhine to Frankfurt, Heidelberg, and Strasbourg. The family visited Basal, Switzerland, during July, climbed the Alps to play in the snow, traveled across southern France, and spent November in Paris. The Roosevelts also visited Italy but liked Switzerland best. The trip was a success, but it was hard on Roosevelt's health because he suffered recurring bouts of asthma while in Europe.

The Roosevelts returned to New York on May 25, 1870, the same year the first subway opened in the city. That summer, the Franco-Prussian War started, and the French Army collapsed in the face of attacks led by Frederick the Great. Roosevelt suffered additional asthma attacks after he returned home and began a strenuous regimen of exercise to strengthen his body and improve his health. His father had a gymnasium built in their home so Roosevelt could exercise regularly. Roosevelt suffered fewer asthma attacks as he grew older and exercised more. In the summer of 1872, Roosevelt was fitted with glasses, and suddenly he could see clearly for the first time. How a wealthy family could have missed his visual handicap is difficult to understand, but the transformation was amazing. In addition to being able to see, Roosevelt experienced a growth spurt and enjoyed better health.

Roosevelt entered Harvard College on September 27, 1876, studying science, philosophy, rhetoric, Latin and Greek. [161] He rowed and boxed while at Harvard, joined Alpha Delta Phi Literary Society, edited the *Harvard Advocate*, was a member of Phi Beta Kappa Honor Society, and graduated *magna cum laude*. When his father died, Roosevelt inherited sixty-five thousand dollars, equivalent to almost two million dollars today—enough to live comfortably for the rest of his life if he just wanted to live the life of a wealthy gentleman. Instead, Roosevelt enrolled in Columbia Law School but found parts of the law illogical. He spent time in law school writing *The Naval War of 1812*, a technical work that remains a standard text on the war today. [162] The publication of Alfred Thayer Mahan's *The Influence of Sea Power on History* in 1890 greatly influenced Roosevelt's thinking about war and international relations. He was impressed with the idea that a strong navy would allow a nation to control the oceans, exert diplomatic influence, and protect itself from attack by sea. The doctrine of a strong navy became a guiding principle for Roosevelt the rest of his life.

Marriage to Alice Lee. Roosevelt met Alice Lee, daughter of George Cabot Lee, at her home in Oyster Bay, New York, on October 18, 1878. George Lee was a Democrat, manager at State Street Bank, and a wealthy New Yorker. Alice was seventeen, and Theodore was nineteen when they met, and he fell in love with her at first sight. She was attractive, tall for a girl, bright, cheerful, and energetic. They spent their first day together walking in the woods, having tea, dinner, and dancing. Roosevelt spent a good deal of time at the Lee mansion that fall and was invited for Thanksgiving dinner with the Lee family. Roosevelt said he decided to marry Alice at that event. They played tennis, walked in the woods, danced, went rowing on Oyster Bay, took horseback rides, and had a grand time that fall. The formal announcement of their engagement was made on February 14, 1880. [163]

Roosevelt's mother was delighted with the marriage and began making arrangements for the wedding. She hosted dinner parties, teas, and other festivities prior to the wedding itself. Theodore Roosevelt married Alice Hathaway Lee on October 27, 1880. She gave birth to Alice Lee Roosevelt on February 12, 1884, and died two days later of kidney failure. Roosevelt's mother had died of typhoid fever the day before, so he was devastated by two tragic deaths so close together. He withdrew from society and grieved alone, leaving his newborn daughter with his sister in New York City.

At that time, he was a member of the New York State Assembly, working on an investigation into corporate corruption, especially among Wall Street financiers. Roosevelt won reelection in his district at the same time Grover Cleveland became Governor of New York. Roosevelt introduced a civil service reform bill in the New York Assembly, aimed at establishing a professional bureaucracy and doing away with the political spoils system run by Tammany Hall. He continued to grieve over the loss of his wife and mother, and he decided to leave New York for the Wild West to become a rancher.

Dakota Rancher. In 1884, Roosevelt retired from New York politics and moved to the Dakota Territory to manage a large cattle ranch he had recently bought and to recover from the loss of his wife and mother. [164] He learned to ride, rope, and hunt, although his cowhands were not impressed with Roosevelt's skills on a horse. Roosevelt hunted buffalo and other large game that were plentiful in the territory at that time. He invested around fifty thousand dollars in his ranching venture, buying large tracts of land and hundreds of purebred cattle. Local citizens wanted Roosevelt to serve as the first Congressman from the territory, but he was not interested. He did organize a cattlemen's association to stop rustling of livestock, wrote magazine articles, and three books: *Hunting Trips of a Ranchman*, *Ranch Life and the Hunting Trail*, and *The Wilderness Hunter* while in the Dakota Territory.

He formed the Little Missouri Stockmen's Association, and the Boone and Crocket Club, whose goal was the conservation of large animals and their habitat for hunting. The severe winter of 1886-87 killed most of his cattle and ruined his ranch. Roosevelt spent the summer of 1887 winding up his affairs in the Dakota Territory and selling the remaining cattle and the ranch at a loss. He decided to return East and reenter politics, his ultimate passion. Roosevelt's ranching experience in the West gave him a new perspective on life, and he voiced no regrets about buying the ranch because he received intangible benefits to his health and mental well-being while in the West. He returned to civilization a changed man, recovered from his grief and ready to begin political life anew.

Edith Carow Roosevelt. Edith Carow, daughter of a wealthy shipowner, had been a childhood companion of Theodore Roosevelt while he was growing up. The Roosevelt and Carow families knew each other socially, traveled to Europe together, and lived in the same neighborhood in New York City. Edith's father began drinking excessively, his business declined, and the family was forced to live with a wealthy relative of Edith's mother as their fortune declined. When Roosevelt returned from the Dakota Territory after his failed ranching venture, he met Edith in New York City and resumed a romantic relationship he had enjoyed before enrolling in Harvard College. [165] They fell in love all over again and were married in London on December 2, 1886.

Coming so soon after the death of his first wife, Roosevelt's sisters opposed the marriage to Edith, but Roosevelt went ahead with the ceremony anyway. Edith and Theodore enjoyed a long honeymoon in Europe and then returned to New York City to live in the mansion Roosevelt had built for his first wife, Alice. Edith was quiet and reserved but strongly supportive of Roosevelt as he gained political power. When he became President after McKinley died, she oversaw construction of the West Wing of the White House, which included a new President's office and more space on the second floor of the White House for the family's private living quarters.

Soon after he returned to New York, Republican politicians asked Roosevelt to run for mayor. He accepted the challenge but ran a distant third in the balloting. Fearful for his political future, he decided to write a book and give politics a rest for a few years before running for another political office. Roosevelt published *The Winning of the West* in 1889, describing the westward movement of Americans after the Civil War. The book was a huge success, earning him a reputation as a first-class writer and bringing in needed money. However, he could not remain out of politics for long.

In 1889, Roosevelt accepted an appointment as the U.S. Civil Service Commissioner and set about moving government workers into the merit system away from political patronage. Roosevelt attacked the Postmaster General as a terrible example of political corruption because he rewarded supporters with lucrative jobs in the post office. Roosevelt also revised civil service examinations to make them more representative of the requirements for each job. For example, he added horsemanship and marksmanship to the border patrol and custom service examinations.

Roosevelt was appointed to the Police Board of New York City in 1895 and set about reforming the police department. He began a program of regularly inspecting police firearms, instituted annual physical exams for all policemen, recruited new policemen based on good mental and physical abilities, established a system of Meritorious Service Medals, and fought corruption in the ranks. [166] Roosevelt regularly walked New York City beats at night to make certain the assigned policemen were awake and on duty. Roosevelt created so much resistance to his actions among New York City politicians that they finally eliminated the police board to get rid of him. Roosevelt liked the taste of power, however, and accepted an appointment by President McKinley to be Assistant Secretary of the Navy in 1897.

Spanish-American War. Since Secretary of the Navy John D. Long was ill, most decisions about the navy were left to Roosevelt, who was delighted with the power and authority the new appointment brought. Influenced by Mahan, Roosevelt began lobbying Congress to build more battleships for the U.S. Navy. He also suggested to President McKinley that the U.S. should consider ejecting Spain from Cuba and administering the island itself. He got his chance on February 15, 1898, when the cruiser *USS Maine* exploded in Havana Harbor, killing hundreds of crewmen and sinking the ship. Roosevelt blamed Spain for the explosion and demanded Congress declare war. [167] However, McKinley wanted to find a diplomatic solution to the crisis if possible, so he ignored calls for war. Roosevelt sent secret instructions to several navy ships to prepare for war and continued to call for war with Spain. It soon became clear to President McKinley that there was no diplomatic solution to the problem because inflammatory newspaper articles published by Joseph Pulitzer and William Randolph Hurst had aroused the public against Spain.

The final straw happened in April 1898, when the Spanish Ambassador wrote that President McKinley was weak and catering to the American rabble. Congress was incensed by the insult and immediately declared war on Spain. Roosevelt resigned his post as Assistant Secretary of the Navy and formed the First U.S. Volunteer Cavalry Regiment (the Rough Riders). The group included polo-playing Ivy League graduates, professional athletes, former cowboys, retired soldiers, reformed outlaws, and sheriffs from around the country. After they assembled and trained for several weeks in San Antonio, Tx., the Rough Riders sailed for Cuba, landing on the island June 23, 1898. After the regiment landed, Roosevelt was promoted to Colonel and took command. He became famous for leading a charge up San Juan Hill (actually, Kettle Hill next door) on July 1, 1898. [168]

Roosevelt led his men up the hill on horseback on his own orders, without clear authorization from higher command. His horse became entangled in barbed wire near the top of the hill, so Roosevelt had to hike the last few yards on foot. He won the battle with a loss of two hundred men killed and one thousand wounded. In 2001, he was belatedly awarded the Medal of Honor for his victory. He was nominated for the medal at the time, but the award was blocked by superior officers because they viewed Roosevelt as a headline-grabbing subordinate. For the rest of his life, Roosevelt preferred to be called Colonel Roosevelt because he was so proud of the Rough Riders and their victory in Cuba. Roosevelt was not interested in staying in the army when the war was over, but he and the Rough Riders returned to New York to march through the streets in triumph before they were disbanded. Roosevelt intended to use his newfound military glory to run for public office.

Governor Roosevelt. Shortly after Roosevelt returned from Cuba, New York Republicans asked him to run for governor of the state. He campaigned with many of his Rough Riders in attendance wearing their army uniforms. Roosevelt stressed his victory at San Juan along with national issues during the campaign. He toured the state by train and won by a small margin. As Governor of New York, Roosevelt learned how to manage economic and political issues that would help him later in the White House. He had to deal with business trusts, monopolies, labor unions, and conservation while Governor of New York. Roosevelt promised that every citizen of New York would receive a square deal from an honest government. He wanted his administration to be free of corruption, treat all citizens equitably, and avoid putting politics above state interests. He held daily press conferences to stay in touch with the voters, supported a tax on franchises, and appointed public servants without paying attention to political bosses who wanted to place their friends in lucrative government jobs.

As Governor of New York, Roosevelt tried to limit the excesses of large corporations, protect the poor, regulate railroad rates, mediate conflicts between capital and labor, and conserve natural resources. These doctrines served him well as Governor of New York and later as President of the United States. He was considering running for president in 1904 after President McKinley had served his second term. At that time, Roosevelt had three options: run for reelection as Governor of New York, serve as Secretary of War in the McKinley administration, or run as Vice-President with McKinley in the coming presidential election.

Vice President Hobart had died in 1899, leaving an open spot on the 1900 ticket that McKinley needed to fill. Roosevelt attended the 1900 Republican National Convention and reluctantly agreed to run as Vice President with McKinley. He won the nomination unanimously and campaigned vigorously for the ticket in 1900. [169] Roosevelt proved to be a worthy rhetorical opponent for William Jennings Bryan, the Democratic Presidential nominee that year. Roosevelt called Bryan a radical who would ruin the country with his extreme policies and emphasized his own role in the Spanish-American War and his service as Governor of New York. McKinley and Roosevelt easily won the Presidential race.

President Roosevelt. Roosevelt became Vice President knowing the job brought little power and would not suit his aggressive personality, but determined to soldier on anyway. His six months as Vice President in the McKinley administration were uneventful; he presided over the Senate and made speeches for Republican causes. On September 2, 1901, he made the famous statement that the U.S. should "speak softly and carry a big stick." On September 6, 1901, President McKinley was attending the Pan-American Exposition in Buffalo, New York, when he was shot by Leon Czolgosz, an American anarchist who was angry at the federal government and blamed McKinley for the country's troubles. Roosevelt immediately visited McKinley in the hospital, and was assured by physicians that the President was expected to recover, so Roosevelt resumed his vacation in upstate New York. However, McKinley's condition worsened, and he died on September 14, 1901.

Roosevelt was sworn in as the 26th President of the U.S. in Buffalo, New York, soon after McKinley died. He served his first term without a Vice President because there was no constitutional provision for filling the vacancy until the 25th Amendment was passed in 1967. Roosevelt was the youngest President in history (Kennedy was a year older when elected), and he assured Republicans he would follow McKinley's policies and keep his cabinet ministers in office. However, Roosevelt was too energetic and strong-willed to follow anyone's lead for long. He soon set out to make his own mark on the country as President of the U.S.

Trust Busting. Soon after taking office, Roosevelt began to use the relatively new Sherman Antitrust Act to regulate monopoly trusts. [170] He believed large corporations were a useful and necessary part of American business and only wanted to regulate those trusts that engaged in restraint of trade or used unfair business practices to gain an advantage over competitors. He often said success by fair competition was fine with him, but he objected to unfair monopoly practices and restraint of trade. During his first term as President, Roosevelt broke up Northern Securities Company, a large railroad monopoly, and Standard Oil, the largest oil refining company in America. After the 1902 midterm election, Roosevelt asked Congress to establish the Department of Commerce and Labor to oversee trusts and labor unions.

In 1903, Congress passed the Elkins Anti-Rebate Act, which forbids railroads from giving large corporations discounts below the published freight rates and authorized the Interstate Commerce Commission to enforce the new law. In 1906, Congress passed the Hepburn Act granting the ICC power to set maximum railroad rates so carriers could not raise rates unilaterally. He was probably the most active President in American history, at least until FDR was elected during the Great Depression. In May of 1902, American coal miners struck, threatening an energy shortage during the coming winter. Roosevelt threatened to bring in federal troops to settle the strike if the two sides didn't agree to binding arbitration of their dispute. They settled the strike by giving the miners a pay raise but not allowing them to form a union.

During his second year in office, Roosevelt uncovered corruption in the Bureau of Indian Affairs, the U.S. Land Office, and the U.S. Postal Service. He vigorously prosecuted corrupt Indian Agents, forced the General Land Office Commissioner to resign, and indicted forty-four employees of the Post Office on charges of bribery and fraud. Roosevelt moved quickly and decisively to prosecute corruption in his administration whenever he found it. He also convinced Congress to give the Interstate Commerce Commission power to set "just-and-reasonable" rates for railroads and pressured Congress to pass the Meat Inspection Act in 1906. Later the same year, Congress passed the Pure Food and Drug Act in response to Upton Sinclair's book, *The Jungle*, which exposed misleading labeling of meats and the use of harmful preservatives in processed meats that were damaging human health. Roosevelt also spent time preserving American lands in their natural state.

Land Conservation. Of all his achievements, Roosevelt said he was most proud of his work in conserving America's natural resources. He worked closely with James Garfield, Interior Secretary, and Gifford Pinchot, U.S. Forestry Service Chief, to enact conservation programs throughout the U.S.

Together, they established the U.S. Forest Service and created five new National Parks: Crater Lake, Oregon; Wind Cave, South Dakota; Sully's Hill, North Dakota; Mesa Verde, Colorado; and Platt, Oklahoma. Roosevelt also supported the Antiquities Act, which was passed by Congress on June 8, 1906, allowing Presidents to designate historic landmarks as national monuments without further action. [171] Roosevelt created Devils Tower in Wyoming, El Morro in New Mexico, Montezuma Castle in Arizona, and the Petrified Forest in Arizona as National Monuments.

Roosevelt signed Executive Orders protecting 150 million acres of forestry land, despite criticism from Congress that he was limiting economic development in the West. During his two terms as President, Roosevelt issued one thousand eighty-one Executive Orders, by far the most of any president until Franklin D. Roosevelt. By comparison, the first twenty-five presidents combined had issued one thousand two hundred sixty-two Executive Orders. One of Roosevelt's greatest achievements was initiating the building of the Panama Canal between the Atlantic and the Pacific Oceans.

The Panama Canal. Roosevelt believed the U.S. had a vital national interest in building a canal to allow warships and commercial transports to travel from one ocean to the other more quickly. [172] He was prepared to guarantee free passage for all nations during peacetime but insisted that the canal remain under American control for national security purposes. In 1903, Roosevelt was still considering two routes for the canal: the Isthmus of Panama, where the French government had already begun work on a canal years earlier, but failed because of yellow fever and financial problems, or Nicaragua, which would be a longer canal, but one that could be built without huge locks to raise and lower ships. Either route would shorten the travel time for U.S. Navy ships from one ocean to the other and offer cheaper transportation of goods from coast to coast. He convinced Congress to pass the Spooner Act approving the Panamanian alternative and waited for Colombian approval of the proposal.

After months without formal approval of the plan by Colombia, Roosevelt began working covertly to separate Panama from Colombia and negotiate a separate treaty with the new country. When the Colombian government rejected Roosevelt's offer of almost ten million dollars indemnity and annual payments of two hundred-fifty thousand dollars for the rights to build the canal in Panama, the region rebelled. Roosevelt sent a message to the rebels supporting their efforts and dispatched several American warships to "maintain peace." The rebellion was successful, and Panama declared independence from Colombia. The U.S. quickly recognized the new country of Panama, and Roosevelt signed a treaty giving America the right to build a canal across the Isthmus. Most of the forty million dollars paid for the right to build the canal went to stockholders of the original French Panama Canal Company, while substantial fees were paid to attorneys representing the French Canal company in its negotiations with the U.S.

Building the Panama Canal was an enormous challenge. It posed financial and engineering issues and required the Panama Canal Company to solve the medical problem of yellow fever. The French attempt to build the canal years earlier had failed because of financial and medical problems. Building the Panama Canal required constructing huge locks to raise and lower ships from sea level to the height of the canal. The Panama Canal opened for traffic in 1914 and brought enormous financial and strategic benefits to the world. President Carter gave ownership of the Panama Canal to the government of Panama in 1999 as a goodwill gesture.

Roosevelt made good use of the media during his time as President. He had a room set aside within the White House for journalists and invented the idea of holding frequent press briefings, giving the press access to his staff on a regular basis. He was a writer himself and enjoyed talking with reporters and other informed people about Washington affairs. However, he hated scandal-mongering journalists who did nothing but publish sensational exposes of government officials. He coined the term "muckraker" for writers who made wild charges against government officials with little or no evidence to support their claims. He called these journalists "liars" and said they were no better than thieves. The only time the press criticized Roosevelt was for his handling of the Panama Canal, saying he had misled the public. He was so angry at the attacks that Roosevelt brought a charge of libel against the *New York World*, which was ultimately dismissed by the courts. He was popular throughout the country and decided he wanted a second term to finish what he had begun.

Roosevelt was nominated for a second term by the Republican party in 1904 with little opposition. Even though he didn't campaign personally, Roosevelt controlled the campaign message by restricting access to journalists who didn't clear their statements with the White House before publishing a story. The Democrats nominated Alton Brooks Parker as their candidate for President, who promptly accused Roosevelt and the Republicans of extorting contributions from large corporations. Roosevelt denied the charge but did return a "gift" of one hundred thousand dollars to Standard Oil Corporation. Allegations of corruption against Roosevelt were not credible and had little effect on the election. He made frequent trips across the country by train to meet with local political leaders and ordinary voters, won fifty-six percent of the popular vote, and three hundred thirty-six Electoral College votes to Parker's one hundred forty.

During his second term as President, one that he felt he had earned in his own right, Roosevelt wanted Congress to regulate corporations, pass a federal incorporation bill, a federal income tax, and an inheritance tax. He also wanted to limit injunctions against labor unions that forbid them from striking because they tended to cripple the union's power to force wage increases. None of these bills passed even though the Republican Party controlled both houses of Congress because Congressional Republicans were more conservative than Roosevelt, favored big business over labor unions, and didn't want to raise taxes on the American people. Roosevelt wanted to increase America's influence on the world stage and acquire new territories in the Pacific.

Imperial America. During the 1890s, Roosevelt supported American Imperial ambitions in the Pacific, including the acquisition of Hawaii in 1898 and the Philippines in 1900. While he was President, Roosevelt increased the size of the U.S. Navy and searched for ways to avoid military confrontation with Japan because he believed Russia was a more serious threat to American ambitions. [173] He made it a priority of his administration to maintain friendly relations with the Japanese Empire so it would act as a counterbalance to the Russian Empire. In 1904-05, Russia and Japan went to war over conflicting claims in the Korean Peninsula and China. The Japanese Navy attacked the Russian fleet in Port Arthur before war was declared and destroyed most of the Russian Pacific Fleet. Roosevelt believed that the

Japanese were doing America's work for it and was delighted. He wanted America to play a leading role in world diplomacy. Early in his career, Roosevelt had felt Japan was the more dangerous nation in the Pacific, but he later decided Russia posed a greater danger to American interests in the region and tended to favor Japan after that.

After several battles on land and sea, Russia and Japan asked Roosevelt to mediate a peace treaty between the two powers. He believed American interests were best served by maintaining the balance of power between Russia and Japan, so Roosevelt wanted to make the treaty fair to both sides. He agreed to hold the conference in Portsmouth, New Hampshire, and successfully negotiated peace between the warring parties by establishing open lines of communication among Russia, Japan, and the major powers of Europe. Japan was given a protectorate over Korea and Russia's rights in Port Arthur but was forced to give up Manchuria to China. Japan wanted an indemnity from Russia, but Roosevelt felt that was unfair and said no. He negotiated the transfer of half the island of Sakhalin, off the coast of Siberia, to Japan as compensation. [174] Roosevelt was awarded the Nobel Peace Prize for mediating the Russo-Japanese Treaty.

The Japanese Menace. In the fall of 1906, the idea of Yellow Peril appeared in California, and anti-Japanese sentiment grew among Americans living on the West Coast. After Tokyo protested how California was treating Japanese laborers, Roosevelt felt he needed to maintain good relations with Japan, so he negotiated an agreement that limited immigration of Japanese into America in return for stopping explicit discrimination against Japanese in California. Anti-American riots broke out in Tokyo over the Portsmouth Treaty. Another source of tension was that Japanese fishermen were illegally killing seals on the coast of Alaska and being driven off by American patrol boats. In one such skirmish, several Japanese fishermen were killed by American sailors. Diplomats in Europe were warning America that the Japanese intended to invade Hawaii and the Philippines, and Roosevelt started worrying about war with Japan.

He found the rumors of imminent war between Japan and the United States were greatly exaggerated, however. The cause of these rumors was fear in Europe that a major war was about to break out between England, France, and Russia on one side and Germany and Austria on the other. The main source of friction between Japan and America was that many Japanese wanted to migrate to America where they could enjoy a higher standard of living compared with migrating to Korea or China, or staying in Japan. In 1906, about seventy-five thousand Japanese lived in California, and school boards in major cities were becoming concerned with overcrowding in their schools. To resolve the issue, the school boards decreed Japanese students must attend special Oriental schools alongside Korean and Chinese students in America. The Japanese felt this was an insult because they considered Koreans and Chinese inferior races. Roosevelt pointed out correctly that Japanese residents in California were entitled to all the rights of other people, save naturalization, but Californians were not impressed by his logic. Roosevelt negotiated a compromise to placate both sides by barring Japanese laborers from entering California and convincing California school boards to allow Japanese students to attend classes with white children. Roosevelt also sent the American Navy around the world in a show of force that impressed the Japanese.

Roosevelt felt America had become a world power after the Spanish-American War, and he wanted to exert more influence in world affairs. He mediated a conference in Algeciras, Spain, that avoided war between Germany and France over Morocco and worked hard to build an alliance with England because that country had supported America during the Spanish-American War. The British agreed to withdraw its fleet from the Caribbean to focus on neutralizing the German naval threat in the North Atlantic, and America took over naval affairs in the Western Hemisphere. Roosevelt also resolved a dispute over the boundary between Alaska and Canada.

In 1908, as he was nearing the end of his second term, President Roosevelt saw his power diminish because he had pledged not to run for a third term during his last campaign. Roosevelt had little power over Congress and the bureaucracy because he would be out of office after March 5, 1909. He was not yet fifty years old and believed he was too young to retire but didn't know what to do next. Not only did Roosevelt face opposition from Congress, but the Supreme Court was invalidating some of his pet legislation, such as the Employers' Liability Act of 1906 (worker's compensation) and the monetary fine against Standard Oil Company of Indiana. Early in 1908, Roosevelt sent a message to Congress requesting that they revise and reenact the Employers' Liability Act of 1906 limited to interstate commerce alone. He also called for workmen's compensation for all government employees. Congress ignored him.

Roosevelt in Retirement. Roosevelt honored his pledge not to run for a third term and energetically supported William Howard Taft as the Republican nominee for President in 1908. [175] Taft won the nomination and easily defeated Democrat William Jennings Bryan, who was running for President a third time. After the election, Roosevelt embarked on a safari to Africa, visiting the Belgian Congo, traveling up the Nile to Khartoum in Sudan, and hunting big game. He collected over eleven thousand specimens for the Smithsonian Institution and the American Museum of Natural History, ranging from insects to elephants. Roosevelt wrote an account of his safari in *African Game Trails*, describing the thrills of the hunt and flora and fauna of Africa in detail. Finished with Africa, Roosevelt traveled to Europe, meeting an Emperor, a Kaiser, and a King during his visits to Russia, Germany, and England. He was invited to see the Pope but declined because he would not agree to avoid mentioning the Methodist Church in the Pope's presence.

When Roosevelt returned to America, he was concerned by President Taft's policies. Rather than following in the footsteps of Roosevelt, Taft had charted his own course, and this alienated Roosevelt. He particularly disliked Taft's conservative policies and Congress' raising of tariffs on manufactured goods. Roosevelt wanted to wrest control of the Republican Party from Taft but hoped to avoid a split in the party that would give the Democrats the presidency in 1912. He was uncertain how to go about achieving that end because Taft was not inclined to step aside voluntarily. In 1910, Roosevelt broke openly with Taft by supporting labor unions' right to strike, the regulation of corporations, and banning corporate campaign contributions to politicians.

The Democrats gained control of the House of Representatives in 1910 for the first time in twenty years and blocked many Republican initiatives. Roosevelt supporters interpreted loss of the House as a mandate for them to take over the Republican Party. Taft wanted to negotiate treaties with other nations that called for arbitration of international disputes rather than going to war, but Roosevelt ridiculed the idea, saying international disputes were too important to leave to the courts. Roosevelt also wanted more regulation of corporations and supported labor unions, while Taft opposed the formation of unions. Roosevelt had drifted to the left in his views, abandoning policies and ideas he supported earlier in his political career.

Many Republicans wanted Roosevelt to run for a third term, and he declared in early 1912 that he would run if drafted, believing that he could save the party from defeat. The direct primary system was being used for the first time in several states, and Roosevelt won Illinois, Minnesota, Nebraska, South Dakota, California, Maryland, Pennsylvania, and Ohio. However, the presidential nomination would be decided by Republican Party leaders rather than the results of these early primaries, and Republican Party leaders were mainly Taft people. A majority of the rank-and-file in the Republican Party preferred Roosevelt, but the Republican Credentials Committee gave almost all contested delegates to Taft, and he won the nomination on the first ballot. Roosevelt had been defeated by Republican Party bosses, he was mad about losing and decided to form a third party.

Once it was clear Taft had won the Republican Party nomination for President in 1912, Roosevelt set about forming the Bull Moose Party to oppose him. [176] By splitting from the Republican Party and forming a Progressive Party to run against Taft, Roosevelt effectively gave the election of 1912 to Woodrow Wilson and the Democrats. Roosevelt was so angry at Taft that he most likely didn't care. While campaigning in Milwaukee, Wisconsin, on October 14, 1912, Roosevelt was shot by a psychotic saloonkeeper named John Schrank, who reported that the ghost of McKinley had told him to kill Roosevelt. [177]

Roosevelt's life was saved by his steel glasses case and a folded copy of his speech, which together stopped the bullet from killing him. The crowd would have lynched Schrank if Roosevelt had not ordered the police to take the shooter into custody and make certain he was not harmed. Roosevelt knew the bullet had not entered his lung because he was not coughing blood, so he continued his speech and went to the hospital after he finished. The surgeons discovered the bullet was lodged in his chest and decided to leave it alone—believing removing it would be too dangerous.

The Democrats nominated Woodrow Wilson, then Governor of New Jersey, as their candidate for President. Wilson favored many of the same policies as Roosevelt, and the campaign developed into a two-way contest between these remarkable men. Roosevelt won twenty-seven percent of the popular vote, Taft collected twenty-three percent, and Wilson got forty-two percent of the vote and four hundred thirty-five Electoral College votes. Wilson's landslide victory was the first for a Democrat in over twenty years. Roosevelt performed well, winning more votes than any other third-party candidate in history, and he denied Taft a second term as president. However, he had not won a third term and was out of a job. [178]

After his defeat, Roosevelt decided to go hunting in South America. During a trip down the River of Doubt in Brazil, Roosevelt injured his leg and it became infected. He also contracted what modern physicians believe was malaria. Roosevelt's health declined, he developed a high fever and became delirious. Feeling he was a threat to the safety of the expedition, Roosevelt asked to be left behind. The group talked him out of that plan, and they proceeded down the river toward civilization. Eventually, the explorers were found by plantation workers and guided to safety. Roosevelt returned to America but never regained the vigor he had enjoyed earlier. He experienced recurring bouts of malaria and inflammation of his leg.

Roosevelt was angered by Wilson's expression of regret at how the U.S. had acquired the Panama Canal. He supported Charles Evans Hughes, the Republican candidate for President in 1916, but Wilson won a second term as President by a narrow margin, claiming he kept the country out of war. Roosevelt advocated declaring war on Germany when it began unrestricted submarine warfare and denounced Irish-Americans and German-Americans as unpatriotic, saying by supporting neutrality, they put the interests of their former homelands ahead of America. Roosevelt wanted to raise a mounted infantry division and lead it into war against the German Army. He met with President Wilson to discuss the idea of his leading an infantry division to war, but his plan was rejected by Wilson, because he didn't trust Roosevelt and didn't want to put General Pershing in a difficult political position.

Roosevelt supported Wilson's idea of a League of Nations and believed it would not succeed unless the U.S. gave it full support. Roosevelt's criticisms of Wilson helped the Republicans gain control of Congress during the midterm elections of 1918. Near the end of his life, Roosevelt announced he supported federally funded pensions for older persons, health insurance, unemployment insurance, public housing for the poor, limits to working hours, aid to farmers, and regulation of big corporations. His health continued to deteriorate; he was deaf in one ear and blind in one eye. Roosevelt died in his sleep the morning of January 6, 1919, at the age of sixty years of an embolism in his coronary artery at his family home in Oyster Bay, New York. [179]

Oliver Wendell Holmes, Jr.

Justice. Oliver Wendell Holmes

Oliver Wendell Holmes, Jr. was born in Boston on March 8, 1841, the eldest of three children to Dr. and Mrs. Oliver Wendell Holmes. [180] His mother inherited money from her family, and the house where he was born was a gift from her father, Judge Charles Jackson. Nineteenth-century Boston was prosperous but primitive, with wells in the back yard to supply water, whale oil lamps to light rooms at night, and outhouses. Holmes' mother bought a New England farm near Pittsfield, Massachusetts, with hills, meadows, streams, and the Housatonic River flowing through it. Holmes grew to love the New England countryside from his early years visiting the family farm.

Holmes' Education. His early education was handled by private tutors and a boys' school associated with Park Street Church, located a block from his family home. Holmes entered Harvard College in 1856, [181] studying Latin, Greek and rhetoric. The best and brightest young men in Boston went to Harvard because they gained social acceptance and made life-long friends at the college. Students were graded for intellectual performance and had points deducted for disciplinary violations. Holmes published an essay in *Harvard Magazine* encouraging his classmates to think for themselves about religion rather than blindly following the teachings of others. His family position and social status guaranteed Holmes' induction into Harvard's exclusive social clubs. Holmes worked hard, was an excellent student, and made friends easily. The issue of slavery was on everyone's mind because of the presidential election of 1860, which Abraham Lincoln won.

Slavery. Boston society was generally opposed to slavery, but New England's businessmen depended on cotton imported from the South for their mills, so they avoided criticizing the institution. New

England citizens opposed violence and believed slavery would gradually fade away if given time and they were concerned that open opposition might cause a dissolution of the Union and trigger a civil war. Holmes opposed slavery while he was at Harvard, but the attack on Fort Sumpter by the Confederate Army on April 14, 1860, inflamed the North and ended any uncertainty about how to deal with the issue of slavery—there was going to be a war and everyone was excited about it. Holmes withdrew from Harvard and enlisted as a private in the Massachusetts Volunteer Militia. He mistakenly believed the war would be over in a few months.

Of the five hundred seventy-eight Harvard men who served in the Union Army during the Civil War, thirty-six percent were killed or seriously wounded, including Holmes three times. In the spring of 1861, however, war seemed like a grand game for these bright young men; they trained hard, were in superb physical condition, and felt a strong sense of purpose. Learning how to keep their camp clean and their muskets in working order gave the young aristocrats a sense of competence they had never experienced before. Over half the officers in the Massachusetts Volunteers were Harvard men, while the enlisted men and the remaining officers were mainly Irish or German immigrants who had prior experience in the British or Prussian Army. These more experienced soldiers had a low opinion of the Harvard men's military skills because they had seen war first hand. Only the senior officers of the regiment had any military training or experience and it showed during Holmes' first battle, which was a disaster from start to finish.

Ball's Bluff. [182] For Holmes and his comrades, this minor battle on the banks of the Potomac River was their first taste of combat. Most performed with extraordinary bravery and Holmes felt the battle was a personal triumph because he had been brave, even though his regiment was badly defeated. The Battle at Ball's Bluff was a model of how not to conduct a military operation. The objectives were vague, the placement of men on a bluff with no way to retreat was a serious tactical error, their orders were ambiguous, the chain of command confused, logistics poorly planned, and there was no reconnaissance prior to the battle. The inexperienced soldiers were put in a difficult situation and everything went wrong from the start.

There were too few boats to move men across the river and only a narrow trail to reach the bluff. When the battle began, Union troops were committed piecemeal and killed or captured quickly by well-organized Southern troops. Holmes was hit by a nearly spent bullet in the ribs, and a few minutes later, he was shot through the chest. Bleeding badly, Holmes was carried down the bluff to a boat and taken to a field hospital. Like many Union soldiers, Holmes carried a small bottle of laudanum with him to hasten his end if the pain became too horrible. He later recalled that being moved in an ambulance was torture. Holmes spent weeks recuperating in Philadelphia at the home of a Quaker family friend and then his father moved Holmes to Boston to finish his recovery. Over two hundred Union men were killed or wounded in the battle at Ball's Bluff, and another seven hundred captured. Holmes rejoined his regiment on March 35, 1862, near Washington, D.C.

The campaign around Washington and Richmond was a sobering introduction to war for the Union Army. General McClellan procrastinated in the face of Confederate threats and tried to avoid battle. Holmes admitted years later that he was more afraid in later battles than he had been at Ball's

Bluff because of his wound. Shortly after Holmes rejoined his unit, the regiment faced a severe test at Antietam, the bloodiest single day in the history of the U.S. Army. The casualties that day were more than twice those suffered by the Allies while landing in Nazi-occupied France on June 6, 1944. During the Civil War, Union troops were often marched into battle in close formation, giving the enemy fine targets. Holmes' regiment was subjected to flanking fire from Confederate troops hidden along the trail while they were advancing at Antietam, and many were killed before they reached the main fighting. Holmes was hit in the neck but managed to walk back to a small field hospital for treatment. He was neglected by the surgeons because they felt Holmes had no chance to survive his wound. However, he surprised them and lived. Antietam was a bloody draw, but because the Union Army was not defeated, England and France avoided recognizing the Confederacy, which was one of the few positive developments for the Union early in the war.

After Holmes recovered from his neck wound, he returned to his regiment across the Rappahannock River near Fredericksburg, Virginia. He came down with dysentery the day before Union troops attacked the city and were slaughtered by Confederate soldiers in trenches on the high ground across the river. After the battle, when General Burnside reviewed his troops, they called him "butcher" as he rode past. Holmes came to hate war after the battle at Fredericksburg because of the needless slaughter he had witnessed. When he recovered, Holmes returned to war and was wounded by shrapnel in his heel. This wound was not life-threatening, but it took eight months to heal. Everyone called Holmes "Achilles" because of the wound.

The heel injury kept Holmes out of the Battle of Gettysburg, but when he returned to the regiment, Holmes was promoted to Lieutenant Colonel and offered command of a colored regiment. He declined, saying he wanted to stay with the Massachusetts Militia. In the Spring of 1864, Holmes was assigned to a general's staff and no longer faced enemy fire on the battlefield. However, it was still dangerous work because staff officers scouted roads ahead of the troops and delivered messages to commanding officers in the front line, often under enemy fire. Holmes met President Lincoln while serving as a staff officer and it's reported he told Lincoln to get down or you will get your head blown off. Good advice from a combat veteran, but we don't know how the Commander-in-Chief reacted to an order from a junior officer.

Lincoln appointed Ulysses S. Grant commander of the Union armies and the new general instilled a fighting spirit in the Union Army--they began winning battles. Grant followed the Confederate Army into the Wilderness where he fought a series of bloody battles over a nine-week period that ended in a draw with heavy Union casualties. However, the Union Army had not retreated in the face of fierce pressures from the Confederate Army and this encouraged Lincoln and the Northern voters. Holmes spent the remainder of the war carrying messages and getting little sleep. During one of his rides, Holmes ran into twenty Confederate soldiers who told him to stop and surrender. Instead, he galloped right through the line of soldiers, riding on the side of his horse Indian style to avoid getting shot. This episode convinced Holmes he should leave the army when his enlistment expired on July 23, 1864.

Holmes said his experience during the war taught him to face the ordinary hardships of life with courage and not worry about problems. He never suffered post-traumatic stress after the war in spite of being wounded three times. Holmes learned that life is a struggle and challenges give it meaning. He concluded from his years at war that everything has a price, and it's best to know the cost before undertaking the task. After the war, Holmes decided to attend law school and become an attorney.

Harvard Law School. Even before the war, Holmes had expressed an interest in law, so he entered Harvard Law School when the war ended. [183] At that time, Harvard Law offered a two-year program of study in the law. Holmes applied himself diligently because he wanted to succeed as an attorney. He learned during the war that technical expertise was more important than gentlemanly behavior and he applied that idea to studying law. Harvard changed under the leadership of President Eliot, who discarded the classics and introduced science and modern languages to Harvard students. He wanted Harvard graduates to be skilled professionals who were well trained in science and mathematics rather than gentlemen schooled in the classics.

After graduating from law school, Holmes went on a grand tour of Europe. He visited the House of Commons, saw the Magna Carta, and toured London art museums. Holmes climbed mountains, stayed with the Duke of Argyll, and went fishing and hunting in Scotland. When he returned, Holmes was admitted to the bar in March 1867, but he had already been contributing regular book reviews to the *American Law Review*. [184] While preparing to take the bar exam, Holmes began working for the law firm of Chandler, Shattuck and Thayer specializing in commercial litigation. Holmes married Fanny B. Dixwell in June of 1872. [185] Fanny contracted a serious case of rheumatic fever right after they were married, and it was two years before they were able to take a honeymoon to Europe.

While practicing law in Boston, Holmes met Henry and William James at a men's club in the Parker House. He was busy with his law practice, edited the *American Law Review*, lectured on constitutional law at Harvard, and prepared a revised edition of *Commentaries on American Law*. [186] Holmes rewrote the *Commentaries*, adding legal analysis and referring readers to legal articles that supplemented the cases he was describing. Holmes compiled relevant cases on the doctrine of warranty, property, and tort law. When the book was published by Little, Brown and Company, Holmes placed his own name on the title page, which irked Thayer and Kent, prior authors of the work. Years later, they were still irritated with Holmes because they felt he should have included their names as prior authors. Holmes felt he had totally revised the work and felt it was his book.

Holmes became a wealthy man when his father and sister died. He inherited a trust from his father and a house and commercial property from his sister. Later, other properties came to him from a cousin and uncle, and Fanny's father left them a substantial estate as well. Holmes was prudent with money and avoided spending his capital. He decided to embark on an ambitious analysis of the common law in a series of articles published in the *American Law Review*.

The Lowell Lectures. An invitation to deliver twelve public lectures to the Lowell Institute motivated Holmes to finish his work on the common law. Holmes delivered the first Lowell Lecture on November 23, 1880, [187] and had them published in book form when he finished. The reviews were generally favorable, although a few critics complained the writing was obscure. Holmes defended his book by pointing out that his work was original and therefore bound to be obscure in places because he had not completed his analysis of the legal issues involved.

In his lectures, Holmes argued that the common law was a summary of procedures and decisions developed by judges to settle disputes rather than a systematic theory of law that followed deductive logic. He believed judges create the common law by deciding individual cases, so he set out to study the history of English common law and tried to understand the purpose of legal decisions. Holmes covered all major areas of the common law, including liability, crime, contracts, property, wills, and bailments. He organized the common law around three principles: first, Holmes argued that the common law changes, but conceals that fact by explaining old rules in new ways; second, judges develop policies to resolve real problems in a fair and consistent way; and finally, he believed the common law should not be concerned with moral responsibility or evil intent but instead ought to deal with objective standards of guilt that can be applied fairly by all judges.

Holmes began his lectures with the statement that the common law has developed to resolve the "felt necessities of the time." He believed trying to create logical coherence and consistency in the common law was doomed to fail. As an example, Holmes stated that under the common law, a ship can be seized, detained, and sold if it was at fault in causing a collision because the foreign owner is beyond the jurisdiction of a court and cannot be forced to appear. He argued that seizure of the ship ensures the injured party is compensated if the other party was at fault, giving the injured person a remedy. Holmes wrote that the common law seeks a balance between competing social interests and tries to develop rules to resolve disputes and avoid future conflicts.

He argued that tort law balances the need for compensating injured persons, the goal of controlling reckless behavior, and the wish to carry on normal business activities. In the case of inherently dangerous activities, such as pulling the trigger of a pistol without first checking to see if it's loaded, Holmes felt the person pulling the trigger should be held strictly liable. His lasting contribution to tort law was the concept of a "reasonable man." Modern jury instructions tell jurors to consider what a reasonable man would have done in the same or similar circumstances in making their decision about guilt or innocence. Holmes stated that the reasonable man is an embodiment of a community standard of appropriate behavior.

When Holmes published *The Path of the Law* [188] in the *Harvard Law Review*, he introduced the doctrine of legal realism, which opposed the idea that law derives from formal legal theories. Legal realism proposed that the common law develops through legal decisions made by judges who balance social interests and public policy in deciding cases. Judges soon began using the balancing tests suggested by Holmes to decide cases rather than trying to make logical deductions from legal theories. This represented a departure from the earlier doctrine of legal formalism.

Judge Holmes. In the fall of 1881, President Eliot invited Holmes to join Harvard Law School as Weld Professor of Jurisprudence at a salary of $4,500 annually. A few months later, Holmes was appointed to the Supreme Judicial Court of Massachusetts by the governor. [189] Holmes had reserved the right to resign if he was offered a judgeship, and he loved his new job. Besides setting *en banc* with the full court on important hearings, each judge had a full docket of divorces, torts, and criminal cases to try. The job required each judge to travel around the state, so Holmes became familiar with the lives of people he would ordinarily not encounter while presiding over disputes involving shady stock transactions, bloody accidents, contract disputes, messy divorces, and terrible crimes. Holmes was a trial judge for two decades before being appointed to the U.S. Supreme Court.

Justice Holmes. In February 1902, Justice Horace Gray suffered a stroke and resigned from the U.S. Supreme Court. Because Gray was from Massachusetts, another man from that state was expected to fill the position. Holme's old friend, Senator Henry Cabot Lodge, was a close advisor of President Teddy Roosevelt and lobbied him to appoint Holmes. Roosevelt arranged for Holmes to meet him at his Long Island summer home, Sagamore Hill. Holmes impressed Roosevelt and his appointment to the Supreme Court was announced on December 4, 1902, and confirmed unanimously by the Senate on December 8, 1902. [190] Holmes was sixty-two when he joined the U.S. Supreme Court.

He was delighted to be a Justice of the U.S. Supreme Court but sad to leave his home and friends in Boston. When Holmes arrived in Washington, he was met by a Black gentleman who said he had been Justice Gray's messenger, and would perform the same services for Holmes. He told Holmes that messengers performed personal tasks such as valet, cook, barber, or any other service the Justice required, and Holmes agreed to keep him on as messenger. Holmes accompanied Fanny on sightseeing trips around Washington, including a visit to Ball's Bluff on the Potomac River, where he first faced enemy fire in the Civil War. Holmes said the place looked enchanting years later without people shooting at him, and he enjoyed the visit. Holmes and Fanny bought a house at 1720 Eye Street in Washington and Fanny took charge of remodeling the place. She hired an architect and contractor to renovate the house and supervised decorating the finished rooms. She included a study and library on the second floor where Holmes could work.

The Supreme Court met in the old Senate chambers until 1935 when a new building was constructed specifically for the nine Justices. The Senate chambers contained no offices for the Justices, so they had to work from home. The Court convened at noon every day and worked until four-thirty. The Justices met every Saturday in the Court's library for deliberations. Holmes continued his practice of writing short, clear judicial opinions, believing it was only necessary to deal with the basic issues of the case. His opinions were well received by other Justices, who said they were "clear as a bell." Holmes' colleagues trusted him so much he sometimes wrote both the majority opinion and the dissent.

Otis v. Parker. His first opinion was *Otis v. Parker* [191] which upheld a provision of the California Constitution that banned buying stock shares on margin. Holmes ruled that the statute was consistent with the Fourteenth Amendment of the United States Constitution. He wrote twenty-nine opinions during his first term, despite starting three months late. Holmes felt humbled by his decisions, stating that he gave the same consideration to a case involving $25 as one that concerned a person's life or the welfare of a state. After Holmes joined the Court, it began to consider the meaning of due process in detail.

During the 19th century, the Supreme Court had avoided declaring a Congressional statute unconstitutional unless the Justices reached the decision beyond reasonable doubt. Beginning in the late 1880s, the Justices began to protect private property against state regulation by invalidating Congressional statutes which violated the Due Process Clause of the Fourteenth Amendment. The Court held that the Due Process Clause of the Constitution forbids government interference with private property or the functioning of the economy unless the regulation is essential to protect public health. Many of these decisions indirectly undermined protections offered to newly freed slaves after the Civil War.

Holmes believed in judicial restraint, feeling that judges had a duty to examine the practical effects of their rulings and that all judicial decisions ultimately come down to weighing competing interests and deciding between them. During his first term in office, President Teddy Roosevelt vowed to break up the railroad, oil, and shipping trusts in a crusade to reform business practices in America. In 1904, the Supreme Court heard *Northern Securities v. United States* [192] concerning a trust organized by J.P. Morgan that owned two Northern railroads. The government accused National Securities of violating the Sherman Antitrust Act by creating a monopoly. In a 5-4 decision, the Supreme Court ruled that the trust created a monopoly on railroad traffic across the Northern part of the country and must sell the railroads. Holmes dissented, writing that the Sherman Act is "an imbecile statute." Teddy Roosevelt was not amused.

Swift & Co. v. United States. [193] Another antitrust case involved six meatpacking companies that agreed to control the price of beef and pressure railroads to offer low transportation rates to them. In a unanimous decision written by Holmes, the Court held that under the Commerce Clause, Congress has the power to regulate trusts. Holmes also expanded the meaning of "interstate commerce" to include any activity that is part of the "stream of commerce" and interstate in character. After the Court's decision, Congress passed the Pure Food and Drug Act and the Meat Inspection Act in 1906. Roosevelt was delighted with Holmes after this decision.

Holmes was getting so much personal mail he hired a secretary to handle his correspondence. It was not until 1919 that Congress appropriated funds to hire a law clerk for each Justice. Holmes used his clerk to find citations for his legal arguments and took him on walks around Washington for company. Holmes wanted to know about the latest fashions and used his clerks as sources of ideas. His clerks had to be single because he wanted them to have no distractions. Holmes was respected at Harvard Law School because his opinions often appeared in their casebooks and his clerks liked his independent thinking. Law clerks often joined prestigious law firms or became professors at major law schools after working with Holmes.

On July 4, 1910, Chief Justice Fuller died, setting off a search for his replacement. President Taft had promised he would appoint Charles Evans Hughes Chief Justice if he didn't run against Taft, but when the opportunity occurred, Taft appointed Justice Edward Douglas White instead. Holmes didn't want to be Chief Justice, but he was hurt by not being considered. His mood changed after Oxford University offered him an honorary degree, and he found a kindred spirit in Felix Frankfurter, a twenty-eight years old Harvard Law School graduate who shared his judicial philosophy.

The appointment of White as Chief Justice was just one of six Taft appointments to the Supreme Court. These new Justices didn't change the basic outlook of the Court; it remained conservative. However, the appointments added new ideas to the Supreme Court. Holmes complained privately that his new colleagues used repetitious arguments, and he resented having to submit his opinions to the criticisms of others, even though he accepted most of their suggestions so he could maintain a majority and write the opinion. Holmes worked hard to convince a majority of the Justices to accept his view of a case by making strategic compromises. He sometimes changed or removed important legal arguments so he could maintain the majority for his opinion, but he was never happy to make changes in his legal arguments. Holmes enjoyed writing dissents because he could express his ideas without compromises. His dissents became famous during his later years on the Court.

Holmes' dissents were crafted to persuade the next generation of judges that his view of the law was correct and his ideas often became the majority opinion decades later. Beginning in 1914, Holmes wrote a series of important dissents that had a lasting influence on Constitutional law.

Abrams v. Unites States. [194] In 1918, the U.S. military conducted a military operation in Russia even though that country was no longer participating in the war. Russian immigrants to America called for a general strike at U.S. munitions plants to protest the American action on Russian soil. They were charged with espionage because the strike harmed the war effort. Justice John H. Clarke wrote that there are limits to free speech during a war, because First Amendment protections are lower when the country is threatened. He ruled that inspiring unrest and undermining the American war effort was counter to the national interest and could not be permitted during wartime. Holmes and Brandeis dissented, with Holmes arguing that rights protected in the First Amendment are at the foundation of freedom and require the right to dissent even when the country is at war. He argued that free speech should not be curtailed unless there is a present danger of immediate evil or the defendant intends to create such a danger. Holmes stated that the actions in *Abrams* did not create a present danger of immediate evil, so the defendants should have been acquitted.

Holmes pointed out that the First Amendment did more than merely formalize English common law concerning prior restraint, arguing that free expression of ideas is essential to a healthy democracy. He believed free speech should be protected at all times, so unpopular ideas can be heard, debated, and accepted or rejected on their merits. Holmes believed that only when speech poses a clear and present danger of creating immediate evil could it be suppressed by a government. Otherwise, he argued, all speech is protected by the First Amendment, even in time of war. Holmes' dissent was welcomed in some circles, but others warned that unfettered free speech was dangerous to the safety and welfare of the country.

After Warren Harding was elected, Taft asked the president to name him Chief Justice of the Supreme Court and Harding obliged him. The Senate confirmed Taft, who joined the Court for the 1921 term. Holmes was skeptical of Taft's qualifications, but came to appreciate the former president's administrative efficiency and good humor during conferences. Taft controlled the Court's agenda and eliminated repetitive arguments, endearing him to Holmes. Taft also cleared the backlog of cases and cut the time needed to get a hearing before the Supreme Court to around six months. He canceled the automatic right of appeal to the Supreme Court and gave Justices the authority to decide which cases they should accept.

Congress passed the "Judges Bill" in 1925 that required the filing of an application for certiorari to appeal a case to the Supreme Court. Automatic appeals were eliminated so the Court could hear only "important" cases. Certiorari reduced the number of cases heard but required Justices review hundreds of applications. Taft also worked to reduce dissents, although Holmes still insisted on writing them when he felt strongly about a legal issue.

In June of 1922, Holmes learned he had to have his prostate removed. The standard procedure at that time was to insert a drain tube in the urethra to relieve the blockage, and weeks later, operate to remove the prostate. Holmes was depressed and anxious about the operation, but it went well and he was released to recuperate at his farm after a month in the hospital. While he was recuperating, Holmes read Shakespeare and had an elevator installed in his Washington home so he could get upstairs to his office and library. He returned to Washington, D.C., and moved into a hotel while renovations to his house were completed. A few months later, Holmes had recovered and was walking and working on legal opinions as if nothing had happened.

During Taft's nine years as Chief Justice, the Court's majority invalidated nearly one hundred state laws on the grounds they interfered with private business arrangements, freedom of contract, or a person's right to private property in violation of the Fourteenth Amendment. In many of these cases, Holmes and Brandeis dissented, arguing that if the legislature had a reasonable basis for enacting a law to regulate business, the courts should not interfere. A majority of the nine Justices believed the only justification for regulating a business was health, safety, or public morals, so they invalidated numerous state statutes regulating businesses. The Court also strengthened defendants' rights to due process and a fair trial.

Moore v. Dempsey. In the winter of 1922-23, an important habeas corpus issue came before the Court in *Moore v. Dempsey*. [195] On an appeal from an order of a District Court dismissing a petition for habeas corpus, the Supreme Court held that when a jury finds an accused person guilty of murder and a state judge hurries the trial and conviction because of mob pressure without upholding an accused defendant's right to due process, the state court verdict is void. In *Moore*, a group of Black farmers met in a church to oppose extortions by white landlords. Cries that the Black farmers were planning an insurrection incited a mob to surround the church and a gunfight broke out. Federal troops were called in to suppress the riot, and all the Black farmers were arrested. Twelve farmers were convicted of murder and sentenced to death after a one-hour trial. Their court-appointed lawyer called no witnesses and made no challenges to the jury, which decided their fate in less than ten minutes.

Holmes ruled that the verdict was void because no one on the jury could have voted for acquittal and continued to live in the county. He held that if judicial proceedings were influenced by mob pressure, and the state judge failed to correct the injustice, the Supreme Court would uphold the defendant's constitutional rights and order a new trial. *Moore* helped secure the right of criminal defendants to due process and a fair trial. This was the first time the U.S. Supreme Court had intervened in a state court criminal conviction on due process grounds, but it wouldn't be the last. The state court reduced the Black defendants' penalties to twelve years in prison in exchange for dropping the federal habeas corpus proceedings.

Chief Justice Taft expected Holmes to resign following his prostate surgery, but after a few months, he recovered and felt competent to continue. There were rumors Holmes would resign on his eighty-fourth birthday, but he continued to work for several years. He appeared on the cover of *Time Magazine* on his eighty-fifth birthday, but refused to give interviews, no matter how famous he became. Holmes said he was happier than he had ever been and was enjoying his life. He became interested in a book by John Dewey titled *Experience and Nature,* that was influenced by the ideas of William James and Charles Pierce concerning pragmatism. Holmes observed but didn't participate in the infamous Sacco-Vanzetti case.

The notorious criminal case was watched closely by the legal community in 1927, although it was not before the U.S. Supreme Court. Nicola Sacco and Bartolomeo Vanzetti were accused of robbing a factory payroll in Braintree, Massachusetts, killing the paymaster and guard. The state trial was plagued by prosecutorial misconduct and biased comments by the presiding judge and many liberal jurists believed Sacco and Vanzetti had not received a fair trial. Holmes reviewed the case transcript and concluded that judicial prejudice was not sufficient to invalidate the jury's conviction of the pair for murder. However, many legal scholars disagreed and the case became a cause celebre for criminal justice reform. The next important case Holmes authored upheld the right of Blacks to participate in primary elections for Democratic candidates.

Nixon v. Herndon. In 1927, Holmes wrote the majority decision in *Nixon v. Herndon,* [196] ruling that a Texas statute, barring Blacks from participating in Democratic primary elections violated the Fourteenth Amendment. He wrote that the Fourteenth Amendment was intended specifically to protect the rights of Blacks from discrimination by state governments and rejected the state's argument that the statute was political and therefore outside the jurisdiction of the Court. Holmes ruled that a state cannot deny a citizen the right to vote because of race. The decision was unanimous.

In October 1928, Holmes became the longest-serving Supreme Court Justice in history, and he began to delegate more work to his clerks, asking them to prepare one-page summaries of applications for certiorari that were assigned to him. Holmes continued to deliver his opinions on the first Tuesday after receiving a case, even though he was getting older and had less energy. His mind remained sharp and he still loved the work of the Court. On April 21, 1929, his wife Fanny fell and broke her hip. Holmes moved her to a bed and called a doctor, who came the next day and put her in a plaster cast. Fanny never recovered from the fall and died on April 30, 1929. Taft kindly arranged her funeral because Holmes was so distressed by his loss. Fanny was buried in Arlington Cemetery in a plot next to one reserved for Holmes. Despite his despair, he still participated in Court deliberations and wrote several dissents.

United States v. Schwimmer. Holmes wrote a strong dissent in an appeal of the denial of citizenship to Rosika Schwimmer, a Jewish Hungarian pacifist who refused to swear she would defend the United States because she didn't believe in war. Holmes wrote that freedom of conscience is a fundamental right necessary for a free society, and "it is the principle of free thought—not free thought for those who agree with us, but freedom for thought that we hate." which is most important. [197] Schwimmer testified that she was willing to be treated as a conscientious objector who refused to take up arms to defend the United States, but that was not sufficient for the Court majority, so they denied her U.S. citizenship. Holmes had fought in the Civil War and was not a pacifist, but he believed Schwimmer was "a woman of superior character and intellect" and should be made a citizen of the U.S. in spite of her refusal to swear she would defend the country in time of war. The case received enormous attention and Holmes' dissent was printed in the *New Yorker Magazine*.

In late 1929, Taft's health began to deteriorate. By 1930, he was too ill to continue working, so Holmes, as senior Justice, assumed his duties as acting Chief Justice until the post could be filled. In February 1930, Taft resigned from the Court and died a month later. President Hoover appointed Holmes' old friend Charles Hughes as Chief Justice of the Supreme Court. When Holmes turned ninety, his friends arranged a national radio broadcast that included tributes from Chief Justice Hughes, the American Bar Association, and the dean of Yale Law School. Holmes received hundreds of congratulatory letters on his birthday. During the summer of 1931, Holmes' health began to decline and although his mind was still sharp, he didn't have the energy to keep up with his work on the Court. On January 10, 1932, Brandeis and Hughes came to see Holmes privately and gently asked him to resign. He agreed, delighted that the decision had been made for him.

On his ninety-second birthday, President Franklin Roosevelt came to visit Holmes at his home on 1720 Eye Street. Holmes contracted bronchial pneumonia in the winter of 1935 and died on March 6th of that year. He was buried two days later on what would have been his ninety-fourth birthday. His private attorney found two musket balls wrapped in a small paper parcel among his personal effects, with the note "these were taken from my body in the Civil War." In his will, Holmes left substantial gifts to his nephews, housekeepers, Court messenger, driver, and clerk, $25,000 to Harvard Law School and another $25,000 to the Boston Museum of Fine Arts. The balance of his considerable estate, including his home, was left to the U.S. government. In 1940, Congress proposed to use the Holmes bequest to fund a history of the Supreme Court in his honor but the work was never finished.

Woodrow Wilson

Woodrow Wilson's mother, Jeanie Woodrow, immigrated from Scotland to Canada in 1836, and later moved to Ohio searching for a warmer climate. Wilson's father, Joseph Ruggles Wilson, also Scottish, lived in Ireland before he immigrated to the United States to escape pressure from the English king to renounce his Catholic religion. The couple married on June 7, 1849, and moved to Virginia where Joseph Wilson served as pastor of a church. Woodrow Wilson was born on December 28, 1856, in Staunton, Virginia. [198] The town contained many slaves, which never bothered Wilson's father, but his mother opposed slavery. Wilson never resolved his ambivalence toward slavery because of the conflicting attitudes he acquired from his parents.

Wilson said his earliest memory was standing in the gateway of the family home in Augusta, Georgia, when he was four years old, watching a rider pass by shouting that Lincoln had been elected president and war was coming. The city of Augusta avoided serious damage during the Civil War, but General Sherman captured Atlanta and burned a swath through Georgia in 1864. Because there was no mandatory schooling during the war, Wilson didn't learn to read until age eleven. Modern experts believe Wilson probably suffered from developmental dyslexia. [199] His early education involved going on rounds with his father and listening to sermons. After the Civil War, Wilson attended a school established by Joseph Derry in Augusta. He took classes in history, Latin, writing, and bookkeeping.

In May 1870, Columbia Theological Seminary in South Carolina offered Wilson's father a professorship of Theology which he accepted. Wilson enrolled in a classical course of study along with about fifty other boys in a barn under the guidance of Charles Barnwell. The Columbia Seminary was not satisfied with Reverend Wilson, so the family moved to Wilmington, North Carolina. Wilson enrolled in Davidson College near Charlotte, North Carolina, in 1873. [200] For the first time in his life, Wilson applied himself seriously to his studies and developed an interest in history and politics. He discovered a talent for debating but fell ill and returned to his family home. There he met Dr. James McCosh, president of the College of New Jersey (now Princeton University), who invited Wilson to apply at his institution the following year.

Princeton University. [201] The College of New Jersey was founded in October 1746, as a seminary for preachers, but later added courses on modern languages, literature, chemistry, and geography. Wilson entered the College of New Jersey in September 1875 and studied Latin, algebra, English, and rhetoric. He developed an interest in British and American history, read Edmund Burke, and followed his advice to study broadly. Wilson read slowly and retained much of what he read. He was not a distinguished student at college but became a good debater and participated in campus politics. Wilson joined the campus newspaper, the *Princetonian,* and published several editorials. He graduated in 1879 and remembered his college years mainly for the friendships he developed.

Virginia Law School. [202] After graduation, Wilson decided he wanted to be a politician and that meant he needed to study law. Law schools were relatively new in America at that time since most young men studied with practicing attorneys rather than attending law school. Wilson entered Virginia Law School in October 1879 and joined a debating group. During his first year at Virginia Law School, Wilson visited his cousin Hattie at her school in Staunton, a forty-mile train ride from Charlottesville. Hattie was talented, religious, and attractive; Wilson fell in love with her and neglected his studies. The Law School dean scolded him for missing so many classes and he promised to do better in the future.

During his second year, Wilson never missed a class because Hattie moved to Cincinnati to study music. Wilson's health failed during his second year at law school and he went home with his law books to undertake a course of self-study. He took a trip to Ohio that summer to see Hattie and asked her to marry him. She said she didn't love him, and he was devastated. Rather than returning to law school, Wilson went to Atlanta and opened a law office with Edward Renick, a distant relative. Atlanta was booming at the time, and Wilson was able to live comfortably on the allowance his father sent every month, so he didn't worry about attracting clients or practicing law. Renick preferred to do legal research and Wilson argued their cases. After practicing law for a few weeks, Wilson decided he didn't like law, but his father advised him to wait a few months, and if he still felt that way, then he could change to another profession.

Wilson decided to study for admission to the bar and on October 18, 1882, he appeared before Judge George Hillyer for an examination. Hillyer and four other attorneys questioned Wilson and agreed to admit him to practice in Georgia. Because his law firm had few cases, Wilson wrote articles and attended sessions of the Georgia legislature. He was tempted to run for office because he was unhappy with law and was thinking about other careers. Wilson decided he wanted to be a professor and applied to Johns Hopkins University as a Ph.D. candidate. Before he left Atlanta, Wilson went to Rome, Georgia, to settle a trust case he had accepted.

While in Rome, Wilson met Ellen Louise Axson, a minister's daughter. [203] Reverend Axson was an old friend of the Wilson family, and Woodrow discovered Ellen was a gifted painter who had won a bronze medal at the Paris International Exposition. She was well-read and an interesting conversationalist-- Wilson fell in love with her. They met in Ashville, where Wilson was vacationing, when Ellen stopped by on her way to visit her father, who had fallen ill. Wilson took Ellen to meet his mother, who was charmed by her. After the visit, Wilson asked Ellen to marry him, and she accepted.

Wilson moved to Baltimore to attend Johns Hopkins University and study history and political science, with the goal of eventually becoming a university professor, marrying Ellen, and spending his life reading, writing, and teaching. While at Johns Hopkins, Wilson wrote a book on congressional government, describing how to make the institution work more efficiently. After his first year in graduate school, Wilson won a scholarship that brought him various academic privileges and Ellen enrolled at the Art Student League in New York to study painting. Wilson was offered a teaching position at Bryn Mawr College while still a student at Johns Hopkins. Although he had not finished his thesis, he accepted the position so he could earn a living and marry Ellen.

Wilson taught economics, history, and politics at Bryn Mawr College. A gifted lecturer, he asked his students to listen to him and think about what he was saying rather than taking notes. He began writing a series of articles that eventually appeared in book form as *The State*, describing the governments of all nations. Dr. Adams, his advisor at Johns Hopkins, told Wilson he could finish his degree by taking a special examination and using his book, *Congressional Government,* as his Ph.D. thesis. He passed the examination and earned his doctorate on May 29, 1886. Wesleyan University in Connecticut offered him a job, and he contracted to write a book covering American history after 1829, with particular attention to the Civil War, one of Wilson's special interests. In February 1890, the Trustees of Princeton University offered Wilson the Chair of Jurisprudence and Political Economy at a salary of $3,000 annually and he immediately accepted. [204]

Princeton Professor. Wilson wrote dozens of historical articles and finished *Division and Reunion*, the history of America after 1829 at Princeton University. Theodore Roosevelt praised Wilson's book in the *Educational Journal*. Next, he began writing *A History of the American People* and a six-part biography of George Washington that was published in *Harper's Magazine*. In May 1896, Wilson felt severe pain in his right arm and his right hand became numb. He was alarmed enough to consult a physician, who dismissed the pain as writer's cramp and told him not to worry about it. Modern physicians believe Wilson may have suffered the first of several mild strokes at that time. A wealthy neighbor offered him a trip to Europe to rest and recover his health, which Wilson accepted. His academic reputation was growing outside Princeton, and he was offered a faculty position at Yale, presidency of the University of Illinois, and the chancellorship of the University of Virginia. Wealthy Princeton alumni offered Wilson an extra stipend of $2,500 annually if he would stay in New Jersey. He agreed and published his *History of the American People* in 1902. The book made him one of the best-known historians in America. It was a commercial success and Wilson began to spend time on university politics rather than writing.

The faculty was concerned about declining academic standards at Princeton University, and Wilson was determined to do something about it. The president of Princeton University resigned and the

Trustees appointed Wilson president of the university. He developed a plan to reorganize Princeton and raise its academic standards. Wilson recommended Princeton adopt the English tutorial system rather than teaching by lectures and planned to strengthen the departments of history, economics, and biology. Wilson wanted to add a law school, a graduate school, a school of electrical engineering, and a museum of natural history to the University to widen its appeal.

He asked Princeton alumni to raise funds to pay for the upgrading of the University and dismissed poor students and underperforming faculty. The fundraising was successful, new faculty were recruited, better students admitted, and Princeton University gained renewed academic recognition. President Teddy Roosevelt attended the annual Army-Navy game at Princeton and had lunch with Wilson. Soon after, Wilson was being mentioned as a candidate for the U.S. Senate, Governor of New Jersey, or even President of the U.S. He decided to run for Governor of New Jersey to gain political experience before he made his next important political move.

Governor Wilson. The Democratic Party in New Jersey nominated Wilson for governor to give him administrative experience outside Princeton University. [205] He planned to serve as Governor of New Jersey and then be nominated as the Democrat candidate for President in 1912. Wilson received more than twice as many nomination votes as any other Democratic candidate for Governor of New Jersey. He resigned from Princeton and began campaigning around the state. Wilson's crowds increased and he became proficient at giving a rousing political speech. He debated the Republican candidate and won the governorship of New Jersey in a landslide. [206]

Wilson began campaigning for the presidency soon after being elected governor by accepting an offer from rich New York residents to go on a speaking tour to raise his national profile. He spoke mainly about what kind of President the country needed and his vision for America. Wilson followed Jefferson's doctrine that the best government is one that governs least. After his speaking tour, many Democrats favored Wilson as their nominee for President because he would be the most scandal-free candidate in decades and they believed he could win.

Wilson entered presidential primaries where there was no favorite son running to avoid offending powerful members of the Democratic party. At the party's convention, his rival Champ Clark of Missouri collected more votes than Wilson on the first few ballots, but then it became clear Clark had peaked while Wilson continued to gain support. Franklin Delano Roosevelt later claimed he engineered the shift of votes that actually nominated Wilson for President. He ran against Teddy Roosevelt and William Taft. [207] On election night, Wilson won forty-two percent of the popular vote to Teddy Roosevelt's twenty-seven percent and collected four hundred thirty-five Electoral College votes, the most ever won by a presidential candidate. The reason Wilson won so many electoral votes was because the Bull Moose and Republican candidates split the conservative vote while Wilson received all the liberal votes. After less than two years in politics, Woodrow Wilson was President of the United States. [208]

President Wilson. Wilson immediately began selecting a cabinet to help him run the administration. His first task was to find a post for William Jennings Bryan, the most important elder statesman in the Democratic Party. Wilson named Bryan Secretary of State because that post carried prestige and would keep Bryan out of domestic politics. Wilson nominated William McAdoo Secretary of the Treasury, the

Postmaster General was Albert Burleson, and the Secretary of Agriculture was David Houston. In his inaugural address, Wilson said he intended to safeguard the health of the nation, keep America safe, and run an honest administration. He began holding regular White House Press Conferences and delivered his State of the Union address to Congress in person. In his first address, Wilson asked Congress to pass tariff reform so American manufacturers were neither protected nor penalized in foreign markets. He also wanted to abolish the monopolistic privileges some businesses enjoyed. Wilson's State of the Union speech lasted only nine minutes—a far cry from the much longer speeches given today.

Wilson regularly met with Congressional leaders to discuss bills he wanted passed and convinced Congress to lower tariffs from forty percent to twenty-five percent on many items. Some tariffs were reduced to zero during his first term as President. [209] To make up the lost revenue from lower tariffs, Wilson asked Congress to pass progressive income tax brackets, with the top rate at seven percent. Wilson also proposed a Federal Reserve Board be established to stabilize the economy and act as a lender of last resort during recessions or bank runs. The Federal Reserve Act was signed into law February 23, 1913. [210] Wilson faced his most serious political challenge when war broke out in Europe in 1914. The country was evenly divided concerning whether to intervene or stay out of the conflict, and Wilson had to tread carefully to avoid offending voters.

World War I. On June 28, 1914, a Bosnian Serb anarchist shot Archduke Franz Ferdinand, killing the heir to the Austro-Hungarian throne and triggering a series of treaty obligations that plunged Europe into a catastrophic war. One bullet started four years of bloody conflict between Germany and Austria on one side and Britain, France, and Russia on the other. When asked if America would try to mediate peace in Europe, Wilson said the United States wanted to stay neutral. In the middle of this political turmoil, Wilson's wife Ellen fell ill and died on August 6, 1914. [211] Wilson was emotionally distraught and had difficulty concentrating for weeks after her death. He was thankful the Atlantic Ocean protected the country and the U.S. could stay out of war. The opening battles of World War I caused massive casualties and were a preview of the horrible slaughter to come. Wilson issued a formal declaration of American neutrality on August 4, 1914, to keep America out of the war.

Both sides instituted naval blockades and American economic activity slowed as a result. Cotton sat in American warehouses, the New York Stock Exchange was closed to prevent a financial panic, and the country fell into a serious recession. During the crisis, Wilson's administration offered money to banks so they could underwrite loans to farmers to store their cotton and pay for planting the following year. The government offered "credits" to warring nations when they bought American commodities. Because of the newly enacted Seventeenth Amendment, Senators were elected for the first time by direct vote of the people rather than by state legislatures. Wilson's Democratic Party gained seats in the Senate but lost seats in the House during the interim election. On December 8, 1914, Wilson delivered his second State of the Union address to Congress, saying the nation needed to prepare its defenses in case it was attacked, but promised to keep America out of war.

In 1915, Wilson sent an emissary to Europe to see if America could mediate peace, but the offer came to nothing because both sides still believed they could win on the battlefield. England and Germany expanded their naval blockades, resulting in the German Navy sinking the American merchant ship

William P. Frye while it was transporting wheat to England. [212] Wilson appreciated that Germany was being starved by the British blockade and that American ships had an obligation to stay out of danger and avoid putting the U.S. government in a difficult situation, but many Americans were angry about the loss of American lives and wanted retribution against Germany. Wilson hoped to avoid war so he did nothing to aggravate the Germans.

Nearly a year after Wilson's wife Ellie had died, Edith Gault was invited by a friend to have tea at the White House. As Edith and her friend were entering the building, she "accidentally" met President Wilson and his physician returning from a round of golf. Wilson was charmed by Edith and invited her to stay for dinner. She declined but asked for a rain check. A few weeks later, Wilson invited Edith to join him at a New York Yankee baseball game where he was to throw out the first pitch of the season, and she accepted. Edith became a regular guest at the White House and after several visits, Wilson told Edith he wanted to marry her. She hesitated because it was only a year since his wife had died. Wilson said that didn't matter because he loved Edith and wanted her to be his wife. Edith said she would think about his proposal and they continued enjoying evening dinners at the White House that eventually lead to marriage. [213] Meanwhile, war in the Atlantic was becoming more serious.

The Lusitania. On May 7, 1915, a German submarine torpedoed and sank the English ship *Lusitania*, taking nearly twelve hundred passengers to their death, including over one hundred Americans. The sinking created an international incident and enraged many Americans. Wilson tried to remain neutral, but Teddy Roosevelt called the sinking an act of piracy and said America needed to declare war against Germany. Some in Wilson's cabinet favored neutrality while others felt the United States had to declare war on Germany because of the repeated naval provocations. Wilson sent a formal letter to Germany reminding them that their current policy was infringing on the rights of neutral nations engaging in lawful commerce and called on Germany to disavow recent acts against neutral shipping, make reparations, and take steps to prevent future maritime incidents.

The German government expressed regret for the loss of American lives, but pointed out that the ship was financed by the British government, owned by an English company, was carrying munitions and Canadian troops to England, and the British were using neutral passengers as a shield for wartime activities. The German government promised it would avoid attacking neutral shipping in the future— which it did for a while, but insisted it would continue to sink British vessels that were carrying war goods and neutral citizens should avoid sailing on such ships for their own safety.

Wilson's State of the Union address in 1915 stressed that he wanted to keep America out of war and asked for money to strengthen the army and navy. He focused on keeping America out of war during the presidential election of 1916 while preparing the military to fight if necessary. Wilson also proposed a conference between the warring sides to see if they could negotiate peace. The presidential campaign of 1916 proceeded against a backdrop of war in Europe, labor unrest at home, and a significant increase in American nationalism. The Republican Party nominated Charles Evans Hughes and the Democrats nominated Wilson as presidential candidates. The major theme of Wilson's campaign was "he kept us out of war." The Democratic Party held the South and the Republican Party won the Northeast, so the battleground states were in the West and Midwest.

On election night, the decision came down to California's thirteen electoral delegates. [214] The vote in California was close, and ballots from Sierra County had not been counted yet because of heavy snow in the mountains. When those votes were finally tallied, the Electoral College vote was two hundred seventy-seven for Wilson and two hundred fifty-four for Hughes, making Wilson the first Democrat re-elected president since Jackson in 1832. After the election, Germany announced it would sink any ship found in waters around Great Britain, whether the vessel was neutral or belligerent, because it believed unrestricted submarine warfare would bring the English to their knees and end the war quickly. However, the German government had not counted on America entering the war because of a diplomatic incident.

The Zimmermann Telegram. On March 1, 1917, the *New York Times* carried a headline announcing that Germany was discussing an alliance with Mexico and Japan against the U.S. [215] The information came from a diplomatic cable Germany sent to its ambassador in Mexico that was intercepted by British intelligence and turned over to the American press. Germany offered Mexico the states of Texas, New Mexico, and Arizona if it joined the war against America, while Japan was offered colonies in the Pacific and concessions in China if it would declare war on America. Americans were angered by the proposed Mexico-German alliance and Wilson asked Congress for authority to arm American merchant ships. The Senate refused, but he armed them anyway. Adding to the general uncertainty, the Russian people revolted against the Tsar and stopped fighting Germany, freeing millions of troops to fight on the Western Front against England and France.

On March 8, 1917, the German Navy torpedoed three American merchant ships, killing over a dozen Americans. Coupled with the Zimmerman affair, that was the last straw, so Wilson asked Congress for a declaration of war against Germany. The Senate voted eighty-two to six and the House three hundred seventy-three to fifty in favor of war. [216] America went to war with less than three hundred thousand men under arms, fewer troops than countries such as Belgium and Portugal had in their armies. The American Navy mobilized quickly and seized ninety-one German vessels in American ports. Wilson seized the railroads and established a War Industries Board to coordinate military purchases. He appointed Herbert Hoover to organize food production and asked Congress to pass a draft law for the first time since the Civil War. Almost four million men served in the American Army during World War I.

In his December 1917 State of the Union address, President Wilson outlined his war objectives, saying America wanted peace based on his published Fourteen Points. In the trenches of Europe, the German Army was winning because of added manpower from the Russian front. The Americans would probably not land in Europe until the summer of 1918, and the German government hoped to defeat the French and English before Americans could enter the war and make a difference. The German generals believed they had a few months before American troops arrived in Europe and tipped the balance of power against them, so they launched a major offensive in the spring of 1918 to break through the Allied lines, flank the British Army, and win the war. The German spring offensive succeeded at first, but eventually failed, and American troops joined the Allies and turned the tide of battle against Germany.

Americans in Europe. By June 1918, one and one-half million American troops landed in Europe equipped and ready to fight. At the same time, the Spanish flu began infecting nearly a billion people and killing over one hundred million worldwide. The first significant clash between American and German troops occurred at the Battle of Belleau Wood. It lasted a month and the American Marines won a major victory. French and British Armies joined the Americans in attacking all along the Western Front, taking advantage of the momentum created by American victories and the arrival of British tanks, which allowed Allied troops to leave the trenches safely for the first time. The Americans had arrived at the critical moment and shifted the balance of military power against Germany. The German government recognized they were being defeated and opened discussions on an armistice.

On October 6, 1918, Germany formally asked Wilson to organize a delegation to negotiate an end to the war, accepting his Fourteen Points as the basis for peace. Wilson personally participated in negotiating the peace treaty because he was concerned Britain and France would insist on a vengeful surrender, and he wanted to avoid provoking another war in a generation. Before he could go to Europe, however, the Republican Party gained control of both houses of Congress in the midterm elections, and they didn't support Wilson's ideas for a just peace. The Republican Senate blocked the peace treaty when it was submitted for approval, and America never joined the League of Nations, even though Wilson personally attended the peace conference and helped negotiate the terms.

The Paris Peace Conference. The peace conference was held in the French Ministry of Foreign Affairs in Paris and included delegations from over two dozen nations. [217] The major Allied nations included France, Great Britain, Italy, the United States, and Japan. George Clemenceau of France, David Lloyd George of England, Vittorio Orlando of Italy, and Woodrow Wilson made all important decisions at the conference. Japan was not given a major role because she had done little to win the war, and Russia was involved in a civil war so it was not invited to attend. The agenda included new territorial boundaries in Europe, changes in colonial possessions, and the establishment of new states in Europe and the Middle East. Clemenceau was elected chairman of the conference and immediately announced his interest in requiring Germany to pay huge reparations to France and England.

At the second session of the conference, Wilson proposed establishing a League of Nations to monitor the peace. He said the U.S. sought no specific territorial gains but wanted the League to protect small countries. The Allied leaders formed a committee to draft a constitution for the League, even though they believed Wilson was out of touch with reality. However, they realized he needed to bring home something to the U.S., and they went along with his idea of a League of Nations to placate Americans. England and France wanted to discuss reparations and annexing parts of the German and Ottoman Empires for themselves but were willing to humor Wilson to get him to agree with their other terms in the treaty.

Wilson was able to convince England, Japan, and Italy that a mandate system was the best way to manage German Pacific and African colonies. He was also concerned about economic conditions in Europe, noting that millions in Europe were facing starvation without food from America. In February 1919, Wilson returned to the U.S. to deal with pressing domestic problems. He faced a hostile Congress and believed he needed to get the American people on his side if he was going to convince the Senate to ratify the Paris Peace Treaty. Two days after he returned to Washington, Wilson hosted the Senate Foreign Relations Committee at the White House. After dinner, Wilson made a speech outlining the Treaty and the League of Nations and opened the floor for questions. Many Republican members of the committees opposed the League and said so openly. Wilson was discouraged when he returned to Europe to complete negotiations for the peace treaty because of the Republican opposition he faced at home.

On his return to Paris, Wilson leaned the American delegation had made compromises he didn't like, so he had to renegotiate these issues. Wilson rejected France's proposal that they separate the League of Nations from the peace treaty and opposed establishing a small nation between France and Germany as a buffer to avoid further conflicts. The other major issues to be resolved were the size of reparations due from Germany, how to separate the Middle East from Turkey, a clause blaming Germany for starting the war, and the establishing of spheres of influence for England and France around the world. Wilson was most interested in rebuilding Poland, so he bought Allied support for that country in return for agreeing to several other English and French demands. France played a waiting game, forcing Lloyd George and Woodrow Wilson to compromise because they needed to return home to deal with important domestic political issues. Wilson warned France and England that demanding ruinous reparations from Germany would only cause another war—which happened when Hitler came to power in the 1930s.

While in Paris, Wilson suffered a serious illness that was never clearly diagnosed. Some experts speculated that he contracted the Spanish flu; others believe he suffered small strokes that caused memory loss. With Wilson temporarily out of commission due to illness, Lloyd George and Clemenceau tried to push through their plan for reparations from Germany, but Wilson recovered in time to oppose them. However, Wilson agreed to several terms after his illness that he had rejected earlier, including ceding territory from Germany to Italy and giving Japan railroad rights in China. England and France both looked after their national interests and forgot their debt to America for winning the war. The German people came to hate America because they believed their country would have won the war without United States intervention, and that was probably accurate.

The Treaty of Versailles contained articles establishing the League of Nations, requiring German disarmament, limiting the German military, blaming Germany for starting the war, and demanding ruinous reparations from Germany to France and England. [218] Wilson suffered another serious illness during the final days of the conference and was unable to address the last session. Germany rejected the harsh terms of the treaty, and even some Allies had second thoughts about the size of the reparations demanded from the defeated country. Many historians believed the treaty was too harsh and were concerned Germany would retaliate once it recovered from the war. After minor modifications, the Germans signed the treaty because they had no choice. The peace agreement left open what to do about Russia. John Maynard Keynes wrote a book predicting that the Versailles Treaty demanded too much from Germany, would not allow the country to recover after the war, and had sowed the seeds of another world war.

Because the Senate was controlled by Republicans, Wilson realized getting the treaty approved would be difficult. He wanted to present the entire treaty to the Senate for an up or down vote, but

Republicans were in no hurry to cooperate. Demobilization caused serious economic problems and inflation in America. Race riots broke out in several cities bringing bloody confrontations between opposing groups. Senate Republicans embarrassed Wilson by calling cabinet members to testify before Senate committees, showing the members didn't understand the treaty or were ambivalent about its terms. Wilson decided he had to take his case to the American people to force Republican Senators to approve the treaty. However, the speaking engagements proved too strenuous for Wilson's health, and he suffered a serious stroke, severe pains in his head, and his left arm and leg became numb. [219] Due to his health problems, the speaking trip was canceled and Wilson returned to Washington.

Wilson avoided press conferences or personal meetings and Edith acted as intermediary between him and the public. After being at the White House for a few days, Wilson fell unconscious in his bathroom, probably from another stroke. When his physician arrived, the left side of Wilson's body was completely immobile. A neurologist called to examine him found Wilson's entire left side was paralyzed and his left eye barely responsive to light. The diagnosis was a clot in an artery of his brain that had caused the paralysis. Wilson's cognitive ability was not seriously impaired, but his personality changed, and his judgment deteriorated. The White House deceived the public about Wilson's physical condition by minimizing his health problems and implying that Wilson would be resuming his duties soon.

Hiding the News. Edith and his physicians kept Wilson's medical information from the public and Congress. He was not in serious danger of dying, but Wilson was exhausted and confused as a result of the brain clot. His physicians suggested Wilson might make a partial recovery if he had time to rest and avoid stress, so they advised Edith to limit his personal contacts, consult with the heads of the various cabinet agencies herself, and resolve issues without involving the president. His doctors recommended Wilson not resign because they felt the emotional shock might kill him. Based on this advice, Edith became de facto President of the United States, initiating a huge conspiracy against the American people. Her rationale was that the President's mind was clear, and he was not cognitively disabled, so he could carry on governing with a little help from Edith and the cabinet. In truth, Wilson's judgment was severely impaired and he was not capable of managing the country. His physicians refused to answer medical questions, fueling controversy and gossip about the seriousness of his illness.

At that time, there was no formal procedure for determining whether a President was fit to perform his duties, so the government muddled along with Edith in charge. Cabinet members delivered messages to government departments and foreign countries after consulting with Edith. Wilson's health deteriorated further when he developed a prostate problem. His physicians decided an operation would be too stressful and left his recovery to nature. Wilson survived, but his health continued to deteriorate. Wilson's energy eventually improved enough that he could attend a short cabinet meeting and receive a few foreign visitors, including the Prince of Wales, who would later become King Edward VIII. These meetings were carefully controlled and presented to the public as evidence Wilson was improving. He was not.

Republican Senators avoided contacting the White House, believing that time would help them defeat the Treaty, and they were right. Senator Henry Cabot Lodge drafted a compromise treaty and sent it to Wilson for review, but he never saw it. Instead, Edith simply asked Wilson if he would accept revisions to the treaty to get it passed and he said "no." As a result, the treaty was rejected by the Senate and the United States never joined the League of Nations. Wilson was upset when the treaty was rejected and felt Congress had intentionally kept him in the dark. That was inaccurate, but Wilson was irrational about the issue and his judgment was severely impaired.

After the treaty was rejected by the Senate, Wilson went into denial, unrealistically planning to reintroduce the treaty and get it passed without changes. He was unable to speak clearly and his health was deteriorating. As the President continued to avoid public appearances, rumors of his death began to circulate. When it came time for Wilson to deliver his State of the Union address to Congress, he sent a published copy that was bland and uninteresting. Important issues were postponed rather than resolved, the American government essentially stopped functioning, and cabinet members considered resigning. When his Secretary of State did resign, other cabinet members took advantage of Wilson's health problems to foster their own political ambitions, including running for President at the next election.

Wilson experienced alternating bouts of euphoria and depression during 1919-20. On February 29, 1920, Democratic Senators met over dinner to discuss making changes in the Treaty of Versailles so it could become law. When the compromises were presented to Wilson, he rejected them all. Because of his stubborn attitude, the treaty was never ratified by the United States and a great opportunity to further world peace was missed. On April 14, 1920, Wilson held a full cabinet meeting and members were shocked by his appearance and behavior. After a few minutes of small talk, the cabinet members realized Wilson could not initiate a coherent discussion or lead the meeting. The Attorney General stepped in and ran the meeting. The public was wondering what had happened to the President, but everyone was kept in the dark.

Freud's Diagnosis of Wilson. Sigmund Freud prepared a psychological diagnosis of Wilson based on public and private information he collected. Freud concluded that Wilson had a mental breakdown outside Pueblo, Colorado, after his stroke, and was no longer an independent human being, was a carefully coddled invalid. Freud believed Wilson was at the mercy of illogical thoughts and was a querulous old man full of anger and self-pity who could not manage the office of the President. [220] Freud's analysis of President Wilson's mental condition created a sensation in America.

In the presidential election of 1920, both parties nominated candidates who had never run for national office. The Democrats nominated James Cox for president and Franklin Roosevelt for vice president while the Republicans nominated Warren Harding for president and Calvin Coolidge for vice president. Harding won the election, and Wilson continued to do nothing, waiting for the inauguration of a new President. Before he left office, Wilson learned the Nobel Committee would award him the Peace Prize for his work in ending World War I. He retired in Washington, and Edith found a house for them. Wilson was now a former President and needed to earn an income because ex-presidents didn't receive a pension until 1958. Publishers urged him to write something, but he refused—probably because he could no longer draft coherent sentences.

Ray Baker was given access to Wilson's papers and published a three-volume series entitled *Woodrow Wilson and World Settlement*, which contributed to Wilson's being seen as a great president by historians.

Wilson hatched one unrealistic plan after another but did nothing constructive or productive. In the summer of 1923, Harding died and Calvin Coolidge became president. Wilson's popularity rose as the Coolidge administration became mired in scandal. Edith limited his social activities and only allowed family members to see Wilson during his last years. On December 28, 1923, Wilson turned sixty-seven. His friends gave him a new black Rolls-Royce Silver Ghost limousine with a small orange stripe on the side. They also provided him with a trust that produced $10,000 annual income for the remainder of his life, resolving Wilson's financial problems.

On Sunday, February 3, 1924, after months of declining health, Wilson died. [221] Flags in Washington flew at half-staff for thirty days and Wilson was buried in the Washington National Cathedral.

Franklin Delano Roosevelt

Franklin Roosevelt was born on January 30, 1882, to James and Sara Roosevelt in Hyde Park, New York. [222] He grew up in a privileged environment and was home-schooled by his mother and private tutors. The Roosevelts traveled annually to Europe, Washington, D.C., and Campobello, their summer estate in Canada. In 1896, Franklin enrolled at Groton, an exclusive preparatory school to begin his formal education. He was fluent in English, French, and German by that time because of private tutoring. Franklin adjusted easily to the rigid regime at Groton and flourished.

After four years at Groton, he entered Harvard College. Since Roosevelt had taken all Harvard's required courses at Groton, he could take any courses he wanted and graduate in three years. Roosevelt avoided philosophy and enrolled in practical courses that interested him. After a summer in Europe, he returned to Harvard and was elected editor of *The Harvard Crimson*, the undergraduate newspaper. Roosevelt was a good administrator and a natural leader even at that young age. After graduating, Franklin married Anna Eleanor Roosevelt, his fifth cousin, on March 17, 1905, with President Teddy Roosevelt attending. [223] After the wedding, Franklin enrolled in Columbia Law School and passed the New York bar but never finished law school.

He joined the New York firm of Carter Ledyard and Milburn, one of the most prestigious in America. Roosevelt voiced an interest in politics so the Democratic Party asked him to run for the New York assembly. However, the current assemblyman changed his mind about giving up his seat, so Roosevelt ran for the New York Senate instead. He campaigned in a red Maxwell automobile, crisscrossed the district, and found he loved campaigning. Roosevelt benefited from a Democratic landslide engineered by Teddy Roosevelt's splitting the Republican votes that year. Franklin was such a successful campaigner that he led the Democratic ticket in New York. [224]

As a reward for helping him win New York, President Wilson offered Roosevelt the office of Assistant Secretary of the Navy, and he accepted, noting that Teddy Roosevelt had been Assistant Secretary of the Navy before becoming President. [225] Roosevelt was unanimously confirmed by the Senate without a hearing. He worked hard to keep Democratic politicians friendly to Wilson since the President didn't take the time to make friends with Congressmen. The U.S. Navy was ranked third in the world behind England and Germany in 1913, but Roosevelt believed many American ships were old and unfit for combat.

World War One. Roosevelt loved being close to power but disliked the day-to-day drudgery of his job. He briefly thought about running for Governor of New York, but war broke out in 1914 and he stayed with the navy. Roosevelt wanted America to get involved in European affairs, but President Wilson issued neutrality declarations aimed at keeping the U.S. out of war. Roosevelt was ordered to deal with Americans stranded in Europe and organize coastal defenses to keep German and British warships offshore. He pushed for a bigger navy to protect America, but Wilson declined to support building more ships.

Wilson's goal of neutrality was challenged when a German submarine sank the British liner, *Lusitania*, killing over one hundred Americans. The German government blamed England, pointing out that the ship was carrying war materials and soldiers as well as civilian passengers. However, the German Navy ordered its submarine captains to avoid sinking large passenger liners until further notice. After this incident, Wilson decided to strengthen the U.S. Navy by building an additional one hundred seventy-six ships, including ten battleships and six battlecruisers.

America Goes to War. Wilson ran for a second term against Chief Justice Charles Evans Hugues and narrowly won. Germany decided it needed to drive Britain from the war or starve, so the German Navy initiated unrestricted submarine warfare against all ships carrying passengers or materials to England. When German submarines sank the freighter *Housatonic*, Wilson severed diplomatic relations with Germany in hopes of stopping the submarine warfare, but it didn't work. Then, the English released an intercepted copy of German diplomat Zimmerman's cable offering Mexico the U.S. states of Texas, New Mexico, and Arizona if it would declare war on America. This made Americans angry. [226] On April 2, 1917, Wilson asked Congress for a declaration of war against Germany.

America began a rapid mobilization, instituted a draft, and rebuilt the navy for convoy duty. Roosevelt managed procurement for the navy and was so successful Wilson ordered him to share materials with the army. In 1917, the war was not going well for the Allies. Russia had collapsed in revolution and unrestricted submarine warfare was taking a terrible toll on British shipping. The answer was to organize ships in convoy with armed escorts, but the Royal Navy resisted that idea for months. When the convoy system was finally tried, it was so successful the tactic was continued for the duration of the war. Roosevelt recommended the Allies lay an anti-submarine barrier of mines across the North Sea from Orkney Island to Norway, and it proved effective in curtailing German submarine activity.

Lucy Mercer. During the war Roosevelt grew distant from Eleanor. They stopped having marital relations after their sixth child and it strained the relationship. In the summer of 1916, Franklin became involved with Lucy Mercer, Eleanor's part-time secretary. [227] Their long-term relationship was kept secret from the public until years after Roosevelt's death. Roosevelt went to Europe to visit the front and caught Spanish influenza on his return trip. Eleanor discovered love letters from Lucy in Roosevelt's suitcase when she unpacked his clothes and she was furious. There are conflicting accounts of what happened next. The truth seems to be that Eleanor was willing to divorce Roosevelt, but Sara, Roosevelt's mother, was opposed and threatened to disinherit him. Also, Roosevelt's advisors told him divorce would be the end of his political career. Roosevelt told Eleanor he would never see Lucy again but began seeing her in 1941, and she was with him when he died in 1945.

Roosevelt traveled to Europe to close the Navy's European installations after World War I, but he had no role in the peace conference. He sailed home on the same ship as President Wilson, who was returning to America to sign legislation passed by Congress. During the trip, Wilson summoned Roosevelt to his cabin to discuss the League of Nations. Wilson asked the ship's captain to land him in Boston because he had a speaking engagement, but the ship had no charts for that harbor. Roosevelt had sailed around Boston Harbor many times, so he was able to help the captain find the port.

Roosevelt began thinking about his political future because he had been mentioned as a possible candidate for the Senate or Governor of New York. He also considered running as vice president on the Democratic ticket but was concerned about a Republican landslide in 1920. Ohio Governor James Cox, who won the nomination for president, asked Roosevelt to run with him as vice president. Roosevelt agreed, resigned as Assistant Secretary of the Navy, and spent the next three months campaigning for Cox. Cox and Roosevelt supported the League of Nations, but the country elected Warren Harding because he promised a "return to normalcy."

Roosevelt believed he would not have been nominated for President in 1932 if he had not run for vice president in 1920 because he made many friends and collected a number of political debts during that campaign. Roosevelt believed the Democratic Party would not return to the White House until a depression drove Republicans out of Washington. He needed to earn money and decided to join Fidelity & Deposit Company, a Maryland bank run by a Democratic friend for $25,000 annually. Roosevelt increased his fortune, stayed in the public eye, and was able to remain active in politics. On July 28, 1921, Roosevelt set sail up the Hudson River to attend the annual Boy Scout Jamboree and contracted an illness that would change his life.

Polio? Roosevelt and his family traveled to Campobello for the summer as usual and engaged in sailing, hiking, picnicking, and swimming. However, he felt tired and lacked energy. He developed a chill and said he might be catching a cold and didn't want to infect the children, so he went to bed. Roosevelt had no appetite, didn't sleep well, and felt worse the next day. When he tried to get out of bed, his left leg collapsed and he recorded a temperature of 102 degrees. Eleanor called two physicians for consultations. One said he had a bad cold and the other a blood clot on his spinal cord. Neither was accurate. Louis Howe called a specialist who diagnosed poliomyelitis. That doctor said Roosevelt might make a complete recovery, but they would have to wait and see what happened. Ultimately, Roosevelt became permanently paralyzed from the waist down. Some modern physicians believe he suffered from Guillain-Barre Syndrome, an autoimmune disease, rather than polio. [228]

By October 1921, Roosevelt was able to sit up, had enough energy to work for an hour a day. He worked hard and learned to pull himself up by a strap and get into a wheelchair. His doctors recommended Roosevelt stay active and try to resume as normal a life as possible. He was fitted with leg braces and learned to swing his hips and walk with crutches. Eventually, Roosevelt could stay on his feet for an hour without feeling overly tired. He returned to Fidelity & Deposit on October 9, 1922, tried to walk from the car to the elevator, but fell and had to be put in a wheelchair. After that experience, he came by wheelchair every day through the back door. Rather than return to his old law firm, Roosevelt organized a new one with Basil O'Connor as his partner. O'Connor was an energetic Harvard Law School graduate who did the legal work while Roosevelt brought in clients and collected a salary of $10,000 annually.

In 1924 Roosevelt visited Warm Springs, Georgia, to take the therapeutic magnesium-laced waters in the area. He found the waters buoyant, he could stand on his weak legs, and enjoyed swimming with his powerful arms. Roosevelt enjoyed the experience so much he bought Warm Springs and established an aftercare facility for polio victims. For years, he spent time at Warm Springs and had a cottage built on the grounds for his use.

Governor Roosevelt. Roosevelt gave the nominating speech in Houston, Texas, for Al Smith for President. Herbert Hoover, the Republican nominee, appeared likely to win because the country was prosperous and people were happy. To help Smith, the Democratic Party begged Roosevelt to run for Governor of New York and win that state. The Republicans attacked Roosevelt's health, but he pointed out that being governor didn't require an acrobat because the job was brain work. He campaigned strenuously across the state, making as many as a dozen speeches every day. On election day, Roosevelt voted at Hyde Park and then went to campaign headquarters in Baltimore to await returns. By noon it was clear the Republicans were going to win the presidency. Roosevelt was ahead of Smith in New York but running behind the Republican candidate for Governor. However, late votes from upstate New York came in, and the final result was that Roosevelt won by around twenty-five thousand votes out of over four million votes cast. [229]

When Roosevelt took the oath of office on January 1, 1929, the New York Times said he was the new leader of the Democratic Party because New York had the most electoral votes. Roosevelt instantly became a major player in presidential politics, although his first priority was to be a good governor. He had to fend off Al Smith's interference, because Smith had been Governor of New York for the past eight years and was reluctant to give up his influence on state politics. Smith wanted Roosevelt to keep his key aides in the new administration, but Roosevelt installed his own people.

Roosevelt's day was well organized. He had breakfast in bed, read the papers, handled his personal correspondence, went to the Capitol at ten, worked until five, went home for a swim, and then had children's time, dinner, and worked until bedtime. He loved movies and had a small theatre installed in the Governor's Mansion so he could watch new releases at home. Roosevelt had the Governor's Mansion modified with an elevator, ramps, and a swimming pool to accommodate his paralysis. Franklin and

Eleanor reached an understanding that she would be hostess at the Governor's Mansion but have total freedom to pursue her own career. Roosevelt began flood control and power projects to produce more electricity for the state of New York and tried to help rural farmers by raising the gasoline tax to fix county roads. He began holding fireside chats to pressure the legislature into passing his proposals. In the summer of 1929, America's economic growth began to falter. Consumer spending slowed, industrial production stalled, commodity prices stagnated, and the Federal Reserve raised interest rates. However, the stock market kept climbing to new heights, fueled by huge margin borrowing.

The Great Depression. The stock market collapse began on October 4, 1929, when panic selling sent stock prices sharply lower. The wave of selling continued the following week, and on Black Friday, October 29, 1929, the stock market dropped twenty percent in one day on heavy trading volume. The severity of the resulting depression caught everyone by surprise. [230] American leaders thought the slowdown would be brief and the economy would quickly resume growing, but that didn't happen. Roosevelt believed the economic downturn might give him a chance to win the 1932 presidential election, believing the Republicans would be discredited for their poor handling of the economy.

He was one of the first governors to recognize the seriousness of the depression and attack President Hoover for saying employment was getting better when it was not. Roosevelt established the first office of unemployment insurance in the country, set up a commission to encourage employment in New York, and began planning how he would defeat Hoover in the 1932 presidential election. However, before he could run for President, Roosevelt had to win reelection as Governor of New York. He spent the summer and fall of 1930 campaigning around the state. Roosevelt ran against Hoover and Washington, stressing the need for farm subsidies, higher employment, and public power. He won reelection in New York by nearly a million votes, and the Democratic Party won control of the state legislature. In Washington, Democrats gained control of the House of Representatives and almost won the Senate. Democratic leaders began considering Roosevelt for President in 1932 to run against Hoover.

Roosevelt delegated the day-to-day management of his campaign for the Democratic presidential nomination to Louis Howe, while he governed New York and focused on the economic problems of the entire country. He asked the New York Legislature to appropriate twenty million dollars to provide work and food for unemployed men and women. This was the beginning of Roosevelt's belief that government had a responsibility to help people when the economy was not functioning properly. Roosevelt also asked for a tax hike to pay for the relief. Harry Hopkins, a social worker from Iowa, was given control of the relief agency. Jesse Straus commissioned one of the first opinion polls and found that Roosevelt was the front runner for the Democratic presidential nomination. The Republicans challenged Roosevelt to be examined by a team of medical experts to determine if he was able to govern the country. He immediately agreed and the medical panel gave him a clean bill of health.

Roosevelt easily won the first primary in New Hampshire by a landslide against Al Smith. Next, he won North Dakota, Georgia, Iowa, and Maine in the following weeks. He established a "brain trust" of college professors who generated new ideas for his campaign. When the Democratic Convention began on June 27, 1932, in Chicago, Roosevelt was one hundred votes short of winning the nomination. The most difficult issue for the Democratic Party was prohibition, but Roosevelt told the delegates to vote as they wished, because he could run on either platform. On the first ballot, Roosevelt collected six hundred sixty votes; on the second, he climbed to six hundred seventy-seven votes, but was still short of victory.

The key to Roosevelt's nomination was John Nance Garner of Texas. Roosevelt's people offered Garner the vice presidency if he would release his votes to Roosevelt, and Garner agreed. California delegates said that in return for veto power over who would be nominated for Secretary of State and Secretary of Treasury, they would back Roosevelt and he would win the nomination. The deal was made and Roosevelt became the Democratic nominee for President in 1932. Roosevelt decided to fly to Chicago to address the convention personally. American Airlines borrowed a Ford airplane and flew Roosevelt from Albany to Chicago. They wanted the publicity because Americans were reluctant to fly, and the CEO of American Airlines believed that a presidential candidate flying on his airline would be good publicity. Roosevelt captured the country's imagination with his dramatic flight to Chicago.

The Democrats made few mistakes during the campaign and Hoover seemed inept. Farley and Howe managed Roosevelt's campaign flawlessly and had a well-organized crew to get out the voters. At first, money was a problem, but as Roosevelt gained momentum, contributions began pouring in, giving the Democratic Party a large advantage over Hoover in the general election. Also, economic conditions were getting worse, and thousands of unemployed veterans were living in Washington and petitioning the government for a bonus. Hoover ordered the Army to evict them, and General MacArthur did just that, using American soldiers wielding sabers and bayonets against unarmed veterans. [231] Newspapers criticized Hoover for using excessive force to evict the veterans from abandoned buildings. The treatment of veterans symbolized Hoover's insensitivity to the unemployed and helped Roosevelt win the presidency, carrying forty-two states and collecting four hundred seventy-two Electoral College votes. [232]

Roosevelt used the time between his election and inauguration to put together a cabinet. He nominated Cordell Hull Secretary of State and William Woodin Secretary of the Treasury. He named Claude Swanson to head the Navy Department and picked George Dern for the War Department. Roosevelt nominated Homer Cummings for Attorney General and Francis Perkins as the first woman Labor Secretary. Then, he took a short Caribbean cruise, landing at Miami on February 15, 1933, to address the American Legion. An unemployed Italian bricklayer tried to shoot Roosevelt but missed.

Roosevelt made a short inaugural address after being sworn in by Chief Justice Charles Hughes, uttering the famous line, "the only thing we have to fear is fear itself." He said the most pressing problem was to put people back to work and Congress must act quickly to pass his New Deal programs. Roosevelt went to the White House to meet with his cabinet, which had already been confirmed by the Senate. During his first hundred days in office, Roosevelt called Congress into special session, asked for a bank holiday, and began looking for ways to get Americans working again, stop farm foreclosures, and pay unemployment insurance to those who lost a job. Democrats had a majority in the House and sixty votes in the Senate, so Roosevelt could pass any bill he wanted. The Secretary of the Treasury decided to print money under the Federal Reserve Act to stimulate the economy.

Congress passed, and Roosevelt signed the Emergency Banking Act to stop bank runs. He also gave a fireside chat during his first week in office. [233] Roosevelt explained the economic situation to the people and promised no one would lose their deposits if it could be avoided. The banks reopened for business and people deposited funds back in the banks. There were no bank runs and the U.S. dollar rose on foreign exchange markets. When the stock exchange reopened, it went up fifteen percent in one day. On March 16, 1933, Roosevelt sent an agricultural bill to Congress designed to reduce food surpluses and raise farm prices by paying farmers not to grow more than a specific allotment of produce. Next, he asked Congress to authorize the Civilian Conservation Corps to employ young men for reforestation and flood control. [234]

Roosevelt also asked Congress to provide mortgage relief to homeowners, establish the Tennessee Valley Authority, and rebuild the country's railroads to put people back to work. Roosevelt then reformed the stock markets by requiring publicly traded companies to disclose their financial status. Company officials were also made personally liable for the truth of their disclosures, which made them think twice about misleading investors. On April 18, 1933, Roosevelt took America off the gold standard, allowing prices to be set by the market. The measure was challenged in the Supreme Court, which upheld the power of Congress to regulate the monetary system in a five to four decision. The Glass-Steagall Act required investment banks to divest their banking functions so that depositors would not be at risk if the stock market crashed. The act also gave the Federal Reserve the power to set interest rates and establish the Federal Deposit Insurance Corporation to guarantee bank deposits up to two thousand five hundred dollars. Roosevelt announced the repeal of prohibition on December 5, 1933. [235]

He met with the press twice a week and held a cabinet meeting every Thursday. Roosevelt loved to play poker, fish, watch movies, and work on his stamp collection for relaxation. In the winter of 1933-34, Roosevelt established the Civil Works Administration with Harry Hopkins in charge and told him to create four million new jobs. The Civil Works Administration installed sewers, upgraded roads, build schools, and airports, creating millions of jobs for unemployed Americans. Congress reconvened on January 3, 1934, and created the Securities and Exchange Commission to regulate the investment industry and the Federal Communications Commission to regulate broadcasting. He asked Congress to fix the price of gold at thirty-five dollars an ounce, effectively devaluing the dollar by approximately sixty percent to increase the supply of money in the economy and stimulate growth.

The Congressional elections of November 1934 provided the first political feedback on Roosevelt's policies. Contrary to expectations and historical precedent, Democrats won an additional twelve seats in the House and nine in the Senate, even though the party in control of the White House usually loses seats during midterm elections. The American economy had not yet recovered and unemployment was over twenty percent, so there was still work to be done. Roosevelt wanted to pass laws that would provide unemployment compensation, old-age pensions, and aid for dependent children to create more jobs. He proposed a Social Security system paid for by employers and employees jointly which would supply a monthly pension payment to all Americans enrolled in the system when they reached age sixty-five. In his State of the Union Address in 1935, Roosevelt said he wanted to replace government relief programs with jobs programs to make Americans feel better about themselves.

Congress appropriated nearly five billion dollars to create more jobs and Roosevelt asked Hopkins to enlist the U.S. Army Corps of Engineers to administer the Works Progress Administration (WPA). [236]

During its first year, the WPA put more than three million men to work building schools, hospitals, parks, playgrounds, and highways. The final accomplishments of the New Deal were the Rural Electrification Administration and the Wagner Labor Relations Act. The Rural Electrification Act brought power to every farm in America by 1940, and the Wagner Act allowed workers to organize labor unions and bargain collectively.

Court Packing. Roosevelt began the 1936 presidential campaign early and made the New Deal his major issue. He had reason to be optimistic because the American economy had grown by almost fifty percent since 1932, and more than six million new jobs had been created under his administration. Moreover, the banking system was solvent, deposits were safe, farm mortgages were being refinanced, and the Home Owners' Loan Corporation had bailed out over three million insolvent households. Roosevelt launched his presidential campaign during his State of the Union address to Congress. The Republican Party nominated Governor Alfred M. Landon of Kansas as their candidate. Landon was not Herbert Hoover, but he was nearly as bland. The Democratic Party nominated Roosevelt and made adding more Justices to the U.S. Supreme Court part of their platform. Roosevelt won over sixty percent of the vote and five hundred twenty-three Electoral College votes to Landon's eight!

Roosevelt was angry at the Supreme Court for declaring several of his New Deal acts unconstitutional and decided to pack the Court by adding new Justices. The number of Supreme Court Justices is determined by Congress, not the Constitution, so Roosevelt believed he could legally add Supreme Court members by simply getting Congress to pass a law. He argued that the number of Justices had fluctuated in the past for political reasons, so why not now? He proposed to appoint a new Justice for every current Justice with over ten years of service who failed to retire after reaching the age of seventy.[237] This scheme would have given Roosevelt six new appointments to the Supreme Court during his second term as president, but the proposal ran into serious opposition in Congress and among the Supreme Court Justices.

Congressional leaders resented the fact that they had not been consulted about Roosevelt's proposal to pack the Supreme Court. Leaders of the House and Senate, and the Vice President turned against Roosevelt's idea of packing the Supreme Court. Bar associations opposed the plan, and the press accused Roosevelt of being a dictator who wanted to politicize the Court. Even the Chief Justice of the Supreme Court opposed the idea of adding new members to the Court and wrote a seven-page open letter arguing that packing the Court would destroy it. Not since Chief Justice John Marshall had defended the Court's right to review the constitutionality of Congressional acts had a member of the Court intervened in a political dispute. Chief Justice Hughes refuted every one of the President's arguments in favor of packing the Court in his letter.

The Court-packing bill failed in Congress and Roosevelt was humiliated by his own party. However, Roosevelt was still able to appoint three new Justices during his second term because three sitting Justices resigned. Roosevelt eventually appointed eight new Justices during his four terms as President.

In 1937 Roosevelt believed the Great Depression was over and he slashed government spending. Social Security taxes also took effect and the Federal Reserve raised reserve requirements at banks by fifty percent, reducing the money available for loans. The stock market went down forty percent that year as a result. Industrial production declined and over two million men lost their jobs. Roosevelt was worried and didn't know whether to restimulate the economy or wait out the recession. Harry Hopkins convinced him to do something and Roosevelt initiated massive new spending to stimulate the economy and create new jobs. He added money to the WPA for low-cost housing and began building ships for the navy to stimulate the economy. There was an even bigger economic stimulus on the horizon as Germany and Japan became more aggressive around the world and war seemed likely.

War Clouds. By 1937, Germany was becoming increasingly assertive in Europe and Japan had attacked China and was occupying large sections of that country. However, isolationism was strong in America and Roosevelt felt he could do little to prepare the country for war. On Sunday, December 12, 1937, Japanese planes bombed and sank the American gunboat *Panay* and three oil tankers in the Yangtze River. The U.S. cabinet met to discuss the incident, and the Secretary of the Navy and the Vice President supported going to war with Japan over the incident. Instead, Roosevelt demanded an apology and compensation for the loss of life and material. The Japanese government apologized and offered full restitution, defusing the situation temporarily. However, it was just a matter of time until tensions rose again because the Japanese government wanted to expand into the South Pacific in search of raw materials to fuel its economy.

In Europe, Hitler annexed Austria and demanded areas of Czechoslovakia inhabited by ethnic Germans be given to Germany. On September 29, 1938, Chamberlain, Daladier, Hitler, and Mussolini signed the Four Powers Agreement at Munich, ceding the Sudetenland to Germany in return for a promise that Germany wanted no more territory in Europe. [238] Roosevelt pledged to support Canada if it was attacked and asked Congress to authorize building more planes. Germany signed a non-aggression pact with the Soviet Union and then, on August 23, 1939, attacked Poland. England and France declared war on Germany and World War II began.

Roosevelt wanted to repeal the Neutrality Act so America could sell arms and supplies to the Allies, but Congress refused. Roosevelt said he would run for a third term if things got worse in Europe. After the quick defeat of Poland, Germany attacked Denmark and Norway in April 1940. Chamberlain resigned and Winston Churchill became Prime Minister of Britain. Germany invaded Belgium and Holland and moved toward Paris later in 1940. Churchill asked Roosevelt for fifty old American destroyers, modern aircraft, anti-aircraft weapons, ammunition, and steel to protect Britain from invasion and starvation. Roosevelt asked Congress for an emergency defense appropriation of over a billion dollars to begin rebuilding America's defenses.

German Armies drove the English from Dunkirk and conquered France in just a few weeks—entering Paris on June 14, 1940. [239] England was now fighting Germany alone and Roosevelt pledged to help them resist Nazi aggression. He also decided to run for a third term after the Republicans nominated Wendell Willkie as their candidate for President. While America was holding its presidential election, the Battle of Britain was fought in the skies over England, and German submarines were sinking British freighters at an alarming rate, threatening to starve England into submission. England once again asked for fifty old American destroyers to keep the shipping lanes open, but Congress refused to authorize it. Roosevelt decided to send the old American destroyers to England anyway in return for naval bases in the Western Hemisphere and Congress didn't object.

Roosevelt won a third term as president with four hundred forty-nine Electoral College votes to Willkie's eighty-two. Shortly after Roosevelt was reelected, he introduced the Lend-Lease program, which gave England the war materials she needed, with the understanding that Britain would return everything when the war was over. [240] Roosevelt sold the idea to Congress by saying that if your neighbor's house is on fire, you would let him borrow a hose to put out the fire provided he returned it later. He argued that Lend-Lease was the same thing. Churchill wanted America to declare war on Germany, but Roosevelt told him to be patient because the country was not yet ready. On June 22, 1941, the German Army invaded Russia and the immediate threat to England was over.

Roosevelt wanted to keep Russia in the war by sending food and war materials, but many Americans were opposed to communism. The Russian Ambassador was invited to the White House to give the president a list of items Russia needed to stay in the war, and Roosevelt sent one hundred planes immediately. Churchill and Roosevelt met off the coast of Canada and the Prime Minister again asked America to declare war on Germany, but Roosevelt resisted, saying the American people were still not ready. On Sunday, December 7, 1941, the Japanese Navy attacked Pearl Harbor, sinking eighteen American ships and destroying over three hundred planes. America declared war on Japan the next day and Germany declared war on America soon after. [241]

Roosevelt underestimated the Japanese military and Japan underestimated the industrial might of America. The "sleeping giant" began building military equipment on a massive scale for the Allies. On December 26, 1941, Churchill addressed a joint session of Congress and discussed war strategy with Roosevelt. They agreed that Germany should be defeated first. England and America established a Combined Chiefs of Staff in Washington to plan and coordinate strategy for the war.

Americans living on the West Coast feared an invasion by the Japanese, so Japanese-Americans were relocated to prevent them from possibly passing secret military information to the enemy. Roosevelt wanted a boost to American morale and asked the Army Air Force is if it was possible to bomb Tokyo. The navy decided they could launch Army Air Force B-25s from a U.S. carrier and bomb Tokyo in a one-way trip. The minor damage to Tokyo forced the Japanese to attack Midway Island to protect their homeland and the decision turned into a disaster for the Japanese Navy. At the battle of Coral Sea, Americans damaged two Japanese carriers and destroyed eighty aircraft. Because American intelligence agents had cracked the Japanese diplomatic code, the U.S. Navy was prepared to ambush the Japanese Navy when it attacked Midway. [242]

American planes arrived over the Japanese carriers off Midway at the precise moment their air cover had landed to refuel. Two squadrons of American dive bombers descended on the Japanese carriers, and in a matter of minutes, three Japanese carriers were sunk and another severely damaged. The Pacific War would continue for years, but the Japanese Navy never regained superiority over the American Navy after Midway. It was the decisive battle of the Pacific War.

War in Russia. News from the Eastern Front was grim because the German Army resumed its offensive in 1942 and made massive gains. Russia lost over seven hundred thousand soldiers, two thousand tanks, and six thousand artillery pieces that spring alone. Stalin sent his Foreign Minister to America asking for a second front in France to relieve German pressure on his country. Roosevelt was sympathetic but didn't believe the Allies could be ready before 1943 at the earliest to invade Europe. Churchill also opposed invading Europe in 1942, feeling the Allies were not yet prepared to cross the English Channel. He convinced Roosevelt that the lack of landing craft and the unpreparedness of American troops made a cross-channel landing impossible in 1942. Churchill proposed the Allies attack North Africa to gain experience and face less resistance compared with a landing on the coast of France. [243]

Roosevelt agreed with Churchill's plan, and the Allies landed near Casablanca on November 8, 1942, against light resistance from Vichy French forces. In response, Hitler seized the remainder of France and moved German and Italian troops to North Africa to defend the area. Meanwhile, the Battle of the Atlantic between German submarines and the Allied convoys continued. The key to winning that battle was small escort carriers for the convoys, because submarines could not remain submerged for long and were easy to spot and sink on the surface by planes. Roosevelt also ordered Admiral King to transfer sixty B-24 long-range bombers from the Pacific to the Atlantic to protect the convoys. These tactics worked, and the German submarine menace was curtailed by a combination of convoys, small carriers, and long-range bomber patrols to attack German submarines on the surface.

American mass production was generating prodigious amounts of war materials and now most of it was arriving in England rather than being lost to submarines in the Atlantic. The next major decision was when to invade France. The Allies agreed to set a target date during May 1944, and in the meantime, continue the campaign against Germany by invading Italy. On July 10, 1943, Allied forces invaded Sicily and captured Palermo. Mussolini was dismissed as prime minister and arrested. The new Italian Prime Minister surrendered to the Allies on September 3, 1943, and declared war on Germany. [244] However, Hitler moved sixteen German divisions into Italy, occupied Rome, and restored Mussolini to power. The Germans resisted the Allied advance in Italy for years before finally surrendering in 1945.

D-Day. Churchill, Roosevelt, and Stalin agreed to meet in Teheran, Iran, during November or December of 1943 to discuss war strategy. When Churchill and Roosevelt met Stalin in Teheran, the three leaders concentrated on the status of post-war Germany. Stalin wanted Germany to be dismembered rather than merely disarmed because he feared another attack on Russia. Churchill wanted Prussia separated from the rest of Germany, and Roosevelt proposed dividing Germany into five parts. Stalin preferred Roosevelt's plan and it was adopted.

Stalin, Churchill, and Roosevelt agreed that the invasion of France would occur no later than May of 1944. Roosevelt named General Eisenhower Supreme Commander of the Allied invasion of France. [245] When he returned to the U.S., Roosevelt's health was poor. His blood pressure was high and he stopped swimming in the White House pool. Roosevelt seemed unusually tired and in March his temperature went up to 104 degrees. He was admitted to Bethesda Naval Hospital for a complete check-up. The diagnosis was congestive heart failure. Roosevelt was told if his condition was left untreated, he would not survive another year. He was prescribed low doses of digitalis, a reduced work schedule, asked to cut down his smoking, limit his drinking, and try to get ten hours of sleep every night. The new regimen helped and the President's health improved.

Roosevelt decided he would run for an unprecedented fourth term because he wanted to finish the war. The fight at the Democratic Convention that year involved who would be Vice President, because many Democrats recognized that Roosevelt was not in the best of health and might not survive another four years. They finally settled on Senator Harry Truman of Missouri because he was believed to be the man who would hurt the President the least during the campaign. Roosevelt didn't attend the Democratic Convention because he was on his way to Hawaii to discuss the Pacific War. [246] The major issue in the Pacific was whether to invade the Philippines or Formosa first. MacArthur wanted to liberate the Philippines while Admiral King supported invading Formosa. Roosevelt decided to liberate the Philippines first and then move toward the Japanese homeland. While giving a speech in Bremerton, Washington, on his way back to Washington, D.C., Roosevelt suffered an angina attack, experiencing serious pain in his chest and both arms. During the presidential campaign he made the most of his role as Commander-in-Chief and won the election easily. Roosevelt collected four hundred thirty-two Electoral College votes to Thomas Dewey's ninety-nine.

After the election, Roosevelt's health declined rapidly. He lost weight, had no appetite, and his blood pressure was high. However, despite these health issues, he continued twice-a-week press conferences and weekly cabinet meetings. Two weeks after the inauguration, Roosevelt left for a meeting with Stalin and Churchill at Yalta to agree on the structure of post-war Europe. [247] The three leaders met for eight days, with Roosevelt presiding. The Russian Army was fifty miles from Berlin, the Allies had won the Battle of the Bulge, and were on the west side of the Rhine River ready to invade Germany. The Allies agreed that Germany would be divided into four parts, with Britain, France, the U.S., and Russia each occupying one section of the country and Berlin separated into four political zones. The status of Poland proved contentious. Russia wanted a friendly Poland to protect its border with Germany, but Roosevelt needed a way to placate Polish-Americans, who wanted an autonomous state of Poland established. The compromise was to promise free elections in every European country to decide what sort of government each nation wanted. However, because the Russian Army was still occupying Poland, it was not clear how free the elections would be when they were held.

Roosevelt wanted Russia to enter the war against Japan after Germany surrendered because he was not certain the atomic bomb would work, and estimates were that it would cost a million dead Allies to invade the Japanese homeland. Russia agreed to enter the war against Japan in return for territorial concessions from China and Japan. When he returned to America, Roosevelt addressed a joint session of Congress and outlined the agreements reached with Stalin and Churchill at Teheran. That was his last public appearance. Roosevelt's health declined and he traveled to Warm Springs, Georgia, for a vacation. Everyone seemed to know they were looking at a dying man. Roosevelt's hands were shaking so badly he couldn't mix drinks, and his memory was poor.

On Thursday, April 12, 1945, Roosevelt suddenly put his hand to his head in a jerky movement and said, "I have a terrific pain in the back of my head." He slumped forward, collapsed, and never regained consciousness. Roosevelt was pronounced dead at 3:35 p.m. from a cerebral hemorrhage at the age of sixty-three. [248]

Earl Warren

Earl Warren's father immigrated from Norway in 1886, married Chrystal Hernlund, and moved his family to Los Angeles, where he worked for the Southern Pacific Railroad. Earl was born on March 19, 1891. [249] In 1894 the Pullman Strike began after the company cut wages. The federal government broke the strike using army troops and the railroad workers were fired. Mathias Warren soon found another job inspecting cars for the Santa Fe Railroad in Bakersfield, California. Earl Warren was not a good student in high school because he spent time running track rather than studying. He worked summers on the Southern Pacific Railroad and entered the University of California, Berkeley after high school.

When Warren arrived at Berkeley, San Francisco was rebuilding after the April 18, 1906 earthquake, which destroyed much of the city. The University of California, Berkeley was already the leading university in the state. Warren made friends easily, dabbled in local politics. and earned a Bachelor of Letters degree in 1912. Warren entered Berkeley Law School the following year. Graduates from Berkeley's law school were automatically admitted to the California Bar without passing a bar exam, so Warren joined the law firm of Robinson and Robinson in Oakland after he graduated. He enlisted in the army when the U.S. entered World War I, earned a commission, and was assigned to Fort Lewis, Virginia, for training. [250] Warren was in Waco, Texas, as the war ended, was discharged, and returned to California where he met an old classmate who offered him a job as a legislative analyst in Sacramento. He also landed a job as clerk to the judiciary committee of the California Legislature. Later, Warren worked in the Oakland City attorney's office, advising officials and defending them in court. [251]

Warren wanted to be a trial lawyer and his opportunity came when he was hired as deputy district attorney for Alameda County. [252] His first case was prosecuting John Taylor, a union leader and member of the Communist Party. Taylor represented himself at trial and insisted he was not violent. However, Warren called witnesses from the International Workers of the World who testified that the Communist Party advocated violence to achieve its ends. Since Taylor was a member of the party, he was convicted and sent to prison. Wilson loved the job, worked hard to be a good trial lawyer, and advanced quickly. He met newspaper owners in the Bay Area and expanding his network of important political contacts in California.

Warren met his future wife, Nina Myers, at the Piedmont Baths in Oakland. [253] He asked a friend to introduce him and Warren immediately asked her for a date. After a few months, Warren proposed and told Nina he wanted to postpone their wedding until he earned enough so she could stay home and take care of their children. His chance came when the Alameda County District Attorney retired. Warren was supported by the Oakland Tribune and won the election. Being a district attorney gave Warren his first taste of political power and he liked it. Nina and Earl were married on October 14, 1925, in the Oakland First Baptist Church. [254] Warren adopted Nina's six-year-old son Jim soon after they married.

Warren again ran for District Attorney of Alameda County in 1926 and won a victory that carried him toward higher office. He was an energetic and tough campaigner who reminded voters of his legal accomplishments and military service. Warren accused his opponent of collecting a "slush fund" from crooks to finance his campaign and won the office of district attorney for Alameda County by a landslide. He attracted the attention of J. Edgar Hoover, head of the FBI, and established a close personal relationship with the Special Agent in charge of the San Francisco office of the FBI.

Warren became involved in the governor's election in 1934 when Upton Sinclair, a Democrat, ran against Frank Merriam, the incumbent Republican governor of California. Warren argued that if Sinclair was elected, all the unemployed in America would come to California to take advantage of his offer of a state-funded job. Warren also accused Sinclair of secretly being a Socialist. Merriam won the election, but the vote was close and party bosses began looking for a new candidate to run in the next election. Their attention focused on Warren, who was a popular district attorney with a handsome family.

Attorney General Warren. Warren needed a state-wide political office to raise his political profile before he ran for Governor, so he decided to run for Attorney General of California. That job would give him the authority to investigate crime anywhere in California, leadership of the state and local police and sheriffs, and state-wide name recognition that would help his run for Governor of California. Warren didn't want to challenge the incumbent Attorney General, so they met privately and he asked Attorney General Webb to let him know when he was ready to retire. When the call came, Warren announced his candidacy on February 17, 1937. During his campaign, Warren learned his father had been murdered, so he sent a team to investigate. [255] No suspect was ever prosecuted, however.

Candidates in California could register for more than one party at that time, so Warren ran on the Republican, Progressive, and Democratic tickets for attorney general. He won all three nominations and was elected Attorney General of California. Warren quickly opened an investigation into allegations the former governor had sold pardons to the highest bidder. After a few months Warren was a favorite to run for Governor of California. To raise his political profile further, Warren attacked dog racing tracks and gambling ships anchored off the coast of Southern California. During the winter of 1939, Warren's mother fell unconscious outside a beauty shop and died in an Oakland hospital. [256] In spite of these family tragedies, Warren worked hard to make California safe for all citizens.

Warren was in Oakland on December 7, 1941, when the Japanese Navy bombed Pearl Harbor and sank a majority of the U.S. Pacific Fleet. Soon after the attack, Attorney General Warren joined California Governor Olson, urging people to stay calm and prepare for an attack by Japan on the U.S. West Coast. Warren was concerned about spying and sabotage by ethnic Japanese, German, and Italian immigrants. Anger increased in 1942 against Japanese Americans after a report noted that Japanese Americans in Hawaii had supplied secret information to the Japanese Navy about the location and movements of U.S. ships prior to the surprise attack on Pearl Harbor. Calls for Japanese Americans to be interred increased and they were placed in concentration camps by the U.S. government for the duration of the war. The internment was ordered by Franklin D. Roosevelt by Executive Order 9066. [257]

Governor Warren. As the state's most prominent Republican, Attorney General Warren had a good chance to become governor in the next election. He announced his candidacy on April 9, 1942, running as a Republican against Democrat Olson. [258] Warren organized his campaign around a record of fighting crime and the corruption of the Olson administration, which had been selling pardons. Warren loved campaigning and speaking on issues of the day. He developed a political machine that collected names and information about his supporters and used his photogenic family in the campaign, having their pictures published regularly in California papers. Warren also sent out three million pictures of his family to voters and easily won the election for Governor of California.

In Warren's inaugural address, he made a commitment to nonpartisanship, lower taxes, and support for the American war effort. He also wanted better health care for Californians, more money for education, and crime prevention rather than punishment of criminals. Warren said he wanted to help every man, woman, and child in California have a better life. He reduced taxes but kept them high enough to fund his favorite programs. Wilson found money for state universities, new prisons, social welfare for the poor, and a "rainy day" fund for emergencies because state revenue increased during the war due to a growing economy.

By the end of his first term as Governor of California, the national press was beginning to discover Warren and his attractive family and never lost interest in him. Warren appeared on the cover of *Time* in January 1944 when the newsmagazine began printing in California. [259] The article inside suggested Warren was destined for national office. However, FDR was running for a fourth term to finish the war, despite his failing health, and Warren didn't want to run against a popular president. Warren avoided joining Dewey as vice president because he didn't want to lose the election. He delivered a key-note address at the Republican Convention and campaigned for Dewey, but FDR won all but twelve states in the 1944 presidential election.

On May 7, 1945, Germany surrendered and World War II was nearly over. Victory came at a terrible price in lives and treasure but ended the Great Depression and made California prosperous. The state gained over eight hundred thousand new residents after the war, many settling in the suburbs of San Francisco, Los Angeles, and San Diego to raise families and work in the thriving California economy. They bought homes and cars, and the state constructed roads for them. Warren ran for a second term as Governor of California and won both the Republican and Democratic votes by wide margins. He was now the unquestioned political leader of California, combining financial prudence with generous support for education and health care.

Ambitious California Republicans looked to Warren for help, including a young Navy veteran named Richard Nixon. Although both men became important national figures, they had different personalities and didn't like each other. Warren was open and friendly while Nixon was closed and mistrustful. Nixon asked for an endorsement, but Warren refused. Despite the refusal, Nixon defeated Jerry Voorhis following debates that Nixon won.

Before the 1948 Republican Convention, Warren was mentioned as a possible presidential candidate by a few party leaders. He went to the convention hoping for a deadlock that would make him the compromise candidate. The plan didn't work because Dewey collected so many votes on the first ballot it was clear he would be the Republican nominee. Warren campaigned vigorously for Dewey and attracted large crowds. The Republicans believed they would win against President Truman but didn't campaign effectively, while Truman worked hard and labeled Republicans the "do nothing" Congress. Truman won because the Republican vote was divided between Dewey and Strom Thurmond, a Southern senator who ran on a third-party ticket.

The Communist Menace. Soon after the war, Americans began to feel threatened by communism at home and abroad. Communist China and Russia were hostile to the U.S. and American officials were concerned that communists had infiltrated the U.S. administration and were spying for the Russians and Chinese. American patriots decided every American should take an oath of loyalty to the U.S. and if they refused, that was evidence they were sympathetic to communism. In California, state Senator Jack Tenney believed that communist subversives had infiltrated the University of California, Berkeley and wanted faculty and staff to swear allegiance to the U.S. Gordon Sproul, the President of Berkeley, defended the University, saying there were no communists on campus.

To defuse the issue, President Sproul proposed requiring all employees of the University to sign an oath rejecting communism to remain employed by the University. [260] The Board of Regents approved the oath and required that all staff and faculty sign it. However, some members of the university faculty believed requiring an oath infringed their academic freedom and was a challenge to tenure, so they refused to sign. Sproul was caught between his liberal faculty and conservative regents. With a small number of university faculty opposing the oath and the Board of Regents insisting on it, the Berkeley oath became a national issue of loyalty and anti-communism. To resolve the problem, two members of the Board of Regents asked Sproul to get Governor Earl Warren involved.

Warren hesitated to tackle the issue because it could turn into a political disaster if handled badly. He finally decided to attend a Board of Regents' meeting in January 1950, and publicly said that the oath required of university staff and faculty was different from the oath other state employees were required to take, and he believed the loyalty oath singled out faculty members for suspicion. Warren also argued that requiring them to sign a loyalty oath was inconsistent with the faculty's civil rights. He tried to calm emotions by stating that he was an alumnus of the University of California, Berkeley, three of his children were attending the university, and two more would attend soon. Warren said he would not let his children be taught by a communist faculty and did not believe any faculty members at Berkeley were communists.

At the next regents' meeting, there was an emotional debate over the oath, and when a vote was taken, it was tied, meaning the faculty would be required to take the oath or be fired. Warren and Sproul began looking for a way out of the impasse. The issue became even more incendiary after the Korean War began because American troops were now actively fighting Asian communists. The problem was solved when a regent resigned and Warren was able to appoint a new liberal regent who voted to reject the loyalty oath. The loyalty oath issue faded away and Warren avoided a political disaster.

He ran for reelection as Governor of California by promising to be nonpartisan, and arguing that he had added twenty thousand new classrooms and teachers, improved health care, created over a million new jobs, improved roads, and supported the construction of more than six hundred thousand new homes in California. He also voiced support for minority civil rights and attacked his opponent, Jimmy Roosevelt, as a rich man who knew little about ordinary working people. Warren was the first person to win a third term as governor of California when he was reelected. [261]

He attended the 1952 Republican National Convention in Chicago with the hope of gaining the nomination for president. At the convention, Eisenhower and Taft were competing for the nomination, while Warren waited in the wings, hoping for a deadlock so he could be the compromise candidate. Richard Nixon, working behind the scenes, persuaded a number of California delegates to support Eisenhower's nomination, and those votes were enough to put Eisenhower over the top and avoid a deadlocked convention. Because of his help for Eisenhower during the nominating process, Warren felt Nixon had the inside track to be selected as vice president, so he didn't attend the meeting where it was decided. Eisenhower and Nixon formed a strong team and easily won the 1952 election. However, Eisenhower viewed Warren as a threat in the next election.

Chief Justice Warren. Eisenhower wanted to eliminate Warren as a rival for the next presidential election, so he offered him a cabinet post, with the confidential understanding that Eisenhower would nominate Warren to the United States Supreme Court when a vacancy occurred. Warren accepted the deal and Chief Justice Fred Vinson died soon after. True to his word, Eisenhower named Warren Chief Justice of the Supreme Court to remove him from politics. [262] Warren left California for a very different life in Washington as Chief Justice. As Governor, Warren administered a massive bureaucracy, managed a billion-dollar budget, and oversaw the welfare of millions of Californians. As Chief Justice of the U.S. Supreme Court, he employed one government secretary, three law clerks, messengers, security guards, and his own personal secretary. And Warren was one of nine Justices who each had a vote and jointly decided cases. Most members of the Court had been nominated by Democrats during the administrations of FDR and Truman. Earl Warren and Harold Burton were the only Justices appointed by a Republican president.

Warren joined four of the brightest and most assertive Justices who ever served on the Supreme Court: William O. Douglas, Hugo L. Black, Robert H. Jackson, and Felix Frankfurter. The main division within the Court was between judicial activists and those advocating judicial restraint. Jackson and Frankfurter were for judicial restraint, while Douglas and Black believed the Court should break new legal ground and not be bound by precedent or the plain text of the Constitution. It was not clear which camp Warren would join when he took the oath of office on October 5, 1953. He met Justice Black, the senior member of the Court first, and Black introduced Warren to the other Justices. Warren immediately began making friends and bringing a more collegial tone to Court deliberations, although he moved slowly to forge alliances. Shortly after Warren took office, one of the most contentious civil rights cases in a century came before the Court: racial segregation in American schools.

Brown v. Board of Education of Topeka. The Declaration of Independence states that all men are created equal, but a disconnect had developed between the ideals of the Constitution and the reality of how America treated Black school children. History and legal precedent suggested that school segregation would continue for generations because the Supreme Court had declared that separate but equal schools for Blacks were constitutional. Thurgood Marshall, Charles Houston, and the NAACP went looking for cases to bring before the Supreme Court to show that separate but equal schooling for Black children was harmful to their development and therefore, unconstitutional.

Thurgood Marshall found appropriate cases in Kansas, South Carolina, Virginia, Delaware, and the District of Columbia, and he combined these cases into a single cause of action titled *Brown v. Board of Education of Topeka*. [263] The issue in these cases was whether it was constitutional to deny admission of Black children to white schools based on race alone. Lower federal courts had followed *Plessy v. Ferguson* and ruled that racially segregated public schools were constitutional so long as they were truly equal. When *Brown v. Board of Education of Topeka* reached the Supreme Court, Warren opened deliberations by saying it was time to face the issue of racial segregation directly. He also argued that if the Court supported continued racial segregation of America's schools, it was embracing white racial superiority. Justice Black would normally have spoken next, but he was absent dealing with a family matter, so he had sent word he would vote to overturn racial segregation in public schools. Reed came next, saying segregation was based on racial differences, not inferiority. Frankfurter followed, arguing that racial segregation was constitutional so long as school facilities were equal. Douglas reported he would vote for the end of racial segregation and Jackson agreed that ending racial segregation was the right thing to do. Burton, Clark, and Minton also voted to end racial segregation.

Warren now had a seven to two majority in favor of desegregating public schools, but he wanted a unanimous ruling if possible, so he suggested they wait and take a formal vote. He had two reasons for postponing the vote: Warren was not yet confirmed by the Senate, and if he voted to end racial segregation, Southern Senators would likely reject his nomination to the Court; and, he wanted to persuade all nine Justices to end racial segregation, because he felt the decision needed unanimous support to stand against Southern opposition. Warren scheduled a series of lunches with each Justice, personally supported junior Justices who were not firm in their views, and worked to convince Reed and Frankfurter to switch their votes. He even invited his colleagues to a duck and pheasant dinner at his Washington home.

At their weekly conferences, Warren steered the discussion toward how to draft an opinion that would be acceptable to the public rather than moving to take a formal vote on *Brown*. Eisenhower wanted to avoid government intervention in race relations and shared his attitude with Warren; however, he ignored Eisenhower and went forward with his plan to desegregate American schools.

After Warren was confirmed by the Senate in March of 1954, he scheduled *Brown v. Board of Education of Topeka* for a formal vote, because he had a majority in favor of overturning racial segregation and he believed the opinion could be unanimous if it was carefully worded. His colleagues urged Warren to write the opinion, feeling it would carry more authority if drafted by the Chief Justice himself. Warren agreed and opened his written opinion with a factual summary of the five cases. Next, he traced the history of the Fourteenth Amendment and argued that separate but equal schools were inconsistent with the intent of the Fourteenth Amendment. Warren pointed out that widespread free public education had not been available when the original concept of separate but equal was proposed after the Civil War. He concluded the opinion in *Brown* by stating that separate educational facilities for Black children violated the Equal Protection Clause of the Fourteenth Amendment and was therefore unconstitutional.

Warren also wrote in his opinion that segregated educational facilities based on race created a feeling of inferiority among Black students that harmed their intellectual and personal growth. He based the Supreme Court decision on social science rather than legal precedent, giving opponents ammunition to attack the ruling and delay school desegregation. Jackson and Frankfurter were impressed with Warren's arguments and joined in a unanimous decision overturning school segregation. However, the fight over racial segregation in public schools was far from over, just because the Supreme Court had ruled it was unconstitutional.

The basic flaw in *Brown v. Board of Education of Topeka* was first articulated by James Reston, a reporter for the *New York Times*. He pointed out that *Brown* used social science to support its conclusions rather than legal precedent and wrote that the decision sounded more like an article on sociology than a Supreme Court opinion. Southern opponents seized on the idea that the Court's decision was based on social science rather than legal precedent to attack the ruling in Congress and the press. Eisenhower said the Supreme Court has spoken and he was bound to uphold its decisions--hardly a ringing endorsement of the Court's opinion.

Southern legislators began a resistance campaign, vowing not to send white children to Black schools or allow Black children into white schools. State and local authorities in the South tried to delay and modify the ruling to avoid integrating their schools. To counter this resistance, the Supreme Court issued a second decision ordering that integration be carried out "with all deliberate speed." *Brown II* moved the issue from Southern streets and legislatures into federal district courts. Federal judges faced hostile opposition when they demanded compliance with the Supreme Court's decision in *Brown v. Board of Education of Topeka,* and they had difficulty enforcing their rulings in Southern states.

Earl Warren became internationally famous because of his decision in *Brown*, and his ambition to run for president grew, especially after Eisenhower suggested he might not seek a second term. Warren and his old rival Richard Nixon would be competitors for the Republican nomination. Nixon believed he was the natural choice of the Republican party to succeed Eisenhower because he had been vice president and Warren was already Chief Justice of the Supreme Court. The issue became critical when Eisenhower suffered a mild heart attack and Republican leaders feared he might not be able to serve a second term. Warren told a journalist he would consider running for president to keep Nixon out of the office, but Eisenhower recovered and decided to run again.

In 1955, the Court was faced with the emotionally explosive issue of inter-racial marriage between a Chinese man and a white woman. The couple lived in Virginia but traveled to North Carolina to marry because interracial unions were legal in that state. When they returned to Virginia, the couple argued that the federal Equal Protection Clause prevented Virginia from prosecuting them for marrying. However, the Virginia Supreme Court ordered the couple to dissolve their marriage because it was against state law. The couple appealed to the U.S. Supreme Court, but the Justices refused to hear the case. Warren was furious with his colleagues for their cowardice but was powerless to do anything about it because the votes to accept the case were not available. The issue of minority civil rights was not going away, however.

In December 1955, Rosa Parks was tired after a long day at work and refused to give up her seat to a white passenger on a bus in segregated Montgomery, Alabama. She was promptly arrested, and Martin Luther King, Jr. organized a boycott of the Montgomery bus company, beginning direct political action to integrate Montgomery buses. Southern politicians attacked the Supreme Court for meddling in state affairs and blamed Warren for the Montgomery bus boycott. The Warren Court was attacked from all sides in the South. A case involving an avowed communist made matters worse for Warren and the Supreme Court.

Pennsylvania v. Nelson. [264] Hostility toward the Warren Court increased after it heard the case of a communist who was convicted of subversion in a state court. The Supreme Court ruled that state law was preempted by the Smith Act, concluding that only the federal government had jurisdiction to try cases of subversion, and it overturned the state court conviction of the communist. The nation was outraged when the Supreme Court released an admitted communist who had been sentenced to twenty years in prison by a state court. Congress tried to pass a bill to set aside the decision in *Nelson*, but the attempt failed. Calls for Warren to be impeached for treason and removed from the bench increased, and Eisenhower refused to defend the Supreme Court decision because he was seeking reelection and the *Nelson* opinion was unpopular. During his campaign, Eisenhower had the opportunity to nominate another Justice to the Supreme Court. He told the selection committee to find a conservative Catholic with judicial experience. The committee recommended William J. Brennan, Jr., Chief Justice of the New Jersey Supreme Court. Brennan was nominated by Eisenhower and quickly confirmed by the Senate.

Chief Justice Warren tried to maintain friendly relations among the Justices, but Justice Frankfurter felt Warren was not intellectually distinguished enough to be Chief Justice and privately made it clear he thought Warren was a fool. Frankfurter believed he could impose his superior intellect on the other Justices and lead the Court in spite of Warren being Chief Justice and having considerable political experience. However, Warren adroitly isolated Frankfurter and built coalitions among other Justices by his good cheer, hard work, and fairness. Warren never lost control of the Court, even when it was under attack by Southern politicians from without and Frankfurter within.

Little Rock Resistance. On July 17, 1957, at a news briefing, Eisenhower said, "I can't imagine any set of circumstances that would ever induce me to send federal troops into any area to enforce the orders of a federal court." Soon after, the governor of Arkansas decided to test the president's will. The school board in Little Rock had tried to comply with the Court's ruling in *Brown* by developing a plan to integrate schools in the city. Although residents didn't like the decision, they expected to allow the plan to proceed. However, Arkansas Governor Faubus asked the legislature to pass laws blocking integration of all the state's schools, arguing that the admission of nine Black students into Little Rock's Central High School would threaten the state's safety. He mobilized the Arkansas National Guard to turn the Black students away when they tried to enter the high school to attend classes.

Eisenhower didn't care much about racial segregation, but he couldn't let a state governor defy a federal court order, so he was forced to respond. Eisenhower tried to negotiate a solution and force Faubus to acknowledge that *Brown* was the law of the land. But Faubus refused, withdrew the National Guard, and turned the city over to an angry mob that blocked Black children from entering Little Rock high school. Eisenhower urged the citizens of Little Rock to end their resistance and allow law and order to prevail, but the mob ignored him. Eisenhower had no choice but to order federal troops to intervene by sending one thousand paratroopers from the 101st Airborne Division to the city to restore order. The mob backed down and nine Black students were escorted into classrooms and guarded by federal paratroopers while they studied. Integration was achieved at the point of a gun in America. However, the Arkansas governor was not through resisting desegregation.

Cooper v. Aaron. [265] Arkansas filed suit in the Eastern District of Arkansas, asking for suspension of the plan to integrate the Little Rock school system. The case came before the Supreme Court and all nine Justices held that Arkansas officials must carry out federal court orders under the Supremacy Clause of Article VI of the Constitution. The Court asserted its power in *Cooper* but lost the support of Congress and much of the nation in the process. A clear sign that public support for Warren's Supreme Court was fading occurred when Judge Learned Hand delivered the Oliver Wendell Holmes Lecture at Harvard University in 1958. Hand expressed concern with Supreme Court activism—saying he didn't believe nine "Platonic Guardians" on the U.S. Supreme Court should rule America.

Hand's criticism encouraged Southern Senators to introduce a bill limiting the power of the Supreme Court. When the bill came up for a vote, Learned Hand refused to testify in favor of the act, and Majority Leader Lyndon Johnson was able to defeat the bill. Black activists pushed further by initiating sit-ins throughout the South to protest racial segregation.

Lunch Counter Sit-Ins. On February 1, 1960, four young Black men entered a Woolworth store in Greensboro, North Carolina, and sat at the lunch counter waiting to be served. They were ignored and walked out when the counter closed at five. However, they returned with sixteen other classmates the next day and sat down, waiting for service. Within weeks, sit-ins at lunch counters were being staged all across the South. After a few months, a Woolworth store in Greensboro, North Carolina, served two Black waitresses who worked there and lunch counters were soon integrated throughout America.

The Kennedy-Nixon presidential election of 1960 triggered a realignment of Black voters within the Democratic Party, and Black voters in battleground states helped Kennedy defeat Nixon by a narrow margin. Unlike Eisenhower, President Kennedy vigorously supported federal enforcement of civil rights in America. As the Kennedy administration consistently supported civil rights in America, conservatives launched a campaign to impeach Warren.

Impeach Warren. In 1961, the John Birch Society initiated a publicity campaign to drive Warren from the Court. Billboards calling for his impeachment were erected across the country. There was only modest public support for impeaching Warren outside the South, but the John Birch Society was the public face of opposition directed against the Supreme Court and Chief Justice Warren. Eisenhower had been passive in his support of Supreme Court decisions, but Kennedy actively enforced Court rulings concerning desegregation and this increased resentment against Warren. Meanwhile, the Supreme Court began to expand criminal defendants' civil rights.

Gideon v. Wainwright. [266] Gideon was charged with felony breaking and entering and appeared in court without an attorney because he was too poor to afford one. He asked the Florida court to appoint an attorney for him, but the judge refused because the right to a public defender only existed for capital cases in Florida. Gideon was found guilty and sentenced to five years in prison. Civil rights attorneys filed a habeas corpus petition in the Florida Supreme Court, arguing that the refusal to appoint an attorney to defend Gideon violated his right to counsel. The Florida Supreme Court disagreed, so his attorneys appealed to the U.S. Supreme Court. In a unanimous opinion, Justice Black held that the U.S. Constitution requires state courts to appoint attorneys for all criminal defendants if they cannot afford one. Gideon was tried again with representation and was acquitted. That same year a lone gunman shot President Kennedy in Dallas.

The Warren Commission. On November 22, 1963, the Justices were discussing whether the right to vote fell within the Equal Protection Clause of the Fourteenth Amendment when there was a knock on the door, and a note was handed to Warren saying Kennedy had been shot and was dying. Newly elevated President Lyndon Johnson asked Warren to form a Commission to investigate the assassination. The Warren Commission hired a special counsel, reviewed the FBI investigation, and initiated an independent review of the facts. The FBI learned about the commission's deliberations because Gerald Ford leaked them to Hoover.

The Warren Commission investigated several explosive rumors, including that Oswald had been an undercover agent for the FBI, and more than one gunman was involved in the shooting. The first witness was Marina Oswald, widow of the shooter. She identified the rifle as belonging to her husband, described his anger, his tendency to violence, and his alienation from society. She believed her husband had shot Kennedy. All testimony was taken behind closed doors but was subjected to intense scrutiny by the press. Another witness, Arthur Rowland, was standing below the Texas Book Depository and saw a man in a window holding a gun. He didn't report the sighting to police, however.

After extensive investigation, the Warren Commission concluded that Oswald acted alone, although, in response to pressure from commission members Russell and Ford, the report stated that the Commission found no evidence that either Lee Harvey Oswald or Jack Ruby was part of a domestic or foreign conspiracy to assassinate President Kennedy, leaving open the possibility that new evidence might change that conclusion. The Commission delivered its report to President Johnson on September 24, 1964, and the initial public reaction was positive. The FBI never accepted the theory that a single bullet had killed Kennedy and wounded Connally, and attitudes toward the Warren report became more skeptical for a while, although today, the Warren Commission's findings are generally accepted as accurate. The next case before the Warren Court involved voting districts in minority areas of Alabama.

Reynolds v. Sims. [267] Sims filed a case alleging that Alabama had created large population differences among various electoral districts to disenfranchise Black voters. Sims showed that Jefferson County, which contained a large minority population, had forty-one times as many voters as other districts in the state. The Supreme Court held that the Equal Protection Clause of the Fourteenth Amendment requires roughly equal populations in each voting district so all votes count. In an eight-to-one decision, Warren wrote that the right to representation is the foundation of America's political system, and state voting districts have to be apportioned in an "honest and good faith" way to create districts that are nearly equal in population. *Reynolds* triggered a battle over the right of all citizens to have their vote count. The next important case before the Warren Court involved the definition of libel.

New York Times Company v. Sullivan. [268] The *New York Times* published an ad asking for contributions to pay for the legal defense of Martin Luther King, Jr. The ad contained factual errors and Sullivan, the City of Birmingham Public Safety Commissioner, asked the *Times* for a formal retraction because he alleged his subordinates had been unfairly criticized. By asking for a retraction, Sullivan set the stage for a libel suit. The *Times* refused to retract the ad and Sullivan filed suit in Alabama state court. An Alabama jury awarded Sullivan $500,000 in damages and the state Supreme Court affirmed the verdict. The *Times* appealed to the U.S. Supreme Court. In a unanimous decision, Justice Brennan wrote that to prove libel, a plaintiff must show a defendant knew a statement was false or was reckless in deciding to publish the information without investigating whether the information was accurate. Moreover, when the statement involves a public figure, the Court said that a plaintiff must show the statement was made with knowledge of its falsity or in reckless disregard for its falsity to prove libel. In other words, the defendant must have published the information with "actual malice," a nearly impossible standard to meet in proving libel. Next the Court expanded the rights of criminal defendants even further.

Miranda v. Arizona. [269] *Miranda* was a consolidation of four cases where defendants had confessed during police interrogation without being told they had a right to remain silent. In a 5-4 decision, Warren ruled that the Fifth Amendment requires law enforcement officials to advise suspects of their right to remain silent and to have an attorney with them during interrogation when they are in police custody. He concluded that a suspect must be warned of his right to remain silent and have an attorney present during interrogation, and if a defendant cannot afford an attorney, he must be told that one will be appointed for him. Finally, Warren held that all evidence obtained as a result of interrogation without this warning cannot be used at trial. The dissent argued that the Fifth Amendment should not be so strictly interpreted and there was no legal precedent requiring police officers to inform a suspect of his rights.

Warren's Retirement. Warren decided to retire from the Court to give President Johnson the opportunity to nominate a liberal Justice before the next election. Johnson nominated Justice Abe Fortas as Chief Justice and named Homer Thornberry to fill the vacancy left by Fortas. When Fortas testified before the Senate, the hearing was a disaster. Then it was discovered his old firm had given him $15,000, so the Senate voted against Fortas' confirmation as Chief Justice. Warren was now in a difficult spot because he could hardly refuse to resign at this late date. Nixon was elected president and his administration attacked Justice Fortas for signing a lifetime contract with a criminal. When Warren showed Fortas the contract he had signed, Fortas resigned from the Supreme Court. President Nixon paid personal tribute to Warren's long service in 1969, and his departure from the Court was a national event, celebrated before the Lincoln Memorial on the National Mall. Warren decided to write a memoir of his life in the form of a short essay entitled *A Republic, If You Can Keep It.*

By 1973, Warren's health was failing and in January 1974, he was hospitalized in Los Angeles, treated, and released. In July of 1974, Warren was again hospitalized and died on July 9, 1974, only hours after the Supreme Court forced President Nixon to turn over a secret recording discussing the Watergate burglary, which eventually led to his resignation as president.

John Fitzgerald Kennedy

John Kennedy was born May 29, 1917, in Brookline, Massachusetts. [270] His father, Joe Kennedy, became wealthy trading stocks and selling liquor after prohibition ended in 1933. The family moved to New York from Boston, hoping to escape the stigma of being Irish Catholic. John enrolled in private Riverdale Country Day School, Canterbury School, and then Choate for his early education but developed an unknown illness that slowed his growth and weight gain. [271] John's grades were uneven in prep school—good in English and history but poor in Latin and French. His grades didn't really matter because John Kennedy was assured admittance to Harvard College since Joe Kennedy, Sr. was a prominent alumnus, and Joe, Jr. was already attending the school.

John didn't take his academic work at Harvard seriously because he was too busy chasing girls. His honors thesis discussed the origins of Britain's appeasement of the Nazis prior to World War II, and he turned the thesis into a book titled *Why England Slept*. In 1937, President Roosevelt appointed Joe Kennedy ambassador to England, the most prestigious diplomatic post in the U.S. State Department. [272] The appointment gave the Kennedys a chance to participate in British high society. The family was vacationing in Southern France when Germany invaded Poland, starting World War II. John asked his father to pull political strings so he could join the Office of Naval Intelligence. He was assigned to the Foreign Intelligence Branch of ONI in Washington, D.C.

Kennedy began an affair with Inga Arvad, a Danish blond whom Hitler described as "a perfect example of Nordic beauty." [273] Joe and Rose were unhappy with the relationship because they didn't want one of their sons marrying a divorcee. There were also concerns she might be a German spy, so the navy sent John to South Carolina to get him away from Inga. While in South Carolina, Kennedy decided he wanted to captain a PT boat, so he asked his father to get him into the program. Joe pressured the navy to admit John into the program but asked them to make him an instructor so he would stay in the U.S. However, Kennedy asked his grandfather, Honey Fitz, to have him transferred to the South Pacific near the Solomon Islands. Kennedy spent seventeen months in combat on his PT boat and became a hero after his boat was sunk by a Japanese destroyer.

PT 109. Kennedy was not impressed with PT boats once he was involved in combat because they were easy to detect speeding through the water, too lightly armed to do much damage to a Japanese destroyer, and PT boat attacks were poorly coordinated. Kennedy's boat was cut in half by a Japanese destroyer while on patrol. He was criticized later for having only one motor running at the time because that made escape from an oncoming destroyer nearly impossible. Kennedy and five other crew members clung to the damaged hull for several hours before PT 109 began sinking. Kennedy organized the men into two groups, and they swam to a small island in about five hours. Kennedy then swam to a larger island nearby and found a canoe, a fifty-gallon barrel of water, some crackers, and local natives who guided Kennedy and his surviving crew to an army base where they were given medical attention. [274]

The navy made heroes of Kennedy and his crew for the hardships they endured and the courage of their rescue. Then they sent Kennedy home because he had a stomach ulcer. The Mayo Clinic, where he was medically evaluated, recommended surgery to relieve pain in his spine. Kennedy was declared unfit for service and retired from the navy on March 1, 1945. After the war, Kennedy began thinking about what he wanted to do with his life. Politics was attractive because his grandfather, Honey Fitz, had good connections and his father had the money to finance his campaigns. Joe Kennedy recommended John run for a seat in the House of Representatives to start his political career. Joe persuaded James Michael Curley to vacate his House seat and run for mayor of Boston so his son could campaign for that seat immediately. Kennedy's main advantages during the election were his grandfather's political connections, his father's wealth, and his status as a war hero. The deciding factor in the race was Joe Kennedy's money; he spent over three hundred thousand dollars on Kennedy's first political campaign.

During the general election, Kennedy began speaking about the threat from the Soviet Union and won more than seventy percent of the votes in his Congressional district. [275] He always thought of the House seat as a springboard to the Senate but worked hard while he was in the House of Representatives to avoid appearing too ambitious. Kennedy's father hired reliable aides to help him deal with constituent queries and organized a speaking campaign to raise John's profile nationally. Kennedy was able to hire a large competent staff because his father paid for everything. Joe also pressured the U.S. Chamber of Commerce to name John Kennedy one of the ten outstanding young men of 1946, and planted favorable articles about him in the *New York Times*, the *Boston Globe*, and other major papers. Kennedy avoided Catholic issues while he was a Representative, even though his district was heavily Catholic, because he feared his religion could be a negative factor when he ran for the Senate. He developed a reputation as a womanizer and many politicians in Washington considered him a playboy rather than a serious member of the House.

Kennedy concentrated on being anti-communist, and his timing was good because concern about the Soviet Union was growing, and the country worried about the communist challenge. Events in Europe seemed to favor the Soviet Union, and the Chinese Communists were winning against the Nationalists in China. The Korean War started badly because the North Korean Army was larger and better trained than the South Korean military. After the U.S. and other nations sent soldiers to Korea to drive the North Korean Army back to the Chinese border, the war went well for a while. When U.N troops approached China, several hundred thousand Chinese soldiers staged a surprise attack and drove the United Nations forces back to the 38th parallel, where the war developed into a stalemate. [276]

Kennedy decided to run for the Senate against Henry Cabot Lodge and the race was again decided by his father's money. Joe Kennedy even loaned five hundred thousand dollars to John J. Fox, owner of the *Boston Post*, which promptly endorsed John Kennedy two weeks before the election. Kennedy's brother, Robert, worked long hours as campaign manager to keep things organized, get out the vote, and make sure nothing bad happened during the campaign. John Kennedy won by a margin of 51.5 percent to 48.5 percent, despite Eisenhower winning Massachusetts by two hundred thousand votes over Stevenson. [277] During the Senate campaign, the major issues involved relations with the Soviet Union, Communist China, and the Korean War. Kennedy hired Ted Sorenson to advise him because he needed to become more liberal if he wanted to win a Senate seat. After being elected, Kennedy concentrated on helping Massachusetts grow economically by expanding defense manufacturing in the state. He also suggested America increase foreign aid to Indochina but make the aid contingent on the French giving more freedom to the peoples of Vietnam.

Marriage to Jacqueline Bouvier. Kennedy was advised he needed a wife to project an image of a family man rather than a womanizer. He was attracted to Jacqueline Bouvier because she was young, pretty, bright, socially prominent, and Catholic. Kennedy's campaign for the Senate interfered with their courtship, and his casual attitude toward dating bothered Jackie, but the most difficult barrier might have been rumors of Kennedy's womanizing. However, that trait seemed to make Kennedy more attractive to Jackie. They were married on September 12, 1953, at St. Mary's Roman Catholic Church in Newport, Rhode Island, in a lavish wedding attended by America's rich and famous. [278] The reception was held for two hundred guests on the terrace of her stepfather, Hugh Auchincloss, on his three-hundred-acre estate. John and Jackie spent their honeymoon in Acapulco.

Marital tensions appeared almost immediately, because Kennedy was rarely home and he left Jackie alone at parties while he went off with other women. Kennedy's back pain also caused friction because he was irritable a good deal of the time. He was continuing to take steroids for Addison's disease (which was never disclosed to the public), and X-rays showed his fifth lumbar vertebra had collapsed, causing him increased pain. Surgeons operated on Kennedy and inserted a metal plate to stabilize his lumbar spine, but the surgery was only moderately successful. Kennedy contracted a urinary tract infection after the surgery because steroids had suppressed his immune system. He went to Florida to recuperate, where his surgery created public sympathy when it was disclosed.

While Kennedy was recovering from surgery, he published *Profiles in Courage*, a book describing the careers of eight senators, including John Quincy Adams, Daniel Webster, Thomas Hart Benton,

Sam Houston, Edmond G. Ross, Lucius Lamar, George W. Norris, and Robert Taft. [279] In the book, Kennedy argued that each Senator had shown uncommon courage by risking his career to vote for unpopular issues. Published in 1956, the book was a national best-seller and raised Kennedy's political prominence even further. Critics asked where he found the time to write a book while recovering from back surgery? The answer was that Ted Sorenson and Professor Jules Davids of Georgetown University gathered research materials and drafted most of the chapters for him. At best the book was a joint effort rather than Kennedy's work alone.

Because Kennedy was considering a campaign for President, his health problems were kept secret. His back pain continued because the steroids he was taking weakened his bones and caused his spine to collapse. Kennedy began campaigning for the Democratic presidential nomination in 1956, contacting party leaders and members of Congress to develop a plan to win southern support for his election. He avoided the issue of school desegregation as much as possible because race relations were a sensitive issue in the Democratic Party at that time, especially in the South. Kennedy decided he had to support some Black civil rights issues if he wanted to win the nomination, but he was concerned that strong support for civil rights might damage his chances among South Democratic voters. Consequently, Kennedy tried to do no more than was absolutely necessary to placate the Black community and win the nomination.

Kennedy believed he would be better off stressing economic issues and national security during the 1960 presidential campaign rather than civil rights. He accused the Eisenhower Administration of allowing a missile gap to develop between the U.S. and the Soviets, claiming America was falling behind in missile technology. [280] Although the polls showed most Americans had a positive view of Kennedy in 1959, the family recognized there were formidable obstacles to winning the Democratic nomination, and they knew he would face a tough campaign against Richard Nixon in the fall. Kennedy's main liabilities were liberal opposition to his voting record and his Catholic religion.

Many liberal Democrats believed Kennedy was a rich playboy who had done little to further Black civil rights or support working-class Americans. Kennedy believed foreign relations and the arms race with Moscow were better issues to emphasize during his campaign for the Democratic nomination. At that time, there were only sixteen state primaries, but Kennedy decided he needed to win several of them to impress state party leaders if he hoped to be nominated at the Democratic Convention. Most Democratic leaders believed Nixon would beat Kennedy in the 1960 campaign, so he had to win several primaries in Protestant states to convince them that he would be a viable candidate in the general election.

Candidate Kennedy. His main competitors for the Democratic presidential nomination were Hubert H. Humphrey and Lyndon B. Johnson. Kennedy believed Humphrey was too liberal to win the nomination and thought Johnson was the more competitive candidate. New Hampshire was the first test of whether Kennedy could get Protestants to vote for him. He won the state with eight-five percent of the vote. Since Kennedy was from next-door Massachusetts, that victory was not a good test of his national appeal, however. He ran unopposed in Nebraska and Indiana, so Kennedy needed to win an important contested primary to prove he was a viable candidate. He decided to run in Wisconsin, where Humphrey attacked Kennedy for being a recent convert to farming issues. Kennedy ignored these attacks, stuck to his own issues, and won fifty-six percent of the votes in Wisconsin's primary.

The loss in Wisconsin essentially finished Humphrey's campaign for the presidential nomination. However, Kennedy still had to convince party bosses he could win in mostly Protestant states, so he contested the remaining primaries. Kennedy spent two weeks campaigning in West Virginia and won more than sixty percent of the votes, proving he could win in a Protestant state. He went on to win Maryland with seventy percent of the votes and Oregon with fifty-two percent of the votes. However, Lyndon Johnson was still a major threat to Kennedy's nomination because, at that time, primaries didn't determine who would be nominated at the convention; that decision was up to the Democratic leaders and they could still nominate someone else. At the convention in Los Angeles, Kennedy, Johnson, and Stevenson competed for the nomination. On the first ballot, Kennedy gathered more ballots than Johnson and clinched the nomination when Wyoming cast its votes, giving him two more than he needed to win.

Kennedy immediately began thinking about how his Vice-Presidential selection could help in the general election. Humphrey, Johnson, and Stevenson were all potential candidates, but since the liberal wing of the party would be expected to vote for Kennedy rather than Nixon, the family decided Johnson was likely to be the candidate who would help win the presidency for Kennedy because Johnson was popular in Texas and the South. Johnson accepted the offer to run as vice president because the Democrats wanted to beat Nixon. In his acceptance speech for the Democratic nomination, Kennedy addressed the Catholic issue head-on, saying his decisions as President would not be influenced by his religion. Liberal support for Kennedy was weak, and after the Republicans nominated Nixon and Lodge, opinion polls showed them leading Kennedy and Johnson fifty-three to forty-seven percent. Republican support was stronger for Nixon than Democratic support for Kennedy, and the family needed to do something to change that dynamic.

Republicans accused Kennedy of being influenced by the Catholic Church. To counter that criticism, he organized a group of prominent Protestant ministers in Houston, Texas, and made a speech about Catholicism and public office. Kennedy said state and religion are absolutely separate in America and he intended to keep them that way. He also said religion was a private affair and not relevant to political office. [281] At the end of his presentation, the Protestant ministers gave Kennedy a standing ovation. The Houston speech temporarily suppressed the religious question during the campaign and allowed Kennedy to concentrate on other issues. To counter his relative lack of experience, Kennedy challenged Nixon to a series of debates. Eisenhower advised Nixon to refuse, since he was better known nationally, but Nixon accepted four televised debates. Kennedy believed he won the presidency as a result of his performance in those televised debates. [282]

President Kennedy. Right before the 1960 election, a Gallup poll showed Kennedy's lead over Nixon was under one percent. Although Kennedy won three hundred three electoral votes to Nixon's two hundred nineteen, his margin of victory in the popular vote was less than one hundred twenty thousand votes out of over sixty-eight million cast. Kennedy won because Johnson brought in southern votes, an economic slow-down hurt Nixon, and American voters believed the U.S. was falling behind

Moscow in the arms race. After the election, Kennedy said he was in excellent health and rumors that he suffered from Addison's disease were false, but that claim was not true.

Kennedy asked Allen Dulles to remain as head of the CIA and J. Edgar Hoover to continue as Director of the FBI. During an hour-long personal meeting, Eisenhower was impressed with Kennedy, believing the new President was well informed on national and international issues. Kennedy retained key people who had been with him during his Senate and presidential campaigns, including Sorensen, O'Brien, O'Donnell, Powers, and Salinger. Along with McGeorge Bundy, who became special assistant for national security, this group worked on important issues for Kennedy during his presidency. He named C. Douglas Dillon Secretary of the Treasury, Walter Heller Chairman of the Counsel of Economic Advisers, Robert McNamara Secretary of Defense, and Dean Rusk Secretary of State. [283] Kennedy also needed to decide what to do with Bobby, who wanted to be the U.S. Attorney General. Kennedy finally claimed his father forced him to name his brother as Attorney General to deflect criticism of nepotism, but that claim was false because Kennedy wanted his brother to protect him from legal problems.

Kennedy wanted his inaugural address to instill hope and confidence in America, so he asked Sorenson to draft a patriotic speech and make it short. Kennedy opened his address by mentioning shared national values and promised to pay any price to guarantee the survival of freedom. He pledged to help third-world countries, promised to oppose aggression by communist nations, and invited the Soviet Union to search for common ground and avoid nuclear war. In closing, he said, "Ask not what your country can do for you—ask what you can do for your country." Almost three-quarters of Americans approved of Kennedy after his inaugural address. [284] To maintain his high approval ratings, Kennedy concentrated on foreign issues because the President has more control over foreign affairs.

Kennedy made little progress on civil rights because Southern Democrats opposed any bill giving rights to Black Americans. He did issue an Executive Order establishing the Committee on Equal Employment Opportunity to monitor discrimination in federal hiring. The economy was a major concern of the President because he wanted to avoid a recession during his first term in office. He ordered the federal government to spend more money on roads and bridges to increase employment and stimulate economic activity. To keep his approval ratings high, Kennedy inaugurated weekly televised news conferences that were a hit with the press and public. He also established the Peace Corps to help poor countries meet their needs for skilled labor. Many young Americans volunteered to help less advantaged people in poor countries and the idea was widely approved by the public.

Nuclear war with the Soviet Union was Kennedy's biggest concern. He moved control of all nuclear weapons into the White House so he could make certain some mid-level military commander didn't start a nuclear war without presidential authorization. Kennedy also increased the number of Polaris submarines and Minutemen ballistic missiles in America's inventory to deter a nuclear war. Khrushchev promised to support "wars of liberation" around the world, and in response, Kennedy asked the military to develop counter-insurgency forces, which led to the development of the Green Berets, who were trained to fight limited wars all over the world. [285]

South Vietnam demanded a good deal of Kennedy's attention as President because Eisenhower had promised that America would supply military equipment, financial aid, and advisors to the South

Vietnam government, and Kennedy decided to continue that commitment. He sent Johnson to Vietnam on a fact-finding mission with a letter to the Vietnamese government promising continued financial aid. Johnson urged Kennedy to stand firm in Vietnam and oppose Communism in that country. But Cuba was destined to be a bigger problem for Kennedy than any other country.

The Bay of Pigs. The CIA recommended Kennedy move against Castro because Cuban exiles were already training in Guatemala to invade the island. The CIA wanted to use American troops to invade Cuba, but Kennedy vetoed that idea. The CIA and the U.S. military believed an invasion by Cuban mercenaries would create a general uprising on the island, but the State Department warned Kennedy that the invasion was likely to fail. Kennedy wanted to keep U.S. hands off the invasion as much as possible so failure would not damage his reputation. He insisted that the invasion appear to be an internal uprising rather than a foreign attack by America, but that's not what happened. The Bay of Pigs invasion went wrong from the beginning. [286] Planes tasked with destroying Castro's air force missed most of their targets, so Cuban planes were able to attack the invaders before they reached shore. The CIA also canceled air support promised for the invaders after landing on the beach. To make matters worse, there was no uprising among the civilian population, the Cuban Army was stronger than expected, and surprise was lost before the troops even landed at the Bay of Pigs. Kennedy faced a meeting with Khrushchev in Vienna soon after the fiasco in Cuba, and the Soviet leader was emboldened by the Bay of Pigs defeat.

Soviet Summit. Kennedy and Khrushchev met on June 4, 1961, in Vienna for a face-to-face discussion of U.S.-Soviet relations. Khrushchev told Kennedy the Soviet Union was growing stronger and America would have to live with the fact that Communism would win in the end. Khrushchev battered Kennedy with accusations and said he came to Vienna to compete with Kennedy, not to negotiate. Khrushchev clearly won the first debate, and Kennedy had to decide what to do to counter Soviet aggressiveness. On the second day of the summit, the Soviets threatened to sign a unilateral agreement with East Germany if the Allies didn't agree to participate in a general peace treaty with Germany. [287] Khrushchev also warned that a treaty between the Soviet Union and East Germany would negate prior agreements concerning Germany and Berlin. Kennedy told Khrushchev the U.S. would not accept a change in the status of Berlin under any circumstances.

On June 10, 1961, Khrushchev announced the Soviet Union planned to sign a separate treaty with East Germany that would alter Allied right of access to Berlin. On June 28th Kennedy announced that changing Allied access to Berlin threatened world peace and challenged the Soviet Union to compete economically as a safer alternative. Some military advisers recommended a general U.S. mobilization to counter Soviet threats, while others advised caution. Kennedy wanted a diplomatic solution to the Berlin crisis rather than nuclear war, so in a speech to the nation on July 25, 1961, he tried to strike a balance between negotiation and confrontation. Kennedy said the U.S. would not permit the Soviet Union to overturn its right of access to Berlin, but he was ready to discuss the issue with the Soviet Union at any time. Over the next few weeks, Khrushchev threatened confrontation and hinted at negotiations.

The Berlin Wall. On August 13, 1961, East German forces blocked access from East to West Berlin by building a concrete wall around the Soviet sector of Berlin, closing the border to communist citizens fleeing into West Berlin. [288] Kennedy believed erecting the Berlin Wall signaled the Soviet Union didn't intend to close Allied access to Berlin. Otherwise, why would they erect a wall enclosing East Berlin? Kennedy sent American troops and Vice President Johnson to West Berlin, demonstrating that Allied access to Berlin was still open. Khrushchev invited Drew Person to his summer home and told him: "There isn't going to be a war." Khrushchev also sent a private message to Kennedy that the "storm in Berlin is over." The Soviet Union postponed signing a separate peace treaty with East Germany and allowed the crisis over Berlin to subside for the moment.

Once the pressure on Berlin eased, Kennedy focused on Vietnam as the next likely place where the Soviet Union would bring diplomatic or military pressure against the U.S. He was concerned that communist aggression might produce hostile states in Asia, Africa, and Latin America, which would surround the United States and limit its ability to defend the homeland from attack. To counter that threat, Kennedy continued Eisenhower's strategy of resisting communist military pressure in South Vietnam. His plan was to commit more military "advisors," give covert air support to the South Vietnam Army, and increase financial aid to the South Vietnamese government. But he wanted to avoid publicly acknowledging American involvement in the war. American military commanders believed more was at stake than just South Vietnam; they wanted to halt Russia's "wars of liberation" around the world and South Vietnam appeared to be the best place to stop Soviet advances. [289]

Kennedy resisted committing American ground troops in South Vietnam, believing the communist threat could be controlled by money and advisors alone. He approved planning for the commitment of U.S. ground forces to South Vietnam but didn't want to take such a drastic step unless it was absolutely necessary. After the Bay of Pigs failure, the confrontation with Khrushchev in Vienna, and difficulties over Berlin, Kennedy felt he had little choice but to defend South Vietnam against a communist takeover to prove he was no push-over in international affairs. Kennedy ordered U.S. military forces to help South Vietnam make military, political, and financial decisions concerning the war. However, the South Vietnamese President resisted ceding control over his country's affairs to America and didn't trust the U.S. commitment to continue fighting against the North Vietnamese.

When asked directly during a press conference if American troops were in South Vietnam, Kennedy said "no," even though it was well known over three thousand American "advisors" were helping the South Vietnamese defend themselves and occasionally getting involved in fighting. The press also reported seeing American planes in the skies over Vietnam. Kennedy tried to keep American involvement in Vietnam secret, but that was impossible because of press coverage of the war. John K. Galbraith advised Kennedy to establish a neutral coalition government in South Vietnam and withdraw American troops from the area to avoid being seen as the new colonial power in Asia, but Kennedy ignored that sage advice. He didn't want to withdraw advisors or commit more troops, but at the same time, he didn't want to appear weak on communism. Kennedy eventually decided to continue financial support and advice to the South Vietnamese government but not to commit ground forces to the area. [290]

To bolster U.S. economic growth, Kennedy proposed cutting corporate and personal taxes, but economists worried publicly about the resulting federal deficit. Kennedy felt he needed to cut taxes after the economy grew slowly during 1962 if he was to avoid a recession. The U.S. press continued to report that the situation in South Vietnam was going badly, and these negative reports added pressure on Kennedy to increase America's commitment to South Vietnam. At the same time, the Soviet Union raised tensions in the Cold War by shipping nuclear missiles to Cuba, creating the most dangerous situation of the Kennedy Presidency.

Cuban Missile Crisis. In 1962, because Khrushchev believed the U.S. was planning to invade Cuba, he decided to build nuclear missile bases on the island that could threaten the U.S. homeland. The Soviet military secretly planned to install forty nuclear missiles in Cuba which would double the number of Soviet nuclear weapons capable of striking the U.S. mainland. Khrushchev intended to use these missiles as a bargaining chip over Berlin and to deter an American invasion of Cuba. He also believed having nuclear missiles in Cuba would prevent America from starting a nuclear war. Khrushchev tried to keep the missiles in Cuba secret until they were operational, and then he planned to speak privately with Kennedy at the U.N. and tell the American President about them to improve his bargaining position.

Khrushchev expected that Soviet activity in Cuba would be interpreted by the CIA as an increase in Soviet ground forces to defend the island from American attack rather than the deployment of offensive nuclear missiles. In fact, U.S. intelligence analysts believed the Soviets were installing anti-aircraft missiles in Cuba to defend against air attacks on the island. [291] Public statements by Soviet leaders characterized the build-up as normal military activity and not a significant change in military strategy on the part of the Soviet Union. The CIA sent Kennedy an intelligence analysis saying they believed the U.S. was not under any increased threat from Cuba because of Soviet military activity in the area. Kennedy warned Moscow that the military build-up in Cuba would preclude any agreements with Russia about Berlin or Germany, but he refused to go any further in threatening Khrushchev at that time.

On October 1, 1962, Defense Secretary McNamara received intelligence suggesting there were Soviet offensive weapons being deployed in Cuba. [292] To confirm these sightings, Kennedy authorized high altitude U-2 reconnaissance flights over Cuba on October 14, 1962, which produced photographs showing five missile sites under construction and twenty-one crated medium-range bombers at a Cuban air field. Kennedy was briefed by the CIA on October 16, 1962, concerning these developments and immediately realized the planes and missiles could start a nuclear war. Kennedy asked if any of the missiles were ready to launch, and CIA experts said they believed warheads were not available, so there was time to discuss the issue before acting. Kennedy ordered additional U-2 flights to determine whether the missiles were armed and began considering four options to eliminate the missiles: an air strike against the missiles, an air strike on major Cuban targets, a blockade, or an invasion of the island by American marines. [293] Kennedy believed that if nuclear missiles were allowed to remain in Cuba, the Soviet Union would gradually increase its military capability on the island, damaging U.S. national security.

McNamara proposed that the U.S. establish a naval blockade around Cuba and step up U-2 flights over the island to make certain no more missiles were delivered. On October 18, 1962, reconnaissance photos suggested the Soviets would have between sixteen and thirty-two missiles ready to fire within a week. The Joint Chiefs recommended a full-scale invasion of Cuba, but Kennedy said he preferred a naval blockade and asked how best to communicate with Khrushchev about the crisis. On Saturday,

October 20, 1962, Kennedy ordered a naval blockade as a first step, with air strikes to follow if the Soviets did not remove the missiles from Cuba. It was decided to call the blockade a "quarantine" to make it appear less war-like. [294]

Kennedy considered removing missiles from Turkey or Italy if Russia raised the issue, but he wanted the missiles in Cuba removed first. Kennedy delivered the news of the quarantine and the presence of the missiles in Cuba on Monday evening, October 22, in a nationally televised address and demanded the missiles be removed immediately. Kennedy also condemned the Soviets for lying about the missiles, saying it was a major breach of faith, since Russia had promised to supply Cuba with defensive weapons only. By Tuesday, October 23, there was still no response from the Soviet Union, so Kennedy authorized U.N. Ambassador Stevenson to show U.S. reconnaissance photos to the General Assembly. At the same time, Soviet ships with additional missiles were sailing toward Cuba with Soviet submarines screening the ships, making the situation dangerous for the U.S. Navy. After many tense hours, McNamara announced that the Soviet ships had stopped or reversed course away from Cuba. [295] Khrushchev proposed the U.S. remove its Jupiter missiles from Turkey and agree not to invade Cuba in return for the Soviet Union removing the missiles from Cuba and Kennedy agreed to that proposal.

At a news conference on November 20, 1962, Kennedy announced that Khrushchev had agreed to remove the medium-range bombers and nuclear missiles from Cuba and allow American observation flights to confirm they had been removed. The main reason the Soviets had backed down was that America was militarily superior to the Soviet Union in the Caribbean and keeping nuclear missiles in Cuba was not a vital Soviet national interest. Khrushchev gambled that Kennedy would back down when confronted with the missiles, but he was mistaken. Historians agree that the Cuban Missile Crisis was the most dangerous moment in the entire Cold War and could have resulted in World War III. [296] Cool heads and a naval blockade defused the situation peacefully.

Domestic Politics. Kennedy believed he could no longer ignore the demands of Black Americans for more civil rights, so he signed an Executive Order integrating federally supported housing. Kennedy also denied rumors he was having an affair with Marilyn Monroe, but records of phone calls from Marilyn to the White House suggest their relationship may have been more than just a friendship. [297] Kennedy told his brother Robert to keep sex scandals out of the papers at all costs and decided to push for a tax cut to get the American economy growing again. Early in 1963, he began arguing that federal deficits were caused by slow economic growth rather than spending and taxes were too high. His economic advisors expected a recession in 1964 during the presidential election if taxes were not lowered, and Kennedy wanted to avoid that because it would threaten his chance for a second term.

To complicate matters further, Martin Luther King, Jr. launched a campaign to desegregate Birmingham's city services and increase the number of Black police and elected representatives in the city. When Black Americans demonstrated in the streets of Birmingham, police and firemen attacked them with dogs and high-pressure hoses. [298] Kennedy immediately called for a compromise to defuse the situation, believing that Black American unrest was bad for the country's image and that Martin Luther King, Jr. was under communist influence. Kennedy sent Burke Marshall to settle the dispute. The City of Birmingham agreed to desegregate department store fitting rooms, lunch counters, washrooms, restrooms, and drinking fountains. However, these concessions angered die-hard segregationists and Birmingham's mayor announced he would not enforce the settlement.

In response, Blacks attacked police and firemen, so Alabama state troopers and anti-riot squads were called in to quell a riot that left several blocks of the Black community in Birmingham burning. This was the first time in a century Blacks had turned violent, permanently changing the rules of civil disobedience in America, and Kennedy was worried that might be major race riots in the streets of America. King pledged to stop Black violence and Kennedy prepared to federalize the Alabama National Guard, but these actions did little to calm the situation since Governor George Wallace continued to inflame racial hatred. Kennedy decided to make an issue of admitting Black students to the University of Alabama because that gave him the moral high ground. On June 10, 1963, the Justice Department obtained a federal court order prohibiting Governor Wallace from interfering in the integration of the University of Alabama and Kennedy enforced the order with armed soldiers. He decided to concentrate on foreign affairs to burnish his image before the coming election by trying to negotiate an agreement with the Soviets to ban nuclear testing in the atmosphere.

Partial Nuclear Test Ban. In January 1963, Kennedy went to Europe to assure America's allies it didn't intend to reduce military spending and ask European nations to increase their defense spending. Kennedy also announced he wanted to ban nuclear weapons testing and discovered Khrushchev was interested, but would not agree to on-site inspection of Soviet test facilities, believing that would be an invitation to American spying. Khrushchev offered a limited ban on above ground nuclear testing without inspections because both countries were concerned about China developing nuclear weapons. [299]

In the fall of 1963, Kennedy was growing more concerned that the U.S. economy would fall into recession during the presidential campaign. Growth in the first quarter of 1963 had been moderate, but without a tax cut Kennedy worried the economy might falter later in the year. During his State of the Union address in 1963, Kennedy said things were going better in Vietnam, but that Cuba, Berlin, Laos, and the Middle East were still potential trouble spots. He said South Vietnam could not survive without substantial American help, although he didn't want to commit American ground forces to the war.

South Vietnam. Kennedy was still undecided about how to deal with Vietnam. Henry Cabot Lodge, the American Ambassador to Saigon, suggested the U.S. replace the civilian leadership in Vietnam, and Kennedy gave him authority to do what he thought best. [300] Kennedy pressured Diem to reform his government and at the same time, encouraged Vietnamese generals to overthrow the civilian government by force. Kennedy believed the Diem government was incapable of winning the war, so he allowed the U.S. to support a military coup in Vietnam. However, he insisted it must succeed or the damage to American prestige would be enormous. Ambassador Lodge told Kennedy the U.S. would be blamed no matter what happened and could exert little influence over the outcome. The coup was launched on November 1, 1963, and Diem quickly offered to surrender if the generals would guarantee him safe passage out of the country. Before arrangements could be made to fly him out of Vietnam, Diem and his staff were assassinated. [301] At that time, Kennedy began his campaign for a second term as President.

Kennedy's Assassination. Kennedy planned campaign trips to Florida and Texas in November 1963 because he feared his civil rights stance would make it difficult for him to win Southern votes, and he wanted to keep Texas and Florida if possible. Johnson opposed the trip to Texas, feeling Kennedy could do little to heal the breach within the Texas Democratic Party caused by civil rights issues. Kennedy ignored Johnson's advice and flew to San Antonio, Houston, Fort Worth, and Dallas for campaign events. The plan was for Kennedy to greet crowds at the various airports and then spend time in a motorcade waving to crowds lining the streets in each city. [302] The Secret Service missed the threat that Lee Harvey Oswald, a mentally unstable person who had lived in Russia for almost three years and was impressed by Castro's Cuba, might attempt to kill Kennedy in Dallas.

Oswald worked in the Dealey Plaza building of the Texas School Depository, which overlooked the street where Kennedy would be passing in his motorcade. Oswald fired three shots from the sixth-floor window of the Book Depository building at President Kennedy, who was traveling in an open car directly below. The second shot hit Kennedy in the neck and the third shot hit him in the back of the head, fatally wounding the President. Doctors at Parkland Memorial Hospital in Dallas pronounced Kennedy dead at 1:00 p.m. on November 22, 1963. [303] His death shocked the public in a way similar to Pearl Harbor and the assassination of Abraham Lincoln. Johnson believed that Kennedy's assassination was in retaliation for the killing of Diem in South Vietnam, while Robert Kennedy believed Castro or the Mafia was involved. The Warren Commission concluded Oswald acted alone, but many Americans never accepted that conclusion and conspiracy theories still surround his death even today.

Ronald Reagan

Ronald Reagan was born February 6, 1911, in Tampico, Illinois. His mother read to Reagan every night and by the age of five he could read the newspaper by himself. World War I ended when he was seven. Soon after the war, they moved to Dixon, Illinois, and Reagan spent a lot of time in the wilderness swimming, fishing, and skating on the river. When he was eleven, Reagan came home to find his father passed out in the snow near their house. His mother said Reagan's father couldn't control his drinking and that when he did something to embarrass the family, they should remember their father when he was sober and loving.

Reagan's mother was a natural entertainer and invited Ronald to participate in plays with her. Reagan walked on stage, said his part, and the audience applauded. Acting changed his life that day. When Reagan was thirteen, the family took a Sunday drive. His mother had left her glasses in the back seat and Reagan put them on. He immediately let out a shout because, for the first time, he saw the world clearly. Now he knew why he always wanted a desk in the front row at school and why he couldn't hit a baseball no matter how hard he tried. Reagan was called "four eyes" by his classmates, but the ability to see was more important than being called names.

At Dixon High School, Reagan played right guard his junior and senior years and loved it. He also worked as a lifeguard for seven summers at Lowell Park and saved seventy-seven people who were drowning. Reagan was determined to attend college, even though only about seven percent of high school students went to college in the 1920s. Eureka College offered him a scholarship and a job to help pay for the cost of his education, and he accepted. During Reagan's second year at Eureka College, the stock market crashed and the Great Depression began. He didn't notice the economic change at first because Reagan was busy with football, acting, and studying. However, when he graduated, Reagan had to decide what to do with his life. He wanted to be an actor but didn't know if he could make it in Hollywood or New York, so he considered other options.

Radio broadcasting was a coming thing, so Reagan went to Chicago to get a job in radio. He was advised to go work in the "sticks" to gain experience in broadcasting and then come back to Chicago. Reagan interviewed at WOC Radio in the Tri-Cities area of the Midwest, described a football game he played at Eureka and got the job. He was soon broadcasting sports on a 50,000-watt radio station in Des Moines, Iowa, that became so popular Reagan began getting speaking engagements on the side. He spent summers working with the Chicago Cubs in California and was introduced to Max Arrow, a Hollywood agent. Max gave Reagan a screen test and sent the film to Warner Brothers Studio. A week later, Reagan was offered a contract for $200 a week. The studio gave him a new haircut, new shirts, and new suits. It was a dream come true for Reagan. He was cast in B movies to give him a chance to learn acting and the studio an opportunity to assess his crowd appeal. Reagan drew good reviews, and his contract was renewed.

He made thirteen pictures his first eighteen months at Warner Brothers. Reagan couldn't wear glasses before the camera, so he bought contacts which were large pieces of glass that fit over the whites of his eyes. He wore the contacts when he had to see long distances; for close-ups, he was almost blind because he couldn't wear the lenses. Shortly after Reagan starred in *King's Row*, the Japanese attacked Pearl Harbor. He was drafted into the army and assigned to Army Air Force Intelligence in Los Angeles. His job was to make training films and teach camera crews how to film bombing missions over Germany. Reagan helped develop a new method of briefing pilots before a mission by showing the actual terrain the pilot and bombardier would see as they flew to their target.

After the war, Reagan returned to Hollywood and became involved in contract negotiations for the Screen Actors Guild, beginning his transition from screen star to politician. He began speaking out about the dangers of Communism after he realized that many organizations in Hollywood were being infiltrated by Soviet sympathizers. The American Communist Party was trying to take over the movie industry as a propaganda tool and Reagan opposed them.

Reagan met Nancy Davis, because another actress with the same name was suspected of being associated with the American Communist Party. She wanted to clear her name. Reagan agreed to investigate her case and found this Nancy Davis was not associated with Communism. Her agent told Reagan to take Nancy out to dinner and tell her himself, saying she will feel better hearing it directly from you. He took her to dinner and they started dating soon after. A few months later, Reagan said, "Let's get married." and Nancy said, "Let's." They married on March 4, 1952, and Nancy suggested Reagan be more selective about the pictures he made. He was offered roles in television series, but turned them down because he felt that doing a television show would be the kiss of death in the movie industry.

Reagan's career took a dramatic turn when GE offered him the job of hosting General Electric Theatre, which ran for eight years at nine p.m. Sunday evenings. In addition to hosting General Electric

Theatre, GE management asked Reagan to travel around the country visiting manufacturing plants in various states as a spokesman for the company and giving speeches at the local Chamber of Commerce, United Fund, or Executive Club. These speeches turned out to be an apprenticeship for Reagan's later political career. At first, his speeches were about Hollywood, but then Reagan decided to begin warning Americans about the dangers of communism. As Reagan spoke, more and more people came up to him to say the government was interfering in their businesses. He heard about how expanding government was causing troubles for businesses all over the country.

Reagan made a major change in his political thinking in 1960 when Richard Nixon ran against John Kennedy. He realized that the Democratic Party was responsible for growing the government, and at that moment, he became a Republican--saying he didn't leave the Democratic Party, the party left him. After the 1960 election, Reagan began to get invitations to speak at Republican functions. He also began hosting Death Valley Days, another popular TV program that raised his profile even higher. Senator Berry Goldwater asked Reagan to co-chairman his election committee when he ran for President in 1964. Reagan gave speeches saying that America was at a crossroad and would either continue to grow government until it ran the country or return to free enterprise and smaller government. Goldwater lost the election to Lyndon Johnson.

Shortly after the 1964 presidential election, a group of prominent Los Angeles Republicans told Reagan he should run for governor against Pat Brown. They said the Republican Party in California was in shambles, and Reagan was the only one who stood a chance of beating Brown. At first, he said, "No," but Republicans kept pressuring him to run, and Reagan finally said he would go on the road for six months and if he thought he could beat Brown, he would run. Reagan gave his standard speech about the abuses of big government and got the same positive reactions from his audiences, except this time, people kept asking why he didn't run for governor. On January 4, 1966, Reagan agreed to run for Governor of California.

In the California primary, Reagan ran against George Christopher, a liberal former mayor of San Francisco who tried to paint Reagan as a right-wing extremist. The attacks became so nasty that the state Republican chairman proposed the Eleventh Commandment: *Thou shall not speak ill of a fellow Republican.* Reagan beat Christopher in the primary and turned his attention to Brown, who attacked Reagan as an actor who knew nothing about politics. Reagan said, "I am running for governor as an ordinary citizen because you politicians have made such a mess of things." Brown accused Reagan of just reading speeches others had written. Reagan suggested he make a short speech, and then take questions from the audience to show he had command of the important issues of the day, because no one could write answers for questions that were asked at the spur of the moment. His advisors were skeptical, but Reagan insisted he had to do it if he wanted to win.

To everyone's surprise, Reagan beat Pat Brown and became Governor of California in 1966. His first job was to learn how California's government worked. At a Governor's Conference held just before Reagan took office, he talked to Jim Rhodes of Ohio, who told Reagan he was forming a committee of businessmen to evaluate the bureaus of his state and let him know what was wrong with them. Reagan thought that was such a good idea he did the same thing in California. After he took office, Reagan learned California was broke. Brown's administration had known about the fiscal crisis for a year but hid the problem to get reelected. Reagan promised to cut government spending and balance the budget, but he needed cooperation from the legislature to do that.

Governor Reagan set broad policy and allowed his staff to carry out their jobs. He was always willing to meet with someone when there was a problem, but he didn't look over their shoulders all the time. Reagan encouraged his cabinet to speak up and gave them ample opportunity to tell him what their constituents wanted. Reagan made the final decisions about policy himself, trying to avoid doing things because they were politically advantageous.

Two years before Reagan arrived in Sacramento, large parts of Los Angeles had gone up in smoke during the Watts Riots. He wanted to find out what had caused these racial difficulties, so Reagan talked privately with Black and Latino families in Los Angeles. He learned that minorities felt they were not being given a fair shot at state government jobs. Reagan promised to give them a level playing field in applying for jobs. He had to ask for a tax increase to balance the state budget, but promised to give back any surplus money once the financial crisis was over, something unheard of at the time.

During his second year in Sacramento, Reagan realized he had to go over the Democratic legislature's head and appeal directly to the people of California if he wanted his agenda passed. He decided to follow Franklin Roosevelt's example by going on television and radio to tell the people of California what was happening in Sacramento. Reagan believed the people wanted government to be fair, not waste money nor intrude in their lives. In the spring of 1968, a group of prominent Republicans said they wanted him to run as a favorite son in the California presidential primary to stop the intra-party feuding that had erupted in 1964 between the liberal and conservative wings of the Republican Party. The Republicans in California decided they would treat Reagan as a real candidate for president and campaign for him. Nixon won the Republican nomination, but Reagan became a viable presidential candidate as a result.

Near the end of his first term as Governor of California, Reagan decided he had more to accomplish, so he ran for a second term. He was reelected by fifty-three percent to forty-five percent, a clear vindication of his policies over the past four years. During his second term, Reagan wanted to reform the California welfare system because the number of people receiving welfare payments had quadrupled in the last ten years. California had one of the most generous welfare systems in America and was a magnet for people who wanted a handout rather than a job. The first thing he did was eliminate fraud in the program by cross-checking who was employed and receiving welfare payments. Reagan found that there were many people working and receiving a welfare check. The Democrats agreed that the welfare system was expensive but wanted to fix the problem by increasing taxes. Reagan said, "No." and negotiated a compromise that tightened eligibility standards and actually decreased welfare recipients in California.

After Reagan left the governor's office, he and Nancy bought a ranch in the Santa Ynez mountains as a retirement home and a place to ride. During the spring of 1975, people kept saying Reagan should challenge Gerald Ford for the Republican Party presidential nomination in 1976. He decided to run and organized his campaign around attacks on Democrats and big government. Reagan promised smaller government, lower taxes, a balanced budget, and more freedom from government interference if he was elected. After a hard-fought campaign, Ford collected enough delegates to win the Republican nomination. Reagan campaigned for him in twenty states during the general election, but Ford lost to Jimmy Carter in November. Reagan began writing a newspaper column and speaking out on the evils of big government. Soon, party leaders came knocking on Reagan's door, telling him he should run for president in 1980. He was not ready to make up his mind but said he was interested.

Candidate Reagan. The Carter administration called for a fairer distribution of wealth, income, and power—code words for the redistribution of money from wealthier producers to people who didn't work. The Democrats were also cutting back on military spending, increasing the threat of nuclear war with the Soviet Union. Inflation and interest rates were climbing and President Carter was sending a message to the people that America was in decline and people needed to get used to it. Reagan didn't agree and announced his decision to run for president on November 13, 1979, at the New York Hilton Hotel. Two major issues facing Reagan in his campaign for the Republican nomination were his age and New England Republicans' mistrust for someone from California.

Reagan lost the Iowa caucus to George Bush and knew he must win the New Hampshire primary if he wanted to gain the Republican nomination. Bush and Reagan were the front runners in New Hampshire, and the Nashua Telegraph offered to sponsor a debate between them. Both candidates accepted, but the other candidates objected. Reagan agreed to pay for the debate and invited all the candidates to attend. When the debate was scheduled to begin, the Bush campaign objected to having the other candidates on the stage, but Reagan said he wanted them there. He began to address the crowd, and the editor of the Nashua newspaper said, "Turn off Mr. Reagan's microphone." That made him angry, and Reagan said, "I am paying for this microphone, Mr. Breen." The crowd went wild and yelled approval. When the polls closed in New Hampshire, Reagan won fifty-one percent of the votes cast in a seven-way race. After New Hampshire, all the other candidates dropped out except Bush, who finally quit in May after further primary losses. Reagan began thinking about who he wanted for his vice president. He considered Gerald Ford, but Ford wanted to be co-president and Reagan said that won't work. The other obvious choice was George H.W. Bush.

During the 1980 campaign, the country was experiencing inflation over thirteen percent, high unemployment, and slow economic growth. Reagan claimed the American military was underfunded, and fifty-two American hostages were still being held captive in Iran. Carter said there was a "malaise" in the country, but Reagan disagreed. He said America's greatest years are still ahead. During the last months of the campaign, Reagan concentrated on what was wrong with the country. Carter claimed Reagan was a war monger who would plunge the country into a nuclear conflict. Reagan wanted to debate Carter, but the President refused. Finally, Carter was forced to debate Reagan on October 28, just a week before the national election.

Carter claimed Reagan had opposed Medicare benefits for Social Security recipients, and Reagan replied, "There you go again." At the end of the debate, Reagan told the audience if they were better off now than they were four years before, then they should vote for Jimmy Carter. If they were not better off, then it was time for a change and they should vote for him. Reagan campaigned hard that final week and returned to Los Angeles to await the results of the election. While he was in the shower, President

Carter called to tell him he was the fortieth president of the U.S. Reagan had collected four hundred eight-nine electoral college votes to Carter's forty-nine.

President Reagan. During his inaugural address, Reagan said government was not the solution, but the problem. He wanted to lower taxes, reduce government regulations, and restore power to the states. His first executive order was to lift price controls on oil and gasoline. He also announced that the fifty-two American hostages held by Iran had been released and were flying home. Reagan's immediate priorities were dealing with inflation, unemployment, and high interest rates. He wanted to reduce taxes, believing that would grow the economy. Since the Democrats controlled the House of Representatives, Reagan went around them to the American people with televised chats to pressure Congress to cut taxes.

On March 30, 1981, Reagan gave a speech before the Construction Trades Council at the Hilton Hotel. As he was leaving, Reagan heard what sounded like firecrackers behind him. Secret Service agents shoved him into his limousine and told the driver to go to the White House. On the way, Reagan coughed and saw blood on his hands. Seeing blood on Reagan's hands, the car was immediately directed to George Washington University Hospital. Reagan was taken to the emergency room, where doctors placed a breathing tube in his throat. When he recovered consciousness, Reagan learned that he had a bullet in his lung that had ricocheted through a gap between the car and the door hinges, struck him under his left arm, hit a rib, tumbled through his lung, and stopped near his heart. Reagan believed God had been looking out for him that day.

Soon after Reagan entered the White House, the Soviet ambassador told Secretary of State Haig that the Russians were interested in discussing nuclear arms control. Reagan decided to write a personal letter to Chairman Brezhnev saying that America also wanted to reduce the threat from nuclear weapons. He lifted the grain embargo on the Soviet Union as a gesture of goodwill. Reagan got a reply blaming the U.S. for starting the Cold War and said America had no right to tell the Soviet Union what it could do anywhere in the world.

During his campaign, Reagan had promised to appoint a woman to the Supreme Court, and shortly after taking office, Justice Potter Stewart sent word he intended to retire. Reagan asked Ed Meese and Bill Smith to find a woman for the Supreme Court who would follow the Constitution rather than rewrite it. On June 21, 1981, Reagan met with Bill Smith and reviewed a list of potential judicial nominations. He tentatively decided to nominate Sandra Day O'Connor, and after Reagan met her personally, he nominated her to be the first woman Justice on the Supreme Court. She was bright, honest, fair, and nonideological, all the things Reagan wanted in a Supreme Court Justice.

On the same Sunday he decided to appoint Sandra Day O'Connor to the Supreme Court; Reagan learned that air traffic controllers were threatening to strike because they had not been given a huge salary increase. Reagan supported unions but believed air traffic controllers had no right to strike because Congress had passed a law forbidding strikes by government employees. The air traffic controllers went on strike anyway, threatening the safety of thousands of flights daily. Reagan told the FAA to reduce flights to ensure the safety of the air passengers, and then told reporters that any air traffic controllers who were not at work in forty-eight hours would be fired. Enough air traffic controllers returned to work to keep the airlines flying, and over the next two years, new controllers were trained and hired. The

FAA discovered that they had employed almost six hundred too many controllers, because the system ran better and more efficiently with fewer air traffic controllers after the strike.

Reagan was still trying to get his tax and spending cuts passed by Congress, so he asked for an opportunity to speak to a joint session. Shortly after his speech, sixty-three Democratic House members voted with Republicans to pass a bill cutting billions of dollars in federal spending in 1981. Reagan had convinced a block of conservative Democratic House members, called the "boll weevils," to vote with him. Immediately, House Democrats offered to cut taxes over three years, with a five percent cut the first year, and then two ten percent cuts the next two years. Reagan accepted the compromise.

He also proposed eliminating all intermediate-range nuclear missiles in Europe and beginning negotiations to reduce all nuclear arms by the U.S. and the Soviet Union. Reagan also asked Congress for money to modernize American nuclear weapons, saying he wanted to negotiate from a position of strength. Near the end of his first year in the White House, Reagan had some significant successes. The first phase of the largest tax cut in history was taking effect, Congress had approved significant cuts in domestic spending, interest rates were falling, and inflation was in single digits for the first time in years. And George Bush was leading a task force to cut federal regulations.

At the same time, there were still many problems to resolve. Relations with the Soviet Union were difficult,Cuba was trying to export Communism to Latin America, there was fighting in the Middle East, and the Sandinistas were exporting their revolution to El Salvador. The CIA developed a plan to train and support Nicaragua's Contra freedom fighters to resist the Sandinistas in El Salvador. On Christmas Day, Reagan sent a cable to Moscow saying that the United States had no intention of intervening in Poland if the Soviet Union did not and proposed that the Polish people be given the right of self-determination through free elections. On New Year's Day, Reagan announced he was imposing economic sanctions on Poland and the Soviet Union in response to the repression of Polish civil rights by the Soviet Union.

Reagan got his tax cuts in 1981, but the American economy didn't begin to climb out of a deep recession until November 1982, months later than expected. During most of 1982, Reagan faced political pressure to increase taxes and spending to get the economy moving, but he resisted. The Democratic Party nominated Walter Mondale as their presidential candidate in 1984, and almost immediately, articles began appearing in major newspapers saying Reagan intended to raise taxes if he was reelected. In his acceptance speech after being nominated as the Republican candidate for president, Reagan promised he would not raise taxes and pointed out that Mondale had said he would raise taxes if elected. Reagan's advisors said he was in good shape politically because the economy was growing, inflation was down to 4.6 percent, unemployment and interest rates were lower, and Reagan had a substantial lead over Mondale in the polls. However, Reagan still campaigned hard because he hated to lose.

During their second debate, in response to a question about whether age was going to be a handicap for him, Reagan said, "I am not going to exploit for political purposes my opponent's youth and inexperience." The crowd roared in laughter, and even Mondale enjoyed the joke. During the campaign, Reagan attracted blue-collar workers who traditionally voted for Democrats because he asked them if they were better off than they had been four years before. Polls showed that Reagan was leading Mondale by a substantial margin, but he still worked hard on the campaign. On election day, Reagan won forty-nine states and fifty-nine percent of the vote. In his second inaugural address, Reagan promised to continue the policies of his first four years and bring peace and prosperity to the country.

The economic expansion that began in 1982 was one of the longest in American history and began about a year after Congress reduced income tax rates for most individuals by twenty-five percent. The economy created over eighteen million new jobs and brought prosperity to America. The tax cuts created more revenue for the government, but Congress kept increasing entitlement programs rather than balancing the federal budget. Reagan's goal during his second term was to keep the economy growing, cut the expansion of big government, lower taxes, and reduce the threat of nuclear war.

In the spring of 1984, Reagan flew to Communist China to see for himself whether the country was opening itself to free enterprise and foreign capital. The formal meeting between Reagan and Chairman Xiaoping began with the Chairman criticizing America for supporting Israel, its treatment of developing nations, and its failure to achieve an arms control agreement with the Soviet Union. Reagan aggressively defended American policy and after that rebuttal, Xiaoping became friendlier, although he still raised the issue of America's friendship with Taiwan. Reagan said that was a Chinese issue, but it had to be worked out peacefully because reunification by military force would seriously damage relations between the U.S. and China.

The Middle East. No region of the world has presented more problems for an American president than the Middle East. Disputes have been going on in that area for centuries. In 1948, the Jewish people achieved their ancient goal of establishing the State of Israel. However, Palestinians who had been occupying that territory for centuries became refugees, and that angered many Arab countries. They declared war on Israel in 1948, 1967, and 1973. On all three occasions, the Israelis drove the Arabs back. The Arab-Israeli conflict flared again after Israel invaded Lebanon in 1982 to drive the Palestinian Liberation Organization more than twenty-five miles from their border so the Arabs could not fire artillery shells into Jewish settlements. The Israeli invasion was successful and the U.S. believed this might be the beginning of a comprehensive settlement in the Middle East. However, on September 14, 1982, a terrorist bomb destroyed the building in Beirut where the president-elect of Lebanon was speaking.

Israel immediately sent troops into Lebanon to find those responsible for the bombing. To make matters worse, Christian Phalanges militia entered a refugee camp and massacred men, women, and children while the Israelis did nothing to halt the bloodletting. Both Israel and Syria refused to leave Lebanon after that incident and the fighting continued. George Shultz went to the Middle East to negotiate a settlement of the conflict and withdrawal of all foreign forces from Lebanon. After intense talks, he was successful and both sides withdrew.

Grenada. On October 21, 1983, Reagan was contacted by George Shultz and Bud McFarlane to discuss a request from the Organization of Eastern Caribbean States to intervene militarily in Grenada, a small island north of Venezuela. During the previous week, Marxists in Grenada had invited Cuban workers to build a huge new airport as part of a military build-up on the island. Reagan was concerned about eight hundred American medical students who were attending school on the island, fearing they could become hostages. The U.S. Navy already had ships and marines moving toward the island as part of a regular rotation of troops from Lebanon, so the President authorized a mission to rescue the medical students. He imposed total secrecy on the operation because he didn't want Cuba to send more troops to the area or have them take the students hostage. Nineteen hundred marines and rangers landed in Grenada, took control of the airport and medical school, and neutralized the Cuban troops on the island. Documents showed the Soviet Union and Cuba were planning to begin terrorist attacks from the island into Latin America.

Iran-Contra. The CIA told Reagan that Nicaragua was sending military arms and financial support to the Sandinistas in El Salvador, so he authorized his intelligence agents to covertly interdict the flow of arms. The CIA organized Central American soldiers into a fighting group called the Contras. However, Congress refused to supply funds needed to continue the operation. Reagan told his staff there ought to be a way for private citizens to help the Contras independently of Congress. At the same time, Israel contacted National Security Advisor Bud McFarlane to let him know that a group of moderate Iranians wanted to establish a secret relationship with the U.S. government and negotiate the release of hostages held in Lebanon.

Israel wanted to send anti-tank missiles to Iran, and Reagan agreed to the transfer because he wanted to establish a secret channel between the U.S. and Iran. In January 1986, Reagan approved a second shipment of weapons to Iran in return for the release of the remaining American hostages in Lebanon. The deal fell through when the Iranian negotiators demanded that Israel withdraw from the Golan Heights in return for the hostages being released. Reagan continued to pursue the negotiations with Iran and was able to achieve the release of some hostages. However, while conducting an audit of the Iran negotiations, the Justice Department discovered a memorandum showing that money received from Iran for the military equipment had been diverted to pay for supplies shipped to the Contra forces in Central America and that members of the National Security Council knew about the transaction.

No one had mentioned this to Reagan, so he decided to make the entire affair public and avoid a cover-up. John Poindexter resigned as National Security Advisor and Colonel Oliver North was relieved of his duties as a result of these revelations. The Iran-Contra affair frustrated Reagan because he believed his actions had been lawful. However, the press and many Americans didn't believe Reagan when he said there was no trading of arms for hostages. Christmas of 1986 was a difficult time in the White House as Reagan waited for the Tower Board to release its report. The report concluding that Reagan had no personal knowledge of the Iran-Contra transactions and was not to blame for the scandal. The report vindicated what Reagan had been saying all along, but the cloud over his administration during the investigation limited his ability to get legislation through Congress. The "moderate" Iranians had been dealing with America under false pretenses and were merely trying to obtain weapons to use against Iraq.

Strategic Defense Initiative (SDI). In 1983, Reagan decided America should develop a missile defense system called SDI to protect the homeland from nuclear attack. He didn't like the idea that deterrence alone provided safety from nuclear missiles. Reagan asked the Joint Chiefs of Staff to explore developing a defensive weapon that would intercept nuclear missiles before they hit the United States.

They said that was an interesting idea and the military would look into it. In March 1983, the Joint Chiefs told Reagan that his idea of a strategic defense against nuclear missiles was probably feasible, so he decided to make the plan public. The Soviet Union claimed the missile defense system would destabilize the world, but Reagan said the missile defense system was only intended to protect against a rogue nation such as Iran or North Korea launching a nuclear missile at the United States. He wanted to be able to shoot it down rather than destroy the other country.

Reagan also sent word to the Soviets that he was interested in real arms reduction. He felt no one would "win" a nuclear war because the loss of life and destruction would change civilization for a generation. On November 13, 1982, Chairman Brezhnev died, and Yuri Andropov, former head of the KGB, was elected chairman of the Communist Party. On August 31, 1983, a Soviet fighter plane shot down Korean Flight 007, killing two hundred sixty-nine passengers, including sixty Americans. The Soviet government denied that its aircraft had been involved in the incident, even though Japanese air traffic controllers had recorded radio transmissions among the Soviet pilots. When Andropov finally admitted that their planes had shot down the Korean airliner, he claimed it was justified because the plane was on a spying mission in Soviet territory. The U.S. and European allies imposed economic sanctions on the Soviet Union because of the incident.

On February 9, 1984, Chairman Andropov died, and Konstantin Chernenko was placed in charge of the Kremlin. Reagan felt this gave him another chance to open a dialogue with the Soviets about controlling nuclear arms. Despite difficult relations with the Soviets, Reagan felt it was time to explore holding a summit with Chernenko because America was now on a par with the Soviet Union in terms of nuclear missiles. Reagan also decided he was going to deal with the arms reduction talks through a White House group rather than the State Department. However, the Soviets rejected the idea of a summit so long as America continued work on the Strategic Missile Defense System or deployed intermediate-range missiles in Europe.

Reagan was adamant that he would not give up the Strategic Missile Defense System under any circumstances. He believed it was imperative that the U.S. develop a defense against nuclear missiles. Reagan knew that the system would not be totally effective but believed it would protect the homeland from catastrophic damage. On March 11, 1985, Chairman Chernenko died, and Mikhail Gorbachev became leader of the Soviet Union. Reagan sent George Bush to Moscow with a private letter inviting Gorbachev to meet with him. Gorbachev said he was interested in meeting Reagan and discussing ways to improve relations. As a gesture of goodwill, Gorbachev proposed that both countries continue to abide by the Strategic Arms Limitation Treaty, stop nuclear bomb testing, ban space weapons, negotiate a reduction of troops in Europe, and continue the process of building mutual trust between the U.S. and Russia.

Reagan and Gorbachev began a lengthy private correspondence about issues between America and the Soviet Union and agreed to personally work out differences between the two countries. On his way to Geneva to meet Gorbachev, Reagan decided he wanted to follow an old Russian proverb, "trust but verify." Reagan wanted to negotiate directly with Gorbachev because he felt they were the only ones with authority to make big changes in the issues facing America and the Soviet Union. Reagan immediately liked Gorbachev when they met. The first day involved Reagan and Gorbachev arguing that the other side was the aggressor and that was the main reason for the Cold War. Reagan pointed out that when the U.S. had a monopoly on atomic weapons, it had not used that advantage to become expansionist. Instead, America had helped Europe rebuild through the Marshall Plan.

During their discussions, Reagan and Gorbachev agreed to hold two more summits, one in Washington, D.C. and one in Moscow. Gorbachev didn't believe Reagan when he said the U.S. would share the Strategic Missile Defense System with the world if it worked, because he said no country would do that. Reagan said the U.S. would. They agreed in principle to a fifty percent reduction in nuclear weapons at the first summit. Reagan felt he had found a Soviet leader he could work with and addressed a joint session of Congress when he returned, reporting that they had made good progress toward resolving major issues between the two countries. A week after returning from the summit in Geneva, Reagan sent a private letter to Gorbachev saying it would help relations between the Soviet Union and America if he would withdraw his forces from Afghanistan. Gorbachev responded by objecting again to the Strategic Missile Defense System—a continuing point of dispute in these bilateral talks.

By 1986, the CIA reported that the Soviet economy was in bad shape and this gave Reagan hope Gorbachev would eventually come around to an arms control agreement that would lighten the economic burden on both economies. He felt that the U.S. economy could sustain the burden longer than the Soviet Union's economy. In April of 1986, the nuclear accident at Chernobyl occurred, and Reagan sent a letter of condolence to Gorbachev. At a meeting in Reykjavik, Iceland, Reagan was initially optimistic that they could work out a comprehensive arms control agreement. Reagan and Gorbachev agreed to limit nuclear weapons, and then Gorbachev said, "This all depends, of course, on your giving up SDI." Reagan got angry and said SDI was not a bargaining chip and that would not happen. Then, he walked out of the meeting.

In June 1987, Reagan made a trip to Berlin and, standing before the Berlin Wall, said, "Mr. Gorbachev, tear down this wall." It required more than a year after Reagan walked out in Iceland before relations between the Soviet Union and America warmed enough to resume discussions of arms reductions. Reagan felt that the time spent in Iceland was not wasted, because eventually the U.S. and Moscow agreed to terms for arms reductions that eliminated all intermediate-range nuclear weapons and a framework for the reduction of long-range nuclear missiles as well.

In September of 1987, Gorbachev sent a letter to Reagan asking for America to give up the Strategic Missile Defense System and Reagan, said "No." On October 31, 1987, Gorbachev set a date for the next summit in Washington where the U.S. and Soviets would sign an agreement eliminating intermediate-range nuclear missiles and begin discussions on reducing long-range nuclear missiles by fifty percent. On January 25, 1988, Reagan gave his last State of the Union address to a joint session of Congress. He reported that the state of the union is good, the country is strong, and there is a good chance we will achieve a significant reduction in long-range nuclear missiles in the coming year. Shortly after, Reagan read *Perestroika*, a book written by Gorbachev, that outlined his goals for remaking the Soviet Union. Gorbachev admitted that the Communist system was failing and needed changing.

Several other positive events happened in 1988: the Soviet Union withdrew from Afghanistan, the people of Poland were striking for freedom, and the Berlin Wall would eventually come tumbling down. In Latin America, there was a return to democracy among many of the countries in that region. All was not good news, however, because Pakistan, Taiwan, and Israel were believed to have acquired nuclear weapons. Another summit was scheduled for late May of 1988, where Reagan expected to sign a treaty reducing long-range missiles by both sides by fifty percent. Seventy years of Communism had bankrupted the Soviet Union, and Gorbachev wanted to change the Communist system to make its economy grow by introducing democracy, freedom, and capitalism. Gorbachev saw that the current system was not working, and he made the decision to try something new.

Gorbachev gave Reagan the opportunity to lecture students at Moscow State University, where the brightest Russian students were trained as future leaders of the Soviet Union. Reagan spoke to them about democracy, individual freedom, and capitalism. In the fall of 1988, Reagan went on the campaign trail for George H.W. Bush to ensure his policies were continued for another four years. Reagan and Gorbachev met one last time at the U.N. in New York. By then, the Soviet Union was undergoing major changes in its foreign policy. When Reagan left the White House, he put a note on the desk in the Oval Office that said: "don't let the turkeys get you down."

Reagan and Nancy moved back to Los Angeles, and he spent the next few years speaking about democracy, freedom, and capitalism. Reagan began developing Alzheimer's isease in 1995 and died June 5, 2004, in Bel Air, California.

Sandra Day O'Connor

Sandra Day O'Connor

Sandra Day was born March 26, 1930, in El Paso, Texas, in a hospital four hours from her parents' Lazy-B Ranch in Arizona. [304] She was an only child for nine years and kept bobcats, hawks and tortoises as pets. She loved to ride horses on her father's ranch, but during the summer she stayed in the house reading to avoid the heat. When it came time for Sandra to attend school, the nearest public school was not adequate. Her mother homeschooled Sandra for a year, but she was so bright they decided she needed to attend a first-rate school with other children her age, so they sent her to live with her grandmother in El Paso, Texas.

Sandra's grandmother was emotionally distant and demanding. She told Sandra it was important to work hard and strive for success, and it didn't matter whether you were a female, you could still succeed. After four years attending public school, Sandra was enrolled in the Radford School for Girls, where she studied Latin, Greek, piano, ballet, elocution, and enunciation. Graduates of Radford often went to Smith or Wellesley College in the East. Sandra was homesick most of the time while she was living in El Paso and was shy. She skipped two grades, graduated from high school at fifteen years of age, and returned to her parents' ranch in Arizona for the summer before going to college.

In the fall of 1946, Sandra's parents drove her to Palo Alto, California, to attend Stanford University. [305] The campus was full of older veterans attending college on the G.I. Bill and Sandra was younger than most of the other girls. She especially loved her History of Western Civilization class and liked studying and learning new ideas. She majored in economics and her conservative father was unhappy when he heard her talk about Keynesian deficit spending as a good thing. She scored in the top fifteen percent on the Law School Aptitude Test and applied to Stanford Law School because graduates from Stanford could finish both college and law school in six years. The accelerated program was designed to allow veterans to make up time lost during the war. Sandra studied law because she didn't want to be a housewife or secretary. She was one of four women accepted at Stanford Law School among a class of approximately one hundred fifty students.

Stanford was not on the same academic level as Harvard or Yale Law Schools at the time because it accepted half the students who applied. She earned high grades in her classes, was active in moot court, and was a member of the Stanford Law Review. William Rehnquist was the top student in her class and they dated in the summer of 1950, but Rehnquist failed to impress Sandra's father. She met John O'Connor, the man she would eventually marry when they were paired to cite check a law review article. They met at the library to discuss the article and immediately hit it off.

Sandra was thinking about her own future and wanted a job at a leading California law firm when she finished school. She applied to several law firms in Los Angeles and San Francisco, but heard nothing, even though she was one of the top students in her class at Stanford Law. She had a friend whose father was a partner at Gibson, Dunn, and Crutcher, a top Los Angeles law firm, and Sandra went to see him. The partner told her that even though she had a good resume, the firm would never hire a woman because their clients wouldn't stand for it. He did offer to hire her as a legal secretary, but Sandra said no thanks. There were legal jobs available for women in the public sector, such as clerking for a judge or working as an attorney for the U.S. government, but prestigious private law firms would not hire women in the 1950s.

She married John O'Connor at her father's ranch and they traveled to Mexico City for their honeymoon. When she returned to California, Sandra went to the San Mateo County District Attorney's office to ask for a job. She was told that she could have a job but would not be paid. [306] She accepted the offer because she wanted to gain experience doing research and writing legal memos for senior partners. After a few months, they began paying her a salary because the district attorney was impressed with her work. After John finished law school, he was commissioned in the Judge Advocate General's Corps, completed basic training, and was posted to Frankfurt, Germany. Sandra was hired by the Army Quartermaster's Corps in Germany to write contracts. They returned to the U.S. in 1957, and John got a job with a Phoenix law firm. Sandra decided to stay home with her children while they were young.

State Senator O'Connor. Sandra was a housewife, mother, and volunteer for a few years before she went to work in 1965. She wanted a job at a first-rate private law firm, but they would not hire a woman. Sandra finally formed a partnership with a graduate of Michigan Law School, and in 1966 she was hired by the State Attorney General as an assistant. In 1969, Sandra was appointed to the Arizona Senate representing an affluent district in Phoenix. [307] Three years later, she was elected majority leader of the Senate, the first female leader of a state upper house in the U.S. The national media continued to ignore her, however. In October 1971, President Nixon appointed William Rehnquist to the U.S. Supreme Court.

In 1972, the Equal Rights Amendment passed the U.S. Congress and was sent to the states for ratification. Sandra made a speech on the floor of the Arizona Senate urging the state legislature to support it. However, the amendment sat in committee for months and nothing happened. When support for the ERA began to decline, she cut her losses and stopped pushing for passage of the Amendment. In 1973, the U.S. Supreme Court ruled seven to two in *Roe v. Wade* that women have a Constitutional right to an abortion based on a discovered right to privacy. The Court believed the decision would be supported by a wide majority of Americans, but there was an immediate backlash from the Christian Right that brought cultural and social issues to the forefront of American politics. Sandra tried to keep a low profile about abortion in the Arizona Senate. She backed bills limiting the right of women to have an abortion while also supporting pro-choice legislation that was not controversial. Sandra worked to eliminate laws that discriminated against women.

Judge O'Connor. In 1974, Sandra ran for office as a Phoenix judge. She disliked campaigning but was good at making speeches, collecting money, and getting out the vote. She won over 70 percent of the vote, but admitted later she was anxious about making judicial rulings because she had little experience in the courtroom. She was neither a soft touch nor a strict legalist but tried to be fair and make the legal system work for people. The Watergate scandal was unfolding in Washington and Republicans were losing control of state legislatures, even in traditionally Republican states such as Arizona. In 1977, President Carter appointed the governor of Arizona to be ambassador to Argentina, and his successor died in office shortly after. The Republicans sensed an opportunity and approached O'Connor to see if she was interested in running for governor of Arizona. She agreed to run if the party raised enough money, but conservative donors didn't contribute because they believed she could not win since she was a woman.

In 1979, Arizona Governor Babbitt appointed Sandra Day O'Connor to the Arizona Court of Appeals to keep her from running against him in the next election because polls showed she was twenty points ahead. That summer, she met Chief Justice Warren Burger, who was in Arizona at a judicial conference. John and Sandra entertained Burger on a houseboat on Lake Powell, a man-made reservoir on the border between Arizona and Utah. O'Connor and the Chief Justice liked each other and discussed law and politics late into the evening. Burger thought she would make a good first woman Justice because the country was getting tired of an all-male Supreme Court. He appointed her to important judicial committees so she could meet the right people and become better known before she joined the Court.

President Reagan promised to put a woman on the U.S. Supreme Court during his campaign, so when Justice Potter Stewart resigned, Reagan's staff began compiling a list of qualified women for the Court. Justice Rehnquist and Chief Justice Burger both supported Sandra Day O'Connor for the position, even though she was not well known. Their support carried considerable weight with the selection committee, and by the time Reagan's top advisers met to discuss potential nominees, she was at the top of their shortlist of preferred candidates. O'Connor had a personal meeting in Phoenix with Ken Starr and Jonathan Rose so they could learn her views on the Constitution, abortion, and other sensitive political issues. She passed with flying colors and they recommended President Reagan nominate her to the Court.

O'Connor met President Reagan in the Oval Office during June of 1981. He asked about her judicial philosophy, and she said judges should not make law but interpret exiting statutes, precedents, and the plain text of the Constitution. In August of 1981, O'Connor was nominated to be the first women Justice on the U.S. Supreme Court. [308] She faced opposition from pro-life senators and a few conservatives such as Jesse Helms, but O'Connor was an effective advocate when she met each Senator. Senators Berry Goldwater and Strom Thurmond supported her nomination and escorted her into the room for the confirmation hearing. She made it clear in her opening statement that she would not comment on any particular case that might come before the Court but would otherwise answer all their questions. Sandra said she was opposed to abortion, but because she was older, it was easy for her to feel that way. The Senate confirmed her nomination unanimously. President Reagan worked hard behind the scenes to make sure her nomination succeeded.

Justice O'Connor. On September 25, 1981, Chief Justice Burger walked Justice O'Connor down the Supreme Court steps as photographers snapped pictures of the historic event. She met each Justice in his private chamber accompanied by President Reagan. When she was escorted to the grand chamber of the Court, Justice O'Connor sat in the chair originally used by Chief Justice John Marshall. After she took the oath of office and donned her black robe, O'Connor was escorted to a seat on the far right alongside the other eight Justices. Sandra's office was bare, except for a huge stack of petitions for "writs of certiorari" requesting a Supreme Court review of a lower court decision. A vote of four Justices is required for a case to be accepted for review by the Supreme Court, and she had to read and decide whether to accept or reject each of the petitions on her desk.

In her first meeting with other Justices to review cases, she took notes of which cases they agreed to review. By silent agreement, everyone got their own coffee—no one dared ask O'Connor to do it. The Justices don't necessarily like each other because they have different judicial philosophies, but they mask their feelings with formal rituals and politeness whenever possible. Bitter fights between Justices occur from time to time, but for the most part, they try to get along because they hold lifetime appointments. Shortly after she joined the Court, Chief Justice Burger sent her a memo about the dynamics of a lone female among a group of males in a work environment. The article recommended she take a passive role to accommodate the men and make the group more productive. She ignored the memo, but felt isolated because Justice Rehnquist was being distant and O'Connor didn't understand why. The reason was Rehnquist wanted to keep their interactions formal because of his past personal relationship with her at Stanford University and wanted to avoid the appearance of impropriety.

Justice Lewis Powell stepped forward to help O'Connor organize her office by assigning one of his best legal secretaries to help her office run smoothly. Justice O'Connor was grateful for his help and they became good friends. Powell was impressed by O'Connor's intellect and upper-class manners. He was a Virginia gentleman himself and appreciated good breeding. Justice O'Connor retained Justice Stewart's law clerks because it was too late to select her own. She started an aerobics class for women open to all females associated with the Supreme Court. Female clerks, secretaries, and an occasional Senator's wife joined the group. Justice O'Connor listened to her law clerks' advice because they were fresh from first-rate law schools and had been taught by the brightest Constitutional Law professors in the country, and she learned quickly.

Her law clerks were concerned about how O'Connor would perform during questioning of attorneys in oral arguments, because East Coast lawyers and Ivy League graduates looked down on her as having an inferior education from Stanford Law School. In the Court's weekly conferences, the junior Justice votes last according to tradition. On the first case before the Justices with O'Connor in the room, she was the deciding vote and felt a keen sense of power. The first civil rights case that came before the Court after she joined was *Plyler v. Doe*, which raised the issue of whether undocumented aliens had a right to free public education in America. [309] By a five to four vote, the Court said "yes." Justice O'Connor was often the swing vote at judicial conferences because she was moderate, which gave her significant power on the Court.

Engle v. Isaac. The first case Justice O'Connor felt strongly about was *Engle v. Isaac*, which involved a writ of habeas corpus, an age-old right of all citizens to be brought before a court of law to force the government to show why they are incarcerated. [310] The writ gives every arrested defendant the right to appear before a judge and have his or her case heard. The writ had become a favorite tactic of prisoners on Death Row to have their cases moved from state to federal court where they believed their civil rights were more likely to be protected. Writing for a five to four majority, Justice O'Connor limited the right of a prisoner to use a writ of habeas corpus to move a case to federal court until he or she had exhausted all state remedies.

When she joined the Supreme Court, women were beginning to enter law schools in increasing numbers and some were even being appointed to lower courts. Sandra wanted to be a role model for these women and she made numerous speeches across the country encouraging women to consider law as a career. O'Connor was cautious about crusading aggressively for women's rights because she felt it would be counter-productive. In March of 1982, O'Connor heard her first sex discrimination case on the Supreme Court.

Mississippi University for Women v. Hogan. [311] Joe Hogan was a 26-year-old male who wanted to be a nurse. He applied to Mississippi University for Women but was rejected because the college only enrolled females. He won admission to the university in state court, but the women's college appealed to the U.S. Supreme Court to reverse the decision. During oral arguments, Justice O'Connor asked the attorney for Mississippi University for Women, "What level of scrutiny do we apply to this case?" Her question went to the heart of the case, because in racial discrimination, the courts always apply "strict scrutiny," meaning that there must be a compelling reason for any discrimination and it must be narrowly tailored to achieve the stated goal. Public schools that discriminate against Blacks by providing separate but equal facilities flunk the test. Should the Supreme Court apply the same strict standard to discrimination on the basis of sex, she wondered?

When *Mississippi University for Women v. Hogan* was considered in chambers, Chief Justice Burger and Justices Rehnquist, Powell, and Blackmun voted to allow the university to remain all female. Justices Brennan, White, Marshall, and Stevens voted to allow men to attend the all-female school—a four to four tie. O'Connor held the deciding vote, and she followed Justice Brennan's lead by arguing it was not necessary to decide the issue for all same-sex schools in America, since Mississippi University for Women was the only one in the state, and they could decide the issue for it alone. By narrowing the grounds for the decision, she was able to get five Justices to allow men to enter the university without deciding the issue for all women's colleges. Brennan, as the senior Justice in the majority, assigned the case to Sandra so she would not change her mind.

The pressure on O'Connor to do a good job was enormous because she was the first woman on the Supreme Court, and if she failed, there might never be another. To make certain she didn't make legal errors, Sandra personally checked every citation her clerks proposed before she accepted the case as support for an argument. When O'Connor decided a case, she considered both legal precedents and real-world consequences, rather than only thinking about the legal precedents involved. She realized that Supreme Court rulings have serious consequences for people's lives, especially for women in the case of abortion.

City of Akron v. Akron Center for Reproductive Health, Inc. [312] This abortion case was accepted by the Court a decade after *Roe v. Wade*. The issue involved restrictions passed by the City of Akron to discourage women from having an abortion. The City of Akron required women to sign a consent form, listen to a lecture that a fetus is "human life from the moment of conception," and wait twenty-four hours before receiving an abortion. When *Roe v. Wade* had come before the Court, Justice Blackman devised a three-stage system to govern a woman's right to an abortion. During the first three months of pregnancy, Blackman believed women have an absolute right to an abortion. During the second three months, the state could intervene to protect a woman's health, and during the last trimester, when the baby might be viable, the state had a right to intervene to protect both the mother and her child.

Justice O'Connor disagreed with Blackman's analysis, believing there is no legal justification in the Constitution for different standards over the three trimesters of pregnancy, but that was already settled precedent. O'Connor believed that Blackman's system governing abortion made the Supreme Court a medical review board rather than a court of law. She thought the state has an interest in protecting a fetus at all stages of life, not just during the third trimester, and supported state regulations that didn't unduly restrict a woman's right to an abortion at all stages of pregnancy. Justice O'Connor wanted to get the courts out of the business of deciding when a fetus is "viable," because she believed medical science will ultimately change the age of viability and a changing standard is not a proper foundation for a legal doctrine.

O'Connor was willing to allow states to pass restrictions on abortion, so long as the restrictions didn't place an "undue burden" on a woman's right to access an abortion. Six Justices voted to strike down Akron's restrictions on abortion, while O'Connor, White, and Rehnquist voted to sustain the restrictions. *Roe v. Wade* survived unchanged.

Female law clerks flocked to Justice O'Connor's court, wanting to be among those who shared her legal thinking. She hired males and females in equal numbers, looking for bright, well-trained attorneys who had experience outside the law. She hired clerks with advanced degrees in economics, clerks from impoverished families, and clerks who had practiced law for a few years. Her law clerks gave O'Connor loyalty and affection but were concerned because she could be impatient with a clerk when she heard enough about a case. She would simply say, "move on" when that happened. Because she was a junior Justice and the first woman on the Court, her law clerks double-checked every citation to make certain they were accurate and on point, so O'Connor would not be criticized by the senior male Justices.

O'Connor and Brennan were considered the best politicians on the Court. O'Connor was direct, while Brennan was subtle, but both were able to lobby other Justices to their cause and hold a majority of the Court in their favor once it formed. Justice O'Connor worked hard to remain friends with Brennan, asking her husband John to send Brennan Irish jokes, and she gave a party in her chambers to celebrate Brennan's thirty years on the Court. They were friendly but didn't trust each other when it came to writing opinions because both Brennan and O'Connor tried to write constitutional law into their footnotes, hoping the other Justices wouldn't object. O'Connor joined the Court majority striking down a "moment of silence" in public schools on the grounds that it was a disguised way to sneak prayer back into the classroom.

Wallace v. Jaffree. [313] One of the most unpopular decisions ever issued by the Warren Court was *Engel v. Vitale*, which prohibited prayer in public schools. To get around the *Engel v. Vitale* prohibition on school prayer, the Alabama Legislature introduced a "moment of silence" at the beginning of class. Justice O'Connor joined a majority of the Court in declaring that a "moment of silence" in public schools violates the establishment clause of the U.S. Constitution. The Court majority argued that the true purpose of the "moment of silence" was to reintroduce prayer in the classroom in contravention of the earlier ruling in *Engel v. Vitale*.

Chief Justice Burger decided to retire at the end of the 1986 term, and Justice Powell told O'Connor he intended to support her nomination as the next Chief Justice. She was flattered, but William Rehnquist was nominated as Chief Justice instead because Edwin Meese was upset that O'Connor voted to overturn the "moment of silence" in Alabama public schools. Chief Justice Rehnquist was not always a reliable conservative vote because he developed a "live and let live" libertarian philosophy on the Court. Chief Justice Rehnquist kept judicial conferences short and avoided long debates before asking for a vote. He also convinced Congress to cut the Court's workload by eliminating mandatory review of some cases. Justice O'Connor faced serious health problems in 1988.

Breast Cancer. O'Connor scheduled a routine mammogram but discovered she had a mass in her right breast. [314] The biopsy found a small tumor and she consulted several physicians about how to deal with the problem. She got conflicting advice, from removal of her breast to having another biopsy. She chose a second biopsy, which found that the cells were invasive, and she decided to undergo a mastectomy to remove the cancerous tissue. The operation went well, although it took longer than expected and left scar tissue. During recovery after surgery, her clerks brought briefing materials to the hospital for her to review. When she was released, O'Connor's law clerks came to her house to have Saturday lunches. Her physicians found cancer cells in her lymph nodes and recommended chemotherapy to increase her chance of survival. She became emotionally distraught at the thought of having to endure chemotherapy because she would lose her hair and feel tired all the time.

Her physician said that aggressive chemotherapy would increase her chance of survival to over seventy-five percent, so she decided to go ahead with treatment. O'Connor scheduled her sessions on

Friday so she could recover over the weekend and return to work Monday morning. She was lethargic, looked pale, and had little energy during the chemotherapy, but kept working in spite of these obstacles. She bought a wig to cover the hair loss from chemotherapy but was dissatisfied because it looked different from her natural hair. She was determined not to miss oral arguments, but Justice Scalia advised Sandra to put her health first and not worry about the Court. When chemotherapy was finished, her hair grew back thicker than before, and O'Connor was delighted. The first important case she drafted after her cancer treatment involved restrictions on abortion passed by the State of Pennsylvania.

Planned Parenthood of Southeastern Pennsylvania v. Casey. This case raised the issue of abortion before a Supreme Court with a conservative majority, and many legal scholars believed the Justices might overturn *Roe v. Wade* in 1992. [315] Pennsylvania had passed a restrictive law requiring women who wanted an abortion to wait twenty-four hours, receive a lecture on the development of the fetus, and notify her husband if she was married before having an abortion. At the conference after oral arguments, five Justices wanted to overturn *Roe v. Wade*. However, Justices Kennedy, Souter, and O'Connor secretly drafted an opinion that preserved the right to an abortion with restrictions, and it attracted five votes at the next conference. The following year, Justice O'Connor had another female Justice join her on the Supreme Court.

Ruth Bader Ginsburg. President Bill Clinton nominated Ruth Bader Ginsburg to replace Justice Byron White in 1993, adding a second female to the U.S. Supreme Court. O'Connor welcomed Ginsburg to the Court as another female even though she was more liberal and activist than O'Connor. Both women wanted to stop gender discrimination because they had similar difficulties in law school and finding a job after graduating because they were female. During oral arguments, O'Connor and Ginsburg cooperated in asking attorneys difficult questions if the case involved women's rights.

In 1996 Justice O'Connor began considering retiring because she would turn sixty-six and felt she had been on the Court long enough. However, Bill Clinton was president and she didn't want him to appoint a liberal Justice to replace her. Moreover, legal scholars were calling it the O'Connor Court because she was so often the swing vote in a five to four majority. Justice Kennedy was the other potential swing vote, but he was more reluctant to cast the deciding vote than O'Connor. She was a moderate Justice in the center of the political spectrum, and as a result, joined neither camp consistently. Justice O'Connor tried to follow the facts and the law and believed the Court ought not to make law but follow precedent. However, she was careful to protect the rights of women and children when these cases came before the Court.

A good example was *Davis v. Monroe County Board of Education*, where Justice O'Connor ruled that a school could be liable for student-on-student sexual harassment under Title IX of the Civil Rights Act. Perhaps the most important case to come before the Supreme Court during her tenure was *Bush v. Gore*, which decided who would be President of the United States.

Bush v. Gore. [316] The presidential election of 2000 between Al Gore and George Bush was a tie because neither candidate had won a clear majority of Electoral College votes. Florida voted for Bush by so few votes that an automatic recount was required under state law. Bush and Gore both hired attorneys to contest the Florida recount. The problem in Florida was caused by old voting machines, older voters, and confusing ballots, which produced chaos during the counting process. The voting machines were unable to count paper ballots that contained hanging or dimpled chads, so these ballots had to be counted by hand. The Republican secretary of state was prepared to certify that Bush had won the election, but the Florida Supreme Court, dominated by Democratic judges, ruled that the state authorities had to hold a recount over the entire state, which would favor Gore. The Bush legal team appealed the Florida Supreme Court's decision to the U.S. Supreme Court, asking for an injunction. The Supreme Court is supposed to be non-political, but in most votes, liberal and conservative Justices end up on opposite sides.

When the Justices met on Saturday, December 9, 2000, all five Republican Justices voted to issue a stay and stop the state-wide Florida recount with no debate. Based on that vote, George Bush won the presidency. However, the five Republican Justices had to find a legal reason to justify their decision. They scheduled oral arguments for two days later. The judicial conference after oral arguments in *Bush v. Gore* was heated. Justice O'Connor finally suggested the Court use the Equal Protection Clause of the Fourteenth Amendment to argue that the State of Florida, by using different standards in the various voting districts of the state, had violated Bush's right to equal treatment under the law and that justified stopping the statewide recount. O'Connor wrote the Court's opinion, holding that the ruling was "limited to the present circumstances" and was a one-time solution to a difficult political problem.

The negative reaction from liberal newspapers to the Supreme Court's decision was harsh. Some called it a travesty, others pure politics, and liberal papers ridiculed Republican Justices. Gallup found that the approval ratings for the Supreme Court dropped for a while and then regained its prior level after *Bush v. Gore*. Justice O'Connor decided not to attend any social or political events involving the Bushes after the decision, to avoid the appearance of impropriety. She also decided not to retire because it might look like a quid pro quo—her voting to give Bush the presidency so he could choose a conservative replacement. The next important case before the Court involved how to deal with past racial discrimination against Black Americans.

One answer to past racial discrimination was the doctrine of affirmative action, which allowed business and law schools to use race as a factor to increase the number of Black students in these schools. However, this doctrine triggered resentment among white and Asian students who were denied admission because lower-scoring Black students were admitted instead. These students who were denied admission because of affirmative action policies at business and law schools filed litigation to stop the practice of giving preference to minority students in admission policies. Justice O'Connor wanted to fix the problems caused by past racial discrimination but had difficulty finding a least intrusive means of doing it. She had plenty of experience with discrimination against Hispanics in Arizona while serving in the legislature and on the court of appeals. She turned to Thurgood Marshall for advice about the experience of Blacks and how best to remedy the situation. Racial segregation in public schools had been declared unconstitutional by the Warren Court in *Brown v. Board of Education of Topeka*, but the current issue involved the use of racial preferences at the University of Michigan to fix the problems associated with a history of slavery in America.

Gratz v. Bollinger. [317] Two white Michigan residents filed suit against the University of Michigan, alleging that the school's admission policy was racially discriminatory and violated their civil rights. The University of Michigan used a 150-point scale to rank students and gave bonus points to African American, Native American, and Hispanic students based on their race or ethnicity. The Court, in a six to three decision, ruled that the university's admission system violated the Equal Protection Clause of the U.S. Constitution and Title VI of the Civil Rights Act of 1964. Chief Justice Rehnquist authored the opinion, writing that giving extra points to minority students had the effect of making race the main factor in the University's decision to admit a student and was therefore unconstitutional.

Justice O'Connor voted with the conservative majority to reject the undergraduate admission policy of the University of Michigan. However, when it came to the admission policy of Michigan's Law School, she voted with the liberal wing of the Court to uphold a flexible affirmative action plan where race could be considered, but must not be the deciding factor in admission to the law school. Her reasoning was that law schools provided national leaders and they needed to reflect the country as a whole. She believed that a "critical mass" of minority law or business students was necessary for the welfare of all students on campus. O'Connor also suggested there should be a twenty-five-year time limit on the affirmative action plan at law schools in America. Her time limit has been ignored, however. The next important case before the Court involved the legal status of enemy combatants who were also American citizens.

Hamdi v. Rumsfeld. [318] Yaser Hamdi was captured in Afghanistan and held by the U.S. military as an enemy combatant. However, he had been born in Louisiana and was an American citizen, so the issue before the court was whether Hamdi, who was classified as an enemy combatant by the U.S. Military, was entitled to due process rights afforded other U.S. citizens. Justice O'Connor wrote the plurality decision using a balancing test. She held that Hamdi had a right to due process because he was an American citizen and must have a meaningful opportunity to challenge his status as an enemy combatant. She wrote that a court must consider the interests of the government, the rights of the individual, and whether additional legal procedures will improve the chance of reaching a just outcome. O'Connor reduced the burden of proof on the government by allowing the use of hearsay evidence and required that the government establish separate tribunals to review the status of all enemy combatants. She also held that these enemy combatants have the right to an attorney in these hearings. She believed that even during a war, individuals have basic rights to due process, even if they are not American citizens.

During this time, John O'Connor, Sandra's husband, began showing signs of advancing Alzheimer's disease. He was still friendly, cooperative, and good-natured but was unable to care for himself and was becoming a serious burden. Justice O'Connor became depressed because of the pressures she faced caring for John and working full time on the Court. She tried having friends stay with John, but he became agitated when she was not with him. Her husband also began saying inappropriate things at social gatherings, and it was becoming difficult for Sandra to do her work on the Court and take care of John at the same time.

In August of 2004, O'Connor decided she had to leave the Court to take care of John because she could not do both jobs properly. When the new Supreme Court term began in October of 2004, Chief Justice Rehnquist was not feeling well and announced he was going to the hospital for thyroid surgery. During the operation, his surgeons discovered Rehnquist had developed cancer and his future on the Court was questionable. After George W. Bush was inaugurated in January of 2005 for his second term, O'Connor and Rehnquist discussed who should resign first because they didn't want two vacancies on the Court at the same time. Her husband's situation continued to deteriorate and O'Connor decided she would have to retire. When Rehnquist returned to the Court, he announced that he intended to stay for another year, so Sandra decided she would retire immediately. She received warm letters from Ruth Bader Ginsburg and Antonin Scalia, announcing they were saddened she was leaving.

President Bush nominated John Roberts to replace O'Connor and she was planning to resign once he was confirmed. However, at the end of August, Chief Justice Rehnquist was rushed to the hospital suffering from a recurrence of aggressive thyroid cancer that appeared terminal. Before Rehnquist died, he suggested President Bush nominate John Roberts as the new Chief Justice and Bush agreed. Under these changed circumstances, O'Connor told President Bush she would continue to serve on the Court until her replacement was confirmed. Before she left, another abortion case appeared on the docket.

Ayotte v. Planned Parenthood of Northern New England. [319] Justice O'Connor's last Supreme Court opinion was *Ayotte v. Planned Parenthood of Northern New England.* The issue was whether minors must notify their parents before getting an abortion. Justice O'Connor wrote an opinion for a unanimous Court sending the decision back to the lower court to find a remedy that did not invalidate the entire state statute requiring parental notification but was narrowly tailored to meet the needs of the state, the minor, and the parents.

After another term on the Court, Justice Samuel Alito was confirmed as Justice O'Connor's replacement so she could retire. On January 31, 2006, Sandra Day O'Connor retired from the Supreme Court after decades of service. She and John took a boat trip off the coast of Turkey, but it was a disaster because John was developing late-stage Alzheimer's disease and Sandra was concerned he might jump overboard and drown. Sandra realized she could no longer take care of John herself, so she asked her children to help find suitable assisted living for him. The family persuaded John to enter the Huger Mercy Living Center in Phoenix by telling him they were taking him to a hotel while Sandra went fishing because John hated to fish. After a few weeks being retired and having John in an assisted living center, Sandra realized she didn't know what she was going to do with herself for the rest of her life. She had an office and two secretaries at the Court, but she had no purpose there and felt like an outsider. She felt unimportant now that she was not a Supreme Court Justice.

Sandra became concerned her legacy would be undone by more conservative Justices, but her rulings on affirmative action and abortion were not disturbed. The working of the Court changed without Justice O'Connor as a swing vote. After she left, the court shifted from a liberal to a conservative majority, depending on how Chief Justice Roberts and Justice Kennedy voted.

John continued to deteriorate mentally and became romantically attached to another patient at the Huger Care Center, which is not unusual for a late-stage Alzheimer's patient. When Sandra learned of the attachment, she was understanding and realized the husband she knew was not there anymore. She didn't become upset by his behavior but became a modern-day female Teddy Roosevelt, doing public service, giving speeches, and loving the West. John O'Connor died on November 11, 2009, in Phoenix. [320] Sandra was in Washington at the time, and decided not to fly home to be with him while he was dying because he would not recognize her, and she saw no point in being there to watch a stranger die.

By March of 2013, Sandra began to show early signs of failing health and became forgetful and irritable. By the late spring of 2013, she was increasingly forgetful, not recalling she had taken a trip the year before and not recognizing people she had known for years. Sandra was diagnosed with dementia and fell into denial for a while before acknowledging she couldn't remember anything. Retired Justice O'Connor is currently living in Phoenix, Arizona.

Barack Obama

Barak Obama, Jr. was born in Honolulu, Hawaii, on August 4, 1961. [321] His father, a citizen of Kenya, was studying economics at the University of Hawaii when he met and married Barak's mother, Ann Dunham. They began dating, Ann became pregnant, and they married on February 2, 1961, when interracial marriage was unusual in America. Ann's parents opposed the marriage but accepted and loved Barak. When he was two, Barak's parents separated and later divorced. Ann and Barak went to Seattle, Washington, where she enrolled in the University of Washington while his father finished his studies at the University of Hawaii, transferred to Harvard University for further studies, and then moved back to Kenya. [322]

Barak and his mother returned to Hawaii to live with her parents, and in 1967, Ann married Lolo Soetoro, an Indonesian studying at the University of Hawaii. Lolo, Barak, and his mother returned to Indonesia, and Barak attended a local Catholic school. His mother gave Barak lessons in English every morning so he would not forget his native language. She began to worry about her son's education when he turned ten, recognizing he was bright and needed a better school than those available in Indonesia. She contacted her parents, and they agreed to enroll Barak in a first-class private school in Hawaii—the Punahou School, which he attended while he lived with his grandparents. [323]

Obama's Education. Barak played basketball at Punahou and was happy during his high school years. He graduated in June 1979 and enrolled at Occidental College near Pasadena, California. Barak began to read about Black history at Occidental and became interested in the U.S. civil rights movement, studying the biographies of civil rights leaders such as Richard Wright, Langston Hughes, Malcolm X, and Martin Luther King, Jr. He also became interested in South Africa's system of apartheid, which separated Blacks and whites. Barak invited speakers from South Africa to lecture at Occidental College about the evils of apartheid and gave his first public speech condemning separation of the races. He was excited when he noticed people were paying close attention to his speech and applauded him. That was the first indication Obama had a talent for public speaking. [324]

Obama transferred to Columbia University for his final two years of college because he wanted to be close to Black culture in America. He majored in political science, international relations, and English literature. After graduation from Columbia University in 1983, Obama traveled around the world and then began working as a financial researcher and writer in New York City. After a year, he was a project coordinator for the New York Public Interest Research Group before moving to Chicago to become a community organizer. [325]

He was employed by the Developing Communities Project, financed by a group of Catholic parishes in Chicago, and designed to help Black families resolve problems with landlords, find jobs, or enroll in job training programs. Obama decided he could make a bigger difference in people's lives through law rather than social work, so he decided to become an attorney. He applied and was accepted at Harvard Law School for the fall of 1988. Obama was older and more mature than most of his classmates, studied hard at Harvard, and was research assistant to Lawrence Tribe, a well-known Constitutional scholar at Harvard Law School. [326] After his first year, Obama returned to Chicago to work at Sidley Austin Law Firm as a summer intern. He was introduced to members of the firm by Michelle Robinson, who would later become his wife. He invited her to lunch; they were attracted to each other and carried on a long-distance romance while he finished law school at Harvard.

During his senior year, Obama was elected supervising editor of the Harvard Law Review, the first Black American to hold that office. He graduated from Harvard Law School in 1991, and Boston newspapers ran a story about him being the first supervising editor of Harvard Law Review. A New York City publisher saw the newspaper story and asked Obama to write a book about his early life in America. He wrote *Dreams from My Father*, published in 1995. [327] When Obama finished law school in 1991, he returned to Chicago, married Michelle, and took a job with a Chicago civil rights law firm. He also taught Constitutional Law at the University of Chicago Law School. Obama's mother Ann died in November 1995, and he regretted not being with her during her last year, but couldn't travel because he was in the middle of a political campaign running for the Illinois State Senate from Chicago.

Obama ran as a Democrat in an area of Chicago that was predominantly Black and won the election at age thirty-five in 1996. He spent his weeks in Springfield, Illinois, where the state legislature met and then traveled to Chicago to be with Michelle on weekends. Obama found he liked being a state senator because he could work on solving problems and help the people in his district. He was active in the state legislature, passing laws that created after-school programs for children with working parents and allocating money to remove dangerous asbestos from poor families' homes. Obama thought about running for mayor of Chicago but decided to enter national politics instead. He ran for a seat in the U.S. House of Representatives in 2000 against a well-known Black civil rights leader and lost. [328] Obama stayed in the Illinois Senate until another attractive political opportunity appeared where he could run for national office. International terrorists attacked America on 9-11, crashing hijacked airplanes into the Twin Towers in New York City, killing thousands of people and changing politics.

September 11, 2001. The world changed after terrorists crashed hijacked airplanes into the Twin Towers of the World Trade Center and the Pentagon, shocking and angering the U.S. In early 2002, America declared war on Afghanistan because Osama bin Laden, the leader of Al Qaeda, was using the mountains of that country as a sanctuary for planning and executing terrorist activities around the world. These important events caused Obama to think about running for higher office so he could participate in making important decisions for the country. When President George W. Bush declared war on Iraq, Obama opposed the war, not believing the country had weapons of mass destruction. He decided to run for higher national office to have a voice in the future of his country and began looking for the right place to serve.

Senator Obama. Obama saw an opportunity to win an important political office when Peter Fitzgerald, one of two U.S. Senators from Illinois, decided not to seek another term. During his campaign for the U.S. Senate, Obama was invited to give a keynote speech at the Democratic National Convention in Boston. Obama was selected to deliver the speech because he was young, popular, Black, and a critic of President George W. Bush and the Iraq war. [329] Obama talked about his dreams for America in his keynote speech and was seen by millions across the country, instantly gaining valuable name recognition that helped his Senate campaign. Overnight, he became a well-known Democrat, and in November won a seat in the U.S. Senate from Illinois.

While in the Senate, Obama served on the Foreign Relations Committee, the Veterans Affairs Committee, Governmental Affairs Committee, Homeland Security Committee, and Health, Education, Labor, and Pensions Committee. He supported legislation that encouraged equality among the races and state assistance to the poor. On February 19, 2007, Obama announced he intended to run for President of the U.S. from the spot where Abraham Lincoln made his famous "House Divided" speech. Obama favored ending the war in Iraq, reforming health care in America, and supported progressive policies that would bring change and hope to America. His chief opponent for the Democratic nomination was Hillary Clinton. The contest was close at first, but then Obama began accumulating significant Democratic delegate support, so Hillary Clinton withdrew from the campaign and endorsed him.

President Obama. Barak Obama was the first Black American to be nominated as a presidential candidate by a major political party in the U.S. and his campaign created a sensation around the world. [330] On August 23, 2007, the Democratic Party announced that Joe Biden would be his vice-presidential running mate to add experience to the Democratic ticket. Obama ran against Republicans John McCain and Sarah Palin. Democratic candidate Obama used social media platforms such as Facebook and Twitter to connect with his supporters in a new way and was effective in getting out his message of hope and change. On November 4, 2008, the American people elected Barak Obama, the first Black president of the U.S. with fifty-three percent of the popular vote and three hundred sixty-five electoral college votes. The election was a historical first and signaled that the American people were ready to move beyond racial differences toward a more equal society.

Barak Obama was inaugurated as the 44ᵗʰ President of the United States on January 20, 2009. The first one hundred days of Obama's presidency were marked by several significant events, including issuing an Executive Order instructing the U.S. military to begin removing troops from Iraq and pledging to begin closing Guantanamo Bay detention camp in Cuba. However, Congress blocked the closing of Guantanamo Bay detention camp by denying the Obama administration funding to carry out the closure. President Obama increased state aid to international family planning organizations that performed abortions and provided contraception counseling. He also created a White House Council on Women and Girls, which formed a task force to investigate sexual assaults on American campuses. President Obama appointed Hillary Clinton Secretary of State, Timothy Geithner Secretary of the Treasury, Robert Gates Secretary of Defense, and Eric Holder Attorney General. [331] His first priority was to help American workers recover from the 2008 recession by fostering private sector job creation. He wanted to spend money on infrastructure projects and health care for uninsured Americans.

American Recovery and Reinvestment Act. In 2009, Congress passed the American Recovery and Reinvestment Act, which inserted $787 billion into the U.S. economy to help unemployed Americans overcome the 2008 recession by increasing federal spending on infrastructure, education, and health care. [332] The primary purpose of the Recovery Act was to increase employment and provide temporary financial relief for Americans impoverished by the recession. The Act, which became law on February 17, 2009, was initiated during the George W. Bush administration in collaboration with the incoming Obama administration. The stimulus bill was controversial because supporters felt it was not large enough, while opponents believed it was wasteful, inefficient, and would be hampered by government bureaucracy. Studies of its effectiveness in creating jobs concluded that unemployment was no lower after the Recovery Act had passed than it would have been had the act not passed. There is little agreement among economists about whether the money was well spent, and the U.S. economy took years to recover from the worst recession since the Great Depression of the 1930s. Another pressing issue was the survival of the American auto industry.

Auto Industry Rescue. To help the American auto industry avoid insolvency, Obama's administration gave money to Chrysler, General Motors, and Ford to allow the companies to continue operating while they reorganized. In December 2008, the U.S. government nationalized General Motors and Chrysler Corporation, and injected eighty-one billion dollars into the two companies. [333] The auto industry rescue package cost taxpayers over ten billion dollars in the end, although it succeeded in keeping the American auto industry functioning and saved thousands of American jobs. Ford Credit, a subsidiary of Ford Motor Company, received money from the government to support auto loans to customers, but Ford was never in danger of bankruptcy. Chrysler Corporation was merged with Fiat Motors of Italy to save expenses and create a more viable auto company, and General Motors reorganized and became more competitive. The auto companies agreed to design and build more energy-efficient autos as part of their bargain with the government. The rescue was believed to be necessary because auto sales fell forty-six percent after the 2008 recession and the auto companies were losing money. President Obama also nominated two Justices to the U.S. Supreme Court during his first term in office.

Justice Sonia Sotomayor. [334] To further his policy of equality in the American government, President Obama appointed Judge Sonia Sotomayor, then serving on the U.S. Court of Appeals of the Second Circuit to the U.S. Supreme Court. She was confirmed by the Senate in August 2009 by a vote of sixty-eight to thirty-one. Sotomayor attended Princeton University as an undergraduate and Yale Law School, where she was editor of the Yale Law Review. After law school, she worked for five years as a prosecutor in the Manhattan District Attorney's Office and then became a partner in Pavia and Harcourt, a private law firm handling corporate and general litigation cases. President George W. Bush appointed Sotomayor to the U.S. District Court for the Southern District of New York, and President Clinton appointed her to the U.S. Court of Appeals of the Second Circuit, which is often used as a proving ground for future Supreme Court Justices.

Justice Elena Kagan. [335] Elena Kagan attended Princeton University for her undergraduate studies and Harvard Law School where she was supervising editor of the Harvard Law Review. She served as a law clerk for Abner Mikva of the U.S. Court of Appeals for the District of Columbia and Justice Thurgood Marshall of the U.S. Supreme Court. After her experiences as a law clerk, Kagan joined the firm of William Connolly, LLP, as an associate before being appointed professor of law at the University of Chicago Law School in 1995. She served as associate counsel to President Clinton before joining the faculty at Harvard Law School in 2001. Kagan was appointed Dean of Harvard Law School in 2003 and served in that position until President Obama appointed her to the U.S. Supreme Court in May 2010. The Senate confirmed Justice Kagan on August 5, 2010, by a vote of sixty-three to thirty-seven. Perhaps the most controversial action taken by the Obama administration was passage of the Affordable Care Act (ACA), designed to lower health care costs and increase health insurance coverage for uninsured Americans.

The Affordable Care Act. On March 23, 2010, Congress passed the Affordable Care Act, expanding the availability of health care to millions of uninsured Americans. [336] Health care reform had been a priority of the Democratic Party for years, and with a majority in the House of Representatives and a super-majority in the Senate, President Obama asked Democratic Congressional leaders to draft a comprehensive health care bill that would lower costs and increase health care coverage for low-income Americans. The House of Representatives passed a health care bill 220-215 and the Senate passed its own bill by 60 to 39, enough to override a Republican filibuster. Both bills were reconciled in committee, and the ACA expanded Medicaid coverage to include families earning higher levels of income, provided health care subsidies for low-income families, mandated that all Americans must buy health insurance or pay a fine, established health care exchanges to offer health insurance policies to the public, and banned denying coverage for any person suffering from a preexisting health condition.

The Affordable Care Act met severe Republican opposition after it was passed and was challenged in the Supreme Court. The Court voted five to four to uphold the constitutionality of the Affordable Care Act, ruling that the mandate to buy health insurance was a legal tax authorized by Congress and therefore constitutional. The health insurance website, established to offer government-designed health care plans to Americans, was heavily criticized because it often failed and was difficult to navigate by individuals looking to enroll in the ACA. However, the percentage of Americans without health insurance dropped from twenty percent to thirteen percent by 2015, even though Republican congressmen continued to oppose the ACA and tried to repeal it on several occasions. The liberal wing of the Democratic Party pushed for a single-payer government health care plan that would replace all private health insurance in the U.S. with a federal health plan. However, President Obama only supported single-payer health insurance as an option along with private health insurance. The single-payer health insurance option was not adopted during his presidency because of opposition in the Senate. President Obama also worked to limit nuclear weapons during this tenure in office.

Russia-U.S. Relations. On April 8, 2010, President Obama and Russian President Dmitry Medvedev signed the Strategic Arms Limitation Treaty (SALT) to limit the number of long-range nuclear weapons possessed by the two countries and establish a monitoring system to oversee compliance with the treaty. [337] Congress ratified the treaty by a 71-26 vote in December 2010. In 2012, President Obama normalized trade relations with Russia and invited the country to join the World Trade Organization. When Vladimir Putin regained the presidency of Russia in 2012, he intervened militarily in Ukraine and annexed Crimea. The U.S. punished Russia by imposing economic sanctions on the country in an attempt to reverse the aggression against Ukraine, but with limited success. President Obama refused to arm Ukrainian forces, even with defensive weapons, so Russian military forces remained in Ukraine and Russia retained Crimea without serious consequences. President Obama justified his reluctance to intervene to counter Russian aggression in Ukraine by arguing that America has many interests in the world and to achieve anything important, the country needed to make difficult choices among competing priorities. Obama believed that domestic priorities were more important than countering Russian aggression, pointing out that America has limited resources to resolve conflicts.

The Democrats lost sixty-three seats in the House of Representatives during the mid-term elections of 2010, losing control of Congress and making it more difficult for Obama to pass significant legislation. There were several reasons for the mid-term losses by Democrats in the House of Representatives, including continued economic problems in the country, high unemployment, difficulties implementing the Affordable Care Act, and the historical fact that during mid-term elections, the party holding the White House tends to lose seats in the House of Representatives. In spite of these losses, Obama announced that he would seek a second term as President on April 4, 2011. A year later, he had secured enough primary delegates to win nomination as the Democratic candidate for President in 2012. Senator Mitt Romney from Massachusetts was nominated by the Republican Party to run against President Obama. President Obama won a second term in November 2012. During the mid-term elections of 2014, the Republican Party increased the number of seats it held in the House of Representatives and won control of the U.S. Senate for the first time since 2006. During this time, several Arab nations began revolting against their authoritarian governments and triggered what was called the "Arab Spring." These revolts created bloody civil wars in several Arab countries, including Syria.

Syrian Civil War. When the Syrian people revolted against President Assad on March 15, 2011, Obama issued a statement asking Assad to abdicate and allow the people to form a new government. Assad refused and ruthlessly suppressed the rebellion with overwhelming military force, including using chemical weapons on his own people. Assad used chemical weapons on several occasions, even though

President Obama had warned him that the use of chemical weapons by the Syrian government on its own people would be a "red line" and lead to serious consequences. [338] However, when Assad attacked his own people with chemical weapons after Obama issued his warning, America did nothing, and the Syrian civil war continued with mass killings of civilians. In 2014, Obama authorized an air campaign intended to target ISIL troops operating in regions of Syria but refused to commit American ground troops to the Syrian conflict. By combining American airpower with logistical support for indigenous American allies in Syria, especially the Kurds, President Obama was able to halt the advance of ISIL in Syria.

Osama bin Laden. In March 2011, the CIA discovered the secret hiding place of Osama bin Laden by careful observation of couriers who delivered messages to him. Osama bin Laden was living in a luxurious compound in Abbottabad, Pakistan, and directing terrorist activities from that location. President Obama discussed the intelligence with advisors and authorized U.S. Navy Seals to raid the compound and either capture or kill bin Laden. On May 1, 2011, Seal Team Six killed Osama bin Laden and collected documents, computer drives, and disks that contained important intelligence information about his terrorist operations. [339] The body of bin Laden was buried at sea to avoid his grave becoming a religious shrine for terrorists. President Obama also encouraged Congress to pass regulations to reform large financial firms in America and protect American consumers from fraud.

Dodd-Frank Wall Street Reform and Consumer Protection Act. Wall Street firms and large banks were accused of engaging in risky lending practices which were blamed for causing the mortgage crisis of 2007. The resulting severe recession was triggered by lax lending practices among American banking institutions, leading to defaults by many homeowners who could not afford the payments on extravagant mortgages they had assumed. Easy lending practices caused many people to buy homes they couldn't afford, and the resulting financial crisis caused a serious recession. President Obama wanted to reform Wall Street, and he signed the Dodd-Frank Wall Street Reform and Consumer Protection Act on July 21, 2010.

The Wall Street Reform Act increased regulations and reporting requirements on large financial firms, increased capital requirements for major banks, established a mechanism to liquidate bankrupt financial institutions in an orderly manner, and created the Financial Stability Oversight Council charged with measuring systematic risk in the banking sector and the economy. [340] The statute was designed to make it less likely financial institutions would cause another severe recession through lax lending practices by regulating the nation's financial institutions and protecting American consumers from fraud and abuse by banks. While this was happening, the Obama administration had to deal with the accusation it was spying on U.S. citizens.

Domestic Surveillance. In 2009, shortly after Obama took office, the *New York Times* reported that the NSA was collecting private communications among American citizens, including at least one member of Congress. The Obama Justice Department investigated and reported that the program was consistent with the Patriot Act, although civil libertarians criticized the government for conducting any type of domestic surveillance. In June 2013, Edward Snowden, who worked for the NSA as a private contractor, released documents showing that a program called PRISM was secretly collecting electronic information about communications between foreign citizens and Americans. [341]

In the face of international criticism, the Obama administration argued that PRISM could not read any American citizen's communication without a court-issued warrant, the program was essential to combat domestic terrorism, and the domestic surveillance program was controlled by the executive, legislative, and judicial branches of the government. However, civil libertarians continued to criticize the government's surveillance of American citizens in the name of counterterrorism. The balance between privacy and safety is difficult in a democracy, and there is often conflict between the government, which is responsible for safety, and the public which is primarily concerned with its own privacy. The Obama administration continued to face increased unemployment and slow economic growth due to the severe recession.

Taxes and the Economy. During President Obama's first term between 2008 and 2012, the unemployment rate in America increased from 4.6 percent to over 9.6 percent before it began slowly falling to 4.9 percent by the end of his second term. U.S. GDP fell during most of his first term and increased at around two percent annually during his second term. The federal debt increased from $10 trillion dollars when he took office to $14 trillion dollars when he left eight years later. Median household income declined during Obama's first term before beginning to increase slowly during his second term as the economy began to recover from recession.

President Obama and Congress clashed over tax policy during his two terms as president. Obama wanted to extend the Bush tax cuts for Americans earning less than $250,000 but increase the tax rate for persons earning more than that amount. Ultimately, he compromised with Congress and extended all the Bush tax cuts for an additional two years, accepted a thirteen-month extension of unemployment insurance benefits, and a one-year reduction in FICA payroll taxes in December of 2010. In 2012, President Obama and Congress agreed to make the Bush tax cuts permanent for all taxpayers earning below $400,000 annually and increased the income tax rate for persons earning more than that amount to 39.5 percent. The tax bill also increased the estate tax exemption to $5.12 million, indexed for inflation, and limited deductions for individuals earning more than $250,000. During Obama's first term, terrorists killed an American diplomat in Libya, and this created an uproar in Congress.

Libya. In February 2011, anti-government forces began protests in Benghazi, Libya, and the local government responded with military force to suppress the rebellion. In March 2011, the United Nations called for a no-fly zone over Libya to protect the rebels from air attacks by Gaddafi's government. The no-fly zone was enforced by NATO, Sweden, and some Arab countries. They suppressed air-defense forces and maintained a no-fly zone over the entire country. With NATO support, the Libyan rebels captured Tripoli and removed Gaddafi from power. In September 2012, Islamic terrorists burned the American Consulate in Benghazi, killing Ambassador J. Christopher Stevens and three American personnel who were attempting to protect the ambassador. [342] Congressional Republicans criticized Obama for his handling of the Libyan intervention, and he admitted his management of the Libyan affair was faulty.

Immigration Policy. President Obama supported comprehensive immigration reform, including a path to citizenship for illegal immigrants living in the U.S., but his administration and Congress were unable to agree on a plan. Consequently, President Obama issued several executive orders, including one that implemented the DACA policy covering approximately 700,000 illegal immigrants who had been brought to America while they were under the age of sixteen and were still living in the country. In 2014, Obama issued an executive order protecting over four million illegal immigrants from deportation, but the order was declared unconstitutional by the U.S. Supreme Court. Despite Obama's executive orders concerning immigration, deportation of illegal immigrants continued at a high level during his presidency. Over 400,000 illegal immigrants were deported from the United States in 2012 alone. Obama tried to develop clean energy sources in the U.S. during his presidency.

Energy Production. President Obama's administration supported the development of renewable energy sources such as solar and wind power by subsidizing the purchase of electric autos, the construction of wind towers for generating electricity, and the installation of solar panels on homes and industrial buildings. However, the major increase in energy production during Obama's presidency was created by private American oil producers who developed fracking, a procedure which allows the production of significant quantities of oil from wells that had previously been declared nearly dry. The Obama administration issued regulations aimed at increasing the efficiency of internal combustion engines, electricity generation plants, electrical appliances, and home or factory heating and cooling systems. These regulations led to a lessening of demand for energy in the U.S.

The Obama administration also stopped issuing drilling permits on federal lands and opposed the Keystone XL pipeline that would have moved oil from Canada to the Gulf of Mexico. President Obama vetoed a bill authorizing the pipeline when it was passed by Congress, saying it would damage the environment, although Canada would continue to produce the oil and it would be shipped to the U.S. by other means. President Obama tried to end the wars in Iraq and Afghanistan during his time in office but was not successful.

Iraq and Afghanistan. Obama inherited wars in Iraq, Afghanistan, and a war on terror authorized by Congress during the George W. Bush administration. Obama attempted to establish better relations with Muslim countries, limit military activities in the Middle East, and rely on diplomacy rather than military action to support America's goals against terrorists. During his 2008 campaign, Obama criticized the war in Iraq, and after winning the presidency, withdrew most American troops from that country by 2011, leaving only a small force to guard the American embassy. In 2014, President Obama was forced to reintroduce American troops into Iraq to combat growing aggression by ISIL. During his second term in office, there were over 335,000 American troops in Iraq advising and training the Iraq army and defending the country against the terrorist forces of ISIL. [343]

After a lengthy review, President Obama also increased the number of U.S. troops in Afghanistan to over 35,000 in an effort to stabilize that country and stop the Taliban from taking over the government. By 2010, the number of American fighting men in Afghanistan was over 100,000. In 2012, the U.S. and Afghanistan governments signed an agreement to turn over combat operations to the Afghanistan Army, with U.S. troops serving as advisors and trainers. President Obama announced that all American troops would be out of Afghanistan by 2016. However, Obama later announced that American troops would remain in Afghanistan indefinitely to suppress the war against the Taliban, ISIL, and al-Qaeda. One of President Obama's major goals was to delay the development of nuclear weapons by Iran and he negotiated a treaty with that country to slow the development of nuclear weapons.

Iranian Nuclear Agreement. Iran and America endured a difficult relationship since the Iranian Revolution when Muslim clerics assumed control of the country and revolutionary activists overran the American embassy in Tehran and held embassy workers hostage for months. During President Obama's administration, Iran accelerated the development of its nuclear program and increased support for state-sponsored terrorism in the Middle East, especially against Israel and Iraq. President Obama organized a group of allies to negotiate a pause in Iran's nuclear program in return for lifting economic sanctions on Iran and releasing funds owed Iran by the U.S. Negotiations continued from 2012 through 2015, when the allies, the U.S., and Iran announced an agreement to limit Iran's nuclear activities for a decade. [344] The U.S. Congress and Israel were opposed to the Iranian nuclear agreement, claiming it would not stop Iran from developing nuclear weapons and gave Iran billions of dollars to support terrorism in the Middle East.

Under the Iranian nuclear agreement, Iran promised to limit its nuclear program and give the International Atomic Energy Agency access to some Iranian nuclear facilities for inspections. America and its allies agreed to lift economic sanctions on Iran and release billions of dollars to Iran immediately. Congress refused to ratify the treaty, so it remained an agreement between the Obama administration, the allies, and Iran and could be rejected by the next U.S. administration without Congressional action. Republican congressional leaders criticized the agreement as too favorable to Iran, not guaranteed to stop Iran's nuclear weapon development, and lacking any limits on Iran's sponsoring of terrorism in the region. Also, critics said that the negotiations had not addressed Iran's ballistic missile program, which was designed to develop long-range missiles that could deliver nuclear weapons against Iran's enemies, including Israel and the U.S. The Obama administration also moved away from close relations with Israel.

Israel. President Obama and Israel's Prime Minister Benjamin Netanyahu disliked each other and disagreed about how to deal with Iran and the Palestinian issue. Obama appointed George Mitchell special envoy to the Middle East and ordered him to discuss settlement of the Israeli-Palestinian conflict, but he was unable to make any progress. Israel opposed any nuclear agreement with Iran that didn't eliminate that country's nuclear weapon program. President Obama instructed his U.N. ambassador not to veto a resolution calling for Israel to stop building settlements in the occupied territories captured during the Six-Day War of 1967. This policy shift created heated debate within the U.S. about whether America had abandoned its long-time friend Israel. President Obama negotiated major trade agreements with other countries during his administration.

Trade Agreements. The Obama Administration negotiated two major free trade agreements, the Trans-Pacific Partnership (TPP) with eleven Pacific nations, including Japan, Mexico, and Canada, and the Transatlantic Trade and Investment Partnership (TTIP). The goal of TPP was to establish free market capitalism as the basis of trade in the Pacific region, establish enforceable standards for the protection of intellectual property such as trademarks and patents, impose rules and norms on international trade, and block China from establishing a competing trade agreement that would exclude the U.S. [345] In 2015, twelve nations reached an agreement on TPP and Congress passed a bill giving the president authority to negotiate trade deals through 2021. After Obama left office, the next president withdrew the U.S. from TPP.

When Obama assumed office, he promised to manage the "most transparent" administration in history. However, his administration's actions failed to meet this standard. For example, although he promised to post all executive orders and other non-emergency actions on the government website for five days to allow public comment, he violated this pledge twice during his first month in office. The Obama administration also aggressively pursued whistleblowers and prosecuted individuals for leaking documents to the press, charging several persons under the rarely used Espionage Act of 1917. For example, Edward Snowden was charged with theft and unauthorized release of classified government documents, which showed the NSA was collecting private electronic communications among Americans without their knowledge. Some Americans called for Snowden to be prosecuted as a traitor, while others wanted him pardoned for alerting the public to massive domestic surveillance by the U.S. government. Mr. Snowden currently resides in Russia and has been given citizenship in that country.

After President Obama finished his second term as president of the United States, he has remained active in American politics, speaking out on public issues, raising money for the Democratic Party, and writing books about his life and presidency. The first volume, entitled *A Promised Land*, was published in 2020 by Crown, a division of Penguin Random House, L.L.C. in New York City.

Ruth Bader Ginsburg

Joan Ruth Bader was born March 15, 1933, in Brooklyn, New York, the second daughter of Celia Amster and Nathan Bader. [346] She grew up in an observant Jewish family, attended synagogue, and participated in traditional Jewish rituals, but abandoned her faith when she faced gender discrimination within the synagogue. There were several girls in her class named Joan, so Celia suggested the teacher call her Ruth. She excelled in school, was involved in student activities, and went to the local library weekly to check out books. Her mother encouraged Ruth to get a good education and become independent.

Ruth's mother was diagnosed with cancer when Ruth entered James Madison High School, and Celia died around the time Ruth graduated. [347] Before she died, Celia told her daughter to be civil and not let anger or envy damage her relationships. Celia also told Ruth to be independent, something few girls were encouraged to do at that time. Celia wanted Ruth to be a high school history teacher, which was a respectable job for a woman and would allow her to work, manage children, and run a household. However, Ruth wanted more.

Ruth's Education. She was offered a scholarship to attend Cornell University where she met her future husband, Martin Ginsburg. Ruth was a member of Phi Beta Kappa and the top female student in her class at Cornell. She said that the women at Cornell were smarter than the men because there was so much competition for the few slots open to females. Ruth studied hard and made excellent grades. [348] She was strongly influenced by Vladimir Nabokov, the author of *Lolita*, and Robert Cushman, an attorney who sparked her interest in law. It was Cushman who pointed out that lawyers were protecting victims of McCarthyism from censorship and economic oppression, and Ginsburg was so impressed she spent her life helping victims of discrimination.

Ruth and Martin married in June 1954, shortly after she graduated from Cornell. While working in New York over the summer, Ginsburg failed her driving test five times, and for the rest of her life, she was a terrible driver. Martin was drafted into the U.S. Army after he graduated from Cornell and they spent two years in Oklahoma. [349] He taught at the Fort Sill artillery school and played golf while Ruth worked for a local law firm, had difficulty learning to type, and decided to take the civil service exam and work for the federal government. When the Social Security Office discovered she was pregnant, they demoted her. She was furious and decided she wanted to do something about protecting women's rights when she became an attorney.

After finishing his tour in the army, Martin and Ruth moved to Boston, where they both entered Harvard Law School. [350] Ruth studied law, served on the staff of Harvard Law Review, and was caregiver for her husband when he was diagnosed with testicular cancer. After Martin's recovery, he graduated from Harvard Law School and accepted a job as a tax attorney with a New York law firm. Ruth transferred to Columbia Law School to be with Martin in New York and became the first woman to serve on two major law reviews. She graduated in a tie for first in her class at Columbia Law School in 1959. Despite graduating at the top of her class, Ruth couldn't find a job with a law firm because she was female and a mother. [351]

Legal Clerkship. Gerald Gunther, a constitutional law professor at Columbia, pressured Judge Edmund Palmieri of the U.S. District Court of the Southern District of New York to offer Ginsburg a clerkship in 1959. [352] Gunther said if Judge Palmieri didn't offer Ruth a clerkship, he would never send another clerk to him. Palmieri agreed to try her and she was his law clerk for two years. The judge said later Ginsburg was one of his best clerks. After the clerkship, Ruth worked as associate director of Columbia Law School's Project on International Procedures and was invited to co-author a book titled *Civil Procedure in Sweden* with Anders Bruzelius. She became fluent in Swedish and spent a year at Lund University in Sweden studying Swedish civil procedures. Ginsburg saw that Swedish women had the same freedoms as men and she wanted similar status for American women. When she returned to New York, Ginsburg taught civil procedure at Rutgers School of Law and spoke at international conferences about her work. [353]

Ginsburg was one of only twenty female law professors in America at the time she earned tenure in 1969. She founded the *Women's Rights Law Reporter* in 1970, the first journal in the U.S. to focus on women's issues. She moderated a law student discussion of "women's liberation" and in 1971 published two law review articles and taught a law school seminar about woman's rights.

The Women's Rights Project. In 1972 Ginsburg joined the American Civil Liberty Union's Women's Rights Project and co-authored a casebook on gender discrimination. [354] She became the first tenured female professor at Columbia Law School and authored several articles on gender discrimination, drafted court briefs, and argued six cases before the U.S. Supreme Court, winning five of them. Ginsburg established three goals for the Women's Rights Project: public education, changing discriminatory laws, and filing cases to stop gender discrimination. She attacked gender discrimination in education, credit, mortgages, renting a home, and serving in the military. Rather than trying to end all sex discrimination at once, Ginsburg developed a strategy of overturning specific gender discrimination statutes one at a time. One of the first cases she argued before the U.S. Supreme Court was about an Idaho law that preferred males when selecting an executor for an estate where there was no will.

Reed v. Reed. [355] The case concerned an Idaho law that explicitly preferred men when selecting who should administer the estate of a deceased person who died without a will. The bias she attacked was the assumption that a man is the independent member and a woman the dependent member in a marriage. In a unanimous decision, the Supreme Court ruled that Idaho's dissimilar treatment of women violated the Equal Protection Clause of the Fourteenth Amendment. Ginsburg argued that denying women equal rights suggested they are inferior to men and their work is less valuable. Once she had established that women should be treated the same as men, she set out to find a case where men were the victims of gender discrimination so she could apply the doctrine of equal treatment to men as well as women.

Moritz v. Comm'r of Internal Revenue. Her husband Martin found the ideal case in *Moritz v. Comm'r of Internal Revenue,* [356] and Ruth convinced the ACLU to fund the case. The facts were simple: Moritz, an unmarried male, needed a caretaker for his invalid mother so he could continue working as an accountant. This would have given him a tax deduction if he had been a woman, a widower, divorced, or had a wife who was incapacitated, but he was a single man and was prohibited by the tax code from taking the deduction. Moritz deducted $600 for the care of his invalid mother anyway, but his claim was denied because he didn't fit into the specified categories of the tax code. Ruth argued the Constitutional issues while Martin argued tax law before the courts. It was soon clear the Justices were not listening, so when it was Ruth's turn for final rebuttal, she appealed to their common sense by reviewing a hundred years of gender discrimination cases.

She began by discussing Myra Bradwell, the first woman who tried to pass the bar exam in Illinois in the 1860s but was refused the opportunity to take the exam and became the first woman to challenge gender discrimination. Ginsburg argued that denying Bradwell the right to attempt the bar exam established a legal precedent of gender inequality that was followed over the years. Next, she reminded the judges of the one hundred seventy-eight laws on the books which discriminated on the basis of sex and said these laws are outdated and need to be changed or overturned by the courts. Then she referred directly to Section 214 of the I.R.C., which she argued was unconstitutional. Ginsburg pointed out that the goal of the law was to give caregivers the opportunity to work outside the home, and the law should be revised to reflect its true intent by extending the deduction to unmarried men.

They lost the case in tax court and appealed to the U.S. Court of Appeals for the Tenth Circuit. [357] The Appellate Court ruled that Section 214 of the I.R.C. was unconstitutional under the Equal Protection Clause of the Fourteenth Amendment because it discriminated against Moritz on the basis of his gender. To generalize the Moritz decision, which applied only to the Tenth Circuit, to the entire nation, Ginsburg took another male gender discrimination case to the U.S. Supreme Court.

Frontiero v. Richardson. In *Frontiero v. Richardson,* [358] Ginsburg convinced the Supreme Court that not allowing the husband of a female Air Force officer military dependent status was unconstitutional gender discrimination because all wives of male Air Force officers already qualified for military dependent status. The government defended its policy of treating only women as dependents by pointing out that most men were the breadwinners in the family and the case before the Court was an exception. The nine male Justices didn't ask a single question as Ginsburg argued that gender, like race, is independent of abilities and should not be used to discriminate against anyone. She used the analogy with race because the Court had already said any law that classified individuals by race was automatically suspect and subject to strict scrutiny, and she wanted the same strict standard applied to gender discrimination. The Supreme Court ruled that the government must treat military husbands and wives the same.

Ginsburg's Views on Abortion. In 1973, Ginsburg delivered the Madison Lecture at New York University School of Law, where she argued that the Supreme Court's ruling in *Roe v. Wade* should have been limited to allow state legislatures to address the details of when and how a woman could receive an abortion, thereby avoiding many of the controversies surrounding the issue of abortion in the U.S. She was optimistic that a new morning-after pill would resolve the abortion controversy, but that didn't happen. Many women still wanted an abortion.

Ginsburg also asked what would happen if a woman became pregnant and wanted to continue working? Could a woman's constitutional right to privacy be used to protect a pregnant worker from being forced to take unpaid leave during her pregnancy? In *Geduldig v. Aiello* [359] the Court ruled, in a six to three decision, that the rule making women ineligible for benefits from the California Disability Fund did not violate the Equal Protection Clause of the U.S. Constitution. The Justices reasoned that California could constitutionally choose which disabilities to insure in order to keep its disability fund solvent and maintain workers' contributions at a reasonable level. The Court also stated that pregnancy was voluntary, so a woman had a choice about becoming pregnant.

After this loss, Ginsburg lobbied Congress to pass the Pregnancy Discrimination Act, which would require employers to treat pregnant women exactly like other temporarily disabled workers. She believed gender discrimination needed to be tackled through Congress as well as the courts. Ginsburg also realized that the Equal Rights Amendment was not going to be passed by the states.

The Equal Rights Amendment. For years feminists argued the U.S. needs an Equal Rights Amendment (ERA) that said: "Equality of rights under the law shall not be denied or abridged by the United States or by any State on account of sex." The ERA was introduced in 1923 but never made it out of a Congressional committee for years. When the ERA was finally passed by Congress and sent to the states for ratification, not enough legislatures approved the law in a timely manner, so it failed as an Amendment to the U.S. Constitution.

Ginsburg had another idea. Rather than try to amend the Constitution by adding the Equal Rights Amendment, why not argue that because the preamble to the Constitution begins with "We the people," and since women are people, they already have a right to equal protection under the Fourteenth Amendment, which promises equal treatment of all people. With this new strategy, Ginsburg began looking for cases that could be brought under the Equal Protection Clause of the Fourteenth Amendment. She found three cases where state laws discriminated against men and women and brought them to the Supreme Court.

Equal Protection Under the Fourteenth Amendment. In *Weinberger v. Wiesenfeld* [360] Ginsburg argued that denying Social Security benefits to a husband who had never worked was contrary to the Equal Protection Clause of the Fourteenth Amendment because women who had never worked were eligible for Social Security benefits from their husbands, and the Court agreed. In *Califano v. Goldfarb*, [361] Ginsburg argued that the Social Security Administration could not deny survivor benefits to widowers based on a different standard than the one applied to widows. She won that case. Finally, in *Duren v. Missouri*, [362] she convinced the Supreme Court that women should not be treated differently from men in selection for jury duty. The Court ruled that automatically excluding women from jury duty on their own request violated the Sixth and Fourteenth Amendment guarantees of a jury chosen from a cross section of the community. Next, she attacked a gender discrimination law concerning drinking age in Oklahoma.

Craig v. Boren. Ginsburg cooperated with counsel and filed a brief in *Craig v. Boren* [363] challenging an Oklahoma statute that established different drinking ages for men and women. The Court developed a new standard of review in this case known as "intermediate scrutiny" which was to be applied to state laws that discriminate on the basis of gender. This is a higher standard of review than "rational basis" but lower than the strict scrutiny standard applied in racial discrimination cases, making it easier for civil rights attorneys to win sex discrimination cases. Oklahoma law prohibited the sale of beer to males under the age of 21, but allowed women over the age of 18 to buy and consume beer. Craig, a male under the age of 21, challenged the law as discriminatory. Chief Justice Brennan wrote the seven to two decision, holding that the Oklahoma statute discriminated against males in violation of the Fourteenth Amendment. Ginsburg's strategy of using the Fourteenth Amendment seemed to be working.

In 1978, Congress passed the Omnibus Judgeship Act, substantially increasing the number of federal judges serving on district and appellate courts in America. The law required that a portion of these new judges be women and minorities. The act also required that the president and Congress consider the character and experience of judicial candidates when nominating and confirming them. In 1977-78 Ginsburg was spending a year as a fellow at the Center for Advanced Study in the Behavioral Sciences at Stanford University in Palo Alto, California, working on an article about her crusade against gender discrimination. Martin was a visiting professor at Stanford Law School and was lobbying to get Ruth appointed to the federal bench after the new judgeships were approved. Because there were vacancies, Ginsburg got her chance.

Judge Ginsburg. On April 14, 1980, President Jimmy Carter nominated Ginsburg to the U.S. Court of Appeals for the District of Columbia Circuit in Washington, D.C., and she was confirmed by Congress on June 18, 1980. During her time on the D.C. Court of Appeals, she formed close friendships with conservative Judges Robert Bork and Antonin Scalia and earned a reputation as a moderate jurist. After serving thirteen years on the D.C. Court of Appeals, President Bill Clinton nominated Ginsburg to the U.S. Supreme Court on June 14, 1993, to replace retiring Justice Byron White.

Ginsburg was recommended to President Clinton by U.S. Attorney General Janet Reno, based on discussions with Orrin Hatch, a Republican Senator from Utah. Clinton said in his speech introducing Ginsburg that he was nominating her because she was a moderate, and he wanted to increase diversity on the Court by naming a Jewish woman as a Justice. In her acceptance speech, Ginsburg discussed her role in the women's rights movement. She was confirmed by a vote of 96-3 in the U.S. Senate as the first Jewish and second woman Justice after Sandra Day O'Connor. During her testimony before the Senate Judiciary Committee, Ginsburg refused to answer several questions about her views on the Constitutionality of executions because she felt the issue might come before the Court, and she didn't want to prejudice a case. This tactic established the "Ginsburg precedent" which has been used by Supreme Court nominees on many occasions since.

Justice Ginsburg. After she joined the Court, Justice Ginsburg always wore a jabot (an ornamental ruffle) with her judicial robes during oral arguments. Supreme Court experts soon noticed she wore different jabots when she was in the majority and when she was dissenting. When Ginsburg issued a dissent, she wore a black jabot with gold embroidery and faceted stones. When she was in the majority, she wore a crochet yellow and cream jabot with crystals that was a gift from her law clerks. Both Ginsburg and O'Connor faced subtle gender issues during their early years on the Supreme Court.

When Sandra Day O'Connor was confirmed by the Senate in 1981 as the first female Supreme Court Justice, spouses of judges had a role similar to the First Lady. They sat in a special reserved section of the Supreme Court during oral arguments, they met for lunch three times a year in the Lady's Dining Room at the Court, and their photographs were published in women's magazines such as *Good Housekeeping*. Nothing changed while Justice O'Connor was the sole woman on the Court because it was not clear if the trend would continue. However, after Justice Ginsburg was confirmed and it appeared that women were going to be a permanent fixture on the Court, the Justices began to make changes, including finding a new name for the Lady's Dining Room. When John O'Connor, Sandra's husband, was diagnosed with Alzheimer's disease a few years after Ginsburg joined the Court, Martin Ginsburg became the only male member of the spousal group, but he didn't care because he loved to cook and socialize with the other Supreme Court spouses.

Sandra Day O'Connor and Ruth Bader Ginsburg supported each other on the Court, even though they were often on opposite sides of judicial opinions. Ginsburg said later that O'Connor was like a big sister to her on the court. Aside from being the first two women to serve on the Supreme Court, they had little in common. O'Connor was a Western Republican activist who rejected women's liberation, joking that she still wore a bra and wedding ring, while Ginsburg was an Eastern Democrat and radical feminist. After their first decade together on the Court, researchers found that O'Connor and Ginsburg disagreed with each other more often than any other pair of Justices on the Court. However, both O'Connor and Ginsburg agreed about most women's issues. In 2005, Justice O'Connor left the Supreme Court to care for her husband, who had developed Alzheimer's disease, and Ginsburg became the lone woman on the Court for several years until two new female Justices, Sonia Sotomayor and Elena Kagan, were added during Barak Obama's presidency.

Perhaps the most surprising friendship of two Supreme Court Justices was between Ginsburg, a liberal feminist, and Scalia, a dyed-in-the-wool conservative. Even though they were generally on opposite sides of legal arguments and Court opinions, they genuinely liked each other. Ginsburg found Scalia intelligent and amusing, and he returned the compliment by saying she is an intelligent and considerate woman. They shared a love of opera and people who could make them laugh. Ginsburg and Scalia got along because they never talked about legal or political issues when together. Her friendship for Scalia didn't extend to some of the other conservative Justices, however.

Ginsburg was introduced to rituals of the judicial conference where nine Justices discuss and vote on each case. The only record of what happens in that room are hand-written notes of Justices who choose to take them. Shortly after oral arguments, the Justices meet in conference and vote on the case. The Chief Justice sits at one end of the conference table and the senior Justice at the other. The Chief Justice summarizes the case, and then each Justice votes, with the most senior Justice speaking and voting first. If the Chief Justice is in the majority, he selects a Justice to write the opinion. On the other hand, if the Chief Justice is in the minority, the senior Justice assigns the case. Ginsburg's first-authored opinion concerned a defendant's right to a speedy trial.

Reed v. Farley. Soon after she joined the Court, Justice Ginsburg authored a five to four majority opinion in *Reed v. Farley*, [364] a criminal case in which Reed appealed his conviction, because his trial was not held within 120 days after arriving in a new jurisdiction. The Supreme Court concluded that failure to hold Reed's trial within the 120-day window was not relevant because he failed to object to the delay and suffered no harm as a result. Because Reed had made no objection, the Court ruled that he cannot now complain he was denied a speedy trial. Her next opinion involved whether determining a defendant is in custody involved a question of fact alone or a mixed fact and legal question and whether a confession was obtained properly in an Alaska criminal case.

Thompson v. Keohane. Ginsburg wrote the seven to two Supreme Court opinion in *Thompson v. Keohane*, [365] a criminal case in which Thompson confessed to Alaska State Troopers that he had murdered his wife. He was convicted based on a tape-recorded confession and appealed the conviction to a federal court under a writ of habeas corpus. The state court ruled that deciding whether Thompson was not in custody at the time he confessed was a factual determination and not subject to review by a federal court. However, the Supreme Court held that determining whether Thompson was in custody was a mixed question of fact and law, and therefore subject to review by federal courts. The Court also held that a state court determination of when a person is in custody does not qualify for a presumption of correctness. The next case Ginsburg authored involved gender discrimination by the Virginia Military Institute in its admission policy, an important case fundamental to the issue of women's rights.

United States v. Virginia. Three years after she joined the Court, Ginsburg authored the majority opinion in *United States v. Virginia*. [366] The facts of the case involved a state court ruling that the Virginia Military Institute's male-only admission policy was unconstitutional as was the offer by Virginia to create the Virginia Women's Institute for Leadership as a parallel program open only to women. The state court approved the plan to offer a separate women's program at Virginia Military Institute, but the U.S. government appealed to the Supreme Court, arguing that a women's only school does not satisfy the Equal Protection Clause of the Fourteenth Amendment. In a seven to one decision authored by Justice Ginsburg (Justice Thomas recused himself because he had a son attending the school, and Scalia dissented), the Court held that a separate but equal program for women at Virginia Military Institute was unconstitutional.

Ginsburg ruled that the men-only admission policy of the Virginia Military Institute violated the Equal Protection Clause of the Fourteenth Amendment and discriminated against women. She rejected Virginia's argument that the military education it offered was inappropriate for women, arguing that if women are to become leaders in life and the military, men need to get used to taking orders from them, and that wouldn't happen unless women are allowed to enroll at Virginia Military Institute. In his dissent, Scalia argued that the Court had imported strict scrutiny through the back door in this case and that was inappropriate. Despite the criticism from Scalia, Ginsburg was delighted that she had been able to write the opinion of a nearly unanimous Court to strike down gender discrimination in an important military school. Her next authored opinion involved a medical malpractice case in bankruptcy court.

Kawaauhau v. Geiger. In 1998, Justice Ginsburg wrote a unanimous opinion in *Kawaauhau v. Geiger.* [367] Margaret Kawaauhau was treated by Dr. Geiger for a foot injury that later became infected. She was referred to an infectious disease specialist for treatment, but then Dr. Geiger canceled her transfer to the specialist, and she was forced to have her leg amputated because of the infection. Kawaauhau sued Dr. Geiger for negligent malpractice and won a $355,000 judgment against him. Because Dr. Geiger had no insurance, he filed for bankruptcy. Kawaauhau asked the bankruptcy court to rule that the debt cannot be discharged because it falls under 11 USC section 523(a) of the Bankruptcy Code, which says that debts for willful and malicious injury cannot be discharged.

The Supreme Court determined that debts arising from reckless or negligent injury do not fit within 11 USC section 523(a) because they were not "intentional," so the debt can be discharged in bankruptcy court. Ginsburg's next opinion involved the application of Congressional sentencing guidelines to criminals arrested for crimes involving crack cocaine.

Kimbrough v. United States. In 1986, Congress passed federal sentencing guidelines requiring that crimes involving crack cocaine be subject to stiffer sentences compared with crimes involving powder cocaine. Kimbrough pled guilty to distributing more than fifty grams of crack cocaine but was sentenced to fifteen years, a term well below the guidelines passed by Congress. The government appealed the sentence as too lenient. The Supreme Court had ruled in an earlier case that Congressional sentencing guidelines are advisory but must be considered when setting a sentence. The U.S. Court of Appeals for the Fourth Circuit ruled judges cannot unreasonably depart from the sentencing guidelines simply because they disagree with the Congressional policy, and the government appealed that decision to the Supreme Court. Ginsburg drafted the seven to two opinion reversing the Fourth Court and affirming the fifteen-year sentence issued by the federal district court judge. She argued that because the guidelines are advisory, the Court is willing to tolerate some deviation from guidelines. Ginsburg also was in the majority on a case involving strip-searching of a thirteen-year-old girl suspected of carrying drugs.

Stafford Unified School District v. Redding. Justice Ginsburg joined an eight to one majority opinion in *Stafford Unified School District v. Redding,* [368] which held that school administrators overstepped their authority when they ordered a thirteen-year-old girl strip-searched for drugs. The young girl was allowed to wear only a bra and panties while a female officer searched her person for drugs. Prior to the Court issuing its decision, Ginsburg gave an interview in which she stated that the male Justices don't understand how traumatic it could be for a thirteen-year-old girl to be strip-searched because they had never been a thirteen-year-old girl. The Court ruled that the school violated the Fourth Amendment concerning unreasonable search and seizure and that Redding's suit against the school could proceed, although she could not sue the persons who had ordered the stripsearch in their individual capacities.

Sessions v. Morales-Santana. Morales-Santana was born in the Dominican Republic in 1962 to an American father and a Dominican Republic mother. At that time, the Immigration and Nationality Act stated that a child born to an unwed couple must have a father who is a citizen and has resided in the U.S. or one of its possessions for ten or more years prior to the child's birth. Morales-Santana's father did not meet that requirement, so his son was placed in removal proceedings that would lead to deportation from the U.S. because he had been convicted of felony crimes. Morales-Santana argued that he had derivative citizenship through his father, but his motion was denied by the immigration court.

He filed a motion to reopen his case, alleging that denial of derivative citizenship violated the Equal Protection Clause of the Fourteenth Amendment, pointing out that although his father did not meet the requirements for derivative citizenship, he would have met the requirements if he had been a female because the requirement for unwed citizen mothers was that they must live in the U.S. or a possession for only one year. Morales-Santana argued that this gender-based difference was a violation of the Equal Protection Clause of the Fourteenth Amendment. The U.S. Circuit Court of Appeals for the Second Circuit agreed, holding that gender-based differences in immigration rules violates the Equal Protection Clause of the Fourteenth Amendment. On appeal, the Supreme Court ruled that the different time requirements for being in the U.S. between unwed fathers and mothers violates the Equal Protection Clause of the Fourteenth Amendment, but it is up to Congress to establish a gender-neutral rule to govern the situation. Ginsburg also wrote significant dissents when she disagreed with the majority's legal reasoning in a case.

Ginsburg's Dissents. Ginsburg hated writing a dissent because that meant she had failed to convince four other Justices of her legal position. When Scalia wrote a dissent, his criticism of the majority opinion was often harsh because he believed that if a decision was wrong, it should be attacked vigorously. Ginsburg followed a similar strategy when writing dissents. A majority opinion is usually forged by compromise, but when it was not possible for Ginsburg to join the majority because she disagreed fundamentally with their legal reasoning and could not persuade four other Justices to join her theory of the case, her only option was to write a strong dissent that might change the legal community's thinking in the future. Ginsburg reasoned that sometimes a Justice has to stop arguing with his or her colleagues and begin educating the public and the legal community by writing a well-argued dissent. Her most famous dissent was in *Bush v. Gore*.

Bush v. Gore. *Bush v. Gore* placed the presidency of the U.S. in the hands of the Supreme Court. The presidential election of 2000 was so close it came down to a handful of votes in Florida, and the political fighting ended when the U.S. Supreme Court halted the state-wide Florida vote recount, effectively awarding the election to George W. Bush. The Court could have refused to hear the case, leaving the decision to the state courts, but five Justices voted to accept the case. The Court ruled that the Florida recount violated the Equal Protection Clause of the Fourteenth Amendment because different counties in Florida were using different criteria when counting their votes and that violated Bush's civil rights.

The decision was five to four, with Ginsburg writing one of four dissents. She argued that federal courts routinely defer to state high courts' interpretations of their own laws and should have followed that precedent in this important case. She wrote that deference to state courts is at the core of federalism and accused Republican Justices of being hypocrites by abandoning states' rights when that tactic suited their political agenda. Three years later, Ginsburg drafted a significant dissent in an abortion case.

Gonzales v. Carhart. [369] The Partial-Birth Abortion Act was signed into law in 2003, and Dr. Carhart, who performed partial-birth abortions, sued to stop the law from taking effect. He argued that the Act would ban many abortions and therefore place an undue burden on a woman's right to privacy. A federal district court agreed and ruled the Act unconstitutional. The government appealed to the Eighth Circuit. The Appeals Court agreed with the lower court and ruled the Act unconstitutional. The case went up to the U.S. Supreme Court, which ruled five to four that the Partial-Birth Abortion Act was constitutional and did not place an undue burden on a woman's right to an abortion because the Act applies only to a specific narrow type of abortion performed near the end of a pregnancy.

Ginsburg wrote a passionate dissent arguing that the Act placed unreasonable restrictions on a woman's right to privacy. She stated that the Act's restrictions limited a woman's ability to determine her own life course and enjoy full citizenship. Ginsburg argued that the majority opinion assuming women are emotionally fragile and subject to depression and regret after having an abortion was an outdated idea that had been discredited by science. She argued that the Act was an effort to chip away at the right to privacy which has been upheld by the Supreme Court and is central to the lives of women. Four years later, she dissented in an employment case.

Ledbetter v. Goodyear. Lilly Ledbetter filed an employment discrimination case against Goodyear Corporation, claiming the company paid females less than males for comparable work. She based her claim of gender discrimination on Title VII of the Civil Rights Act of 1964. In a five to four decision, the Supreme Court ruled that the statute of limitations started to run on Ledbetter's case during each pay period, even if she didn't know women were paid less than men for comparable work and therefore, she had no cause of action. Ginsburg said the majority opinion was "absurd" because women often cannot know they are being paid less than men for comparable work because salary scales are secret. She argued that the decision was unfair and called on Congress to amend Title VII to overturn the Supreme Court's decision. In 2008, after President Obama was elected, Congress passed the Lilly Ledbetter Fair Pay Act, making it easier for female employees to file and win sex discrimination cases against employers who pay them less than men for comparable work. In this case, Ginsburg's dissent worked. She also dissented in a voting rights case.

Shelby County v. Holder. In *Shelby County v. Holder,* [370] Ginsburg dissented when the Court majority ruled that part of the Voting Rights Act of 1965, which required some Southern states to receive prior federal clearance before they could change their voting procedures, no longer applied because these states had stopped voter discrimination. In a heated dissent, Ginsburg wrote that getting rid of preclearance for Southern states because it had worked in the past was like throwing away your umbrella because you were not getting wet today. She argued that without the umbrella of preclearance, Southern states would change their voting procedures to discriminate against minority groups as they had in the past. Near the end of her life, Ginsburg became notorious as a liberal Justice of the U.S. Supreme Court and developed a pop culture following on social media.

Cultural Icon. During her last years on the Supreme Court, Ruth Bader Ginsburg became a favorite of feminist progressives and captured the attention of Internet users for ignoring Supreme Court customs. She became famous for reading her dissents from the bench, a clear break with tradition, and a sharp criticism of her colleagues. Justice Ginsburg was perplexed by the attention she received and surprised that she had become popular with social media users. She also faced serious health issues during her later years.

After facing recurring treatments for cancers, several law professors suggested Ginsburg should resign and give President Obama the opportunity to appoint a liberal successor while he was in office. However, she liked her job too much to resign, and because of seniority, she had significant power within the court. When Justice John Paul Stevens retired in 2010, Justice Ginsburg became the most senior liberal Justice and the leader of the liberal wing of the Court. She loved the power and because she believed the Supreme Court was headed in the wrong direction, was reluctant to retire and risk having her work overturned by conservative Justices.

Ginsburg's Legacy. After she founded the Women's Rights Project at the ACLU, Ginsburg developed a plan to give women equal legal and economic rights, sexual freedom, and access to contraception and abortion. She worked for these goals all her life and made enormous progress toward gender equality through teaching, writing, and Supreme Court opinions. After the arrival of two new Republican Justices created a narrow conservative majority, she feared her proudest achievements would be reversed if she resigned, so she decided to stay on the Court to protect her legacy. She believed racial justice, women's reproductive rights, access to affordable health care, and worker protections were under attack by conservatives, and she was determined to stay on the Court as long as possible to protect her legacy.

In 2016, Ginsburg published a book about her life titled *My Own Words*. Her book made the New York Times bestseller list. In 2018, she expressed support for the *Me-Too* movement in America and personally encouraged women to speak out about their experiences with sexual harassment. Ginsburg said that women had been silent too long, and it was time for them to speak up about their experiences with sexually aggressive men. She reported that when she was in college, a chemistry professor had offered to give her the answers to an exam in return for sex and she was disgusted by the offer. Ginsburg developed several maxims during her life: pick your battles, don't burn your bridges, work on what you believe in, set a goal and work for it, don't be afraid to be a leader, develop and enjoy a sense of humor, and do what makes you happy. Sound advice to live a full and productive life.

In 1999, Ginsburg was diagnosed with colon cancer, the first of several struggles with the feared disease. She endured surgery, chemotherapy, and radiation, but never missed a Court session in those years. She became physically weaker because of the chemotherapy and began working with a personal trainer to improve her fitness. In 2009, Ginsburg was diagnosed with pancreatic cancer when a small tumor was discovered. She was treated and returned to the bench to assume full-time work. In 2018, she fell and fractured three ribs. The CT scan of her ribs revealed cancerous nodules in her left lung and part of that lung was removed at Memorial Slone Kettering Cancer Center. In 2020 her cancer recurred. Rather than resign, she chose to remain on the Court so long as she could do her job. She died of complications from cancer on September 18, 2020.

Conclusion

Portraits of Leadership includes biographies of extraordinary men and women who helped America develop into a free and prosperous constitutional democracy. Beginning with George Washington, *Portraits* traces the history of America through the lives of important leaders who shaped U.S. democracy and law. The talented leaders presented in my book applied their talents during critical periods in American history to shape our Constitutional form of government, preserve the Union, free Black slaves, defend the country, ensure equal treatment of all peoples, protect civil rights, and heal tribal divisions.

George Washington gained military experience during the French and Indian War fighting alongside the British, commanded the Continental Army during the American Revolution, chaired the Constitutional Convention of 1787, and was unanimously elected first U.S. President. He opposed English tax policies after the French and Indian War and became an early advocate of independence. Washington was probably the most important Founding Father and led the country as its first elected President. He devised a defensive hit-and-run strategy during the Revolutionary War that avoided defeat until France tipped the balance in America's favor. He was a natural leader, courageous general, excellent judge of talent, even-handed commander, and American patriot. Washington enjoyed the respect of Congress, was diplomatic, able to listen to advice from professional French generals, and ultimately won the Revolutionary War for America.

After the war, Washington returned to Mount Vernon and resumed his life as a wealthy plantation owner. However, the Continental Congress was unable to govern the thirteen states effectively, so he was called from retirement to preside over the Constitutional Convention of 1787. Washington oversaw a compromise that met the needs of New England merchants, Southern plantation owners, yeoman farmers, and different-sized states. The issue of slavery was resolved by giving Southern states three-fifths of a vote for each Black slave in their territory and drafting ambiguous language about the future of slavery. Washington was the unanimous choice to be our first President and established sensible precedents during his eight years in office.

His administration established a National Bank, assumed state and federal debts, avoided foreign entanglements, and Washington limited his tenure as President to two terms, setting a precedent that was not broken until Franklin Roosevelt served four terms during World War II. Washington and Hamilton placed America's finances on a sound footing, created a mint, the Coast Guard, and a customs service. Washington formed the diplomatic corps, subdued Indian uprisings, suppressed a rebellion against the whiskey tax, and avoided war with foreign nations. He was likely our greatest President and a shining example of American leadership.

Alexander Hamilton was a financial genius who guided the young republic through its early economic problems. He fought in the American Revolution, drafted many of the Federalist Papers, was the first Secretary of Treasury in President Washington's cabinet, put the U.S. government on a stable financial footing, founded the Coast Guard, and was killed in a duel with Arron Burr. Hamilton was the manager of Beekman and Cruger, a New York trading house in the Caribbean, where he learned about banking, finance, and money at a young age. He migrated to America, became a successful Wall Street lawyer, aide to General Washington, author of many Federalist Papers, and first Treasury Secretary. Washington asked Hamilton to write memoranda to Congress and orders for his generals during the war because he was able to draft clear prose.

Hamilton attended the Constitutional Convention of 1787, where delegates fashioned a federal government that included a President elected for four years, a bicameral Congress, and a Federal Judiciary with lifetime appointments. As Treasury Secretary, he issued federal bonds to pay off war debts, established a National Bank, formed the U.S. Coast Guard, and collected customs duties on imports. Hamilton supported a strong federal government.

He was a superb administrator, but his private life was a mess. Hamilton had an affair with Mrs. Reynolds while his wife and children were in New York and carried on a life-long dispute with Aaron Burr that ultimately led to his death in a duel. Hamilton accomplished many important things during his short life, but his most important contribution was to organize the Treasury Department and rationalize American finances. Modern politicians occasionally disagreed with his ideas of having a Central Bank to act as a lender of last resort and using deficit financing to stimulate the economy, but today most Americans agree his ideas for managing federal finances were sound and contributed to the development of a strong capitalist economy.

John Adams succeeded Washington as our second President and carried on his policies of avoiding foreign wars and strengthening the central government. He was an early supporter of colonial independence, a delegate to the First Continental Congress, minister to France during the Revolutionary War, Washington's first vice president, and second President of the U.S. Adams paid off the national debt, strengthened the U.S. Navy, and avoided foreign wars. He believed English tax policy was unfair to the Colonies and was one of the first Founding Fathers to favor independence from England.

As a leading member of the Continental Congress, Adams asked Thomas Jefferson to draft the Declaration of Independence because he didn't believe it would be an important document. The Declaration made Jefferson an instant celebrity when it was published. Adams sailed to France in February 1778 to help Benjamin Franklin convince France to join the war against England. France never formally declared war on England but was instrumental in helping America win independence. Adams traveled to Holland while he was in Europe to ask for a loan, but the Dutch Government was reluctant to lend the U.S. money because of English threats. When news arrived in Europe that Washington had defeated Cornwallis at Yorktown, Holland quickly issued a two-million-dollar loan to America, which stabilized U.S. credit.

Congress appointed John Jay, John Adams, and Benjamin Franklin to negotiate peace with England. Adams was a leading delegate at the Constitutional Convention of 1787 and recommended that the new federal government contain an executive, a bicameral Congress, and a judiciary appointed for life. He drafted the Massachusetts State Constitution and served as vice president during President Washington's two terms. John Adams ran against Thomas Jefferson after Washington left office and became the second U.S. President in 1796. He avoided war with England and France, even though both countries were attacking American shipping during the Napoleonic War. In the election of 1800, Adams ran against Jefferson a second time and lost. Before leaving office, Adams appointed John Marshall Chief Justice of the U.S. Supreme Court and the Senate promptly confirmed him. John Adams died on July 4, 1816, fifty years to the day after he signed the Declaration of Independence.

John Marshall helped the U.S. Supreme Court become a co-equal branch of the federal government during his long tenure as Chief Justice. He served in Washington's army during the Revolutionary War, was a prominent attorney, a diplomat, Congressman, Secretary of State, and the most influential Chief Justice in the history of the Court. Marshall gave the Court authority to determine the constitutionality of Congressional legislation and the right to interpret the U.S. Constitution.

Marshall's formal education included one year of grammar school and six weeks of law school, but he was bright and rose quickly in status. He owned household slaves, but supported the gradual ending of slavery and advocated sending freed slaves back to Africa. President Adams nominated Marshall Secretary of State on May 12, 1800. Secretary Marshall had extraordinary authority at that time: his office issued passports, copyrights, land patents, and oversaw the Justice Department. His State Department also ran the mint, handled the census, supervised U.S. territories, and published government documents. He also negotiated treaties with France, England, Spain, and the Barbary pirates as Secretary of State and believed diplomacy was the key to avoiding war.

Marshall's opinion in *Marbury v Madison* established the principle that the Supreme Court could declare Congressional statutes unconstitutional and interpret the U.S. Constitution. His Court also created the doctrine of federal supremacy over state government actions. In 1816, Maryland imposed a tax on notes issued by the Second Bank of the United States, which raised the issue of whether the federal or state governments had superior authority. Marshall issued an opinion stating that the federal government is supreme, and Congress has "all necessary and proper" implied power to carry out its express powers. During his tenure, the Supreme Court issued over one thousand opinions, and Marshall personally authored more than half of them. His Court defended the separation of powers within the federal government, the sanctity of contracts, and established the supremacy of federal statutes. His strengthening of the U.S. Supreme Court made America a more civil place to live.

Thomas Jefferson drafted the Declaration of Independence and became a celebrity when he proposed that all men are equal. This doctrine led to significant reforms in America over the centuries, including the abolition of slavery and giving Blacks and women equal rights. Jefferson was elected Governor of Virginia in 1779 and served as the first Secretary of State in Washington's administration. He favored France over England and was a significant member of Washington's cabinet along with

Alexander Hamilton. These two bright and assertive men were rivals throughout their lives, although Hamilton often prevailed when Washington was President.

Jefferson ran against Aaron Burr and John Adams in 1800 and was elected President by the House of Representatives after twenty-six ballots. In his inaugural address, President Jefferson proposed a smaller federal bureaucracy and said he believed Congress should be the dominant branch of government. The Barbary pirates declared war on American shipping during his first term, and Jefferson sent the U.S. Navy to defeat them. He authorized James Monroe to purchase the Louisiana Territory from Napoleon for $15 million and sent Lewis and Clark on an expedition to map the new acquisition. Jefferson opposed Marshall's idea that the Supreme Court was the final arbitrator of the U.S. Constitution. However, because the Court had already ruled that it had the right to review Congressional statutes and interpret the Constitution, there was nothing he could do to change that fact.

Jefferson's second term as President was a disaster because of the war between France and England. He closed American ports to English and French shipping during the Napoleonic War, but the closures caused a recession in America and made him unpopular. After leaving office, Jefferson claimed he was morally opposed to slavery, but didn't free his own slaves when he died. He designed the University of Virginia in 1819, developing a plan that was far-reaching, brilliant, and unworkable. Jefferson died on July 4, 1816, fifty years after he signed the Declaration of Independence.

Andrew Jackson served in the House of Representatives, the Senate, the Tennessee Supreme Court, and as a general in the War of 1812 before being elected President in 1828. In 1806, Charles Dickinson published an attack on his wife, Rachel, and Jackson challenged him to a duel. Dickinson fired quickly and hit Jackson in the chest, but Jackson waited, took careful aim, and killed Dickinson. In 1814, the British were planning to invade New Orleans, so Jackson imposed martial law on the city and built strong defenses to protect it. The British made easy targets for American sharpshooters, who claimed over two thousand casualties in the battle. The victory at New Orleans made him a candidate for President later.

Jackson won the most votes in the election of 1824, but not enough to win the presidency. The House of Representatives elected John Quincy Adams that year. Jackson ran again in 1828 and won. He shifted power to ordinary Americans, supported agrarian interests, states' rights, a limited federal government, and opposed rich capitalists whom he feared would corrupt the government. South Carolina claimed it had the right to ignore federal laws and secede from the Union if it was not getting fair treatment from the federal government. Jackson feared that would destroy the Union and he opposed the idea.

Because relations between white settlers and Native Americans were often violent, Jackson asked Congress to pass the Indian Removal Act in 1830, authorizing him to buy tribal lands and move the Native Americans to public lands further west. In 1832, Jackson won the presidency for a second time. A week later, South Carolina nullified the Tariff of 1832, saying it would not collect the tax on imported goods and challenging the authority of the federal government. In his State of the Union message, Jackson asked for a peaceful resolution of the crisis. Senator Clay's Compromise of 1833 lowered tariffs and authorized Jackson to use force if South Carolina didn't accept the compromise. The Union was safe for a generation until the issue of slavery started the Civil War.

Jackson withdrew federal funds from the Second Bank of the United States to prevent its rechartering. Clay accused Jackson of trying to establish an elected monarchy. To defend himself, Jackson took his case directly to the people by publishing articles in major papers explaining why he was withdrawing federal funds from the bank. The House of Representatives overwhelmingly supported Jackson's withdrawal of funds from Biddle's bank, and he succeeded in blocking the bank's rechartering.

On January 9, 1835, as Jackson was walking out of the House chamber, Richard Lawrence fired at him from ten feet away. The cap exploded, but the powder didn't. Lawrence withdrew another pistol and fired again, but it also failed. Jackson was probably saved by excess moisture in the Rotunda coming from an empty tomb waiting for the remains of George Washington.

Daniel Webster was an attorney, diplomat, legislator, and staunch enemy of slavery, who wanted to be President most of his life. He served in the U.S. House of Representatives during the War of 1812, became a Senator, was appointed Secretary of State, and argued over two hundred cases before the U.S. Supreme Court. When America faced a severe financial crisis after the War of 1912, Webster drafted a National Bank bill that passed the House with a large majority and was elected to the Senate a second time. Webster argued that slavery is evil and should be abolished by the slave-holding states themselves to avoid destroying the Union. He worked tirelessly to reach a compromise on the issue of slavery among the new states as they were admitted to the Union.

In 1844, Webster had a golden opportunity to be president when Benjamin Harrison asked him to run as his vice president, but Webster refused. Harrison died shortly after taking office and Vice President Tyler became President. Webster regretted that decision the rest of his life. He resigned as Secretary of State to run for another term in the Senate to deal with slavery. The U.S. invaded Mexico, occupied Mexico City, and America annexed Arizona, California, New Mexico, Texas, Colorado, Nevada, and Utah at that time. The addition of these new territories raised the question of whether they would be free or slave states when admitted to the Union.

Webster wanted the territories to be free, but Southern senators wanted to allow each state to decide for itself whether to be free or slave. Webster became Secretary of State again because he believed that office was his ticket to winning the presidency. The Senate admitted California as a free state, abolished the slave trade in Washington, D.C., and passed a bill requiring all states to return escaped slaves to their rightful owners, hoping these moves would placate Southern Senators. Exhausted from his labors at the State Department and his campaign for President, Webster left for a vacation in Boston. On the way North, his carriage broke and Webster fell, striking his head. His health declined and Webster died on October 24, 1852, in Marshfield, Massachusetts.

Abraham Lincoln was one of our great Presidents because he won the Civil War and abolished slavery in America. He was a natural storyteller and leader who worked as a clerk, soldier, carpenter, blacksmith, surveyor, postman, and lawyer before becoming President in 1860. Lincoln was elected to the U.S. House of Representatives from Illinois in 1846 and served in the U.S. Senate before being elected President. Lincoln became prominent through a series of debates with Senator Stephen Douglas about slavery. Lincoln argued that slavery is morally wrong and should be abolished, while Senator Douglas said slavery is beneficial to Blacks and should be preserved. In 1860, Republican Lincoln was

HARRY L. MUNSINGER, J.D., PH.D.

elected because the Democrats split their vote between Northern and Southern candidates. Shortly after Lincoln was elected President, several Southern states seceded from the Union.

The Union strategy during the Civil War was to blockade Southern ports, send an army down the Mississippi River to split the Confederacy, and defeat General Lee's army in the East. Early battles went badly for the Union because Confederate generals were better tacticians and fought an aggressive campaign while Union generals procrastinated. When they did win a battle, Union generals failed to follow up their victory by pursuing Lee's army and destroying it. Slavery was constantly on Lincoln's mind during the Civil War, but he was reluctant to free any slaves while the North was losing battles. After General Grant conquered Vicksburg and closed the Mississippi to Southern shipping, things began to look up for the Union. However, General McClellan did little on the Eastern front, so Lincoln finally replaced him. On July 4, 1863, Lincoln learned Lee had been defeated at Gettysburg and believed that the tide of battle was turning in the Union's favor. Consequently, he issued the Emancipation Proclamation freeing all slaves.

Lincoln appointed General Grant Supreme Commander of Union forces and promoted him to Lieutenant General because he would fight. Lincoln won a second term as President against McClelland now that the Union Army was winning battles and Northern voters supported his policies. On April 9, 1865, Lincoln learned that General Lee had surrendered his army at Appomattox. In a speech shortly after the war ended, Lincoln thanked Grant for his leadership and said he wanted to give freed slaves the right to vote. John Wilkes Boothe was angered by these words and killed Lincoln at Ford's Theatre on April 14, 1865.

Theodore Roosevelt suffered from childhood asthma, but followed a program of exercise and overcame the malady. He graduated from Harvard College in 1876 and went to Columbia Law School, writing *The Naval War of 1812* while studying law. He lost his mother and wife in 1884 and went to the Dakota Territory to manage a cattle ranch and recover. Roosevelt hunted buffalo, raised cattle, organized an association to stop rustling, wrote magazine articles and three books: *Hunting Trips of a Ranchman, Ranch Life and the Hunting Trail,* and *The Wilderness Hunter* while in the Dakota Territory. The winter of 1886-87 killed most of his cattle and ruined his ranch, so Roosevelt returned to New York and reentered politics.

In 1889, he became the U.S. Civil Service Commissioner, and in 1895 he was appointed to the Police Board of New York City. President McKinley appointed him Assistant Secretary of the Navy in 1897. Roosevelt began lobbying Congress to build more battleships and eject Spain from Cuba. On February 15, 1898, the *USS Maine* exploded in Havana Harbor, killing hundreds of crewmen and sinking the ship. Roosevelt blamed Spain for the explosion, and Congress declared war. He formed the First U.S. Volunteer Cavalry Regiment (the Rough Riders) and became famous for leading the charge up San Juan Hill (actually, Kettle Hill next door) on July 1, 1898.

Shortly after Roosevelt returned from Cuba, he ran for Governor of New York and won. As Governor, Roosevelt tried to limit the excesses of large corporations, protect the poor, regulate railroad rates, mediate conflicts between capital and labor, and conserve natural resources. In 1900, he ran as vice president with McKinley. They won, and six months later on September 6, 1901, President McKinley was shot and killed by Leon Czolgosz, an American anarchist who was angry at the federal government. Roosevelt became the youngest President in U.S. history. He said he would follow McKinley's policies and keep his cabinet ministers in office. However, Roosevelt was too strong-willed to follow anyone's lead for long. He soon set out to make his own mark on the country.

Roosevelt used the Sherman Antitrust Act to regulate monopoly trusts and was the most active President in American history until Franklin Roosevelt. During his second year in office, Roosevelt uncovered corruption in the Bureau of Indian Affairs, the U.S. Land Office, and the U.S. Postal Service. He vigorously prosecuted corrupt officials and was proud of his work in conserving America's natural resources. He established the U.S. Forest Service and created five new National Parks. Roosevelt also supported the Antiquities Act, which allows Presidents to designate historic landmarks as national monuments.

Roosevelt believed the U.S. had a vital national interest in building a canal to allow ships to travel from one ocean to the other. He convinced Congress to pass the Spooner Act approving a Canal. After months without formal approval by Colombia, Roosevelt began working covertly to separate Panama from Colombia. The rebellion succeeded and the U.S. quickly signed a treaty giving America the right to build a canal across the Isthmus of Panama.

Roosevelt was nominated for a second term by the Republican Party in 1904 and won easily. During his second term, Roosevelt wanted Congress to regulate corporations, pass a federal incorporation bill, impose a federal income tax, and an inheritance tax. He also wanted to limit injunctions against labor unions that forbid them from striking because they tended to cripple the union's power to force wage increases. None of these bills passed, although the Republican Party controlled both houses of Congress because Congressional Republicans were more conservative than Roosevelt

He made it a priority of his administration to maintain friendly relations with the Japanese to counterbalance the Russian Empire. In 1904-05, Russia and Japan went to war over conflicting claims in the Korean Peninsula and China. Russia and Japan asked Roosevelt to mediate a peace treaty between the two powers. He tried to make the treaty fair to both sides and succeeded in resolving the war. Roosevelt honored his pledge not to run for a third term and supported William Howard Taft in 1908. He took a trip to Africa, visiting the Belgian Congo, traveling up the Nile to Khartoum, and hunting big game. Roosevelt wrote an account of his safari in *African Game Trails*. When Roosevelt returned to America, he was concerned by President Taft's policies, so he decided to oppose him in the next presidential election. Roosevelt and Taft split the Republican party vote and Woodrow Wilson was elected President of the U.S. in 1912.

After his loss, Roosevelt went hunting in South America. During a trip down the River of Doubt in Brazil, Roosevelt injured his leg and it became infected. He also contracted what modern physicians believe was malaria. Roosevelt's health declined; he developed a high fever, became delirious, and never regained his strength.

Oliver Wendell Holmes, Jr. changed the course of American common law through his writings, Supreme Court opinions, and dissents. He fought in the Civil War, practiced law, served on the Supreme Judicial Council of Massachusetts, and was nominated to the U.S. Supreme Court by President Theodore

Roosevelt. Holmes wrote seminal Supreme Court opinions during his long tenure on the Court. He left Harvard College to join the Massachusetts Volunteer Militia when the Civil War started and was wounded at Ball's Bluff in his first battle. Holmes was later wounded in the neck and heel in other battles. After the war, Holmes attended Harvard Law School, became an attorney, edited the *American Law Review*, lectured on constitutional law at Harvard, and revised *Commentaries on American Law*.

Holmes delivered the Lowell Lectures in 1880 and published them in a book titled *The Common Law*. He argued that the common law is a summary of procedures and decisions developed by judges rather than a systematic theory of law. Holmes also developed the doctrine of legal realism, which argued that the common law is not derived from formal legal theory, but develops through judicial opinions made by judges who balance social interests and public policy when deciding cases. Holmes believed in judicial restraint and wanted judges to consider the effects of their rulings on society. In *Swift & Co. v. United States*, Holmes wrote that Congress has the power to regulate trusts and any commercial activity that is part of the "stream of commerce" and interstate in character.

In *Moore v. Dempsey*, an important due process case, the Court held that when a jury finds an accused person guilty of murder and a state judge hurries the trial and conviction because of mob pressure, the verdict is void. In *Nixon v. Herndon*, Holmes ruled that barring Blacks from participating in Democratic primary elections violates the Fourteenth Amendment to the U.S. Constitution. Holmes enjoyed writing dissents because he could express his ideas without having to compromise. His legal reasoning in these dissents was often adopted years later by the Supreme Court. In 1928, Holmes became the longest-serving Supreme Court Justice in history.

Woodrow Wilson served as President of Princeton University, Governor of New Jersey, and President of the U.S. He kept America out of World War I for three years, brought the U.S. into the war in 1918 to help the Allies defeat Germany, participated in the Versailles Peace Treaty, had a stroke while campaigning to get the treaty passed in the U.S. Senate, won the Nobel Peace Prize, and died a disillusioned man. Wilson was the first President to give regular press conferences, personally deliver his State of the Union address to a joint session of Congress, and support establishing the Federal Reserve as a lender of last resort during financial crises.

During Wilson's second term as President, Germany announced unrestricted submarine warfare and began sinking American ships, so Wilson asked Congress for a declaration of war. Germany launched a major ground offensive soon after that, but failed to win because American troops arrived in time to turn the tide in favor of the Allies. Wilson participated in the peace negotiations after the war because he feared Britain and France would insist on a vengeful surrender and he wanted to avoid provoking another war in Europe. The Treaty of Versailles contained articles establishing the League of Nations, forcing German disarmament, limiting the German military, blaming Germany for starting the war, and levying ruinous reparations on the country. The Versailles Treaty was a recipe for disaster that helped Hitler come to power a generation later and start World War II.

Wilson suffered a serious stroke on a speaking tour of the U.S. organized to sell the Versailles Treaty and the League of Nations to the American people. He was unable to function after the stroke, so his wife ran the country during his last months in office. At that time, there was no formal procedure for determining whether a President was fit to perform his duties, so his wife and the Cabinet kept silent and carried on governing in secret. The Versailles Treaty was rejected by the Senate and Wilson went into denial during his last months in office. On April 14, 1920, Wilson tried to hold a cabinet meeting, but the members soon realized he could not conduct a coherent discussion. Sigmund Freud wrote that Wilson had a mental breakdown after his stroke and was no longer an independent person. Wilson was awarded the Nobel Peace Prize for his work in ending World War I, but lived the last years of his life in isolation.

Franklin D. Roosevelt was one of America's great presidents because he led America through the Great Depression and World War II. He served as Assistant Secretary of the Navy during World War I, ran for vice president in 1920, was elected President in 1932, helped America recover from the Great Depression, led the U.S. to victory in World War II, and died of a stroke before the war was over. Roosevelt said he would not have been nominated for president in 1932 if he had not run for vice president in 1920 and lost. During a summer at his Canadian vacation home, Roosevelt was diagnosed with poliomyelitis, although some modern physicians believe he might have suffered from Guillain-Barre Syndrome instead. After his rehabilitation, Democrats began asking Roosevelt to run for Governor of New York. He won the office by twenty-five thousand votes.

Three years into the Great Depression in 1932, Democrats asked Roosevelt to run for President against Herbert Hoover. Roosevelt collected four hundred seventy-two Electoral College votes and won by a landslide. After his inauguration, Congress quickly passed the Emergency Banking Act and the Civilian Conservation Corps. Roosevelt took America off the gold standard, and Congress passed the Glass-Steagall Act requiring investment firms to divest their banking functions to avoid losses to depositors when there was a stock market failure. He announced the repeal of Prohibition on December 5, 1933. During the 1940 Presidential election, the Battle of Britain was fought in the skies over London as England stood alone against Nazi Germany. Roosevelt won a third term as President and immediately began sending old ships and new war materials to England under the Lend-Lease Program to support her efforts against the Nazis.

On December 7, 1941, Japan attacked Pearl Harbor and America entered the war. The American Navy ambushed the Japanese at Midway, and the Japanese never regained superiority over America after that defeat. Stalin, Churchill, and Roosevelt met and agreed that the invasion of France would occur in the spring of 1944. Roosevelt decided to run for an unprecedented fourth term because he wanted to finish the war, although he didn't live to see victory. Roosevelt's health declined rapidly in 1945, he lost weight, had no appetite, and his blood pressure was high. Roosevelt, Stalin, and Churchill met at Yalta and agreed that Germany would be divided into four parts after the war. When he returned to America, Roosevelt addressed a joint session of Congress and outlined the agreements reached with Stalin and Churchill at Teheran. That was his last public appearance. On Thursday, April 12, 1945, Roosevelt said, "I have a terrific pain in the back of my head." He slumped forward, collapsed, and never regained consciousness.

Earl Warren served as Attorney General and Governor of California before being nominated Chief Justice of the U.S. Supreme Court by President Eisenhower. As Chief Justice, Warren desegregated

America's schools, expanded criminal defendants' rights, and chaired the Warren Commission that investigated President Kennedy's assassination. By the end of his first term as Governor of California, Warren was considering running for President. In 1952, Eisenhower became President and decided to eliminate Warren as a rival for the next presidential election, so they reached a confidential understanding. Eisenhower promised to nominate Warren to the United States Supreme Court as soon as a position was available. Chief Justice Fred Vinson died soon after, and Eisenhower named Warren Chief Justice of the Supreme Court.

Shortly after Warren took over as Chief Justice, one of the most important civil rights cases in a century came before the Supreme Court. In *Brown v. Board of Education of Topeka,* the issue was whether it was constitutional to deny admission of Black children to white schools based on race alone. Warren wrote the unanimous opinion of the Court, feeling it would carry more authority if drafted by the Chief Justice. He ruled that separate educational facilities for Black children violate the Equal Protection Clause of the Fourteenth Amendment. Warren based his decision on social science rather than legal precedent, giving Southern opponents ammunition to attack the ruling and delay school desegregation. Southern governors took advantage of the situation and blocked desegregation for months. Arkansas Governor Faubus decided to test the Supreme Court ruling and forced Eisenhower to send armed soldiers to enforce the Supreme Court's authority in Little Rock High School.

Another important Warren Court decision concerned a defendant's rights during police interrogation. In *Miranda v. Arizona,* Warren ruled that the Fifth Amendment requires law enforcement officials to advise suspects of their right to remain silent and have an attorney present during interrogation when they are in police custody. On November 22, 1963, there was a knock on the door of the Supreme Court chambers, and a note was handed to Warren saying President Kennedy had been assassinated in Dallas. President Johnson organized the Warren Commission to investigate the killing. The Commission concluded that Oswald acted alone, although the FBI never accepted the theory that a single bullet killed Kennedy and wounded Connally. Warren died on July 9, 1974, only hours after the Supreme Court forced President Nixon to turn over a secret recording discussing the Watergate burglary.

John F. Kennedy resolved the Cuban Missile Crises without plunging the world into a nuclear war, dealt with the Berlin Crisis, and expanded American involvement in the Vietnam War. He became a hero when his PT boat was sunk in the South Pacific during World War II, served in the U.S. House of Representatives and the Senate before being elected President in 1960. During his short tenure as President, Kennedy faced a crisis in Cuba, dealt with the Soviet Union's building of the Berlin Wall, and expanded America's involvement in the Vietnam War before he was assassinated by Lee Harvey Oswald.

After he returned from the South Pacific and was discharged from the Navy, Kennedy's father recommended he run for a seat in the House of Representatives. Kennedy won and used the position as a stepping stone to the Senate. He needed a wife to project an image of a family man rather than a womanizer, so Kennedy married Jacqueline Bouvier, who was young, pretty, socially prominent, and Catholic. Kennedy took steroids for Addison's disease, and as a result, his back caused him severe pain all his life. He published *Profiles in Courage,* a book describing the careers of eight senators who made unpopular votes because it was the right thing to do. Kennedy won the presidency in 1960 by stressing economic issues and national security.

A CIA-planned invasion of Cuba by mercenaries failed soon after he assumed office, and then Khrushchev threatened to sign a unilateral treaty with East Germany. In 1961, East German forces built a wall around the Soviet sector of Berlin to keep German citizens inside the Soviet sector. A U-2 reconnaissance flight discovered that missile sites were under construction in Cuba during 1962, triggering a crisis. Kennedy ordered a naval blockade to stop Khrushchev from arming the missiles, and after a tense standoff, the Soviets backed down. The Cuban Missile Crisis was the most dangerous moment during the Cold War and could have resulted in World War III had Kennedy not handled the threat carefully.

In 1963, the American Ambassador to Saigon recommended launching a military coup against the civilian government of Vietnam. However, changing the government in Vietnam did little to improve the war situation. Kennedy planned campaign events during November 1963 in Texas to greet crowds at airports and spend time in motorcades at San Antonio, Dallas, and Houston. The Secret Service failed to discover that Lee Harvey Oswald, a mentally unstable person who had lived in Russia for almost three years, was planning to kill Kennedy in Dallas. Oswald fired three shots from the sixth-floor window of the Book Depository building at President Kennedy traveling in an open car directly below, hitting the President in the neck and head. Doctors at Parkland Memorial Hospital in Dallas pronounced Kennedy dead on November 22, 1963.

Ronald Reagan was a movie star, host of General Electric Theatre, Governor of California, and President of the U.S. As President, Reagan cut taxes, deregulated the U.S. economy, managed the longest economic expansion in American history, began development of the Strategic Defense Initiative to destroy rogue nuclear missiles aimed at America, negotiated arms control treaties with the Soviet Union, and won the Cold War. He was introduced to a Hollywood agent while in California and the agent gave Reagan a screen test, earning him a movie contract. After serving in World War II, Reagan became involved in contract negotiations for the Screen Actors Guild, beginning his transition from screen star to politician. Reagan's career took a dramatic turn when GE offered him the job of hosting General Electric Theatre and speaking about freedom and capitalism to the American people.

After the 1964 presidential election, a group of Los Angeles Republicans asked Reagan to run for Governor of California. To the surprise of almost everyone, he beat Pat Brown and served as Governor of California for two terms. In 1980, Reagan announced he intended to run for President against Jimmy Carter. He won by promising to lower taxes, reduce government regulations, curb inflation, lower interest rates, and get the economy growing. Shortly after taking office, Reagan nominated Sandra Day O'Connor as the first woman Justice on the Supreme Court. In 1982, one of the longest economic expansions in American history began under his guidance. Reagan authorized the CIA to sell arms to Iran, but an audit showed that money from the Iran arms sale had been used to pay for supplies shipped to the Contra forces in Central America. The Tower Commission report concluded that Reagan had no personal knowledge of the Iran-Contra transactions, and he was not to blame for the resulting scandal, but the affair hurt his reputation as an honest politician.

In March 1983, Reagan announced plans to build a strategic defense against nuclear missiles. In 1985, Mikhail Gorbachev became leader of the Soviet Union, and Reagan said he was interested in discussing ways to improve relations between the two countries. Reagan and Gorbachev agreed to meet and work out issues between America and the Soviet Union. In 1987, Reagan stood before the Berlin Wall and said, "Mr. Gorbachev, tear down this wall." Soon after, the Berlin Wall fell, and the Soviet Union crumbled. The Cold War was over, and America had won! Reagan spent his last years in Los Angeles speaking about democracy, freedom, and capitalism before developing Alzheimer's Disease in 1995.

Sandra Day O'Connor was an attorney, an Arizona Senator, and judge on the Arizona Court of Appeals before President Reagan nominated her to be the first woman Justice on the U.S. Supreme Court. She worked hard to be a middle-of-the-road Justice who didn't favor liberal or conservative issues. She wrote an important sex discrimination opinion in *Mississippi University for Women v. Hogan,* ruling that Mississippi University must admit males to its nursing program, although she limited the decision to that one university.

The case of *Planned Parenthood of Southeastern Pennsylvania v. Casey* brought the issue of abortion before the Supreme Court, and many experts believed the Court might overturn *Roe v. Wade* at that time. Five Justices did vote informally to overturn *Roe v. Wade,* but Justices Kennedy, Souter, and O'Connor secretly drafted an opinion that preserved the right to an abortion with restrictions and presented their draft to the Justices. The compromise opinion attracted five votes and became law, keeping abortion available in the U.S. but giving states the right to place restrictions on abortion to fit their individual needs.

The 2000 Presidential election between Al Gore and George Bush ended in a virtual tie. In Florida, the margin between the two candidates was so small an automatic recount was ordered. The Florida Supreme Court ruled that all ballots in the state must be recounted, but Bush appealed to the U.S. Supreme Court for an injunction against further recounting. Five Republican Justices voted to issue the stay. Justice O'Connor used the Equal Protection Clause of the Fourteenth Amendment to argue that the State of Florida, by using different standards in various voting districts, had violated Bush's right to equal treatment under the law, and the Supreme Court stopped the state-wide recount, making Bush President. O'Connor decided to leave the Court on January 31, 2006, to care for her husband, who had developed Alzheimer's Disease. In 2013, she was diagnosed with dementia and couldn't remember things. O'Connor is currently living in Phoenix, Arizona.

Barak Obama was serving in the U.S. Senate when he decided to run for President of the U.S. His election as the first Black American President created a sensation around the world in 2008, and many believed it signaled the end of racism in America. During his first term as President, Congress passed the American Recovery and Reinvestment Act in 2009, inserting $787 billion into the U.S. economy. Obama also appointed Judge Sonia Sotomayor and Dean Elena Kagan to the U.S. Supreme Court, passed the Affordable Care Act, signed the Dodd-Frank Wall Street Reform and Consumer Protection Act in 2010, ordered Osama bin Laden killed, and negotiated a treaty with Iran to delay its development of nuclear weapons.

The Affordable Care Act expanded the availability of health care to millions of uninsured Americans. The Act was challenged in the Supreme Court, but five Justices upheld its constitutionality by ruling that the individual mandate was a tax and within the powers given to Congress. In March 2011, the CIA discovered that Osama bin Laden was living in a luxurious compound in Abbottabad, Pakistan, and Obama ordered him killed by Navy Seals and buried at sea. Obama and a group of U.S. allies negotiated a pause in Iran's nuclear program in return for lifting economic sanctions and releasing funds owed Iran by the U.S. Iran promised to limit its nuclear program and give the International Atomic Energy Agency access to some Iranian nuclear facilities for inspections. Republican Senators said the agreement was too favorable to Iran and refused to ratify the treaty. After President Obama finished his second term as President, he began raising money for the Democratic party and writing books about his life and presidency. The first volume, entitled *A Promised Land*, was published in 2020.

Ruth Bader Ginsburg clerked for Judge Palmieri of the U.S. District Court of the Southern District of New York, was associate director of Columbia Law School's Project on International Procedures, founded the *Women's Rights Law Reporter* in 1970, and developed the legal theory that women should enjoy equal rights under the Fourteenth Amendment. She worked all her life to end gender discrimination in America and made significant progress. President Carter nominated Ginsburg to the U.S. Court of Appeals for the District of Columbia in 1980, and President Clinton nominated her to the U.S. Supreme Court in 1993. She authored the majority opinion in *United States v. Virginia,* stopping gender discrimination at the Virginia Military Institute. In response to an earlier state court decision, Virginia had offered to create the Virginia Women's Institute for Leadership as a parallel program open to women. However, in a seven to one decision authored by Ginsburg, the Court held that a separate program for women was unconstitutional.

Ginsburg wrote a famous dissent in *Bush v. Gore*, arguing that the U.S. Supreme Court should have deferred to the Florida Supreme Court's interpretations of state law in this important case because of deference to state court's interpretation of their own laws is at the core of federalism. She accused Republican Justices of being hypocrites by abandoning states' rights when that tactic suited their political agenda. During her last years on the Supreme Court, Ginsburg became famous for reading dissents from the bench. She worked for the equal protection of women all her life and made significant progress. In 2016, Ginsburg published a book about her life titled *My Own Word* that made the New York Times bestseller list. She died of complications from cancer on September 18, 2020.

Endnotes

[1] George Washington-Facts, Presidency & Quotes-Biography. https://www.biography.com/us-president/george-washington

[2] George Washington-Facts, Presidency & Quotes-Biography. https://www.biography.com/us-president/george-washington

[3] George Washington-Facts, Presidency & Quotes-Biography. https://www.biography.com/us-president/george-washington

[4] George Washington-Facts, Presidency & Quotes-Biography. https://www.biography.com/us-president/george-washington

[5] George Washington-Facts, Presidency & Quotes-Biography. https://www.biography.com/us-president/george-washington

[6] George Washington-Facts, Presidency & Quotes-Biography. https://www.biography.com/us-president/george-washington

[7] George Washington-Facts, Presidency & Quotes-Biography. https://www.biography.com/us-president/george-washington

[8] Ten Facts About George Washington and the French and Indian War. https://www.mount vernon.ogr-washington/french-indian-war/ten-facts-about-george-washington-and-the-french-and-indian-war.

[9] webmd.com-a-z-guidelines-smallpox-causes-treatments. https://www.webmd.com/a-z-guidelines/xmallpox-causes-treatment#

[10] History.com, The Boston Tea Party. https://www.history.com/topics/american-revolution/boston-tea-party#

[11] Fairfax Resolves. https://www.loc.gov/collelctions/george-washington-papers/article-and-essays/Fairfax-resolves#

[12] George Washington-Facts, Presidency & Quotes-Biography. https://www.biography.com/us-president/george-washington

[13] American forces occupy Dorchester Heights. https://www.history.com/this-day-in-history/american-forces-occupy-dorchester-heights

[14] Battle of Long Island. https://www.history.com/topics/american-revolution/battle-of-long-island

[15] Battles of Trenton and Princeton. https://www.history.com/topics/american-revolution/battles-of-trenton-and-princeton#

[16] The Battle of Brandywine Begins. https://www.history.com/this-day-in-history/the-battle-of-barndywine-begins

[17] Battle of Saratoga. https://www.history.com/topics/american-revolution/battle-of-saratoga

[18] Valley Forge. https://www.history.com/topics/american-revolution/valley-forge

[19] Franco-American alliances signed. https://www.history.com/this-day-in-history/franco-american-alliances-signed

[20] Benedict Arnold commits treason. https://www.history.com/this-day-in-histgory/benedict-arnold-commits-treason

[21] Battle of Yorktown begins. https://www.history.com/this-day-in-history/battle-of-yorktown-begins

[22] Circular Letter to the States. https://www.mountvernon.org/library/digitalhistory/digital-enclclopedia/article/circular-letter-to-the-states

[23] Constitutional Convention and Ratification, 1787-1789. https://history.state.gov/milestones/1784-1800/convention-and-ratification

[24] Federalist Papers. https://www.history.com/topics-early-us-federalist-papers

[25] Cabinet Members. https://www.mountvernon.org/library/digitalhistory/digital-encyclopedia/article/cabinet-members/#

[26] Mary Ball Washington. https://www.mountvernon.org/library/digitalhistory/digital-encyclopedia/article/mary-ball-washington/

[27] Hamilton vs. Jefferson. www.let.rug.nl/usa/outlines/history-1994/the-formation-of-a-national-government/hamilton-vs-jefferson.php

[28] Edmond Charles Genet. https://www.mountvernon.org/library/digitalhistory/digital-encyclopedia/article/edmond-charles-genet/#

[29] George Washington signs Jay Treaty with Britain. https://www.history.com/this-day-in-history/george-washington-signs-jay-treaty-with-britain

[30] George Washington's Farewell Address. https://www.mountvernon.org/library/digitalhistory/digital-encyclopedia/article/george-washington-s-farewelll-address/

[31] George Washington. https://www.google.com/search?q=washington%27s+death&riz

[32] Alexander Hamilton, Britannica Online Encyclopedia

[33] Alexander Hamilton, A Full Vindication of the Measures of the Congress, Doyle.com https://doyle.com/auctions/14ba01-new -york-city-bar-association/catalogue/87-hamilton-alexander-a-full-vindication-of

[34] A Biography of Alexander Hamilton, American History. www/let.rug.nl/usa/biograpyies/alexander-hamilton/aide-de-camp-to-washington-(1777-1781) php

[35] Benedict Arnold commits treason, history.com https://www.history.com/this-day-in-history/benedict-arnold-commits-treason

36 Shay's Rebellion, U.S. History
    https//www.ushistory.org/US/15a.asp
37 The Federalist Papers: Primary Documents in American History, Library of Congress. https//guides.loc.gov/federalist-papers/full-text
38 Appointment as Secretary of the Treasury (11 September, 1789), Founders Online. https://founders.archives.gov/documents/Hamilton/01-26-02-0002-0147
39 Hamilton, First Report on Public Credit, Online Library of Liberty.
    https://oll.libertyfund.org/pages/1790-hamilton-first-report-on-public-credit
40 Hamilton and the abolition of slavery in New York, statutes and stories.com
    https://www.statutes and stories.com/blog_html./hmilton-and-the-aboliton-of-slavery-in-new-york/#comments
41 History.com Editors, Aaron Burr slays Alexander Hamilton in Duel, November 24, 2009. https://www.history.com/this-day-in-history/burr-slays-hamilton-in-duel.
42 Understanding the Burr-Hamilton Duel, gilderlehrman.org
    https://www.gilderlehrman.org/history-resources/essays/underestanding-burr-hamilton-duel
43 Alexander Hamilton, Britannica Online Encyclopedia
44 John Adams is born, history.com
    https://www.history.com/this-day-in-history/john-adams-is-born
45 John Adams is born, history.com
    https://www.history.com/this-day-in-history/john-adams-is-born
46 Abigail Adams, History.com
    https://www.history.com/topics/first-ladies/abagail-adams
47 A Dissertation on the Canon and Federal Law, Britannica.com
    https://www.britannica.com/A-Disertation--on-the-Canon-and-Federal-Law
48 Boston Massacre, history.com editors
    https://www.history.com/topics/american-revolution/boston-massacre#
49 Paine Thomas, Common Sense, US History.org
    https://www.ushistory.org/paine/commonsense/
50 The Birth of the U.S. Navy. https://www.history.navy.mil/browse-by-topic/commentorations-toolkits/navy-birthday/OriginsNavy/the-birth-of-the-navy-of-the-united-states.html
51 Adams, John, Thoughts on Government, 1776.
52 Lee Resolution, battlefields.org
    https://www.battlefields.org/learn/primary-sources/lee-resolution#
53 Adams, John, Thoughts on Government, 1776.
54 Treaty of Paris, 1783, U.S. State Department.
    http://www.state.gov
55 The Vice Presidency of John Adams, American Experience
    https://www.pbs.org/wgbh/americanexperience/features/adams-vice- presidency/
56 Office of the Historian, The XYZ Affair and the Quasi-War with France, 1798-1800. https://history.state.gov/milestones/1784-1800./xyz#
57 George Washington dies, History.com
    https://www.history.com/this-day-in-history/george-washington-dies
58 Adams Appoints Marshall, American Heritage
    https://www.americanheritage.com/adams-appoints-marshall
59 From the Correspondence of John Adams and Thomas Jefferson, The Library of Congress.
60 Obituary Notice. Mrs. Abigail Adams. Library of Congress
    https://www.loc.gov/resource/rbpe.0520050a/?loclr=blogloc
61 Thomas Jefferson and John Adams died, July 4, 1826. This Day in History
    https://www.history.com/this-day-in=history/thomas-jefferson-and-john-adams-die
62 Historic Valley Forge: John Marshall. U.S. History.org. https//www.ushistory.org/valleyforge/served/marshall.html.
63 Historic Valley Forge: John Marshall. U.S. History.org. https//www.ushistory.org/valleyforge/served/marshall.html.
64 Historic Valley Forge: John Marshall. U.S. History.org. https//www.ushistory.org/valleyforge/served/marshall.html.
65 Historic Valley Forge: John Marshall. U.S. History.org. https//www.ushistory.org/valleyforge/served/marshall.html.
66 Historic Valley Forge: John Marshall. U.S. History.org. https//www.ushistory.org/valleyforge/served/marshall.html.
67 A Biography of George Wythe 1726-1806. American History. www.let.rug.nl/usa/biographies/george-wythe/
68 Marbury v. Madison, 5 U.S. 137 (1803)

69 Office of the Historian, The XYZ Affair and the Quasi-War with France, 1798-1800. https://history.state.gov/milestones/1784-1800./xyz#

70 John Marshall, Secretary of State. U.S. Department of State. https://2001-2009.state.gov/secretary/former/40904.htm

71 Josh Clark, Thomas Jefferson and the Barbary Pirates, How Stuff Works.

72 John Marshall, Chief Justice of the United States, Britannica. https://www.britannica.com/biography/John-Marshall

73 *Talbot v. Seeman*, 5 U.S. 1 (1801)

74 Marbury v. Madison, 5 U.S. 137 (1903)

75 *The Schooner Exchange v. McFaddon*, 11 U.S. 116, (1812)

76 *Martin v. Hunter's Lessee*, 14 U.S. 304 (1816)

77 *McCulloch v. Maryland*, 17 U.S. 316 (1819)

78 *Gibbon v. Ogden*, 22 U.S. 1 (1824)

79 Historic Valley Forge: John Marshall. U.S. History.org. https//www.ushistory.org/valleyforge/served/marshall.html.

80 Thomas Jefferson, History.com Editors https://www.history.com/topics/us-presidents/thomas-jefferson

81 Thomas Jefferson, History.com Editors https://www.history.com/topics/us-presidents/thomas-jefferson

82 Thomas Jefferson, History.com Editors https://www.history.com/topics/us-presidents/thomas-jefferson

83 Jefferson, T., A Summary View of the Rights of British America, Yale Law School. https://avalon.law.yale.edu/18th_century/jeffsumm.asp

84 Declaration of Independence: A Transcription. National Archives. https://www.archives.gov/founding-docs/declaration-tranccript

85 First Lady Biography, Martha Jefferson, firstladies.org www.firstladies.org/biographies/firsstladies.aspx?biography-3

86 Jefferson in Paris, France Today Editors. https://www.francetoday.com/culture/jeffereson_in_paris/

87 Jefferson in Paris, France Today Editors. https://www.francetoday.com/culture/jeffereson_in_paris/

88 Josh Clark, What Was America's First Terrorist Threat? How Things Work/Culture/History/History vs. myth

89 Thomas Jefferson to William Smith, Library of Congress Exhibits https://www.low.gov/exhibits/jefferson/105.htm#

90 Thomas Jefferson, Secretary of State, U.S. Department of State. https://2001-2009.state.gov/secretary/former/40907.htm

91 Industrial Britain, 1750-1900 overview, BBC.com https://www.bbc.co.uk/bitesize/gudelines/zcss7hv/revision/2

92 Jefferson: The Agronomist, Varsity Tutors. https://.varsitytutors.com/earlyamerica/jefferson-primer/agronomist#

93 Josh Clark, What Was America's First Terrorist Threat? How Things Work/Culture/History/History vs. myth

94 Louisiana Purchase, History.com https://www.history.com/topics/westward-expansion/louisiana-purchase

95 From the Correspondence of John Adams and Thomas Jefferson, The Library of Congress.

96 Thomas Jefferson and John Adams died, July 4, 1826. This Day in History https://www.history.com/this-day-in=history/thomas-jefferson-and-john-adams-die

97 Andrew Jackson Biography. https://www.biography.com/us-presient/andrew-jackson.

98 Andrew Jackson Biography. https://www.biography.com/us-presient/andrew-jackson.

99 Andrew Jackson Biography. https://www.biography.com/us-presient/andrew-jackson.

100 Andrew Jackson Biography. https://www.biography.com/us-presient/andrew-jackson.

101 Andrew Jackson Biography. https://www.biography.com/us-presient/andrew-jackson.

102 Andrew Jackson Biography. https://www.biography.com/us-presient/andrew-jackson.

103 Andrew Jackson Biography. https://www.biography.com/us-presient/andrew-jackson.

104 Andrew Jackson Biography. https://www.biography.com/us-presient/andrew-jackson.

105 United States presidential election of 1828. https://www.britannica.com/event/United-States-presidential-election-of-1828.

106 Andrew Jackson's Cabinet. https://www.whitehousehistory.org/andrew-jackson's-cabinet.

107 Andrew Jackson Biography. https://www.biography.com/us-presient/andrew-jackson.

108 Peggy Eaton Affair. www.american-historama.org/1829-1841-jacksonian-era/peggy-eaton-affair.

109 Andrew Jackson Biography. https://www.biography.com/us-presirent/andrew-jackson.

110 Andrew Jackson Biography. https://www.biography.com/us-presirent/andrew-jackson.

111 *Cherokee Nation v. Georgia*, 30 U.S. 1 (1831)

112 United States presidential election of 1832. https://www.britannica.com/event/United-States-presideential-election-of-1832.

113 Ordinance of Nullification. https://www.britannica.com/topic/Ordinance-of-Nullification.

114 Compromise of 1833. https://www.britannica.com/topic/Compromise-of-1833.

115 1833 President Jackson attacked. https://www.rarenewspapers.com/view/575685

116 Senate Censures President. https://www.senate.gov/artandhistory/history/minute/Senate_Centures_President.htm

117 The Quasi War Between France and the United States. https://france-amerique.com/en/the-quasi-war-between-france-and-the-united-states.

118 The Attempted Assassination of Andrew Jackson. https://www.smithsonianmag.com/history/attempted-assassinatin-andrew-jackson-180962526/

119 United States presidential election of 1836. https://www.britannica.com/event/United-States-presidential-election-of-1836.

120 Andrew Jackson Biography. https://www.biography.com/us-presitent/andrew-jackson.

121 Daniel Webster American Politician, Britannica. https://www.britannica.com/biography/Daniel/Webster.

122 Daniel Webster American Politician, Britannica. https://www.britannica.com/biography/Daniel/Webster.

123 Daniel Webster, Encyclopedia.com https://www.encyclopedia.com/people/history/us-history-biographe/daniel-webster#

124 Daniel Webster American Politician, Britannica. https://www.britannica.com/biography/Daniel/Webster.

125 Daniel Webster, Encyclopedia.com https://www.encyclopedia.com/people/history/us-history-biographe/daniel-webster#

126 War of 1812, History https://www.history.com/topics/war-of-1812

127 *The Grotius*, 12 U.S. 368 (1815).

128 Battle of New Orleans, History.com https://www.history.com/topics-war-of-1812/battle-of-new-orleans

129 *Trustees of Dartmouth College v. Woodward*, 17 U.S. 518 (1819).

130 *McCulloch v. Maryland*, 17 U.S. 316 (1819)

131 *Gibbon v. Ogden*, 22 U.S. 1 (1824)

132 Daniel Webster American Politician, Britannica. https://www.britannica.com/biography/Daniel/Webster.

133 Daniel Webster American Politician, Britannica. https://www.britannica.com/biography/Daniel/Webster.

134 The Webster-Hayne Debates, Teaching American History https://teachingamericanhistory.org/library/document/the-webster-haynes-debates/

135 Northwest Ordinance (1787) https://www.ourdocuments.gov/doc.php?flash=false&doc=8

136 *McCulloch v. Maryland*, 17 U.S. 316 (1819)

137 *Proprietors of Charles River Bridge v. Proprietors of Warren Bridge*, 36 U.S. 420 (1837)

138 Webster-Ashburton Treaty, 1842. Office of the Historian https://history.state.gov/milestones/1830-1860/webster-treaty

139 Treaty of Guadalupe Hidalgo (1848). https://www.google.com/search?q=treaty+Guadalupe+hidalgo+1848+summary&oq=treaty

140 Compromise of 1850: Primary Documents in American History, Library of Congress https://guides.loc.gov/compromise-1850#

141 Daniel Webster, Encyclopedia.com https://www.encyclopedia.com/people/history/us-history-biographe/daniel-webster#

142 Abraham Lincoln, History.com Editors https://www.history.com/topics/us-presidents/abraham-lincoln

143 Abraham Lincoln, History.com Editors https://www.history.com/topics/us-presidents/abraham-lincoln

[144] Lincoln Legal Career Timeline, Abraham Lincoln Online
www.abrahamlincolnonline.org/lincoln/education/lawhighlights.htm

[145] Lincoln Legal Career Timeline, Abraham Lincoln Online
www.abrahamlincolnonline.org/lincoln/education/lawhighlights.htm

[146] Lincoln Legal Career Timeline, Abraham Lincoln Online
www.abrahamlincolnonline.org/lincoln/education/lawhighlights.htm

[147] The Life of Mary Todd Lincoln, Kimberly J. Largent, ehistory
http://www.osu.edu

[148] Abraham Lincoln Prepares to Fight a Saber Duel, historynet.com
https://www.historynet.com/Abraham-lincoln-prepares-to-fight-a-saber-duel.htm

[149] The Life of Mary Todd Lincoln, Kimberly J. Largent, ehistory
http://www.osu.edu

[150] Abraham Lincoln-U.S. House of Representatives, History, Art & Archives
https://history.house.gov/People/Details/16982

[151] Lincoln-Douglas Debates, History.com Editors
https://www/history.com/topics/19th-century/loncoln-douglas-debates

[152] Dred Scott v. Sanford 60 U.S. 393 (1857)

[153] Lincoln-Douglas Debates, History.com Editors
https://www/history.com/topics/19th-century/loncoln-douglas-debates

[154] Abraham Lincoln nominated for presidency at Republican Convention, History.com
https://www.history.com/this-day-in-history/lincoln-nominated-for-prsidency

[155] First Inaugural Address of Abraham Lincoln, Yale Law School.
https://avalon.law.yale.edu/19th_century/lincoln1.asp

[156] The Gettysburg Address, Abraham Lincoln Online
www.abrahamlincolnonline.org/lincoln/speeches/gettysbury.htm

[157] Transcript of Abraham Lincoln's Second Inaugural Address
https://www.ourdocuments.gov/doc.php?flash=false&doc=388pages=transcript.

[158] Garber, Julie, Celebrities Who Died Without a Will-Abraham Lincoln, The Balance, 2019
[https://www.thebalance.com/celebrities-who-died-without-a-will-3505108]

[159] Theodore Roosevelt Biography. https://www.biography.com/us-president-theodore-roosevelt.

[160] Theodore Roosevelt Biography. https://www.biography.com/us-president-theodore-roosevelt.

[161] Theodore Roosevelt Biography. https://www.biography.com/us-president-theodore-roosevelt.

[162] Theodore Roosevelt Biography. https://www.biography.com/us-president-theodore-roosevelt.

[163] Theodore Roosevelt's Mother and Wife Died Within Hours of Each Other on Valentine's Day.
https://www.biography.com/news/theodore-roosevelt-wife-mother-death.

[164] Theodore Roosevelt Biography. https://www.biography.com/us-president-theodore-roosevelt.

[165] Edith Roosevelt. https://www.britannica.com/biography/Edith-Roosevelt.

[166] Theodore Roosevelt Biography. https://www.biography.com/us-president-theodore-roosevelt.

[167] Theodore Roosevelt Biography. https://www.biography.com/us-president-theodore-roosevelt.

[168] Theodore Roosevelt Biography. https://www.biography.com/us-president-theodore-roosevelt.

[169] Theodore Roosevelt Biography. https://www.biography.com/us-president-theodore-roosevelt.

[170] Theodore Roosevelt Biography. https://www.biography.com/us-president-theodore-roosevelt.

[171] Theodore Roosevelt Biography. https://www.biography.com/us-president-theodore-roosevelt.

[172] The Panama Canal. https://www.ushistory.org/us/44g.asp.

[173] Theodore Roosevelt Biography. https://www.biography.com/us-president-theodore-roosevelt.

[174] Theodore Roosevelt Biography. https://www.biography.com/us-president-theodore-roosevelt.

[175] Theodore Roosevelt Biography. https://www.biography.com/us-president-theodore-roosevelt.

[176] Theodore Roosevelt Biography. https://www.biography.com/us-president-theodore-roosevelt.

[177] Theodore Roosevelt shot in Milwaukee. https://www.history.com/this-day-in-history/theodore-roosevelt-shot-in-milwaukee.

[178] Theodore Roosevelt Biography. https://www.biography.com/us-president-theodore-roosevelt.

[179] Theodore Roosevelt Biography. https://www.biography.com/us-president-theodore-roosevelt.

[180] Biography, Oliver Wendell Holmes, Jr. Biography.com
https://www.biography.com/law-figure/oliver-wendell-holmes-jr

[181] Biography, Oliver Wendell Holmes, Jr. Biography.com
https://www.biography.com/law-figure/oliver-wendell-holmes-jr

182 Ball's Bluff—Harrison's Island, American Battlefield Trust
    https://www.battlefields.org/learn/civil-war/battles/ball's-bluff
183 Biography, Oliver Wendell Holmes, Jr. Biography.com
    https://www.biography.com/law-figure/oliver-wendell-holmes-jr
184 Biographies of the Robes: Oliver Wendell Holmes, The Supreme Court
    https://www.thirteen.org/wnet/supremecourt/capitalism/robes_holmes.html#
185 Fanny Bowditch Dixwell Holmes, Ancestry
    https://ancestry.com/genealogy/records/fanny-bowditch-dixwell-24-8n53d
186 Oliver Wendell Holmes, James Kent, Commentaries on American Law, Franklin Classics, 2018
187 Oliver Wendell Holmes, Jr., The Common Law, November 23, 1880
    https://www.1215.org/lawnotes/work-in-progress-holmes/index.html
188 The Path of the Law, Oliver Wendell Holmes, Jr. 1897
    https://law.jrank.org/pages11777/Path-Law.html
189 Oliver Wendell Holmes, Jr., Mass.gov
    https://www.mass.gov/person/oliver-wendell-holmes-jr
190 Oliver Wendell Holmes, Jr., 1902-1932
    https://wupremecourthistory.org/timeline_holmes.html#
191 *Otis v. Parker*, 187 U.S. 606 (1903)
192 *Northern Securities v. United States*, 193 U.S. 197 (1904)
193 *Swift & Co. v. United States*, 196 U.S. 375 (1905)
194 *Abrams v. United States*, 250 U.S. 616 (1919)
195 *Moore v. Dempsey*, 261 U.S. 86 (1923)
196 *Nixon v. Herndon*, 273 U.S. 536 (1927)
197 *United States v. Schwimmer*, 279 U.S. 644 (1929)
198 Saladin Ambar, Woodrow Wilson: Life before the Presidency, Miller Center
    https://millercenter.org/president/wilson/life-before-the-presidency
199 Edwin A. Weinstein, Comments on "Woodrow Wilson Re-Examined: The Mind-Body Controversy Redux and Other Disputations."
    https://www/jstor.org/stable/3790941?seq=1
200 Saladin Ambar, Woodrow Wilson: Life Before the Presidency, U.S. Presidents
    https://millrcenter.org/president/wilson/life-before-the-presidency#
201 Saladin Ambar, Woodrow Wilson: Life Before the Presidency, U.S. Presidents
    https://millrcenter.org/president/wilson/life-before-the-presidency#
202 Saladin Ambar, Woodrow Wilson: Life Before the Presidency, U.S. Presidents
    https://millrcenter.org/president/wilson/life-before-the-presidency#
203 First Lady Biography: Ellen Wilson, National First Ladies' Library
    www.firstladies.org/biographies/firstladies-aspx?biography=28
204 Wilson, Woodrow (1856-1924) library.princeton.edu
    https://library/princeton.edu/special-collection/topics/wilson-woodrow-1856-1924#
205 Gov. Thomas Woodrow Wilson, National Governors Association
    https://www.nga.org/goverhor/thomas-woodrow-wilson/
206 Gov. Thomas Woodrow Wilson, National Governors Association
    https://www.nga.org/goverhor/thomas-woodrow-wilson/
207 United States Presidential Election of 1912, Britannica.com
    https://www.britannica.com/event/United -States-presidential-election-of-1912
208 United States Presidential Election of 1912, Britannica.com
    https://www.britannica.com/event/United -States-presidential-election-of-1912
209 Woodrow Wilson: Domestic Affairs, U.S. Presidents, Miller Center, UVA
    https://millercenter.org/president/wilson/domestic-affairs
210 Federal Reserve Act Signed into Law, Federal Reserve History
    https://www.federalreservehistory.org/essays/federal_reserve_act_signed
211 First Lady Biography: Ellen Wilson, National First Ladies' Library
    www.firstladies.org/biographies/firstladies-aspx?biography=28
212 Germans sink American merchant ship, This Day in History
    https://www.history.com/this-day-in-history/germans-sink-american-merchant-ship

213 Edith Bolling Galt Wilson, The White House
https://www.whitehouse.gov/about-the-white-house/first-ladies/edith-bolling-galt-wilson

214 Presidential election of 1916, Britannica
https://www.britannica.com/event/United-States-presidential-election-of-1916

215 The Zimmermann Telegram, National Archives
https://www.archives.gov/education/lessons/zimmermann

216 U.S. Entry into World War 1, 1917, Office of the Historian
https://history.state.gov/milestones/1914-1920ww1#

217 The Paris Peace Conference and the Treaty of Versailles, Office of the Historian
https://history.state.gov/milestones/1914-1920/paris-peace

218 The Paris Peace Conference and the Treaty of Versailles, Office of the Historian
https://history.state.gov/milestones/1914-1920/paris-peace

219 Woodrow Wilson suffers a stroke, History.com
https://www.history.com/this-day-in-history/woodrow-wilson-suffers-a-stroke

220 What Drove Sigmund Freud to Write a Scandalous Biography of Woodrow Wilson? Smithsonian Magazine
https://www.smithsonianmag.com/history/what-drove-sigmund-freud-write-scandalous-biography-woodrow-wilson-180970042/

221 Woodrow Wilson dies, History.com
https://www.history.com/this-day-in-history/woodrow-wilson-dies

222 Franklin D. Roosevelt. https://www.whitehouse.gov/about-the-white-house/presidents/franklin-d-roosevelt/

223 Franklin D. Roosevelt. https://www.whitehouse.gov/about-the-white-house/presidents/franklin-d-roosevelt/

224 Franklin D. Roosevelt. https://www.whitehouse.gov/about-the-white-house/presidents/franklin-d-roosevelt/

225 Franklin D. Roosevelt. https://www.whitehouse.gov/about-the-white-house/presidents/franklin-d-roosevelt/

226 What was the Zimmerman Telegram? https://www.history.com/news/what-was-the-zimmerman-telegram

227 FDR's Secret Love. https://www.usnews.com/news/articles/2008/04/18/fdrs-secret-love

228 FRD Didn't Have Polio? https://www.webmd.com/women/news/20031031/fdr-didn't-have-polio

229 Franklin D. Roosevelt: Life Before the Presidency. https://millercenter.org/president/fdroosevelt/life-before-the-presidency

230 What Caused the Great Depression? https://www.history.com/topics/great-depression/great-depression-history

231 Bonus Army. https://www.britannica.com/event/Bonus-Army

232 Franklin D. Roosevelt. https://www.whitehouse.gov/about-the-white-house/presidents/franklin-d-roosevelt/

233 Franklin Delano Roosevelt and the New Deal. https://loc.gov/classroom-materials/united-states-history-primary source-timeline/great-depression-and-world-war-II-1929-1945/franklin--delano-roosevelt

234 Franklin Delano Roosevelt and the New Deal. https://loc.gov/classroom-materials/united-states-history-primary source-timeline/great-depression-and-world-war-II-1929-1945/franklin--delano-roosevelt

235 Franklin Delano Roosevelt and the New Deal. https://loc.gov/classroom-materials/united-states-history-primary source-timeline/great-depression-and-world-war-II-1929-1945/franklin--delano-roosevelt

236 Franklin Delano Roosevelt and the New Deal. https://loc.gov/classroom-materials/united-states-history-primary source-timeline/great-depression-and-world-war-II-1929-1945/franklin--delano-roosevelt

237 FDR's Court-Packing Plan: A Study in Irony.
ap.gilderlehrman.org/history-by-era/new-deal/essays/frd's-court-packing-plan-study-irony

238 World War II. https://www.history.com/topics/world-war-II-history

239 World War II. https://www.history.com/topics/world-war-II-history

240 World War II. https://www.history.com/topics/world-war-II-history

241 World War II. https://www.history.com/topics/world-war-II-history

242 World War II. https://www.history.com/topics/world-war-II-history

243 World War II. https://www.history.com/topics/world-war-II-history

244 World War II. https://www.history.com/topics/world-war-II-history

245 World War II. https://www.history.com/topics/world-war-II-history

246 World War II. https://www.history.com/topics/world-war-II-history

247 Yalta Conference. https://www.history.com/topics/world-war-II/yalta-conference

248 Franklin D. Roosevelt. https://www.whitehouse.gov/about-the-white-house/presidents/franklin-d-roosevelt/

249 Earl Warren, Chief Justice of United States, Britannica.com
https://www.britannica.com/biography/Earl-Warren

250 Earl Warren, Chief Justice of United States, Britannica.com
https://www.britannica.com/biography/Earl-Warren

251 Earl Warren, Chief Justice of United States, Britannica.com
https://www.britannica.com/biography/Earl-Warren

252 Earl Warren, Chief Justice of United States, Britannica.com
https://www.britannica.com/biography/Earl-Warren

253 Earl Warren, Chief Justice of United States, Britannica.com
https://www.britannica.com/biography/Earl-Warren

254 Earl Warren, Chief Justice of United States, Britannica.com
https://www.britannica.com/biography/Earl-Warren

255 M. H. Warren, Bakersfield is murdered. Madera Tribune,
https://cdnc.ucr.edu/?a=d&d=MT19380516.2.2&e

256 Earl Warren, Chief Justice of United States, Britannica.com
https://www.britannica.com/biography/Earl-Warren

257 Japanese Internment Camps, History.com Editors
https://www.history.com/topics/world-war-II/japanese-american-relocation#

258 Earl Warren, Chief Justice of United States, Britannica.com
https://www.britannica.com/biography/Earl-Warren

259 Time Magazine Cover: Earl Warren-Jan.31, 1944
https://www.pinterest.com/pin/529735974901025437/

260 the loyalty oath controversy, university of California 1949-1951 https://www.lib.berkeley.edu/uchistory/archives_exhibits/
loyaltyoath/index.html

261 Earl Warren, History.com, Editors
https://www.history.com/topics/us-politics/earl-warren

262 Earl Warren, History.com, Editors
https://www.history.com/topics/us-politics/earl-warren

263 *Brown v. Board of Education*, 347 U.S. 483 (1954)

264 *Pennsylvania v. Nelson*, 350 U.S. 497 (1956)

265 *Cooper v. Aaron*, 358 U.S. 1 (1958)

266 *Gideon v. Wainwright*, 372 U.S. 335 (1963)

267 *Reynolds v. Sims*, 377 U.S. 533 (1964)

268 *New York Times Company v. Sullivan*, 376 U.S. 254 (1964)

269 *Miranda v. Arizona*, 384 U.S. 436 (1966)

270 John F. Kennedy. https://www.britannica.com/biography/John-F-Kennedy

271 John F. Kennedy. https://www.britannica.com/biography/John-F-Kennedy

272 President Roosevelt Appoints Joseph P. Kennedy, Sr. Ambassador to Britain.
https://worldhistoryproject.org/1937/president-roosevelt-appoints-joseph-p-kennedy-sr-ambassador-to-britain

273 Meet Inga Arvad, The Woman Who Stole Hitler's Heart And Dated JFK. https://allthatsinteresting.com/inga-arvad

274 John F. Kennedy and PT 109. https://www.jfklibrary.org/learn/about-jfk-jfk-in-history/john-f-kennedy-and-pt-109

275 John F. Kennedy-Congressman and senator. https://www.britannica.com/biography/John-F-Kennedy/Congressman and senator

276 A brief history of the Korean War. https://militarytimes.com/veterans/military-history/2020/06/25/a-brief-history-of-the-korean-war/

277 John F. Kennedy-Congressman and senator. https://www.britannica.com/biography/John-F-Kennedy/Congressman and senator

278 John F. Kennedy. https://www.britannica.com/biography/John-F-Kennedy

279 Profiles in Courage. https://www.jfklibrary.org/events-and-awards/profile-in-courage-award/about-the-book

280 United States presidential election of 1960. https://www.britannica.com/event/United-States-preidential-election-of-1960

281 United States presidential election of 1960. https://www.britannica.com/event/United-States-preidential-election-of-1960

282 United States presidential election of 1960. https://www.britannica.com/event/United-States-preidential-election-of-1960

283 John F. Kennedy. https://www.history.com/topics/us-presidents/john-f-kennedy

284 John F. Kennedy. https://www.history.com/topics/us-presidents/john-f-kennedy

285 John F. Kennedy. https://www.history.com/topics/us-presidents/john-f-kennedy

286 Bay of Pigs: President Kennedy and the Cold War. https://www.history.com/topics/cold-war/bay-of-pigs-invasion

287 Vienna Summit. https://www.historycentral.com/JFK/bio/vienna.html

288 The Berlin Wall: The Partitioning of Berlin. https://www.history.com/topics/cold-war/berlin-wall

289 Vietnam War. https://www.history.com/topics/vietnam-war/vietnam-war-history

290 Vietnam War. https://www.history.com/topics/vietnam-war/vietnam-war-history

291 Cuban missile crisis. https://www.britannica.com/event/Cuban-missile-crisis

292 Cuban missile crisis. https://www.britannica.com/event/Cuban-missile-crisis

[293] Cuban missile crisis. https://www.britannica.com/event/Cuban-missile-crisis

[294] Cuban missile crisis. https://www.britannica.com/event/Cuban-missile-crisis

[295] Cuban missile crisis. https://www.britannica.com/event/Cuban-missile-crisis

[296] Cuban missile crisis. https://www.britannica.com/event/Cuban-missile-crisis

[297] Did Marilyn Monroe Really Have An Affair With JFK? https://www.cheatsheet.com/entertainment/did-marilyn-monroe-really-have-an-affair-with-jfk.html/

[298] Birmingham erupted into chaos in 1963 as battle for civil rights exploded in south. https://www.nydailynews.com/news/national/birmingham-erupted-chaos-1963-battle-civil-right-exploded-south-article-1.1071793

[299] Nuclear Test Ban Treaty. https://www.jfklibrary.org/learn-about-jfk/jfk-in-history/nuclear-test-ban-treaty

[300] Vietnam War. https://www.history.com/topics/vietnam-war/vietnam-war-history

[301] Vietnam War. https://www.history.com/topics/vietnam-war/vietnam-war-history

[302] November 22, 1963: Death of The President. https://www.jfklibrary.org/learn/about-jfk/jfk-in-history/november-22-1963-death-of-the-president

[303] November 22, 1963: Death Of The President. https://www.jfklibrary.org/learn/about-jfk/jfk-in-history/november-22-1963-death-of-the-president

[304] Sandra Day O'Connor, History.com. https://history.com/topics/us-government/sandra-day-o'connor#

[305] Sandra Day O'Connor, History.com. https://www.history.com/topics/us-government/sandra-day-o'connor#

[306] Sandra Day O'Connor, History.com. https://www.history.com/topics/us-government/sandra-day-o'connor#

[307] Sandra Day O'Connor, History.com. https://history.com/topics/us-government/sandra-day-o'connor#

[308] Sandra Day O'Connor, History.com. https://history.com/topics/us-government/sandra-day-o'connor#

[309] *Plyler v. Doe*, 457 U.S. 202 (1982)

[310] *Engle v. Isaac*, 456 U.S. 107 (1982)

[311] *Mississippi University for Women v. Hogan*, 458 U.S. 718 (1982)

[312] *City of Akron v. Akron Center for Reproductive Health*, 462 U.S. 416 (1982)

[313] *Wallace v. Jaffree*, 472 U.S. 38 (1984)

[314] Linda Greenhouse, O'Connor Has Breast Surgery to Stop Cancer, *New York Times*, Oct 22, 1988

[315] *Planned Parenthood of Southeastern Pennsylvania v. Casey*, 505 U.S. 833 (1992)

[316] *Bush v. Gore*, 531 U.S. 98 (2000)

[317] *Gratz v. Bollinger*, 539 U.S. 244 (2003)

[318] *Hamdi v. Rumsfeld*, 542 U.S. 507 (2004)

[319] *Ayotte v. Planned Parenthood of Northern New England*, 546 U.S. 320 (2006)

[320] John Jay O'Connor Dies, https://www.google.com/ssearch?q=when+did+Sandra+Day+O'Connor%27s+husband+die%3F&riz

[321] Barak Obama, Biography. https://www.biography.com/us-president/barak-obama

[322] Barak Obama, Biography. https://www.biography.com/us-president/barak-obama

[323] Barak Obama, Biography. https://www.biography.com/us-president/barak-obama

[324] Barak Obama, Biography. https://www.biography.com/us-president/barak-obama

[325] Barak Obama, Biography. https://www.biography.com/us-president/barak-obama

[326] Barak Obama, Biography. https://www.biography.com/us-president/barak-obama

[327] Barak Obama, Biography. https://www.biography.com/us-president/barak-obama

[328] Barak Obama, Biography. https://www.biography.com/us-president/barak-obama

[329] Barak Obama, Biography. https://www.biography.com/us-president/barak-obama

[330] Barak Obama, Biography. https://www.biography.com/us-president/barak-obama

[331] President Barak Obama with full cabinet 09-10-09. https://en.wikipedia.org/wiki/File.:President_Barak_OBama_with_full_cabinet_09-10-09,jpg

[332] ARRA, Its Details, With Pros and Cons. https://www.thebalance.com/arra-details-3306299

[333] Auto Industry Bailout. https://www.thebalance.com/auto-industry-bailout-gm-ford-chrysler-3305670

[334] Background on Judge Sonia Sotomayor. https://obamawhitehouse.archives.gov/the-press-office/background-judge-sonia-sotomayor

[335] Justice Elena Kagan. https://supremecourthistory.org/history-of-the-court/the-current-court/justice-elena-kagan/

[336] About the Affordable Care Act. https://www.hhs.gov/healthcare/about-the-aca/index.html

[337] New START Treaty. https://www.state.gov/new-start/

[338] More That 300 Chemical Attacks Launched During Syrian Civil War, Study Says. https://www.npr.org/2019/02/17/695545252/more-than-300-chemical-atacks-launched-during-syrian-civil-war-study-says

[339] How SEAL Team Six Took Out Osama bin Laden. https://www.history.com/news/osama-bin-laden-death-seal-tam-six

[340] Dodd-Frank Wall Street Reform and Consumer Protection Act. https://www.investopedia.com/terms/dodd-frank-financial-regulaotory-reform-bill.asp

[341] Everything you need to know about PRISM.
https://www.theverge.com/2013/7/17/4517480/nsa-spying-prism-survellance-cheat-sheet

[342] Benghazi US consulate attack: Timeline. https://www.bbc.com/news/world-africa-19587068

[343] Barak Obama Wars in Iraq and Afghanistan. https://www.britannica.com/biography/Barak-Obama/Wars-in-Iraq-and-Afghanistan

[344] The Iran Nuclear Deal: What's Wrong With It And What Can We Do Now? https://www.unitedagainstnucleariran.com/iran-nuclear-deal?gclid

[345] TPP: What is it and why does it matter? https://www.bbc.com/news/business-32498715

[346] Aaron M. Houck, *Ruth Bader Ginsburg*, Encyclopedia Britannica. https://www.britannica.com/biography/Ruth-Bader-Ginsburg.

[347] Aaron M. Houck, *Ruth Bader Ginsburg*, Encyclopedia Britannica. https://www.britannica.com/biography/Ruth-Bader-Ginsburg.

[348] Aaron M. Houck, *Ruth Bader Ginsburg*, Encyclopedia Britannica. https://www.britannica.com/biography/Ruth-Bader-Ginsburg.

[349] Aaron M. Houck, *Ruth Bader Ginsburg*, Encyclopedia Britannica. https://www.britannica.com/biography/Ruth-Bader-Ginsburg.

[350] Aaron M. Houck, *Ruth Bader Ginsburg*, Encyclopedia Britannica. https://www.britannica.com/biography/Ruth-Bader-Ginsburg.

[351] Aaron M. Houck, *Ruth Bader Ginsburg*, Encyclopedia Britannica. https://www.britannica.com/biography/Ruth-Bader-Ginsburg.

[352] Aaron M. Houck, *Ruth Bader Ginsburg*, Encyclopedia Britannica. https://www.britannica.com/biography/Ruth-Bader-Ginsburg.

[353] Aaron M. Houck, *Ruth Bader Ginsburg*, Encyclopedia Britannica. https://www.britannica.com/biography/Ruth-Bader-Ginsburg.

[354] Aaron M. Houck, *Ruth Bader Ginsburg*, Encyclopedia Britannica. https://www.britannica.com/biography/Ruth-Bader-Ginsburg.

[355] *Reed v. Reed*, 404 U.S. 71 (1971)

[356] *Moritz v. Comm'r of Internal Revenue*, 55 T.C. 113 (USTC, 1970)

[357] *Charles E. Moritz v. Comm'r of Internal Revenue*, 469 /f,2s 366 (10th Cir. 1972)

[358] *Frontiero v. Richardson*, 411 U.S. 677 (1973)

[359] *Geduldig v. Aiello*, 417 U.S. 484 (1974)

[360] *Weinberger v. Wiesenfeld*, 420 U.S. 636 (1975)

[361] *Califano v. Goldfarb*, 430 U.S. 199 (1977)

[362] *Duren v. Missouri*, 439 U.S. 357 (1979)

[363] *Craig v. Boren*, 429 U.S. 190 (1976)

[364] *Reed v. Farley*, 512 U.S. 339 (1994)

[365] *Thompson v. Keohane*, 516 U.S. 99 (1995)

[366] *United States v. Virginia*, 518 U.S. 515 (1996)

[367] *Kawaauhau v. Geiger*, 523 U.S. 57 (1998)

[368] *Stafford Unified School District v. Redding*, 557 U.S. 354 (2009)

[369] *Gonzales v. Carhart*, 550 U.S. 124 (2007)

[370] *Shelby County v. Holder*, 570 U.S. 529 (2012)

www.ingramcontent.com/pod-product-compliance
Lightning Source LLC
Chambersburg PA
CBHW080954120626
46546CB00010B/2890